ADVANCE DIRECTIVES ACROSS ASIA

This book is the first to consider comprehensively and systematically the law and practice of advance directives across Asia. It will thus be important not only as a reference volume that documents how advance directives are regulated and used throughout Asia, but also as an exploration of the concept of the advance directive itself, in context. By examining how advance directives operate in Asian countries, we will also shed light on the principle of personal autonomy in this context, alongside other values and religious and socio-cultural factors that shape health and care decision-making. As such, this book will have broad appeal not only to Asian scholars, students, policymakers and practitioners in the fields of health law and ethics and end-of-life care more generally, but will also be of wider interest to an international academic audience in the fields of law, ethics and health and social care research. This title is also available as open access on Cambridge Core.

Daisy Cheung is Assistant Professor at the Centre for Medical Ethics and Law, Faculty of Law, University of Hong Kong. Her research focuses on the law and ethics of mental health and capacity, and she has published on these topics across a number of contexts, including a funded project on adult guardianship. She is a member of the Mental Health Law Committee of the Law Society of Hong Kong.

Michael Dunn is Associate Professor at the Centre for Biomedical Ethics, Yong Loo Lin School of Medicine, National University of Singapore. He is a internationally-renowned bioethicist, and has made major contributions in clinical ethics, social care ethics and research ethics. He has been a pioneer in establishing and shaping the methodological sub-field of empirical bioethics. He has written over seventy peer-reviewed academic papers, and co-authored or co-edited five other books.

ADVANCE DIRECTIVES ACROSS ASIA

A Comparative Sociolegal Analysis

Edited by

DAISY CHEUNG
The University of Hong Kong
MICHAEL DUNN
National University of Singapore

CAMBRIDGE
UNIVERSITY PRESS

CAMBRIDGE
UNIVERSITY PRESS

Shaftesbury Road, Cambridge CB2 8EA, United Kingdom

One Liberty Plaza, 20th Floor, New York, NY 10006, USA

477 Williamstown Road, Port Melbourne, VIC 3207, Australia

314–321, 3rd Floor, Plot 3, Splendor Forum, Jasola District Centre, New Delhi – 110025, India

103 Penang Road, #05–06/07, Visioncrest Commercial, Singapore 238467

Cambridge University Press is part of Cambridge University Press & Assessment, a department of the University of Cambridge.

We share the University's mission to contribute to society through the pursuit of education, learning and research at the highest international levels of excellence.

www.cambridge.org
Information on this title: www.cambridge.org/9781009152624

DOI: 10.1017/9781009152631

When citing this work, please include a reference to the DOI 10.1017/9781009152631

First published 2023

A catalogue record for this publication is available from the British Library

ISBN 978-1-009-15262-4 Hardback

We dedicate this book to our families.

CONTENTS

CONTRIBUTORS

ABDULLAH ADLAN is chairman of the National Committee of Healthcare Ethics, Saudi Health Council, Saudi Arabia. He has more than 20 years of leadership and research experience, along with two PhDs. He served as the first employee in what became a multibillion SAR research entity in the King Abdullah International Medical Research Center, and in 2018, he was a co-founder of the Saudi National Institute of Health.

MOHAMMAD ASIM BEG is a professor in the Department of Pathology and Microbiology, Aga Khan University, Pakistan. He graduated in 1985 from Nishter Medical College Hospital, Multan, Pakistan with an MBBS. In 1993 he obtained his PhD from the Department of Biological Sciences, Division of Infectious Diseases at the University of Salford, and received his Fellowship from the Royal College of Physicians in Edinburgh in 2011. In September 1997 he joined the Department of Pathology and Microbiology at Aga Khan University as a senior instructor and became a professor in 2013. He is also a Consultant Parasitologist at AKUH. At the Department of Pathology and Laboratory Medicine, he teaches parasitology to undergraduate and postgraduate students, and has been the backbone of parasitic diagnostics in the CAP and JCIA accredited Clinical Laboratory. He has had several PhD students under his supervision and has done extensive research on malaria and parasitic diseases in Pakistan. Asim was former Chair of the Aga University Hospital Ethics Committee and has been an invited speaker both nationally and internationally. He has received many internal and external grants and has around 85 publications, the majority of which are international, to his credit.

MIRIAM ETHEL BENTWICH, PhD, is a senior lecturer of bioethics at the Azrieli Faculty of Medicine, Bar-Ilan University, Israel, with a rich background in political philosophy, along with a proven expertise in empirical ethics and normative philosophically based ethics. She also leads the

Medical Ethics & Humanities programme at the Faculty of Medicine and was responsible for its unique and innovative design as well as its successful application. Miriam is engaged with a broad range of issues in biomedical ethics and medical humanities, and her publications in leading academic journals include varied topics such as coping and evasive strategies in small group learning of medical ethics; teaching art as a source for enhancement of empathy and tolerance to ambiguity among medical students; perceptions of multicultural caregivers on human dignity and autonomy of patients with dementia; physicians' perspectives on enemy patients; vulnerability, integrity and undermining the justification for funding of in vitro fertilisation; and reprogenetics, reproductive risks and cultural awareness. She has published a book (*Reclaiming Liberty*; Palgrave Macmillan, 2012) and articles in leading academic journals (*Nature Biotechnology*, *American Journal of Bioethics*, *American Journal of Public Health*, *Ethnicity and Health*, *Journal of Medical Ethics*, *Nursing Ethics*, *BMC Medical Education*, etc.). Her research in end-of-life (EOL) care spans from regulatory facets of EOL to perceptions and coping mechanisms of multicultural caregivers attending to patients with dementia, as well as perceptions of multicultural nurses and physicians regarding dying patients in Israel.

TRACEY EVANS CHAN is an associate professor in the Faculty of Law, National University of Singapore (NUS), specialising in biomedical law and ethics. He has published in the field both locally and internationally, and served in a number of Singapore expert committees on matters such as surrogacy, transplant ethics, human-animal combinations in biomedical research and mitochondrial germline modification. His recent publications include an article on Singapore's advance care planning initiatives, which appeared in the *Journal of Law & Medicine* (2019). Professionally, he was called to the Singapore Bar in 1998 and then spent two years clerking for the Supreme Court of Singapore before joining academia. He concluded a year-long secondment to the Singapore Ministry of Health as a deputy director in the Regulatory Policy and Legislation Division in 2015, where he assisted in the policy work on the Human Biomedical Research Act 2015. He is also a member of the NUS Institutional Review Board.

BO CHEN is currently an assistant professor at the Faculty of Law, Macau University of Science and Technology and an adjunct lecturer at the Centre for Disability Law and Policy, National University of Ireland

(NUI) Galway. He holds a PhD in law from NUI Galway. Before that, he worked with a China-based public interest law institute that advocates for the rights of persons with mental health issues. His research interests include China's mental health and capacity law, disability law and the United Nations Convention on the Rights of Persons with Disabilities.

DAISY CHEUNG is an assistant professor at the Faculty of Law and deputy director of the Centre for Medical Ethics & Law at the University of Hong Kong. She obtained her Bachelor of Arts in psychology from Amherst College, her Bachelor of Laws (Hons) and Postgraduate Certificate in Laws from the University of Hong Kong and her Bachelor of Civil Law from the University of Oxford. Daisy's research focuses on mental health and capacity law. Her work includes analyses on a number of issues related to Hong Kong's Mental Health Ordinance (MHO), with a focus on the problematic way in which mental capacity is conceived of and assessed in different contexts. She has written on public mental health ethics in the face of the COVID-19 pandemic, and has researched mental capacity law and ethics across several contexts, including her funded research on adult guardianship regimes, an ongoing project on the implications of novel neurointerventions on mental capacity law and ethics and an upcoming funded project on best interests determinations.

LEONARDO D. DE CASTRO is a professorial lecturer in the Department of Philosophy, University of the Philippines Diliman; chair of the Philippine Health Research Ethics Board, the national policymaking body for human research protection; and sits on the National Ethics Committee. When he was vice chairman of the UNESCO International Bioethics Committee, he served on the drafting team for the International Declaration on Bioethics and Human Rights. As member of the UNESCO Advisory Expert Committee for the Teaching of Ethics, he contributed to the development of a Core Curriculum on Bioethics for the agency's Ethics Teacher Training Course (ETTC). In addition to being lecturer for the ETTC, he has participated in UNESCO's programme to provide orientation and training for National Bioethics Committees in resource-challenged countries. As a consultant to the European Commission he assisted in the formulation of national ethics guidelines for health research and conducted training workshops for members of national ethics committees. As a consultant to the World Health Organization (WHO) he contributed to the drafting of the WHO Guiding Principles on Human Cell, Tissue and Organ Transplantation.

He was also on the drafting group for the Declaration of Istanbul on Organ Trafficking and the declaration by the Asian Working Group Against Organ Trafficking. As president of the Asian Bioethics Association and as editor-in-chief of the *Asian Bioethics Review*, he supported the development of young Asian academics. He has done research on bioethics teaching and ethics in global health, healthcare worker migration, organ transplantation, research among indigenous populations and genetic discrimination. His awards include the Takashi Fujii Prize of the International Federation of Social Science Organizations, a National Book Award from the Manila Critics Circle, an Outstanding Monograph Award from the National Academy of Science and Technology and several International Publication Awards from the University of the Philippines.

KELLY AMAL DHRU is a research associate and PhD candidate at the University of Hamburg, Germany. She is a law graduate from Gujarat National Law University in India, and holds the degrees of Bachelor of Civil Law (Distinction) and Master of Philosophy in law with a focus on legal philosophy from University College, the University of Oxford. She was a Fulbright-Nehru Master's Fellow in Bioethics and Public Health Law, as a part of which she completed the Master of Laws degree from Harvard Law School. Kelly is currently a PhD fellow at the AMBSL Graduate School of Law and Research Associate (Wissenschaftliche Mitarbeiterin) at the University of Hamburg, where her PhD thesis focuses on connecting the debates around legal right-holding and legal personhood to the legal rights surrounding the emerging neurotechnologies, particularly concerning decisional and bodily autonomy. Kelly has taught in India, the United Kingdom, and Germany, and her research interests are bioethics, legal philosophy, and legal regulation. In a parallel universe, Kelly has been a theatre artist, and is a co-founder of Lawtoons (www.lawtoons.in), a series of comic books to educate children about laws and rights.

MICHAEL DUNN is an associate professor at the Centre for Biomedical Ethics, Yong Loo Lin School of Medicine, National University of Singapore, where he is also the director of undergraduate education, leading the health ethics, law and professional curriculum for medical students. Michael's research focuses primarily on the ethical dimensions of community-based and long-term health and social care management, practice and law internationally. The other main area of his current work examines questions about the nature of bioethics, the value of empirical ethics research and methodological strategies for answering bioethical questions. He has authored more than 70 peer-reviewed journal articles and book chapters in the fields of bioethics, medical law and health and social care services research. His two most recent books are *Medical Ethics: A Very Short Introduction* (Oxford University Press, 2018) and *Empirical Bioethics: Theoretical and Practical Perspectives* (Cambridge University Press, 2017). Before joining the National University of Singapore in 2022, Dunn was based at the Ethox Centre, University of Oxford, for 13 years. He completed his undergraduate and postgraduate degrees at the University of Cambridge and has held visiting teaching and research positions at universities and research centres in Hong Kong, Tokyo, New York, Oslo, Amsterdam and Bradford.

RAVINDRA B. GHOOI is director of Scientia Clinical Services, India. He is a pharmacologist, with a doctorate from Bombay University and a post-doctorate from Max Planck Institute in Goettingen, Germany. He has spent over 30 years in drug discovery and development, conducting preclinical and clinical research and organising clinical trials and bioavailability and bioequivalence studies. Starting with preclinical research at Haffkine Institute and Max Planck, he shifted to the pharmaceutical industry as a medical advisor. After two decades he made a lateral shift to the clinical research industry. Ravindra was instrumental in setting up a contract research organisation (CRO), CliniRx, in which he headed the clinical operations. From the CRO, he moved to teaching clinical research and retired as professor of drug development and clinical research at the Symbiosis International University. Apart from his professional duties he is involved in social issues, patients' rights and palliative care. In the 1990s, to ensure the supply of morphine to cancer patients, he challenged the Narcotic Drugs and Psychotropic Substances Act, which put morphine out of reach for even cancer patients. This long and difficult fight ended with the Indian Supreme Court amending the law in 2016. He has since been working with groups that have been trying to obtain legal sanction for euthanasia and advance directives in the country. He presently devotes his time to developing a culture of ethics in clinical research and guides ethics committees and research programmes in Pune. He also is involved in teaching ethics and regulations at local universities on a visiting basis. He has contributed to more than 65 research papers in national and international journals and contributed chapters to books on clinical research and related subjects.

He heads a small consulting firm known as Scientia Clinical Services, in Pune, where he lives and works.

ASMA HAMID is the founder and head of litigation at Asma Hamid Associates, Lahore, Pakistan. She received her LLM from Harvard Law School. Before her independent practice, she served as an equity partner in one of the largest law firms in Pakistan and as advocate general for the Province of Punjab – she holds the unique distinction of being the first woman in Pakistan's history to hold this post. Asma regularly advises clients in corporate and commercial laws by reviewing, drafting and negotiating contracts, general advice, opinions, due diligence, structuring and leading complex and high-value transactions. She has carried out extensive work in the areas of public and private sector projects, tax laws, procurement laws, contracts, joint ventures, banking and finance laws, capital markets and securities laws, intellectual property laws, foreign investment, insurance laws, construction and real estate laws, employment and labour laws, and energy, water and environmental laws. Her extensive litigation portfolio includes representing individuals, multinationals and corporates before the Supreme Court, Federal Shariat Court, Lahore High Court, Islamabad High Court, Tribunals and governmental departments.

ERFAN HUSSAIN is a critical care consultant at Aga Khan University Hospital in Pakistan. He is a diplomate of the American Board of Internal Medicine in critical care medicine. He has over 30 years of critical care experience, holding the position of director of critical care medicine at the Northwell Manhasset Hospital in New York. After immigrating to Pakistan, he held the position of director of adult critical care at the Aga Khan University Hospital and Medical College in Pakistan. Having been a member of hospital ethics committees in the United States and in Karachi, he has 20 years of clinical ethical consultation experience. In addition, he has been co-chair of the Aga Khan University Hospital Ethics Committee. While in this position, he devised several policies covering issues such as brain death determination, do-not-resuscitate, end-of-life care and a surrogacy policy. Erfan is also a member of the Aga Khan Medical College Bioethics Committee and recently was a lead author of the hospital's ventilator allocation policy during the COVID-19 pandemic. Erfan is also a visiting lecturer at the Center for Bioethics and Culture at the Sindh Institute of Urology and Transplantation.

GHAIATH HUSSEIN is an assistant professor in medical ethics and law at Trinity College Dublin, Ireland. A medical doctor and bioethicist, he earned a master's degree from the University of Toronto, Canada, and a PhD in bioethics from the University of Birmingham, United Kingdom,. He is the principal co-author of the *Professionalism and Ethics Handbook for Residents* (Saudi Commission for Health Specialties, 2015), the main training and medical licensing examination reference for medical ethics in Saudi Arabia and other Gulf Cooperation Council countries. He has also contributed to other international training manuals, including the WHO's *Training Manual on Ethics in Epidemics, Emergencies and Disasters: Research, Surveillance and Patient Care* (2015). For more than a decade, he has been teaching bioethics to medical students, interns, researchers, postgraduate trainees and public health practitioners. He has been helping medical schools and health institutions in Saudi Arabia establish bioethics departments, develop medical ethics curricula and set examination standards. Regionally, he has helped in developing and delivering the first public health ethics curriculum in the Middle East in collaboration with EMPHNET. His international expertise includes providing consultations and the membership of research ethics committees for such organisations as WHO, UNESCO and Médecins Sans Frontières.

RICHARD HUXTABLE is professor of medical ethics and law and director of the Centre for Ethics in Medicine in the Medical School at the University of Bristol. Qualified in law, sociolegal studies and bioethics, he conducts research primarily regarding end-of-life decision-making, surgical ethics and clinical ethics. He is principal investigator on a Wellcome Trust collaborative project, "Balancing Best Interests in Healthcare, Ethics and Law" (BABEL). In addition to numerous articles, he has authored or edited nine books, including *Healthcare Ethics, Law and Professionalism* (Routledge, 2018) and *Law, Ethics and Compromise at the Limits of Life: To Treat or Not to Treat?* (Routledge, 2012). Richard has served on various ethics committees, including those of the British Medical Association and the Royal College of General Practitioners, and he is chair of the UK Clinical Ethics Network. Richard tweets at @ProfRHuxtable.

MAN TENG IONG is a senior instructor at the Faculty of Law at the University of Macau. He finished his LLB at the Faculty of Law, New University of Lisbon (Portugal) before completing his Masters of Law degree at the Faculty of Law, University of Macau, with a dissertation regarding advance directives in Macau. He is now a PhD student at the School of Law of University of Minho (Portugal) with a dissertation regarding medical liability and ethics. He worked as a legal advisor in the Macao Health Bureau for six years and gained legal experience about medical law issues. His area of interest embraces medical malpractice, patient's safety, patient's rights, human and fundamental rights and criminal law. He published papers about medical law and ethics in international journals, such as *Medicine and Law* and *Biolaw Journal.*

FUTOSHI IWATA is a professor of law at the Kanagawa University, Kanagawa, Japan. He was previously a law professor at Sophia University (Tokyo, Japan) (2000–20). He obtained a PhD from University of Tokyo Law and Political Science Department. He also obtained two master's degrees at the University of Wisconsin Law School (MLI, 1992 and LLM, 1994). He was a research visitor at the Melbourne Law School (Australia) in 2004–5 (issues involving medical errors and the role of law) and at the University of Wisconsin Law School (United States) in 2013–4 as a Fulbright scholar (the ethical and legal issues pertaining to newborn screening). His research interests are mainly in two fields: (1) lay participation in criminal procedure and death penalty and (2) law and medicine, including medical errors, end of life, public health law and newborn screening. He has been a member of several committees at the Ministry of Health, the Ambulance Agency and the Ministry of Justice of Japan. Relating to advance directives, he was a member of the Ministry of Health committee for revising the Process Guidelines of the Decision-Making for the End-of-Life Medicine and Care in 2018.

SHARON KAUR is a senior lecturer at the Faculty of Law at University of Malaya, Malaysia. She teaches medical law and ethics to both undergraduate and graduate students. Sharon's research interests have primarily revolved around medical research ethics and issues of competency and consent. In 2017, she spent a year as a visiting research fellow with the CENTRES programme at the Centre for Biomedical Ethics at National University of Singapore where she developed an interest in issues relating to global health ethics and the rights of marginalised populations.

NOSHIN KHAN is an early childhood education and development consultant and freelance researcher in Pakistan with 18 years of experience in early childhood education (ECE) . She has a Master of Arts degree in early childhood studies and a Bachelor of Arts in ECE from Ryerson University, Toronto, Canada. She is a registered member of the Ontario College of Early Childhood Educators. Noshin has taught early childhood educators in the diploma programme at Sheridan College Toronto and undergraduate ECE students at Ryerson University for several years. She has presented at several international conferences such as the Global Summit on Childhood and Comparative and International Education Society. Moreover, she has represented Pakistan at international forums where the importance of ECE has been at the fore. Noshin is a part of the Early Childhood Development Action Network and a member of its task force working on supporting efforts to invest in and build capacity of the early childhood development workforce to deliver high-quality services to children from birth through school entry. Most recent and notable representation was being part of a team selected by the WHO to develop global guidelines for physical activity, sedentary behaviour and screen time for children aged 0–5 years. Noshin has co-authored "Pediatric Perspectives on Diabetes Self-Care: A Process of Achieving Acceptance", which was published in the *Qualitative Health Research Academic Journal* in 2015. Currently Noshin represents Pakistan at Childhood Education International and is working on projects with UNICEF in Balochistan, which involve primary and secondary research, data analysis, report writing and developing teacher education programmes.

SATOSHI KODAMA has a background in moral and political philosophy. He graduated from Kyoto University and is associate professor in the Department of Ethics in Kyoto University's Graduate School of Letters. Formerly he held a lectureship at the Department of Biomedical Ethics in the University of Tokyo Graduate School of Medicine. His research interests include moral theory (utilitarianism), moral methodology (the role of intuition in moral reasoning), ethics and evolution, end-of-life issues, resource allocation and public health ethics. He has co-authored textbooks on biomedical ethics both in Japanese and English, and he has translated Albert Jonsen's *Clinical Ethics*, Tony Hope's *Medical Ethics: A Very Short Introduction* and Peter Singer's *The Life You Can Save*. His recent work includes *Exploring Bioethics Through Manga: Questions of the Meaning of "Life"* (Kodama, Satoshi and Natsutaka, 2018).

ILHAK LEE is an associate professor in the Department of Medical Humanities and Social Sciences, Division of Medical Law and Ethics,

Asian Institute for Bioethics and Health Law (AIBHL), Yonsei University Medical College (YUMC), South Korea. His major areas of research interest are end-of-life decision making, clinical ethics consultation, and ethical, legal and social implications studies in human genomics. He is trying to find a robust methodology in bioethics to guide practitioners and policymakers. This approach to bioethics aims to bridge the experiences of the local society with philosophical and theoretical ethics. He is also working on practical guidelines that help practitioners with difficult issues in end-of-life care decision-making. Ilhak currently serves as a director of the Division of Medical Law and Ethics, YUMC. He serves as a member of various ethical committees, as well as a member of national bioethics advisory committee expert groups. He is an active board member in many academic societies such as the Korean Association of Medical Ethics and the Korean Association of Medical Law.

REBECCA LEE is an associate professor at the Department of Law of the University of Hong Kong. She holds a Bachelor of Laws degree from the University of Hong Kong) and a Bachelor of Civil Law degree from the University of Oxford. She teaches and researches in equity and trusts, contracts and non-profit law. She is co-editor (with Lusina Ho) of *Special Needs Financial Planning: A Comparative Perspective* (Cambridge University Press, 2019). Her joint research project on special needs trust has led to the successful introduction of a trust scheme for individuals with cognitive impairment. Currently, she is working on research projects on selected issues in trusts law, charity governance and special needs support.

RICHARD BOON LEONG LIM is a consultant palliative medicine physician and the head of palliative medicine in Hospital Selayang. He also serves as the National Head of Service for Palliative Medicine in the Ministry of Health Malaysia. He has been involved in the development of palliative medicine in Malaysia since 1998 and has worked constantly to improve the provision of palliative care and compassionate care within the Malaysian healthcare system. He developed the National Palliative Care Policy and Strategic Plan for Malaysia which was launched in 2019 and among the strategies to improve palliative care and good end-of-life care includes the promotion of advance care planning. He trains other doctors, nurses and paramedical personnel in various aspects of palliative care with a particular interest in ethics, communication skills and end-of-life care.

ALEXANDER ATRIO L. LOPEZ is an instructor in philosophy at the University of the Philippines Diliman. He graduated with a Bachelor of Arts degree in philosophy (summa cum laude). He also has a Bachelor's degree in basic medical sciences from the University of the Philippines Manila.

RENATO B. MANALOTO is an assistant professor of philosophy, University of Philippines Diliman. He has a Master of Arts degree in philosophy and a Bachelor of Laws from the University of the Philippines in Diliman. He specialises in philosophy of law, phenomenology and existentialism, bioethics and research ethics. In 2005, he was an international fellow in bioethics and research ethics administration, a programme implemented jointly by the Western International Review Board, WHO and the University of Washington at Seattle.

REINA OZEKI-HAYASHI is a visiting scholar in the Department of Biomedical Ethics in the University of Tokyo Graduate School of Medicine and an affiliate instructor in the Department of Bioethics and Humanities in the University of Washington's School of Medicine, United States. She obtained an MD from Sapporo Medical University in 2001 and worked as a gastroenterologist and internist from 2001 to 2009. From 2009 to 2011, she pursued her career at the Department of Palliative Medicine, Tsukuba Medical Center Hospital, and obtained a Master of Public Health degree in 2012, and a PhD in social medicine in 2018 from the University of Tokyo. She was an assistant professor at the Department of Biomedical Ethics, the University of Tokyo from 2018 to 2021. She obtained a Master of Bioethics degree from Harvard University in 2022. Her research interests primarily include three fields: (1) medical decision-making process and communication at the end of life, (2) medical futility, and (3) teaching and training for medical professionals in managing moral distress. Ozeki-Hayashi translated into Japanese Lawrence J. Schneiderman and Nancy S. Jecker's *Wrong Medicine Doctors, Patients, and Futile Treatment* (second edition) in 2021. She is a facilitator of the PEACE Project (Palliative care programme Emphasizing symptom management and Assessment for Continuous medical Education) and CST (Communication Skills Training programme for oncologists).

ALIREZA PARSAPOOR is an assistant professor in the Medical Ethics and History of Medicine Research Centre and Department of Medical Ethics,

Tehran University of Medical Sciences. He holds an MD (1998), MPH (2008) and PhD in medical ethics (2014). His research interests include clinical ethics and patients' rights. He is a member of several hospital clinical and research ethics committees and is also secretary of the National Committee of Clinical Ethics. He is a member of the National Committee of Ethics in Research of Iran and a member of the Board of Medical Ethics of Iran.

VERA LÚCIA RAPOSO is an assistant professor at the Faculty of Law of Coimbra University, Portugal and a part-time contributor to the Centre for Medical Ethics and Law, University of Hong Kong. In the past, she was a lecturer at the University of Macau (where she was associate professor) and of-counsel at the law firm Vieira de Almeida e Associados, in Lisbon, in the departments of health law and privacy law. She is a frequent speaker in academic events worldwide and a member of the editorial board of the *European Journal of Health Law*. She is the author of several studies in Portuguese, English and Spanish (some translated into Chinese), particularly on biomedical law (medical liability, patient safety, gene editing and reproductive issues) and new digital technologies (artificial intelligence, digital governance, data protection).

EHSAN SHAMSI-GOOSHKI is an assistant professor of Medical Ethics at Tehran University of Medical Sciences. He graduated as a physician in 2005 and was enrolled in the first PhD programme of medical ethics in Iran in 2009. Until his graduation in 2013, he was involved in several research projects, teaching medical ethics to undergraduate and graduate students, lecturing in a number of national and international workshops/conferences, participating in the UNESCO Ethics Teachers Training Course, interning in the department of ethics at the World Health Organization in Geneva, and visiting as a research fellow at the Institute of Biomedical Ethics, University of Zurich and the Kennedy Institute of Ethics, Georgetown University, Washington DC simultaneously. At the Tehran University of Medical Sciences, he applies ethical standards in practice as the director of the National Committee for Ethics in Biomedical Research at the Ministry of Health and Medical Education, the senior advisor and secretary of the Medical Ethics Committee at the Iran Medical Council and the secretary of the Medical Ethics Group at the Iran Academy of Medical Sciences. Since 2018, the UNESCO Director General has assigned him as one of the 36 members of the

UNESCO International Bioethics Committee. Ehsan has published a number of research articles and book chapters both in English and Persian. His most prominent works include the (1) development of the Code of Ethics for the Iran Medical Council, which has been released recently as an official guideline that Iranian medical professionals are required to consider in their practice and (2) establishment of a national online accreditation system for research ethics committees and a national repository for the committees' approved research projects.

ZAIN ABBAS SYED is a research associate at the ETHOX Centre, University of Oxford, and internal medicine trainee, North-West London Deanery. He graduated in 2013 with a first-class bachelor of arts (Hons) in medical sciences from Christ Church College at the University of Oxford. With the support of Oxford, he then took a gap-study period between 2013 and 2016 and travelled to the Holy City of Qom in the Islamic Republic of Iran to study towards a bachelor of arts degree in Islamic jurisprudence and belief at Qom Seminary. His thesis collates and analyses the opinions of contemporary Shia jurists on the issue of brain death. He returned to Oxford in 2016 to complete his medical degree and successfully graduated with a bachelor of medicine/bachelor of surgery degree in 2019. Zain was then accepted on a highly competitive Academic Foundation Programme at the University of Oxford to, alongside his clinical training, further his research in Islamic medical ethics and law. His current projects include A Comparison between Shia Islamic Law and United Kingdom Law on the Issue of Abortion; Advance Directives and End of Life Decision Making in Muslim Countries and Islamic Law; A Critical Analysis of the Issue of Brain Death according to current Shia Islamic Jurists; and A Pragmatic, Multidisciplinary, Evidence-based approach to Al-Istiftā' on the Issue of Organ Donation after Death. In the future, Zain hopes to pursue an integrated clinical academic pathway in internal medicine, further his Islamic seminary studies and develop his research interest in Islamic law and its application to medical ethics.

MIHO TANAKA is a senior researcher at the Japan Medical Association Research Institute (JMARI), where she has worked since 2013. She received a Master of Public Health degree from the Graduate School of Medicine at the University of Tokyo in 2012. She is also a PhD student at the Graduate School of Core Ethics and Frontier Sciences, Ritsumeikan University. Her research interests include the ethical, legal and social issues around end-of-life care in Japan, other Asian countries and countries in the West, including Korea, Taiwan, the United Kingdom, and the United States. Currently, Tanaka is also interested in the ethical, legal and social issues surrounding the COVID-19 pandemic, such as quarantine; allocation of scarce resources; social isolation; discrimination against disabled people, older people, infected people, and healthcare providers; advance care planning; decision-making in end-of-life care; etc. She has published several articles about ethical issues in end-of-life care in *BMC Medical Ethics*, *Asian Bioethics Review*, *Journal of the Japan Association for Bioethics* and *Journal of Patient Safety and Conflict Management*. She also recently published an academic book, *Choices at the End of Life: Considering End-of-Life Care* in Japanese (Keiso Shobo, 2017) in collaboration with her colleagues. Miho has joined the international collaborative research group, International Joint Research on Ethical and Legal Issues of End-of-Life Care in East Asia (https://en.asian-eolc-ethics.com/). Additionally, she was involved in the research project End of Life Care in the United Kingdom and Japan – Intersections in Culture, Practice and Policy led by the University of Glasgow (www.gla.ac.uk/research/az/endoflifestudies/projects/the-mitori-project/).

THITINANT TENGAUMNUAY has been a law lecturer at the Faculty of Law, Chulalongkorn University, Thailand, since 2014. She received her LLB (First-Class Honours) from Chulalongkorn University before continuing her masters of law at the University of Oxford where she studied medical law and ethics and another LLM in environmental law at New York University. She has recently completed a PhD at the University of Bristol, in the area of environmental law and regulation. Her areas of interest include medical law, criminal law and environmental law.

DANIEL FU-CHANG TSAI (MD, PhD) is the founding professor of the Department & Graduate Institute of Medical Education and Bioethics in the College of Medicine and director of the Center for Biomedical Ethics at National Taiwan University (NTU) and is jointly appointed in the Department of Family Medicine, the Institute of Medical Device and Imaging, and the Graduate Institute of Clinical Medicine. He is also an attending physician in the Department of Medical Research at NTU Hospital and served as the chairman of the Research Ethics Committee. Daniel is a family physician and bioethicist. He graduated from NTU College of Medicine in 1989 and received family medicine resident training at NTU Hospital. He earned his PhD in bioethics from the

University of Manchester in 1999 and has been working in bioethics, clinical ethics and research ethics since. He was formerly head of the Department of Social Medicine. He has been in charge of many national projects commissioned by the Ministry of Education, the Ministry of Health and Welfare, and the Ministry of Science and Technology. He has publications in *Journal of Medical Ethics*, *Hastings Center Report*, *American Journal of Bioethics*, among others and also published 20 books and 15 book chapters on various topics in bioethics. He is on the editorial board of many medical/bioethics journals. He served as vice president of the International Association of Bioethics in 2016–7 and president of the Taiwan Association of Institutional Review Boards in 2018–21. He is a member of the Merck Ethics Advisory Panel and was awarded honorary membership by the UNESCO Chair of Bioethics in 2015, the Goldman-Berland Lectureship in Palliative Medicine in 2019 and Hastings Center Fellow in 2021.

YESIM ISIL ULMAN is a professor of medical history and ethics at Acibadem University School of Medicine, Istanbul, Turkey. She became associate professor in 2005 and has been full professor since 2013. She has studied humanities, political science, history of medicine and ethics. Her MA, MSc and PhD were on the history of modernisation in science and medicine (1986–99). She chaired and contributed to the studies and works of the Turkish Bioethics Association (2006–12); and coordinated in the Training Programme of Health Law Certificate for Acibadem Univ. Continued Education (ASEGEM) (2010–4). She served as vice-chair of the University Research Ethics Committee (2009–14) and a member of the Hospital Ethics Committee (2009–present) and Animal Experiments Ethics Committee (2012–present). She is on the editorial board of *Acibadem University Health Sciences Journal*. She was invited to establish the Turkey Working Group of the Cambridge Consortium of Bioethics Education (2013) in collaboration with a multidisciplinary team. She is an internationally certified trainer of Moral Case Deliberation, an innovative and dialogical approach to teaching ethics and ethics consultation developed by the Amsterdam UMC Medical Humanities. She has contributed to the Horizon VIRT2UE Research Integrity Project as a stakeholder and co-trainer. She initiated the Acibadem University Bioethics Master of Science Programme and was acting director of the Acibadem University Institute of Social Sciences. She serves as referee for European Union Cost Projects and reporter to the Council of Europe Bioethics Committee (DH-BIO). She is the delegate of Turkey at the International Society for the History of Medicine. She has collaborated on numerous international and local research projects on vulnerable groups, gender-based violence, main issues of bioethics, emerging technologies and teaching bioethics. Her latest research projects are on the ethical aspects of Artificial Intelligence in medicine and healthcare and End-of-Life Decision-making and Living Wills.

THOMAS TAN HOOI WANG graduated from the Faculty of Law, University of Malaya in 2020. Currently, he is pursuing a master's degree in commercial law at the same university. During his undergraduate studies, he was the director of University of Malaysia's Consti Team, a student body that aims to raise the constitutional law literacy of the public. He was also very active in volunteering, running a community service project for two years alongside his friends at the residential college level.

MUHAMMAD ATIF WAQAR is an assistant professor and founding chief of palliative medicine, Department of Oncology, Aga Khan University, Pakistan. He completed his residency training in internal medicine at the Brooklyn Hospital Center (an affiliate of the Weil-Cornell Medical School) in New York. He then pursued two successive fellowships in hospice/palliative medicine and geriatric medicine at the University of Nevada School of Medicine in Reno. Muhammad is board certified in internal medicine, hospice/palliative medicine and geriatric medicine with the American Board of Internal Medicine and its subspecialties. He served as a consultant in palliative medicine at the VA Sierra Nevada Healthcare System in Reno. There, he was also appointed as the medical director for the Home Based Palliative Care services. Muhammad has a strong interest in medical education and has previously served as a clinical assistant professor and associate programme director for the fellowship programme in palliative medicine at his alma mater, the University of Nevada School of Medicine. He has extensive experience in the areas of long-term care, home-based medical care and palliative and end-of-life care. Realising the dire need for palliative care services in Pakistan, he relocated to Pakistan to begin setting up the city's first multidisciplinary palliative care service at the Aga Khan University Hospital in Karachi. Under his leadership and vision, the palliative care programme has grown exponentially to now include inpatient palliative care consultations throughout the hospital, as well as admissions to the palliative care service for inpatient end-of-life care as well as intractable symptom management. To address the community-based palliative care needs, his department is now offering daily outpatient palliative care clinics. Drawing from his extensive experience in the realm of non-institutional long-term care, Muhammad helped set up an extensive network of multidisciplinary home-based palliative care services in Karachi, the first of its kind in Pakistan.

JENNY KA YAN YAU is a juris doctor candidate and research assistant at the University of Hong Kong. She has a degree in English and comparative literature from the University of St Andrews. She has extensive experience working with global nongovernmental organisations and charities, and her main areas of interest in law are LGBTQ+ rights and disability rights.

ACKNOWLEDGEMENTS

The ideas behind this book were shaped by an international conference organised by the editors and held online between 30 September and 2 October 2020. This conference involved a number of additional people we would like to thank for their contribution to the development of the book. We would like to thank Olesya Petrol, Sherlynn Chan, Jacqueline Yuen, Albert Lam, Alex Ruck Keene, Urania Chiu, the Centre for Medical Ethics and Law (CMEL) of the Faculty of Law of the University of Hong Kong, the Law Society of Hong Kong and the Ethox Centre and the Wellcome Centre for Ethics and Humanities at the University of Oxford for their contributions and support.

We would also like to express our deepest gratitude for the generous financial support of the Research Grants Council of Hong Kong (Project No. 27611017) and the WYNG Foundation, without which this project would not have been possible.

We would like to thank all our research assistants, Janice Chan, Lok Yiu Lau, Dominic Lo, Kesalan Hui, Dorothy Chan, Nicole Mok, Jenny Ka Yan Yau, Jacky Cheng, Sze Wing Chan and Melissa Lam, who provided us with invaluable assistance throughout the process. We would also like to thank in particular Jane Or and Phoenix To from CMEL and Victoria Kwok from the Faculty of Law of the University of Hong Kong for their administrative support.

We would like to thank Joe Ng, Gemma Smith and the team at Cambridge University Press for their immense patience and guidance throughout the publication process.

Last but not least, we would like to thank our family. In particular, Daisy would like to thank Steven and Jeremy for their love and endless patience. And we would both like to thank our parents for their love, understanding and support.

ABBREVIATIONS

ACP	advance care plan
AD	advance directive
ADRT	advance decision to refuse treatment
AIDS	acquired immunodeficiency syndrome
ALS	amyotrophic lateral sclerosis
AMD	advance medical directive
AMDA	Advance Medical Directive Act
ARAS	Agency for the Registration of Advance Statements for Life-sustaining Treatment
ASLST	Advance Statement for Life-sustaining Treatment
BLWPA	Beijing Living Will Promotion Association
CC	Criminal Code
CJI	Chief Justice of India
CoE	Code of Ethics
COVID-19	coronavirus disease 2019
CPR	cardiopulmonary resuscitation
DNACPR	do not attempt cardiopulmonary resuscitation
DNAR	do not attempt resuscitation
DNR	do-not-resuscitate
DP	dying patient
eHRSS	electronic health record sharing system
ELCP	end-of-life care plan
ELDA	Act on Hospice and Palliative Care and Decisions on Life-Sustaining Treatment for Patients at the End of Life
FHB	Hong Kong Food and Health Bureau
HDI	Human Development Index
HKLRC	Hong Kong Law Reform Commission
HPCA	Hospice Palliative Care Act
ICU	intensive care unit
IEC	Institutional Ethics Committee
IRIMC	Islamic Republic of Iran Medical Council
IRR	Implementing Rules and Regulations

JMFC	Judicial magistrate first class
KAMS	Korean Association of Medical Societies
LGBT	lesbian, gay, bisexual and transgender
LPD	Law on Practicing Doctors
LST	life-sustaining treatment
LSTP	life-sustaining treatment plan
LW	living will
MCA	Mental Capacity Act
MHA	Mental Health Act
MHO	Mental Health Ordinance
MMC	Malaysian Medical Council
MOH	Ministry of Health
MOHME	Ministry of Health and Medical Education
MoNHSRC	Ministry of National Health Services Regulation and Coordination
NCEBR	National Committee for Ethics in Biomedical Research
NCEC	National Clinical Ethics Committee
NCEME	National Committee for Ethics and Medical Education
NCORT	National Committee on Resuscitation Training
NEHR	National Electronic Health Record
NHCO	National Health Commission Office
NHMA	National Mental Health Act
NMEC	National Medical Ethics Committee (Singapore)
OCS	Office of the Council of the State
PAD	psychiatric advance directive
POLST	physician's order for life-sustaining treatment
PRAA	Patient Right to Autonomy Act
PRC	People's Republic of China
ReSPECT	Recommended Summary Plan for Emergency Care and Treatment
SA	Saudi Arabia
SCME	Supreme Council on Medical Ethics
SDM	surrogate decision-maker
SMC	Singapore Medical Council
UHC	universal health coverage
UNCRPD	United Nations Convention on the Rights of Persons with Disabilities

Introduction

DAISY CHEUNG, MICHAEL DUNN & RICHARD HUXTABLE

Population ageing, which has been described as one of the four global demographic "megatrends",[1] is quickly becoming a concern for many countries around the world. The growth in the size and proportion of the elderly has many implications, including the fact that there has been, and will continue to be, a significant growth in the number of individuals who are living longer, and because of that, living with chronic health conditions that often accompany advanced age. With this comes the need to make decisions about the extent to which one wishes to continue receiving treatment towards the end of life, as well as the nature of such treatment. Unsurprisingly, therefore, the development of the advance directive (AD) has been the focus of ongoing discussion in many jurisdictions. In this volume, the AD is defined as a statement in which a competent person makes an advance decision in matters concerning their health and welfare, which is to be implemented in the event that the person becomes incompetent (loses capacity) in the future. In the following, we begin with an explication of ADs in a broad, international context, laying out the origins of the concept and how this is developing over time, as well as some of the conceptual and practical challenges that arise when ADs are implemented.

I.1 Advance Directives in Context: Origins and Challenges

The fundamental idea and purpose of an AD can be usefully understood by invoking the mythical tale of Odysseus and the Sirens in Homer's epic poem *The Odyssey*.[2] Odysseus is warned that his ship will sail past the Sirens, who will attempt to incapacitate the crew and lure them to

[1] United Nations, Department of Economic and Social Affairs, Population Division, *World Population Ageing 2019: Highlights* (ST/ESA/SER.A/430) (New York: United Nations, 2019).

[2] Homer, *The Odyssey: XII Scylla and Charybdis* (Oxford: Clarendon Press, 1963).

shipwreck. The crew plug their ears so they cannot hear the Sirens' fatal song, but Odysseus opts to hear their call – yet, before they reach the Sirens, he directs the crew to bind him to the mast and to not release him if he so requests. The crew honour Odysseus' directive, binding him tighter to the mast when, under the influence of the Sirens, he urges the crew to release him. Odysseus is freed only when the danger has passed.

Odysseus' tale captures the central elements of ADs as we currently recognise them: a directive that is issued by the person to whom it will apply in the future, and who issues it in advance of losing the capacity to make the relevant decision at the critical time. Moving on from ancient mythology, the modern idea of the concept of the AD as conceived in a healthcare setting is typically traced back to the late 1960s and the work of Luis Kutner, an American human rights lawyer and co-founder of Amnesty International. Kutner acknowledged that some patients will not wish to receive life-sustaining treatment, but that they may have lost the ability to convey their wishes at the critical time. "How then can the individual patient retain the right of privacy over his body – the right to determine whether he should be permitted to die, to permit his body to be given to the undertaker?"[3]

In answer to this question, Kutner's "suggested solution is that the individual, while fully in control of his faculties and his ability to express himself, indicate to what extent he would consent to treatment".[4] He offered various labels for this solution, amongst them the "living will" and, notably, the "body trust". Regarding the latter, Kutner drew on an established legal concept, suggesting that an AD is analogous to a conditional or revocable trust, with the patient's body being the "property" that is entrusted, the patient being the beneficiary of that property, and the doctor positioned as trustee and thus acting in accordance with the patient's prior consent.[5] According to Kutner, such a trust could be revoked by the patient, presumably once they regain control of their "faculties", as Kutner puts it.

As this volume will demonstrate, Kutner's idea has increasingly gained support internationally in a variety of different ways, but notably his analogy has not: the concept of a trust is not typically said to ground the

[3] L. Kutner, "Due Process of Euthanasia: The Living Will, A Proposal" (1969) 44(1) *Indiana Law Journal* 539, 550.

[4] Ibid., p. 551.

[5] Ibid., p. 552.

legitimacy of ADs. Rather, there is a settled view within the international community of bioethicists and medical lawyers that advance statements tend to derive their authority from the idea of respect for autonomy, or self-rule, interpreted specifically through the notion of "precedent autonomy" – a specific instantiation of the broader value of autonomy that captures the idea, applicable in some limited circumstances (i.e. where the loss of one's decision-making capacity is anticipated), that it is justifiable to set a precedent for oneself in the future through the exercise of one's autonomous decisions in the present.[6] As an English judge, Munby J, suggested, ADs involve "nothing more or less than the embodiment of the patient's autonomy and right of self-determination".[7] This view is not restricted to England; it is widely invoked in laws formulated in North America and in Europe. As we will see later in this volume, the value of autonomy has been an important, though often complex, component of more recent developments in some Asian countries.

I.1.1 Conceptual Challenges

However, here a first complication arises, because we should not assume that autonomy is a single, straightforward concept. A glance at the international bioethics literature reveals considerable debate over the precise nature of autonomy, with multiple accounts of autonomy being contested. This presents a challenge to advance decision-making: which version of autonomy does and should underpin, inform and constrain decisions made in advance?

There are many accounts of autonomy to choose from.[8,9] Some, taking their lead from Immanuel Kant, view autonomy in principled, objective terms: truly autonomous decisions are (only) those that align with what is objectively "right".[10] Others depict autonomy in fundamentally relational terms, where an individual's decision can be best understood in the context of their relationships. Even relational autonomy is not reducible

6 J.K. Davis, "The Concept of Precedent Autonomy" (2002) 16(2) *Bioethics* 114.

7 *HE* v. *A Hospital NHS Trust* [2003] 2 F.L.R. 408, per Munby J, [37].

8 J. Coggon, "Varied and Principled Understandings of Autonomy in English Law: Justifiable Inconsistency or Blinkered Moralism?" (2007) 15(3) *Health Care Analysis* 235.

9 J. Christman, "Autonomy in Moral and Political Philosophy", in E.N. Zalta (ed.), *The Stanford Encyclopedia of Philosophy* (2020), https://plato.stanford.edu/archives/fall2020/entries/autonomy-moral/.

10 C.M. Korsgaard, *The Sources of Normativity* (Cambridge: Cambridge University Press, 1996).

to a single account, since it is "an 'umbrella term', covering a range of diverse perspectives".[11]

Generally, however, ADs tend not to be associated with relational or principled understandings of autonomy. Rather, ADs usually find their authority in more individualistic, liberal and subjective understandings of autonomy, as emphasised in Munby J's suggested synonym, "self-determination". According to such accounts, an AD expresses – and gains its normative force from – an individual's sincerely and strongly held beliefs and values. Viewed as such, an AD is an expression of different aspects of an individual's personal identity: their preferences, value commitments, desires and beliefs.

This view, of course, involves making a number of assumptions. First, it assumes both that individuals know and can articulate their beliefs and values, and that a person's preferences or desires in the moment will be aligned with more considered values that capture the person's "authentic" commitments over a longer period of time. Second, it assumes that an individual's wishes *should* govern decision-making, irrespective of any other countervailing ethical considerations. Once again, a glance at the extensive bioethics literature on ADs and the value of autonomy reveal that these assumptions are problematic if not interrogated closely. Notwithstanding this point, the role that the principle of "respect for autonomy" plays in grounding and justifying ADs remains largely solid.

But this is not the end of the conceptual story. Beneath this widely supported account lurks another problem. Philosophers have long pondered the nature of personal identity, asking such questions as: what makes me *me*? As with autonomy itself, there are a range of accounts available, at one end locating identity in *bodily* continuity, at the other end locating identity in *psychological* continuity, with others occupying the middle ground in which body and mind interact to constitute identity.[12] If we focus here on the two poles, however, they present problems for ADs. Bodily accounts inevitably underplay the importance of the mind (and brain) and with them the assumed ethical importance of autonomy. Psychological accounts, which arguably command greater

[11] C. Gómez-Vírseda et al., "Relational Autonomy: What Does It Mean and How Is It Used in End-of-Life Care? A Systematic Review of Argument-based Ethics Literature" (2019) 20(1) *BMC Medical Ethics* 76.

[12] A.V. Campbell, "Why the Body Matters: Reflections on John Harris's Account of Organ Procurement", in J. Coggon et al. (eds.), *From Reason to Practice in Bioethics: An Anthology Dedicated to the Works of John Harris* (Manchester: Manchester University Press, 2015), pp. 131–41.

respect, do attend to autonomy, but they present a new challenge: whose autonomy is being respected when an AD is honoured?

According to Davis, invoking the value of "precedent autonomy" can give rise to "cases where the patient decided his or her future treatment, is later treated in accord with that earlier decision, but seems somehow estranged from that decision when treatment is provided".[13] The "estrangement" is typically described in terms of the individual's mental capacity or competence: the individual making the directive has the capacity to do so, which they lack at the time that the directive is to be applied. And this sort of estrangement potentially presents a problem for ADs, as Buchanan has suggested:

> Presumably a point is eventually reached at which the degree of psychological continuity between the author of the AD and the incompetent individual is so small that the AD of the former has no authority at all over the latter.[14]

As such, there are some substantial philosophical questions attending the very idea of ADs. Should they be understood in terms of trust or autonomy? If, as is usually assumed, they are anchored in respect for autonomy, then what account of autonomy is being invoked to justify the AD and its implementation, and why should this be determinative of what should happen? And on what basis can the autonomous individual, such as Odysseus, bind the future non-autonomous individual – are these even the same person? The increasing adoption of ADs worldwide nevertheless suggests that, while some philosophers may be vexed, their concerns do not overly trouble or inhibit lawmakers, policymakers, clinicians and patients – at least in those countries, largely in the West, where regulatory frameworks have gained traction over some years, if not decades. But even if we assume there is some stable basis for honouring ADs across countries, questions remain about what follows for the local implementation of ADs.

I.1.2 Practical Challenges

The real-world adoption of ADs has presented several distinct challenges, "as they can be non-existent, uninformed, imprecise, unavailable,

[13] See note 6, p. 115.

[14] A. Buchanan, "Advance Directives and the Personal Identity Problem" (1988) 17(4) *Philosophy and Public Affairs* 277, 298.

inadequate, [and] unpredictable".[15] These sorts of problems appear to have been detected wherever efforts have been made to adopt ADs, and so it is reasonable to think that the increasing tendency for ADs to gain a foothold in different parts of the world will give rise to similar trends. Here we summarise how designing and implementing ADs in practice in those places where ADs have been examined in some detail has been a far from straightforward journey.

I.1.2.1 Which Model or Form of AD?

"Not every attempted directive will be worth the paper it is written on. And not every attempted directive will be written on paper at all".[16] An AD can take various forms. As in Odysseus' case, the directive might be issued verbally, perhaps also being captured in an audio or video recording. Alternatively, patients might set down their wishes in writing, whether in a bespoke document or in a pro forma, and either on paper or electronically. They might also (or instead) convey the information on a tag that is worn about their person – or even on a bodily tattoo.[17] Questions accordingly arise about the form an AD should take and which mechanism or model of advance decision-making is to be adopted. Not only might the precise form vary, but – to add further complexity – so too do the terms used to capture the phenomenon. Sometimes different labels are used to refer to the same essential idea – for example, the "living will" to which Kutner referred, which is still in use in some contexts,[18] may be synonymous with the "advance directive". On other occasions, apparently neighbouring terms, which deploy the same or similar words, nevertheless refer to somewhat different phenomena.

The situation in England provides a pertinent example of the terminological steps that can be deployed to specify the scope and application of an AD, and to differentiate the AD from other decision-making tools or interventions in healthcare, and in end-of-life care in particular. Fleshing out the English context also helps to demonstrate the complexity that may arise in practice more widely. In that country, the Mental Capacity Act 2005 governs advance decision-making. The Act refers specifically to

[15] R. Huxtable, "Advance Decisions: Worth the Paper They Are (Not) Written On?" (2015) 5 *BMJ End of Life Care* 1, 5.

[16] Ibid., p. 3.

[17] C. Polack, "Is a Tattoo the Answer?" (2001) 323(7320) *BMJ* 1063.

[18] T. Higel et al., "Effect of Living Wills on End-of-Life Care: A Systematic Review" (2019) 67(1) *Journal of the American Geriatrics Society* 164.

the "advance decision to refuse treatment" (ADRT) and sets out the conditions governing their validity and applicability,[19] separate from an advance statement of the person's wishes that are to be drawn upon in making a decision in the person's "best interests".[20] Here we see an immediate qualification to the scope of the AD: it is to be restricted to a decision to *refuse* a treatment or care intervention, essentially on the grounds that a person's positive requests for particular interventions (whether made in the present or in advance) can only be indicative, but not determinative.

The English picture becomes even more complex, bringing with it the potential to confuse patients and professionals alike. A patient in England can make an ADRT, which may be verbal or written. They might also, separately, confer a "lasting power of attorney" – essentially appointing a proxy or surrogate decisionmaker, who is empowered to make decisions on the patient's behalf when they have lost mental capacity.[21] Patients might also be involved in (or subject to) a more specific decision, such as a DNACPR decision (do not attempt cardio-pulmonary resuscitation). While DNACPR decisions are made by practitioners on the grounds of medical futility, in consultation with the patient or those interested in the patient's welfare where possible, they can also be captured in various ways, including – following a recent initiative – in a ReSPECT form.[22] Provided that they meet the relevant conditions, some such forms might amount to legally recognisable ADRTs. But forms like ReSPECT can also be described differently, as an instance of "advance care planning" (ACP). ACP overlaps with, but is distinct from, the ADRT or DNACPR decision. ACP involves a more general reflection, not merely on any specific treatment to which a patient does not consent, but also about the patient's general views, values and wishes regarding their treatment and care.[23] And, in turn, ACP may include some sort of "values history" – and these might also,

19 Mental Capacity Act 2005, sections 24–6.
20 Mental Capacity Act 2005, section 4(6)(a).
21 Mental Capacity Act 2005, sections 9–14. Note, however, that a discussion of proxy decision-making is beyond the scope of this volume.
22 C.A. Hawkes et al., "Development of the Recommended Summary Plan for Emergency Care and Treatment (ReSPECT)" (2020) 148 *Resuscitation* 98.
23 A. Mullick et al., "An Introduction to Advance Care Planning in Practice" (2013) 347 *BMJ* f6064.

on occasion, be appended to a patient's ADRT.[24] Indeed, increasingly, we see a trend internationally to encourage those involved in ACP to make an AD (where one has not been made previously) as part of good practice in planning future care of someone close to the end of life.

Thus, the variety of terms and tools available in England surely complicates efforts there to make provision for a future in which one has lost capacity. Neither patients nor professionals might be sure about where and how the patient's wishes regarding their future care should be captured. Even once this is settled, there then arises the question of what information should be captured within the relevant tool, and what protections should be added if endorsing the AD will have life-changing, even life-ending, implications? A detailed statement, which is sensitive to the patient's particular medical condition, might seem advisable,[25] and it might be judged appropriate for this to be witnessed or signed as part of a formal legal procedure. Yet, choosing a form that is too precise, detailed and voluminous might make it difficult to apply in practice – even more so if legal protections impose time or financial burdens on the person wishing to make it. And even a detailed directive might fail to speak to the situation which later arises – a risk that obviously also presents if the directive is too brief, general or imprecise. In short, there may be risks associated both with over- and under-specification, as subsequent chapters in this volume will demonstrate.

I.1.2.2 Will People Make ADs?

The accommodation of ADs in law, policy and practice will not automatically translate into their uptake. A review of the operation of the law in England suggested that public awareness of advance decisions there remains low, with research showing that only 3% of the public have made an advance decision, even though 82% have "clear views about their end-of-life care preferences".[26]

Similar findings about uptake of ADs have been reported elsewhere. Evans et al.'s systematic review of practice in Germany, published in

[24] D.J. Doukas and L.B. McCullough, "The Values History: The Evaluation of the Patient's Values and Advance Directives" (1991) 32(2) *Journal of Family Practice* 145.

[25] N. Evans et al., "A Critical Review of Advance Directives in Germany: Attitudes, Use and Healthcare Professionals' Compliance" (2012) 87(3) *Patient Education and Counseling* 277.

[26] House of Lords, Select Committee on the Mental Capacity Act 2005, *Mental Capacity Act 2005: Post-legislative Scrutiny* (HL Paper 139) (London: The Stationery Office Limited, 2014), p. 75, [193].

2012, found studies revealing 2.5%–10% of the population had ADs.[27] Citing other studies, the authors saw this range as comparable to uptake in Spain (2%) and the Netherlands (7%), but substantially lower than uptake in the United States (around 20%).[28]

Uptake may, of course, have risen in the intervening years since these studies. Yet, more recent research also points to the low incidence of ADs, at least among some patients. Sutter et al., for example, systematically reviewed studies exploring ADs amongst neurocritically ill patients.[29] They expressed concern about the "limited number of neurocritically ill patients having ADs or defined healthcare agents", given (inter alia) the high burdens imposed by such conditions.[30]

Perhaps there is a fairly straightforward way of enhancing uptake: invest in informing and educating citizens and patients about ADs, so that they can be empowered to set down their wishes. Certainly, such initiatives are underway worldwide, but there are reasons to be sceptical about the likelihood of success. Fagerlin and Schneider, in their forcefully entitled 2004 article "Enough: The Failure of the Living Will", reviewed various attempts in the United States at enhancing uptake and found them wanting:

> If after so much propaganda so few of us have living wills, do we really want them, or are we just saying what we think we ought to think and what investigators want to hear?[31]

I.1.2.3 Can People Make ADs?

The low uptake of ADs might be better understood once one considers the magnitude of the task of making an AD. How easy is it, ask Fagerlin and Schneider, for a patient to "conjure up preferences for an unspecifiable future confronted with unidentifiable maladies with unpredictable

[27] See note 25, p. 286. Although, interestingly, Horn cites data showing that in Germany, there are statistics demonstrating that 93% of the German population are in fact aware of ADs. See further R. Horn, "'Why Should I Question a Patient's Wish?' A Comparative Study on Physicians' Perspectives on Their Duties to Respect Advance Directives" (2017) 24 *European Journal of Health Law* 523.

[28] See note 25, p. 286.

[29] R. Sutter et al., "Advance Directives in the Neurocritically Ill: A Systematic Review" (2020) 48(8) *Critical Care Medicine* 1188.

[30] Ibid., p. 1193.

[31] A. Fagerlin and C.E. Schneider, "Enough: The Failure of the Living Will" (2004) 34(2) *The Hastings Center Report* 30, 33.

treatments?"[32] In response, approaches to making ADs that are disease specific have been proposed,[33] alongside a critical role for specialist clinical input that focuses on discussing treatments that are more predictable.[34] This approach, of course, requires the specialist clinician to be familiar with the provision that has been made for advance decision-making. Unfortunately, research has shown that professional understanding of ADs, alongside a more general awareness of this tool, remains low.[35]

Educational campaigns to better inform professionals and the public about ADs look to be an important intervention, but perhaps only as part of a general attempt to change public and professional attitudes that stress the importance of enabling and empowering people to take control of the future direction of their lives, in light of expected (or unexpected) health crises.

I.1.2.4 Will the AD Be Available When Needed?

Let us assume that an informed patient has been able to set down their wishes in the relevant way, with the relevant support. Will their statement be available to the clinicians at the point that it is needed? Here, too, there is reason to suspect that this cannot be guaranteed. Fagerlin and Schneider, again, put the point pithily: "long can be the road from the drafter's chair to the ICU bed".[36]

Suggestions to close the informational gap have looked to a role for patients' electronic medical records,[37] national registries or new storage systems to enable rapid access to information about the existence of ADs. We might think that this is particularly likely to be important in professional settings, like emergency paramedic response, where time is limited but important decisions about life-saving interventions frequently need to be made. Practices may vary, but it seems fair to suggest that systemic approaches to quickly access information about the existence of an AD will be required.

32 Ibid.
33 See note 25, p. 286.
34 Cf. R. Nowland et al., "Management of Patients with an Advance Decision and Suicidal Behaviour: A Systematic Review" (2019) 9(3) *BMJ Open* e023978.
35 See note 25, p. 284.
36 See note 31.
37 See note 26, p. 77, [200].

I.1.2.5 Will the AD Be Honoured?

Even if a directive can be located, its application in practice is not guaranteed. There are two related challenges here, which build on various points already considered. First, can the directive be applied in practice? Second, even if it is capable of application, will it actually be honoured as intended?

As we have already noted, vague or overly detailed directives might jeopardise their applicability and thus application. Evidence suggests that healthcare professionals are often unsure about how to interpret key aspects of the directive, or of the situation arising – how, for example, should clinicians respond if (despite anything else it might say) the directive does not directly address the specific treatment or presenting condition which is now in view? Moreover, even an apparently clear and specific directive might require some interpretation by the professionals, which has been shown to lead to inconsistent judgements.[38]

Of course, expert involvement, clarity and specificity might help to minimise uncertainty and the need for interpretation.[39] Yet, whenever interpretation *is* needed, this will be shaped by who is doing the interpreting – be they a clinician or, in contested cases, a judge.[40] In interpreting how, or if, an AD should be honoured, these professionals will always be exercising their judgement, and such judgement can be swayed – by the institutional culture, the views of colleagues, the presence of a family member, or how each individual weighs the value of autonomy against competing values like preserving life in challenging decision-making scenarios.[41,42] This is the complex reality of enacting an AD regime that might, on the surface, look compelling from a basic legal or ethical standpoint.

I.2 Advance Directives: The Asian Context

Although more than half of the world's population lives in Asia, and the elderly population in many Asian jurisdictions is growing at an

38 T. Thompson et al., "Adherence to Advance Directives in Critical Care Decision Making: Vignette Study" (2003) 327(7422) *BMJ* 1011.

39 See note 25, p. 285.

40 See note 15.

41 See note 34.

42 L. Quinlivan et al., "Advance Decisions to Refuse Treatment and Suicidal Behaviour in Emergency Care: 'It's Very Much a Step into the Unknown'" (2019) 5(4) *BJPsych Open* e50.

unprecedented rate,[43] there is very little systematic and comprehensive information about the place of ADs in these jurisdictions. As the preceding discussion demonstrates, whilst ADs have been subject to significant reflection and analysis within academic medical law and ethics, much of the writing in this area has come from, or has focused on, jurisdictions in Europe and the Americas, many of which have detailed and well-implemented regulatory regimes for ADs. In contrast, the history of ADs in Asia looks to be a more recent one, though it is a history that also appears to be evolving quickly – in regulatory spaces or in professional practice – in a variety of ways, and at various speeds, across different countries. One of our primary aims in this book is to reveal the various dimensions of this emerging picture across the continent.

But there is also a second reason for wanting to shed light on ADs in the Asian context. The rise of ADs internationally has been the story of a growing international consensus placed on the importance of autonomy to shape new practices of decision-making in the healthcare context, and the subsequent need to invoke policies, laws and practices that accord ADs a central place in the armoury of healthcare decisions available to patients. How precisely does this consensus play out when it reaches Asian shores? Much has been written about the fact that the principle of respect for individual autonomy is not accorded the same primacy in Asian jurisdictions as it is in Western jurisdictions.[44] Relational concepts of autonomy seem to resonate more closely with the communitarian, familial models of decision-making common to Asian jurisdictions, and yet, as discussed, such concepts of autonomy are not generally associated with ADs. Equally, Asia is a continent defined by a rich variety of religious traditions, where the sanctity or prioritisation of the preservation of life has often been taken to play a decisive role in healthcare decision-making. Do these observations explain the relative lack of attention given to ADs across Asian jurisdictions? As increasing attention is given to a potential role for ADs in different Asian jurisdictions, how – if at all – is the ethical foundation of this practice made sense of, or modified, to accommodate different local models and expectations surrounding healthcare decision-making? And what are the implications of these accommodations for the practice of

[43] This is in particular true for the Asia-Pacific region, where it is projected that one in four people will be over the age of 60 by the year 2050. See further www.weforum.org/agenda/2021/10/is-asia-pacific-ready-to-be-the-world-s-most-rapidly-ageing-region/.

[44] See, for example, R. Fan, "Self-Determination vs. Family-Determination: Two Incommensurable Principles of Autonomy" (1997) 11(3) *Bioethics* 309.

ADs, and the future direction of further regulatory, professional or practical developments in Asia that we might expect to see? We hope that we might go some way to interrogating and then answering these important questions in the contributions that follow.

In summary, then, this volume aims to present the first systematic comparative study of ADs in Asia. In order to be both comprehensive and representative in our coverage, we have chosen to include 16 Asian jurisdictions, selecting this sample to take into account various parameters, such as sociocultural influences, religion, and economic status. While the term "Asia" is often associated primarily with East or South/Southeast Asia, with Middle Eastern and West Asian jurisdictions tending to be excluded, we are of the view that adopting this approach would fail to do justice to the breadth of jurisdictions that are correctly identified as being part of the Asian continent, and the richness of the different social, cultural and legal characteristics of this part of the world. Thus, by choosing a wide range of jurisdictions and sociocultural contexts from across the entirety of the Asian continent, we hope to showcase the diversity of views on this issue within Asia. Selecting 16 Asian countries out of a possible 48 countries recognised by the United Nations, a sample that was necessarily limited by accessibility and feasibility, will inevitably mean that there will remain gaps in our understanding. However, by taking a broad-brush approach to the selection of the countries we have chosen, we hope to mitigate the impact of these absences to the greatest degree possible.

The 16 jurisdictions covered are presented in the following three broad categories, which we have chosen to give a robust but basic structure to the insights of the book as a whole:

1. "Well-regulated": this category includes jurisdictions with a clear set of legal rules on or encompassing ADs. It should be noted that the term "well" refers only to the fact that there is comparatively formal regulation of ADs in these jurisdictions, rather than any normative assessment about the quality of such regulation. This category includes the jurisdictions of Israel, Singapore, South Korea, Taiwan, Thailand and India. The first five jurisdictions in this category have legislative frameworks addressing ADs, whereas regulation of end-of-life ADs in India takes the form of detailed, judicial guidelines laid down in the *Common Cause* case of 2018.[45]

[45] Psychiatric ADs in India, unlike end-of-life ADs, are regulated via statute.

2. Semi-regulated: this category covers jurisdictions with other forms of regulation on ADs, including regulation via official regulatory documents and practical guidelines or other forms of guidance from professional societies. This category includes the jurisdictions of Hong Kong, Iran, Malaysia, the Philippines, and Turkey. While the courts in Malaysia and Hong Kong theoretically can be guided by common law case law precedent, there have not been any locally decided cases in this area of the law thus far. Thus, these two jurisdictions have been included in this category rather than the first one.
3. Non-regulated: this category covers jurisdictions where there might be, at best, broad principles contained in legislation or guidelines around healthcare that stress the importance of patient preferences in general terms, but no regulations or guidance which connects to ADs specifically. This category includes the jurisdictions of China, Japan, Macau, Pakistan and Saudi Arabia.

The contributors of each jurisdiction were provided with a broad questionnaire which prompted them to discuss key questions, including the existence (or not) of relevant legal frameworks and professional guidance, the practice of ADs (if any), and the sociocultural and religious context in which decisions regarding regulation (or lack thereof) were made. Contributors were also encouraged to consider the values and normative commitments that underlie the law and practice of ADs (or lack thereof) in their jurisdiction, and to offer critique of the local context, and the values it espouses, where appropriate. It should be emphasised that this volume does not aim to put forward, or advance, the position that ADs *should* be applied in the Asian region. Rather, contributors in each jurisdiction were asked to explore and critique the local directions of travel in relation to ADs, and to do this without being prejudiced by any particular normative ideal.

In shaping the volume in this way, the following chapters provide a rich, contextual landscape of the law and practice of ADs across a number of Asian jurisdictions. The chapters explore the tensions between the secular, individual-focused form of decision-making grounded in the person's own wishes that is the AD and the key sociocultural and religious influences of that jurisdiction, as well as how these tensions are resolved in the local context. Strikingly, however, these chapters demonstrate that many of the practical challenges described here take a similar form in the Asian context.

The final chapter of this book brings the insights of each chapter together in a comparative analysis of the key issues and themes that have arisen, drawing on the experiences of these jurisdictions to better understand the phenomenon of ADs in the Asian context. In particular, this final chapter will explore the ways in which the basic idea and practice of the AD as recognised internationally has been understood, challenged, accommodated or adapted within Asian societies which espouse a broad range of ethical value commitments and distinctive approaches to healthcare practice and decision-making.

PART I

Well-Regulated Jurisdictions

1

Advance Directives in Israel

MIRIAM ETHEL BENTWICH

1.1 Introduction

This chapter explores advance directives in Israel, arguing that, paradoxically, the Israeli state's formal legislative instruments to protect the autonomy of terminally ill individuals by empowering them to make decisions about the scope, nature and extent of medical treatment they wish to accept (or to reject) as they approach the end of life, and affirmed their right to die with dignity, have in fact led to the under-regulation of the use of advance directives. The chapter first discusses the legal and political-religious context that led to the enactment of legislation – the Dying Patient (DP) Act[1] – which constitutes the main legal framework for the use of advance directives in Israel.[2] The main attributes setting the legal framework in which advance directives are incorporated into this law are next explained, followed by a discussion of the state's guidelines for the formulation of advance directives. Finally, the chapter demonstrates how the restrictive nature and the supposed strict regulation of Israeli advance directives have actually led to their under-regulation. Some reasons for this include the practical difficulties posed by the actual implementation of advance directives, the many "shades of grey" faced by healthcare providers when interpreting the law, and legal critiques of, and precedents questioning the DP Act.

[1] Dying Patient Law 2005, *Sefer Hukim* [Book of Laws] 330.

[2] It is interesting to note that, while the "Dying Patient" Act is the literal translation of the law's Hebrew title, some academic English language articles refer to this law by other forms of translation, such as "Terminally Ill Patient" and "Near Death Patient" Act/Law. See O. Asman and Y. M. Barilan, 'End-of-Life Medical Decisions in Israeli Law – How Jewish Law Represents a Balance between Principlist and Situationist Approaches to Medical Law', in N. Emmerich et al. (eds.), *Contemporary European Perspectives on the Ethics of End of Life Care* (Cham: Springer, 2020), pp. 105–15; A. B. Jotkowitz and S. Glick, 'The Israeli Terminally Ill Patient Law of 2005' (2009) 25 *Journal of Palliative Care* 284–8.

1.2 Legal, Religious and Political Background Leading to Legislation

Prior to the introduction of the Patient's Rights Law (1996),[3] Israel had refrained from addressing the issue of end-of-life care, as evident by its ambivalence towards the introduction and enactment of specific legislation to address the matter. In fact, Israeli penal law perceives euthanasia – even for the sake of preventing suffering – to be an act of killing. Similarly, until the 2005 passing of the DP Act, under penal law, even passive euthanasia – namely, the act of refraining from carrying out actions designed to prolong the life of a DP – which was carried out without the explicit permission of the court constituted an act of manslaughter.

The draft of the Patient's Rights legislation originally included a clause entitled "The Right to Die with Dignity". That section (originally, section/clause 10 in the preliminary law proposal) reads as follows:

> A terminal patient is entitled to [can be understood as 'having a right to'] die in dignity and in accordance to their viewpoint and belief, and as much as possible, in the presence of a person that the patient requests. The physician and the medical institution will assist in fulfilling this patient's right, and will refrain from [doing] anything that might infringe this right.[4]

However, this section was subsequently removed, supposedly due to opposition from some ultra-orthodox Jewish parties; notably, the final law that was passed did not include any specific reference to end-of-life care.[5] Indeed, until the enactment of the DP Law – particularly with respect to the matter of prolonging the lives of terminally ill patients – since the mid-1980s and even more so in the 1990s, the main progress made to address this issue was achieved through the courts.[6] Some

[3] Patient's Rights Law 1996, *Sefer Hukim* [Book of Laws] 729.

[4] Quoted in M. Halperin, "The Dying Patient Law – Past, Present and Future from a Systematic Standpoint" (2019) 51 *Refua Umishpat* [Medicine and Law] 124 [in Hebrew].

[5] Patient's Rights Bill 1992, *Hatza'ot Hok* [Legislative Bills] 359; C. Shalev, "Reclaiming the Patient's Voice and Spirit in Dying: An Insight from Israel" (2010) 24 *Bioethics* 134. It should be noted that, according to a later article by Rabbi Professor Mordechai Halperin, the author explicitly denies the objection of these religious parties, though he does admit that he was not present in the specific discussions in which it was decided not to include the "right to die in dignity" clause/section. See note 4, p. 125.

[6] The pivotal influence of the courts during this period is also acknowledged in a document issued by the director-general of the MOH. See Israel MOH, *Treatment of the Dying Patient*, Director-General Circular No. 2/96 (1996).

pivotal cases, such as those of *Tzadok*, *Binyamin*, *Tzadi*, *Gilad*, *Bivas*, *Ploni* ("John Doe"), pushed towards greater acknowledgement of patients' right to personal autonomy in the context of end-of-life care.[7]

The courts' decisions regarding these cases should be understood against the backdrop of the "constitutional revolution", a term often associated with Aharon Barak, the Deputy Chief Justice and later Chief Justice of the Israeli Supreme Court. Chief Justice Barak's employment of this term suggests his preference for a court activism approach.[8] This approach gained favour after 1992 when the "Basic Law: Human Dignity and Liberty" was enacted to express and confirm the judiciary's commitment to upholding the state's main human rights principles. Thus, the governing premise of Justice Barak and many other Supreme Court justices was that the enactment of this Basic Law had opened the way to the court for further interpretations and applications of this law, in specific realms beyond the original written letter of that law. Indeed, during the years 1992–5, various verdicts in the regional courts and in the Supreme Court had expressed a heightened activism approach, which laid stress on strengthening aspects of dignity and liberty in cases addressed by the courts. In fact, the "constitutional revolution" and its emphasis on the court activism approach were explicitly mentioned in the pivotal verdict of the Hamizrahi Bank case of November 1995, a few days after prime minister Yitzhak Rabin was assassinated. Rabin's murder sent shockwaves across the world, for it held potentially major global political implications; its media reporting was so extensive that it overshadowed the court's verdict on the Hamizrahi Bank case, which attracted scant media coverage at the time.

At any rate, the case of *Miriam Tzadok* v. *Beit Hae'la* in 1992 is considered fundamental to the end-of-life care issue for a number of

[7] Motion 759/92 *Miriam Tzadok* v. *Beit Hae'la and others* (10 June 1992); C.A. Motion 1141/90 *Binyamin* v. *Dr Vilenski* (1990) 51(3) 187; C.A. Motion 498/93 *Tzadi* v. *Kupat Holim Clalit* (1993) (unpublished); C.A. Motion 1030/95 *Gilad* v. *Soroka* (1996) 56(1) 441; C.A. Motion (Tel Aviv) 528/96 *Bivas* v. *Tel-Aviv Municipality (Ichilov Medical Center)* (1996); C.A. Motion (Tel Aviv) 1513/01 *Ploni* [*John Doe*] v. *The Attorney General* (1996); I. Doron and C. Shalev, 'Between the Patient's Rights Law and the Dying Patient Law: Advancing Forward or Going Backwards' (2011) 43 *Refua Umishpat* [Medicine and Law] 25 [in Hebrew].

[8] Judicial activism may imply different things and indeed has varied definitions. In what follows, I employ the term "judicial activism" to indicate a stance advocating "judicial review" that allows courts an equal say with the other branches of the state – legislature and government – so that the court (and specifically the supreme court) is not merely following the letter of the law.

reasons.[9] It was the first case regarding end-of-life care that concerned an older person with dementia. The case revolved around the withholding of a feeding tube and raised questions about the authority of healthcare professionals to refrain from offering life-prolonging treatment. Some former cases had focused mainly on the issue of withdrawing ventilator support as death approached. In this case, however, and while still cognitively competent, the patient Ms Tzadok had left clearly written instructions (effectively, directives) requesting that medical staff should refrain from feeding and keeping her hydrated by artificial means, when her dementia had progressed to an advanced stage. The court ruled that although Ms Tzadok was no longer capable of expressing her wishes by the time her case reached the court, her directives – written while she was still cognisant – represented her true desires. It was therefore decided that Ms Tzadok's desires be respected, and that the right to personal autonomy be recognised, in the interests of preventing her further suffering. In accepting Ms Tzadok's written directives, the court not only upheld the principle of personal autonomy as a critical value, but by extension, confirmed the patients' right to refuse life-prolonging interventions. Indeed, the court went even further in applying this value in the context of a non-terminal disease.

Other rulings similarly applied the value of personal autonomy when justifying the withdrawal of ventilator life support for patients with amyotrophic lateral sclerosis (ALS). A landmark case in this respect was the 1996 ruling on the request made by Itay Arad, an ALS patient. Arad had sought the court's permission that he be allowed to be disconnected from a ventilator, once he reached the stage where he was unable to live without requiring the constant support and care of others.[10] The court granted his request, thus upholding his autonomy and dignity, and two years later, his disease having progressed to the stage where he was dependent on medical support to maintain his life, Mr Arad was disconnected from the ventilator, as he had explicitly requested.

Another noteworthy case was that of *Yael Shefer* (1993);[11] the verdict in that case was interpreted as permitting the withdrawal of life support, and was subsequently cited in nine different cases, including that of *Arad.*

[9] Motion 759/92 *Miriam Tzadok* v. *Beit Hae'la and others* (10 June 1992); See Doron and Shalev, note 7, p. 25.

[10] C.A. Motion (Tel Aviv) 2242/95 *Itai Arad* v. *Kupat Cholim Clalit* (1996); R. Gilbar, 'Until Breath Ends' (2015) 42 *Hamishpat Bareshet* [Law in the Internet] [in Hebrew].

[11] CA 506/88 *Yael Shefer* v. *State of Israel* [1993] IsrSC 48(1) 78.

Shefer's case concerned a toddler with Tay-Sachs disease, who had, in fact, passed away before the court could publish its verdict. The court had been asked to decide on the issue of withholding various life-sustaining treatments for the toddler. The written deliberation by Justice Elon of the Supreme Court in this case became of importance because of the decision laid down by him. Judge Elon's deliberation was based on both modern Israeli law and the Jewish religious (*Halakhic*) perspective, derived from biblical commandments, and subsequent Talmudic and rabbinic teachings.[12] Indeed, when referring to the possibility of withdrawing ventilators, Judge Elon offered an in principle interpretation of the Jewish religious law that supported this action be taken, if the patient was suffering. Of interest also is that Judge Elon's written deliberation explicitly addressed both types of euthanasia – active and passive. The latter he referred to as legitimate *in principle, including* from the Jewish religious perspective. As we shall see in the following, Elon's religious perspective in the *Shefer* case departs some distance from the religious viewpoint practically fostered in the letter of the law that was enacted more than a decade later.

The aforementioned courts' rulings and deliberations that fostered the principle of personal autonomy in order to allow passive euthanasia to end suffering were mainly written from a secular perspective. Some representatives of the ultra-orthodox parties within the Israeli parliament regarded these rulings as a "step too far"; their understanding of end-of-life care was primarily grounded in values that stressed the sanctity of life, a philosophical and religious standpoint which emphasised a commitment to preserving and saving human life, regardless of the individual's desires. This perspective offers, at the most, quite limited scope and space for recognising human suffering as a legitimate justification for overriding the commitment to the sanctity of life. Due to the complexity of the *Halakhic* law and its interpretations through varied rulings by rabbis with expertise in this law, it is well beyond the scope of the current chapter and its author's expertise to delve into the specifics and nuances of these interpretations.[13] However, there is no dispute that the *Halakhic*

[12] M. Raz et al., "Dying of 'Old Age' in Israel" (2011) 16 *The European Legacy* 363; Shalev, note 5.

[13] For a more elaborate discussion about the orthodox (and certainly ultra-orthodox) Jewish perspective and/or the embedded tension in the Israeli legal system between this perception and a liberal-secular viewpoint, see Asman and Barilan, note 2; Doron and Shalev, note 7, p. 25; N. Karako-Eyal et al., "The Dying Patient Law 2005: Law, Ethics and Medical Practice" (2018) 41 *Iyuney Mishpat* [Tel Aviv University Law Review] 185 (in Hebrew); C. Shalev, 'End-of-Life Care in Israel – The Dying Patient Law, 2005' (2009) 42 *Israel Law*

law – certainly from an ultra-orthodox religious perspective – is framed less in terms of regard for autonomy and individual rights, but rather, privileges the principle of the sanctity of life as a fundamental value that (in many of the cases) took precedence over other values. It is also not disputed that for the majority of Israeli Jewish citizens (and the 20 per cent of Arabs residing within Israel), the *Halakhic* law does not play an important role in their perceptions and lifestyle values.

Against this backdrop, in 2000, Rabbi Shlomo Benizri, the Health Minister of the ultra-orthodox Shas political party, convened a committee to establish guidelines for a new law to regulate end-of-life care. This regulation can be interpreted as a backlash against what was considered a "liberal-secular" stance, for its support of most court decisions that acknowledged the rights of individuals to refuse life-prolonging treatment, and for that right to be respected and lawful. Rather than appoint a secular bioethicist, physician, or legal expert, Benizri settled on Avraham Steinberg, a rabbi and physician, as committee chairperson. In a demonstration of his political power, Benizri used his position as Health Minister to appoint an individual with a self-declared ultra-orthodox rabbinical viewpoint as chairperson to a committee that set the legal framework of the DP Act. Steinberg's committee held discussions for two years before submitting its main recommendations for the suggested law's framework, eventually leading in 2005 to the enactment of the DP Act. Scholars such as Carmel Shalev have commented on the final version of the legislated DP Act, noting in particular that in substance, this law is conceptualised within a *Halakhic* framework rather than a secular-liberal perspective.[14]

1.3 DP Act: Main Attributes

Israel's DP Act constitutes the main legal framework for advance directives, a legal instrument for a terminally ill patient to explicitly request the extent and nature of medical treatment and interventions at

Review 279; Shalev, note 5; A. Shapira, "The Dying Patient Law – Does It Reflect a Right Bioethical Balance?" (2013) 59 *Refua Umishpat* [Medicine and Law] [in Hebrew]; J.D. Bleich, *Bioethical Dilemmas: A Jewish Perspective* (Brooklyn, NY: Ktav Publishing House, Inc., 1998), p. 1; A. Shaulov et al., "'Death Is Inevitable – A Bad Death Is Not'. Report from an International Workshop" (2019) 8 *Israel Journal of Health Policy Research* 79.

14 Shalev, note 13, p. 279; Shalev, note 5; Shapira, note 13; A. Tichu, "The Dying Patient Law 2005 – The Influence of the Jewish Religion on Euthanasia in Israel" (2008) 1 *Mishpat Refuee Ve-Bioetika* [Medical Law and Bioethics] 107 [in Hebrew].

the end-of-life stage. Patients with a terminal illness are enabled to leave written instructions as to whether they would wish their life to be prolonged (or otherwise) at the point when their suffering becomes unbearable. However, before delving into the details of these directives under this law, it is important to highlight some main attributes and definitions that inform the framework in which advance directives are employed.

A good point to begin with is the definition of the law's goal, as set out in section 1(a) which pertains to "the regulation of medical treatment given to the DP, while striking the right balance between the value of the sanctity of life and the value of a person's autonomy and the importance of the quality of life". Still within the "Goal" section of the law, section 1(b) states that it is "based on the values of Israel as a Jewish and democratic state, as well as on core values in morality, ethics and religion". Thus, in two respects, the DP Act resonates quite well with its legal and political background, as previously described. First, the DP Act acknowledges the tension between the so-called liberal secular viewpoint, which emphasises individual autonomy and quality of life (i.e. where suffering is unbearable to the point that the patient cannot be said to enjoy any quality of life), against the more "religious" perspective which cherishes and privileges the principle of the sanctity of life. Second, the legislature explicitly states that religion (in particular, Judaism) constitutes an important foundation of the law, in line with the reason for which the Steinberg's committee was appointed in the first place.

Following on from the aforementioned tension is the matter of the very definition of a DP according to this law, which distinguishes between two types of DP: a DP and a DP in the "final stage". Section 8 of the law defines a DP as originating from "a patient suffering from an incurable medical problem with a life expectancy of *no more than six months*, even with the provision of medical treatment" [emphasis added]. In contrast, a DP in the "final stage" refers to "a patient with acute systems failure [of his/her body] who, even with the provision of medical treatment, has a life expectancy of *no more than two weeks*" [emphasis added]. Furthermore, the law distinguishes between a "competent" DP and an "incompetent" DP, the determination of which both fall under the jurisdiction of this law. Competent DPs possess adequate mental and cognitive capacity[15] to autonomously reach an informed decision, as well

[15] Under the DP Act, a person is considered competent if s/he (1) has reached the age of seventeen, (2) is able to express his/her will, (3) has not been declared incompetent, and

as having the ability to communicate that decision to medical staff. By contrast, the incompetent DP is without the mental or cognitive capacity to reach an informed decision, or may be unable to communicate their decision to medical professionals. While both a DP and a DP in the "final stage" may choose not to prolong their life, the law is clear that accompanying treatment and nourishment can be withheld only from a DP who is in the "final stage" of life, as will be discussed later. Given that a DP in the "final stage" refers to a patient with acute systems failure of his/her body (also known as "acute multi-organ dysfunction"), for all intents and purposes "final-stage" DPs lack the capacity to express their "choice", since they are usually sedated, a state which implies that they cannot, and therefore do not conform with the definition of "competency", as defined by the DP Act (see note 15).

Sections 9–10 of the law require that a senior attending physician explain to the patient their terminal condition, and to ask the patient how they wish to proceed, should the physician decide that the patient's condition conforms with the DP status as previously defined. In the event that the patient is already incompetent, whether as a DP or if they are DPs in the "final stage", the physician will contact the patient's family and explain the situation to them.

Israeli's legal definition of a DP is quite limited, as it does not extend to the inclusion of patients with chronic illnesses yet without a clear prognosis, such as dementia or ALS. Such a narrow definition seems to be in conformity with more orthodox religious standpoints that regard the sanctity of human life to be a fundamental religious and philosophical principle – a key foundation on which the DP Act rests. The narrowness of this definition prompts the question of autonomy for patients who fall outside the jurisdiction of this law: what rights can they exercise in terms of their ability to fulfil their desire not to have their lives prolonged? This is especially pertinent in instances where patients lack the ability to express their choice (due to incapacitation arising from their disease) since their advance directives cannot be followed, as they do not fit the letter of the law as DPs.[16]

(4) is not excluded from the assumption of legal capacity (section 3). There is a statutory presumption that one is competent (section 6), unless otherwise determined by the responsible physician based on a reasoned and documented medical decision (section 7).

16 Non-DPs who are adults (i.e. age eighteen and above) and who do have the capacity to express their choice and are not deemed incompetent for mental or cognitive reasons may refuse to receive treatment, and their choice will be ultimately respected since the Patient's Rights Law recognises the right of a competent and fully capacitated adult

Yet another important attribute of this law concerns the forbidden and allowed actions that may or may not be taken in weighing the decision whether to prolong (or otherwise) the life of a person deemed to be either a DP or a DP in the "final stage". For both categories of patients, section 19 of the law explicitly forbids euthanasia, which is understood as "an action aimed to kill or that its probable result will lead to death". Section 20 also explicitly forbids physician-assisted suicide. In defining euthanasia as actions taken in the knowledge that the *probable* result will lead to death, Israeli law extends the scope of activities defined as euthanasia. For example, administering morphine in such dosages that will likely kill the patient might be interpreted as an act of euthanasia, even if the intention is to provide comfort and to ease the patient's pain.

The DP Act not only forbids these extended forms of "euthanasia", but also strongly mandates the conditions and manner in which "passive euthanasia" may take place. The legislature has placed significant limits on non-life-prolonging actions, even if they do not involve performing actions intended to bring about the death of the patient (e.g. lethal injection, orally administered poisonous pills). A major restriction, in this respect, is that in some medical contexts, the law does not permit certain actions of withdrawing or withholding treatment. Withholding and/or withdrawing treatment are the main actions in which "passive euthanasia" takes place, and the Israeli legislature has forbidden the withdrawal of a "continuous" treatment (e.g. ventilators). In fact, the distinction between "continuous" and "cyclical" treatments in the DP Act arises from the fact that withdrawal of continuous life-sustaining treatment is prohibited. The rationale here is that a cyclical treatment (e.g. dialysis, chemotherapy) can/could be not renewed; thus, stopping such treatment is not regarded as the withdrawal of an existing treatment, but rather as withholding the next or new cycle of treatment.[17]

That being said, the Israeli DP Act does allow for the withdrawal and withholding of nourishment (feeding and, in case of severe suffering, or

patient to refuse treatment. Depending on the particular circumstances, such refusal may be delegated by the attending physician to the ethics committee (established as part of the Patient's Rights Law).

[17] Originally, when drafting the DP Act, the intention was to employ the use of ventilators with timers, so that this sort of treatment could be withheld, once the cycle set on the timer finishes. However, in reality, timers were not employed on ventilators, rendering this type of medical treatment as "continuous" or "ongoing" rather than "cyclical". For an interesting discussion about timers and ventilators in the context of the DP Act, see V. Ravitsky, 'Timers on Ventilators' (2005) 330 *BMJ* 415.

harm hydration), palliative care, and secondary/accompanying treatment from incompetent DPs in their "final stage". In an article published about the *Halakhic* law basis for the DP Act, Rabbi Steinberg outlined the justification for allowing such exceptions in cases where patients have reached the "final stage".[18] Rabbi Steinberg draws on key *Halakhic* rulings to argue that refraining from giving the aforementioned treatments is allowed, in situations where three or more systems in the human body have failed, and it is clear from a medical perspective that death is inevitable sooner than later. As it stands, the DP Act defines DP patients in the "final stage" as patients with "acute systems failure [of his/her body]", and it is clear that this definition finds resonance with *Halakhic* stipulations that there must be failure of three or more systems in the human body. Rabbi Steinberg's distinction between "final stage" DPs and DPs not in the "final stage" allows for the withdrawal of particular treatment in the DP Act, in accordance with pivotal *Halakhic* rulings.

Interestingly, the DP Act departs from general definitions of the age of consent in a manner distinct from the general legal system. The DP Act allows people from the age of seventeen to autonomously decide whether they wish to accept or reject life-prolonging interventions, as opposed to the general age of consent (and adulthood) in the Israeli law which is legally understood to be when the individual reaches eighteen years of age. This stipulation is relevant for both competent and incompetent DPs (see sections 5 and 14).[19]

Another interesting facet of the DP Act that has ramifications for the employment of advance directives is section 56 of the law that permits individual doctors to declare themselves conscientious objectors. This status permits doctors to withdraw from any involvement in the enactment of an advance directive (which will be discussed in further detail in the next section). Under these circumstances, the physician is obliged

[18] A. Steinberg, "The Halakhic Basis for the Proposal of the Dying Patient Law" (2003) 18 *ASSIA* [Jewish Medical Ethics] 3–4, www.daat.ac.il/daat/kitveyet/assia/habasis-2.htm [in Hebrew].

[19] It is interesting to note that, as part of the preparations process of the DP Act, in a joint meeting of two Knesset (Israeli Parliament) committees – the Welfare and Health Committee and the Law and Justice Committee – it was stated that there were no disputes regarding the lowering of the age of adulthood for this particular law to the age of seventeen. Some participants did raise questions as to the minimal age of mandating that the choice of adolescents under the age of seventeen should be respected and in what circumstances. See Joint Session of Knesset Committee on Welfare and Health and Knesset Committee on Law and Justice – Protocol No. 12 (22 November 2005), http://fs.knesset.gov.il/16/Committees/16_ptv_131323.doc [in Hebrew].

to refer the patient to another physician who is able to respect the patient's choice.

Finally, the law stipulates that the default assumed decision concerning whether a DP wishes to accept or reject life-prolonging treatment is that they would wish to prolong their life. However, according to the law, a DP's wish should be equally respected, as much as possible, regardless of whether they choose to prolong their life or not.

1.4 DP Act: Advance Directives

Advance directives are one mechanism for informing medical staff of the wishes of an incompetent DP regarding the manner in which they should be treated, within the legal framework set by the DP Act (sections 5, 14). The law also stipulates other alternative mechanisms for achieving this end, including assigned durable power of attorney by the patient (when still competent) to a close relative, an institutional or national committee defined as within the law. The latter is particularly relevant in cases where there are disputes, such as between parents of a minor or between two close family members in instances where the patient did not leave an advance directive. In the absence of these mechanisms, a final mechanism is a decision by a senior attending physician, based on a close relative's explicit declaration of the patient's expressed wish to prolong or end their life.[20] This latter option was intended as a last resort when all other options were either unavailable or inapplicable. However, as we shall see, this mechanism was actually applied more frequently than originally expected, at least according to the letter of the law.

Before delving into the manner in which advance directives are completed, it should be noted that, under sections 34(a) and 39(a) of the law, both advance directives and an assigned durable power of attorney by the patient to a close relative are limited for a period of five years, and must be renewed every five years by the patient in order to maintain validity. For certain patients (e.g. patients with dementia), the renewal of advance directives is practically impossible, once the patients' cognitive and/or

[20] To a certain extent this alternative mechanism for deriving the patient's choice in the absence of a clear statement by the patient (whether orally or as an advance directive) resonates with the idea of "consent by next of kin proxy". However, in the DP Act, the close relative does not have a formal legal standing for consenting or not as a proxy for the patient. Rather, it is the attending physician's decision based on the close relative's declaration, if the physician does not deem the relative to be in a potential conflict of interest with the incompetent or incapacitated DP.

mental condition renders them unfit to make an informed decision. Advance directives completed five years previously cannot be renewed, and will become invalid once more than five years have passed since they were originally completed or renewed.

Advance directives are required to be written on a specific designated form which, once completed, must be signed by the patient and two witnesses, and then mailed to the MOH (sections 32, 44), where it is then placed in a national registry, which is designed to record all submitted advance directives in Israel. The form may be completed by a person defined as a DP (while still competent), but it could also be filled out by a healthy person before becoming a patient, let alone a DP (section 31). This form includes thirteen specific actions pertaining to not prolonging the life of an incompetent DP, and eighteen such particular actions for a DP in the "final stage" (of which the first thirteen actions are similar to those available for DP not in the "final stage"). In other words, the scope of legally recognised and applied advance directives is limited to these particular possible actions for not prolonging the DP's life. As noted earlier, the default assumption of the law is that people wish to prolong their life as long as possible (although a DP's decision in this regard should be equally respected whether they want to prolong their life or otherwise). Accordingly, the advance directives mechanism used under the DP Act is formulated in such a way that healthy people or patients (while still competent) must specify for each available action whether they wish to refrain from having that action taken.

Furthermore, the specified actions are quite particular. For example, the person filling out the advance directives form cannot simply state that they wish to refrain from having any form of resuscitation. There are five different actions pertaining to resuscitation, only one of which is defined as "performing resuscitation in any possible way". Other specified actions of resuscitation include, for instance, providing resuscitative medicine, performing defibrillation, and inserting a tracheal tube. Other actions that do not pertain to resuscitation include the following:

1. Being hooked to a ventilator
2. Starting a dialysis treatment and determining whether to continue treatment if it is futile
3. Performing large surgical operations (e.g. amputation of a leg or arm, removing an internal organ)
4. Performing small surgical procedures (e.g. amputation of a finger)
5. Performing radiations for a malignant disease

6. Inducing chemotherapy for a malignant disease
7. Administering antibiotics in a situation of severe sepsis that cannot be treated by usual antibiotic treatment
8. Conducting diagnostic tests (e.g. blood, X-ray)

Treatments that individuals may choose to refrain from (or not) *only* in the case of becoming a DP in the "final stage" include the following:

1. Regular (accompanying) treatment such as antibiotics or transfusion of blood and its products
2. Treatment for a secondary disease, such as the provision of insulin for a diabetic patient
3. Use of a feeding tube (nutrition)
4. Pushing of fluids (hydration)
5. Palliative care

Finally, it is interesting to note that, as part of the advance directives form, future incompetent DPs will have an opportunity to define the physical and/or cognitive conditions that for them would amount to "unbearable suffering", and which would cause them to wish to refuse further life-prolonging treatment. In this section of the form, built-in options include conditions that are not necessarily terminal, and certainly do not comply with the legal definition of a DP, such as severe dementia or quadriplegia. Given that these particular options do not comply with the lawful definition of the DP, they cannot then legally be directly applied by the medical staff, merely on the basis of their stipulation on the form. Rather, these built-in options in the official advance directives forms are at worst, simply moot, or at best, might be used as a basis for appealing to the court; notably, the court, in turn, is obliged to act within the boundaries set by the DP Law. It is therefore unclear to what extent (if any) such personal definitions of what constitutes "unbearable suffering" may be applied in practice, given the narrow definition of a DP, as stipulated under the law.

1.5 Discussion: Over-regulation Leading to Under-regulation in Practice

A key feature emerging from the description of the Israeli DP Act is its extensive regulation in general, and specifically with respect to advance directives. Such extensive regulation also expresses the quite narrow boundaries of practically allowed passive euthanasia in Israel and their corresponding advance directives. This narrowness can be attributed to both the definition of the DP and the limited actions allowed to be taken in order to comply with the patients' stated desire that their life should not be prolonged.

In fact, this extensive regulation – with its emphasis on the limited scope of allowed actions that will not prolong a DP's life, including in the advance directives form – is in stark contrast to the manner with which end-of-life care was handled by the courts before the passing of the DP Act. As previously noted, in the absence of a general official regulation prior to the enactment of the DP Act, the courts simply ruled on a case-by-case basis. No less importantly, these rulings generally covered a wider diversity of patients, including those who did not suffer from terminal illnesses (e.g. dementia, as in the case of Miriam Tzadok), or alternatively, did suffer from a terminal disease but did not have the precise "date of expiry", that is, that the patient was expected to pass away within six months of receiving the prognosis, as required by the DP Act.

Similarly, these courts' verdicts allowed a wider scope of actions for not prolonging the life of patients than the DP Act permits. For instance, this law explicitly forbids any individual from disconnecting a DP from a ventilator, or the withholding of tubal feeding or liquid pushing, except for DPs languishing in their "final stage". In contrast, as already discussed, prior to the DP Act, the courts allowed the disconnection of dying persons from ventilators upon the patient's request (including any written instructions in advance), as well as confirming requests for artificially administered nourishment and liquids to be withheld from patients without a clear life expectancy of two weeks, at most.

Moreover, a gap also exists between the law's presumption to represent a so-called Jewish religious perspective, and the particular interpretation of this perspective by Justice Elon, prior to the enactment of the law. As it may be recalled, Justice Elon's interpretation – also based on *Halakhic* law and rulings, as was the DP Act – nevertheless did not reach the same conclusion, that the *Halakhic*-inspired definition of a DP should be contingent upon a specific time frame (i.e. the up-to six months' life expectancy prognosis). In addition, and again in stark contrast to the DP Act's underlying interpretation of the *Halakhic* law, Justice Elon acknowledged the possibility (in principle) that in the case of severe suffering, DPs could be disconnected from ventilators. This gap is an indication of the complexity and multifaceted nature of the *Halakhic* law, and undermines its somewhat monolithic representation, when it was driven and advocated by the political power of the ultra-orthodox political parties.

Against the backdrop of this observed contrast between the DP Act and many former courts' rulings, some legal experts have argued that precisely because of the law's limited inclusion of patients that it covers, it is entirely possible for different individual interpretations of the law. Instead of the assumption that patients who are not covered by the law are not allowed to request that their lives should not be prolonged (including through advance directives), the suggested interpretation seems to run in the opposite direction. According to some legal experts, this suggested interpretation could allow the courts to revert to the case-by-case rulings that were the norm prior to the passing of the DP Act, since this law (presumably) does not apply to patients who are not covered under its jurisdiction. Such an interpretation also emphasises the right to autonomy, which had been upheld in the Patient's Rights Law, as well as the general spirit that celebrated patients' autonomy (and which characterised most of the courts' rulings), before the DP Act was enacted.[21]

Fundamentally, this interpretation serves to illuminate the unbalanced manner in which the law addresses the tensions between a liberal-secular perspective and a more religious standpoint in favour of the latter, as already noted in this section, and at the end of the "Legal, Religious and Political Background Leading to Legislation" section.[22] Admittedly, in practice, it appears that this interpretation has not secured the support of the courts.[23] Hence, the law's framework regarding the definition of a DP, as well as the allowed and forbidden actions in order to refrain from prolonging life was upheld by the courts, regardless of whether or not the patient was a DP, as stipulated by the DP Law.

Nevertheless, this interpretation reveals the paradoxical possibility that the extensive regulation employed by the law could effectively lead to limiting its application (i.e. under-regulation). On the one hand, there is extremely restrictive regulation regarding the definition of a DP, and the limited permissible actions that may be taken to prolong their life (as demonstrated in previous sections), all of which originate from and are influenced by a particular and strict religious standpoint. On the other

[21] Karako-Eyal et al., note 13, pp. 185–252; Shalev, note 5, pp. 134–44; A. Tichu, "The Dying Patient Law 2005 – The 'Right Balance' Formula between the Sanctity of Life and Autonomy as well as Quality of Life" (2006) 35 *Refua Umishpat* [Medicine and Law] 32 [in Hebrew].

[22] Doron and Shalev, note 7, p. 25; Shapira, note 13; Tichu, note 14, p. 107.

[23] Gilbar, note 10; Shalev, note 5, pp. 134–44; Tichu, note 14, p. 107.

hand, there is the more liberal and secular legal perspective, which undermines the restrictive nature of the DP Act, as evident in its suggestion that precisely because of the narrow definition of DPs, the law holds little relevance for many patients. These legal experts suggest therefore that for patients who do not meet the narrow definition of DP, decisions regarding end-of-life matters should be delegated back to the courts, while not binding them to the letter of the DP Act.

In fact, although this particular legal interpretation remains underutilised by the courts, other aspects concerning the application of the DP Act already reveal its under-regulation in practice. While these aspects are supposedly varied, I argue that – at least to a certain extent – they echo the same tensions between a law that is substantively grounded in religious philosophy, and in its praxis, which is influenced by medical professionals and more secular perspectives of patients and their families. At the very least, the latter side of the tension leads to the under-utilisation of different aspects in the restrictive regulation embedded within the DP Act, and could ultimately lead to the very undermining of this regulation. In other words, such under-utilisations of the DP Act can be interpreted as an under-regulation of it in practice.

Specifically, the discussion here briefly addresses three such aspects: (1) practical difficulties in implementing advance directives; (2) "shades of grey" in healthcare providers' interpretation of the law; and (3) other legal decisions and interpretations undermining the regulation set by the law.

As evidenced by the conclusions of two studies conducted approximately ten years after the enactment of the DP Act, advance directives have rarely been submitted by the potentially relevant population. One study, based on official records of the Ministry of Health, found that as few as 3 per cent of older people had completed advance directives forms.[24] Another study, based on a random sample of 720 people over fifty years of age, found that only 4 per cent of the respondents indicated they had written advance directives, and only 5 per cent had appointed a durable power of attorney.[25] Recall if you will that completion of the advance directives form and the appointment of a durable power of attorney were

[24] P. Shvartzman et al., "Advance Directives – The Israeli Experience" (2015) 49 *Journal of Pain and Symptom Management* 1097.

[25] N. Bentour et al., *Knowledge and Attitudes of GPs and the General Public towards End-of-Life and Palliative Care* (Jerusalem: Myers, JDC & Brookdale Institute, 2016), https://din-online.info/pdf/mb28.pdf [in Hebrew].

supposed to be the main mechanisms through which future incompetent DPs could ensure that their wishes would be respected within the boundaries of the law. Yet, if the low proportion of research respondents who employed these mechanisms in the two aforementioned studies reflect the overall reality, then the main regulative vehicles employed by the law for achieving this end appear to be considerably under-utilised. Furthermore, it would seem that the "last resort", that is, the most under-regulated mechanism, might be the most favoured, possibly against the spirit of the highly regulated law. In the absence of any written documentation, the option for a senior attending physician to act on the best considered decision – on the basis of a declaration made by a close relative that the patient did not want to receive life-prolonging treatment – becomes the most potent mechanism.

In seeking to explain the under-utilisation of advance directives, the studies concluded that low public awareness about DP directives and cultural-religious values represented possible factors underlying their reasoning. Both studies emphasised the need to increase the general public's awareness of the purposes and benefits of advance directives. In fact, the second study (with a random sample of 720 people from the general public), found that only seven respondents (1 per cent) had been contacted by a healthcare provider to discuss their preferences for end-of-life care, and almost half of the respondents (43 per cent) thought that the mass media did not offer sufficient information regarding end-of-life care choices.[26]

In terms of the influence of cultural-religious values, the majority of respondents (73 per cent) in the second study offered the view that from a Jewish-religious perspective (not necessarily reflecting their own viewpoint and certainly not based on expertise in *Halakhic* law) every effort should be made to preserve a life. A small minority of respondents who identified as religious or ultra-orthodox were more likely to deny the need for advance directives,[27] thereby echoing yet again the unresolved tension leading to the under-regulation of the DP Act: in this case, a stricter religious proclivity that is embedded in the law, but in actuality, a viewpoint not shared by the majority of Israelis. Furthermore, it has been suggested that at the very least, the lengthy advance directives form contains too much legalese and medical terminology, and that the

[26] Ibid.
[27] Ibid.

complexity of the form makes it difficult for laypersons to comprehend.[28] This factor may help to explain its low utilisation.

Another practical difficulty appears to stem from the absence of discussion and communication about end-of-life preferences. Some studies carried out among staff of nursing homes in Israel found that staff members were generally unaware of residents' preferences for their end-of-life care.[29] These studies also revealed an overall lack of communication and support resources to facilitate discussions around such care, and which would include conversations with patients about their wishes for end-of-life care. The conclusions of another more recent study, focused on hospital staff, echoes these findings, certainly insofar as lack of sufficient communication with patients regarding their end-of-life care. Therefore, these studies highlight additional barriers to the implementation of advance directives, while stressing the under-regulation of the law – particularly its advance directives mechanism – in practice.[30]

With respect to the shades of grey in healthcare providers' interpretation of the law, at least some elements of the DP Act that are supposedly strictly regulated are not necessarily so, despite being very thoroughly detailed. For instance, the very definition of a DP includes the requirement that the patient has a prognosis of six or fewer months to live. But this raises the question of what happens if – according to the medical literature – the patient receives a prognosis of six- to eight-months life expectancy; how should the physician interpret this range when deciding whether this patient should be deemed a DP? Similarly, let us take for instance, an individual with early-stage dementia, who, while still competent, and wishing to avoid the poor quality of life that is projected with the progression of this disease, completed an advance directive requesting that physicians refrain from all possible actions denoted on the form, including being administered antibiotics when in the "final stage". If this person is hospitalised due to acute pneumonia, where it is uncertain whether the pneumonia can be successfully treated by currently available

[28] Shalev, note 13, p. 279.

[29] R. Nissanholtz-Gannot et al., *The Dying Patient Act – The Letter of the Law and Implementation of the Law* (Jerusalem: The Smokler Center for Health Policy Research, Myers-JDC-Brookdale, 2017); A. Shaulov, *Preparation for End of Life in Nursing Homes at Jerusalem District* (Jerusalem: Hadassah Medical Center, 2012) [in Hebrew]; A. Zigdon and R. Nissanholtz-Gannot, "Barriers in Implementing the Dying Patient Law: The Israeli Experience – A Qualitative Study" (2020) 21 *BMC Medical Ethics* 126.

[30] Karako-Eyal et al., note 13, pp. 185–252.

antibiotics, but without which the pneumonia will possibly cause their death within seven to ten days, how should the medical staff interpret their condition? Should they view the patient's condition as a DP in the "final stage", based on the possibility of pneumonia being acutely terminal, or just as a person with dementia, who is not considered as a DP, let alone a DP in the "final stage"? In the former scenario, the law allows physicians to withhold different medical treatments, including antibiotics. Such a case is hardly clear cut as high dosages of antibiotics may resolve the acute pneumonia, thereby returning the patient to their previous state, as persons with dementia who are not considered to be DPs. The physician is placed in the difficult position whereby s/he is required to make a clear-cut decision on whether the pneumonia is terminal, despite the inherent uncertainty as to whether it is treatable. Thus, these two examples again illustrate how the very specificity of a law that is mainly grounded within a particular and quite restrictive religious cosmology contradicts the uncertainty of some diseases, and might actually lead to problems in interpretation. That the law allows room for clinical discretion in these matters potentially undermines the regulative framework set by the law.

Although the Israeli MOH has issued guidelines for Implementing the Dying Patient Law in 2008, which summarise key provisions of the law and provide instructions to healthcare practitioners on the implementation of advance directives, a study conducted in 2014 found that many physicians remained unaware of the specifics of the law.[31] The majority of physicians surveyed could not provide the correct definition of a DP or the age of competency under the law. This suggests that the complexity and specificity of the law may cause difficulties in its implementation; in other words, stricter regulation (and possibly over-regulation) is, paradoxically, leading to under-regulation.

Finally, a third aspect of this paradox is from a judicial perspective: namely that other legal decisions and interpretations may undermine the regulations set out in the law. In 2014, the court addressed the matter of the legality of a "workaround" suggested by the attorney general to circumvent the restrictive scope of the law. The case concerned a patient with ALS who requested that they be allowed to be disconnected from a ventilator.[32] The employed workaround was that, instead of physically

[31] D. Doron et al., "Israeli Dying Patient Act: Physician Knowledge and Attitudes" (2014) 37 *American Journal of Clinical Oncology* 597.

[32] C.A. Motion (Tel Aviv) 16813-11-14 *Ploni [John Doe]* v. *The Attorney General* (2014).

disconnecting the patient from the ventilator, the percentage of oxygen in the ventilator was gradually decreased until it reached the normal rate in the air (21 per cent), which would not sustain the life of the DP in this case. Here, the court simply confirmed the attorney general's suggested workaround to be lawful. Still, in granting the patient's request, the ruling is essentially at odds with the DP Act in at least two respects.[33] First, this ruling effectively (even if not literally) recognised an ALS patient as being a DP, even though the patient clearly did not have a prognosis of a life expectancy of less than six months. Second, the verdict essentially undermined the legally established principle that non-cyclical treatments should not be stopped or withdrawn. To be sure, this court's ruling is not considered an official legal precedent, as it was issued by a lower court and, therefore, has no binding force for future court verdicts. However, this case cogently demonstrates how the strict regulation embedded within the law has led even the Attorney General of Israel to support the undermining or under-regulating of the law in practice, even if this pertained only to a single case. I would also suggest that this case echoes the same tension between a law that is grounded in strict religious faith, and its actual praxis, that was influenced by the less religious perspectives of patients and their families. In this case, there was an attempt to resolve this tension, but had the tension not existed, the attorney general would not then have needed to resort to an action that undermined the letter of the law.

1.6 CONCLUSION

Israel represents a particularly interesting case study with respect to the legal framework and its implementation insofar as advance directives are concerned. The Israeli case highlights how the interplay of politics and religion may be highly influential in the formulation of the legal framework for advance directives. Such formulation is manifested in relatively restrictive and highly regulated advance directives, certainly when compared to the courts' rulings prior to the enactment of the DP Act. As this chapter has demonstrated, in practice, this restrictive and highly regulated form of advance directives paradoxically leads to an

[33] Roy Gilbar discusses this case thoroughly and offers a robust critique about the verdict in this case, which goes well beyond my critique here. See Gilbar, note 10.

under-regulation of those very same directives. Unfortunately, as long as Israeli politics are plagued by a disproportionate power for religious political parties (as demonstrated in the case of Steinberg's committee appointment and its influence on the phrasing of the DP Act), it would seem that the core reason underlying and leading to this paradox is largely unresolvable.

2

Advance Medical Directives in Singapore: A Faltering Policy for End-of-Life Care?

TRACEY EVANS CHAN

2.1 Introduction

Advance directives rose to prominence in Singapore sometime in the mid-1990s when the National Medical Ethics Committee (NMEC) issued a report recommending enabling legislation that would recognise and give effect to individual patient decisions, made in advance of terminal illness, refusing certain forms of life sustaining treatment while the individual in question still possessed the capacity to do so. After an extensive consultative and legislative process, including deliberations by a Select Committee of Parliament, the Advance Medical Directive Act 1996 was passed and came into force on 1 July 1997. Advance directives considered in this volume encompass statements in which a competent person makes an advance *decision* in respect of healthcare, social welfare and other personal matters, which are to be implemented in the event that that person loses decision-making capacity at some later date. Pursuant to this definition, this chapter will consider the advance medical directive (AMD), which is a legislative instrument, and the common law advance decision. It then analyses reasons for the limited impact these have had on advance medical decision-making in Singapore, and observes the consequential shift to less formal and more consultative advance care planning (ACP) processes promoted by the Agency for Integrated Care in Singapore. Notwithstanding this development, it argues that there remains a legitimate role for an expanded scope of advance directives to offer a better range of options for end-of-life care to meet the needs of an evolving and diverse populace in Singapore.

2.2 The Legal Framework: Types of Advance Directives in Singapore

2.2.1 The Advance Medical Directive

The first advance directive introduced into Singapore law is the AMD, so named to make clear that it pertained only to medical decisions.[1] The impetus for enabling legislation was the need to address difficult ethical and legal issues related to the use and withdrawal of new medical technology that eventually proved futile in preventing death. Affording a patient the ability to indicate her treatment preferences in advance would better guide her physicians in making difficult medical decisions, especially in the face of differences of opinion amongst family members. It was also recognised then that various other jurisdictions facing the very same issues had introduced and legalised advance directives to allow patients the means to be spared futile medical treatment that only prolonged the dying process, and avoid placing such decisional burdens on their families.[2]

At that time, the Singapore courts had not yet addressed the legality and operation of advance directives as a matter of common law. Waiting for a sufficient body of precedents to build up to provide sufficient legal guidance was unpredictable and would take too long. Furthermore, the reception of common law precedents from other jurisdictions may not adequately take into consideration the principles and beliefs of the local community. The NMEC therefore recommended that legislation be introduced to remedy this deficit in the legal framework pertaining to advance medical decisions.[3]

2.2.1.1 The AMDA Framework: Making an AMD

Section 3 of the Advance Medical Directive Act (AMDA) provides that anyone who is not "mentally disordered"[4] and at least 21 years of age may make an AMD in the form prescribed. In the schedule to *AMDA Regulations*, the prescribed form stipulates that the maker of a directive should not be subjected to "extraordinary life-sustaining treatment" if (a)

[1] National Medical Ethics Committee, *Advance Medical Directives* (Singapore: July 1995), p. 1.
[2] Ibid., pp. 9–10.
[3] Ibid., pp. 11–12.
[4] The previous phrase "of unsound mind" was substituted by the Mental Health (Care and Treatment) Act 2008, No. 21 of 2008, s. 33 read with the Second Schedule para. 1(1) .

the person suffers from a "terminal illness" and (b) is unconscious or incapable of exercising rational judgement. Two adult witnesses are required for a valid AMD, one of whom must be a medical practitioner (section 3(2)), and there are various disqualifications for witnesses on the bases of some interest in the estate of the person after her death, or conscientious objection to acting on an AMD (section 3(3)). It is the responsibility of the medical witness to take reasonable steps to assess the person executing an AMD and ensure that she is (a) not mentally disordered, (b) is at least 21 years of age, (c) doing so voluntarily, without undue inducement or compulsion and (d) has been informed of the nature and consequences of making an AMD.[5] Finally, the duly executed AMD must be registered with the Registrar of AMDs appointed under the Act, failing which the directive may not be acted upon (section 5).

2.2.1.2 Capacity to Make an AMD

There is some uncertainty about the capacity threshold required in order to execute an AMD. Section 3 refers to a person who is not mentally disordered. This phrase is not defined in the AMDA, but the amending legislation that introduced it, the Mental Health (Care and Treatment) Act 2008, defines mental disorder as "any mental illness or any other disorder or disability of the mind".[6] Likewise, the required medical practitioner witness is expected under section 4(a) and (d) to take reasonable steps to ensure that the patient "is not mentally disordered" and "has been informed of the nature and consequences of making the directive" respectively. The threshold of mental disorder looks like a status-based conception of capacity, for not all persons suffering from a mental disorder or disability may lack the functional capacity to make an AMD.

Section 5(1) of the Mental Capacity Act 2008 (MCA 2008) adopts a functional conception of capacity, where an incapacitated person must be unable to (a) understand the information relevant to a decision, (b) retain that information, (c) use or weigh it as part of the process of making a decision, or (d) communicate his decision. Confusingly, this latter concept of capacity appears elsewhere in the AMDA, albeit in terms reminiscent of English common law's description of functional capacity:[7] under section 10 of the Act, the medical practitioner who contemplates

[5] Advance Medical Directive Act 1996, s. 4.

[6] Mental Health (Care and Treatment) Act 2008 (note 4), s. 2.

[7] See *Re C (Adult: Refusal of Treatment)* [1994] 1 W.L.R. 290.

acting on an AMD must not have reasonable grounds to believe that "the person was not, at the time of making the directive, capable of understanding the nature and consequences of the directive". Likewise, section 19(1)(c) protects a medical practitioner from liability for a decision made in good faith and without negligence as to whether the patient was "capable of understanding the nature and consequences of the directive". There is no mention in this section of a decision as to whether a patient was mentally disordered at the same point in time, although section 19(1)(d) refers to a decision by a medical practitioner as to whether a directive was valid, which may incorporate the absence of mental disorder prescribed by section 3 of the Act.

This apparently inconsistent conception of capacity within the AMDA could be resolved in two ways: The first is that mental disorder operates as a threshold floor to making an AMD; all mentally disordered persons are precluded from making an AMD, even if they possess sufficient functional capacity to do so. The requirement for functional capacity implied by section 19(1)(c) is then an additional requirement for persons who are not mentally disordered. This interpretation is problematic. It questionably excludes persons by reason of mental disorder, whether permanent or temporary, who are nevertheless functionally capable of making an AMD, and therefore devalues their autonomy. It is submitted that mental disorder should be purposively read, instead, as a mental disorder that prevents a person from being capable of understanding the nature and consequences of making an AMD (i.e. a functional capacity requirement, by reason of a mental disorder). The NMEC in its report recommending enabling legislation did not envisage such nuanced distinctions between status based and functional capacity, but simply required that persons be legally competent to execute an AMD.[8] This interpretation would also render the capacity or competence requirement under the AMDA consistent with that which prevails more generally under the MCA 2008.[9]

2.2.1.3 Safeguards in Making an AMD

There are several provisions that protect the integrity and voluntariness of executing an AMD, which is based on the principle of respect for

[8] NMEC (note 1) p. 16, para. 2.

[9] See Mental Capacity Act 2008, ss. 4 and 5, which prescribe both clinical ("an impairment of, or a disturbance in the functioning of, the mind or brain") and functional components for the requirements of incapacity.

patient autonomy.[10] Section 14(1)(a) makes it an offence to procure or obtain the execution by another person of an AMD, by means of "any deception, fraud, mis-statement, unconscionable conduct or undue influence". It is also an offence to falsify or forge someone else's AMD, or wilfully conceal or withhold knowledge of the revocation of an AMD.[11] Curiously, there is no proscription of deception or undue influence in a patient's decision *not* to execute an AMD. This may have been an oversight, or perhaps reflects an implicit deference to the usual physician-led decision-making together with the patient's family.[12] A conviction under section 14 will deem the AMD revoked and of no effect, while in the interim, no AMD may be acted upon unless it is determined that the AMD was validly and voluntarily made in accordance with the Act.

Section 15 makes it an offence for anyone likely to have medical care of any patient from asking if that patient has made or intends to make an AMD. The underlying rationale was to address a concern that patients who signed AMDs would be neglected by doctors in their medical care. The NMEC was of the view that the medical management of a patient should not be influenced by the existence of an AMD, and so a patient should not be forced to disclose to an admitting hospital or attending physician that she has made one.[13] This seems to be an overreach as patients may not be aware of the need for and facility of an AMD. Thus, the duty or right of a medical practitioner to discuss or explore the concept of directives and the objectives and provisions of the AMDA are preserved in section 15(2) provided they are consistent with good medical practice, held in the context of a physician–patient relationship and in furtherance of the purposes of public education. Further professional ethical guidance in this respect, under the wider rubric of ACP (which may involve the execution of an AMD), was issued by the NMEC belatedly in 2010.[14]

[10] NMEC (note 1) p. 9, para. 2.

[11] Advance Medical Directive Act 1996, 2020 Rev Ed, s. 14(1)(b) and (c) respectively (AMDA).

[12] *Report of the Select Committee on the Advance Medical Directive Bill [Bill No. 40/95]*, Parl. 1 of 1996 (11 Mar 1996), para. 31.

[13] NMEC (note 1) p. 17, para. 7.

[14] NMEC, *Guide for Healthcare Professionals on the Ethical Handling of Communication in Advance Care Planning* (September 2010), para. 17, https://silo.tips/download/national-medical-ethics-committee-guide-for-healthcare-professionals-on-the-ethi.

Section 15(3) also requires that all information pertaining to a patient's making of an AMD, or communications relating to an intention to make one, must be kept confidential by the medical practitioner or other medical worker having care of the patient. This might appear to contradict the recommendation of the NMEC[15] and the Select Committee that the patient be encouraged to involve family members when making an AMD, and physician counselling and advice should extend to these family members.[16] However, section 15(3) can be read harmoniously with this expectation if the patient consents to the inclusion of family members in discussions concerning the execution of an AMD.[17] Finally, section 16 prohibits any person from making an AMD a condition for insurance or receiving medical or healthcare services.

2.2.1.4 Implementing an AMD

Terminal illness, together with incapacity,[18] is the trigger for the eventual implementation of an AMD under section 9 read with section 10. It is defined in section 2 of the AMDA as:

> an incurable condition caused by injury or disease from which there is no reasonable prospect of a temporary or permanent recovery where –
>
> (a) death would, within reasonable medical judgment, be imminent regardless of the application of extraordinary life-sustaining treatment and
> (b) the application of extraordinary life-sustaining treatment would only serve to postpone the moment of death of the patient.

Extraordinary life-sustaining treatment is defined in complementary fashion as treatment that would only postpone imminent death, but *excludes* palliative care – the provision of reasonable medical procedures to relieve pain, suffering or discomfort, and food and water.[19] One immediate implication of the use of "terminal illness" as a trigger for

[15] NMEC (note 1) p. 17, para. 5.

[16] Select Committee Report, note 12, paras. 8–9. This was also acknowledged by the Minister for Health at the Third Reading of the AMD Bill in Parliament: Sing. Parl. Reports, vol. 66(1) col. 116 (2 May 1996).

[17] See also Sing. Parl. Reports, vol. 66(1), col. 115–16 (2 May 1996), Minister for Health George Yeo.

[18] AMDA, s. 9(1)(c) describes this as being "unconscious or incapable of exercising rational judgment".

[19] AMDA, s. 2.

implementing an AMD is the exclusion of patients in a persistent vegetative state and other prolonged disorders of consciousness.[20]

There were suggestions before the Select Committee for the AMDA to define "imminent" in chronological terms, for example, within 6 to 12 months, but the committee preferred to leave this to medical judgement.[21] Instead, the Act prescribes a rigorous process to certify terminal illness. The medical practitioner responsible for the treatment of a patient ('attending physician') must first certify in the prescribed form such terminal illness in order to search the AMD register to determine if the patient has made an AMD (recall, it is unlawful under the AMDA to directly ask a patient whether he has or intends to make an AMD). The attending physician is under a duty to do so where she "has reason to believe that the person is (a) suffering from a terminal illness; (b) requires extra-ordinary life sustaining treatment; and (c) is unconscious or incapable of exercising rational judgment".[22] If the search reveals a valid AMD made by the patient that remains in force, further certification of terminal illness is required from two other medical practitioners. Out of the three certifying physicians, two of them must be specialists recognised by the Director of Medical Services (DMS) for the purposes of the Act.[23] Where the two additional certifying physicians are not in agreement, the matter has to be further referred to a separate panel of three specialists, also appointed by the DMS under section 8 of the Act. Only a unanimous opinion of this separate panel will determine the patient terminally ill under the AMDA.[24] Otherwise, the AMD will not be acted upon.

Once a person who has executed a valid AMD has been certified as terminally ill in accordance with the procedure under the Act and is not pregnant with a viable foetus,[25] it is the duty of the attending physician to act in accordance with the terms of the AMD unless there is reason to believe that (1) the patient has revoked his AMD in any recognised manner or (2) was incapable of understanding the nature and consequences of the AMD at the time of its execution.[26] Recognising that persons do change their minds about preferences for end-of-life care,

20 Select Committee Report, note 12, para. 17.
21 Select Committee Report, note 12, para. 36.
22 AMDA, s. 9(1).
23 AMDA, s. 9(3)-(4).
24 AMDA, s. 9(5)-(7). Similar disqualifications apply to this specialist panel as apply to witnesses to the execution of an AMD: s. 9(9).
25 AMDA, s. 10(3).
26 AMDA, s. 10(2).

revoking an AMD is much easier than making one.[27] Section 7 allows revocation in writing, orally or by any other means of communication so long as there is at least one witness of this. The patient and the witness must notify the Registrar of AMDs as far as practicable of the fact of revocation in writing.

2.2.1.5 Consequential Provisions

In addition to imposing a duty on medical practitioners to implement an AMD once the statutory triggers have been satisfied, the Act makes several important consequential provisions. The physician who implements the AMD in good faith and without negligence shall not be subject to any civil or criminal liability, or professional disciplinary proceedings. A person acting under the instructions of such a medical practitioner is similarly protected in giving effect to an AMD unless he has knowledge of the revocation or intended revocation of the AMD in question.[28] Secondly, the implementation of a patient's AMD does not constitute a cause of that patient's death unless there was negligence in the certification of terminal illness.[29]

2.2.2 The Common Law Advance Decision

Although Singapore has adopted the model of the United Kingdom's Mental Capacity Act 2005 as its framework for handling the care and treatment of mentally incapacitated adults, it chose to omit sections 24 to 26 of that Act which deal generally with advance decisions to refuse specified treatment, which may relate to all medical treatment including the provision of artificial nutrition and hydration.[30] The drafter of the MCA 2008 chose to omit these sections presumably because the prior AMDA already deals with advance decisions in medical situations. However, because of the restrictive nature of the scope and operation of the statutory AMD, it is often asked if other advance decisions that fall outside the AMDA are legally recognised and enforceable at common law.

27 NMEC (note 1) p. 17, para. 8.
28 AMDA, s. 19(1) and (2) respectively.
29 AMDA, s. 20.
30 UK Department for Constitutional Affairs, *Mental Capacity Act 2005 Code of Practice* (London: The Stationery Office, 2007), ch. 9, para. 9.26.

Although the provisions of the AMDA do not address this issue explicitly, it seems reasonably clear that the Act is not meant to preclude advance decisions under the common law. Section 13(1) states that that Act shall not affect the right of any person to refuse medical or surgical treatment, without attempting to restrict it to contemporaneous decisions. This standing common law right to make advance decisions concerning medical treatment is well recognised.[31] In the local case of *Re LP*, the High Court recognised that "[g]enerally, a person who is sufficiently matured is entitled to give or withhold consent to any medical treatment and the doctors are entitled, if not obliged, to respect that person's decision".[32] Although the court left open the question of whether living wills or American-type advance directives distinct from an AMD were applicable here,[33] its reasoning in authorising the amputation of the patient's gangrenous legs held that the patient's *earlier* statements to her doctors did not amount to a clear, express refusal of treatment presently proposed.[34] This appears to be an implicit endorsement of the right of a patient to refuse treatment in advance at common law. Furthermore, the NMEC's proposals to legislate on AMDs made clear that the intention in doing so was to provide a clear and certain legislative route, while allowing for the continued development of ethical principles and common law in relation to advance directives and related issues.[35]

Therefore, patients dissatisfied with the limited ambit of the statutory instrument could have recourse to a common law advance directive.[36] There are no prescribed formalities for this, although the common law places the burden on anyone seeking to rely on the terms of an advance decision to satisfactorily prove its existence and validity. However, where

[31] *Re T (Adult: Refusal of Treatment)* [1992] 4 All E.R. 649 (C.A.); *Hunter and New England Area Health Service v A* [2009] NSWSC 761.

[32] *Re LP (Adult Patient: Medical Treatment)* [2006] 2 S.L.R.(R) 13, [4].

[33] The court did not specify exactly how these American-type advance directives differ from an AMD, but advance directives in the United States encompass both living wills and durable powers of attorney. The former can be broader in ambit, covering both terminal illness and permanent unconsciousness, and other types of treatment apart from life-sustaining treatment: see American Cancer Society, "Types of Advance Directives", www.cancer.org/treatment/finding-and-paying-for-treatment/understanding-financial-and-legal-matters/advance-directives/types-of-advance-health-care-directives.html.

[34] [2006] 2 S.L.R.(R) 13, [8] and [11].

[35] NMEC (note 1) p. 13, para. 10.

[36] The same view was taken soon after the AMDA came into force: K.L. Ter and S. Leong, "Advance Medical Directives in Singapore" (1997) 5 *Medical Law Review* 63, 83.

life is at stake, "clear and convincing" proof is required of its existence and continuing validity.[37] The ethical guidance from the Singapore Medical Council on end-of-life care stipulates that a patient's wishes not to receive specific treatments must be respected,[38] while its *Handbook on Medical Ethics* states that, apart from an AMD, "any advance statement made by patients on care or treatment that they might accept or refuse in particular circumstances" is helpful in determining a patient's values, concerns, wishes, and ultimately what is in their best interests.[39] Although the SMC's *Handbook on Medical Ethics* pronouncements are more likely intended to assist in the determination of a patient's overall best interests under the MCA,[40] the NMEC envisaged that discussions on ACP could lead to the drafting of an advance directive.[41] In particular, the committee described advance directives in broader terms than an AMD, encompassing "oral and/or written instructions that convey treatment preferences in the event of a loss of decision-making capacity".[42]

However, this flexibility of form gives rise to potential evidentiary and interpretational uncertainties concerning the implementation of a common law advance decision. For example, there is no independent witness requirement at common law, and there is no equivalent statutory protection against civil or criminal liability or professional disciplinary proceedings in determining the validity of a common law directive. This may impede the respect for and implementation of such advance decisions. Unlike the AMD, there is also no statutory registration mechanism that might provide assurance that the terms of a written common law directive will be brought to the attention of attending physicians in the

[37] *HE* v. *A Hospital NHS Trust* [2003] 2 F.L.R. 408 (EWHC).

[38] Singapore Medical Council, *Ethical Code and Ethical Guidelines* (2016), p. 20, part A7, para. 3.

[39] Singapore Medical Council, *Handbook on Medical Ethics* (2016), p. 11 (where "best interests" is confusingly stated to be representative of their right to autonomy) and p. 30.

[40] MCA, s. 6(7)(a) requires a doctor determining a patient's best interests to consider the latter's past and present wishes and feelings, and in particular any relevant written statement made by the patient when she had capacity.

[41] See NMEC, note 14, para. 17.

[42] Ibid., para. 12. It is unclear to what extent the medical profession in Singapore appreciates the legality and potential of common law advance directives, although they have been recognised by some: A. Devanand, "Guide to End-of-Life Decision Making", (July 2015) *SMA News* 36–7, www.sma.org.sg/UploadedImg/files/Publications%20-%20SMA%20News/4707/Professionalism.pdf.

appropriate circumstances – but access to the AMD registry is an unwieldy process to begin with.[43]

The *Specific Licensing Terms and Conditions on Medical Records for Healthcare Institutions* instead requires that a patient's medical record include documents pertaining to her advance care plan if prepared.[44] As ACP may result in the documentation of an advance decision to accept or refuse medical treatment, which could arguably amount to a valid common law directive,[45] this must therefore be captured in the medical record as well. The National ACP Steering Committee and Agency for Integrated Care have also rolled out an ACP information technology system that captures key decisions on care options, and catalogues conversation transcripts and other supporting documents into a single record. Since April 2017, this system has been integrated with the National Electronic Health Record (NEHR), thus enhancing accessibility and availability across different institutional care settings.[46] It therefore becomes more likely that any common law advance directives made by a patient in the process of ACP will be brought to the attention of attending physicians throughout the public healthcare system with access to the NEHR. Nevertheless, under the Living Matters ACP initiative, the emphasis has been to deemphasise the completion of legal directives and promote iterative conversations and regular opportunities to review care plans to adapt to changing health and care circumstances.[47] There nonetheless seems to be less concern that any documentation on end-of-life planning will adversely influence the clinical care of the patient. In any case, the proscription on enquiring about the existence of an AMD does not apply to such instruments.

However, unless there is some standardisation of the language and intent behind such common law advance directives, uncertainties as to interpretation and circumstances of implementation will remain. In this

[43] See note 22 and accompanying text.

[44] Ministry of Health, *Specific Licensing Terms and Conditions on Medical Records for Healthcare Institutions Imposed under s. 6(5) of the Private Hospitals and Medical Clinics Act* (6 August 2015), para. 4.2(j).

[45] S. Menon, "Advance Decision-Making in Singapore", in J. Chin et al. (eds.), *Caring for Older People in an Ageing Society*. Vol. 2 of *A Singapore Bioethics Casebook:* (Singapore: National University of Singapore, 2017), www.bioethicscasebook.sg.

[46] See I. Chung, "Advance Care Planning in an Asian Country", in K. Thomas et al., *Advance Care Planning in End of Life Care*, 2nd ed. (Oxford University Press, 2018), ch. 23, 327–8.

[47] Ibid., p. 332.

respect, individual healthcare institutions are in the process of developing and implementing policies on how ACP documents are recorded and implemented.[48] ACP documents preferences and values on types of treatment depending on the stage of illness. Some of these preferences may be stated in directive terms, such as "DO NOT attempt CPR [cardiopulmonary resuscitation]",[49] or indications that proxy decision-makers are to strictly follow the patient's wishes.[50] On the other hand, the terms advance directive or decision are eschewed, and standard forms begin with the overarching statement that physicians "will always act in the patient's best interests…".[51] This reference perhaps alludes to the best interests standard of proxy decision-making in the MCA 2008, where prior statements of wishes and feelings are to be considered but have no binding authority.[52] This leaves some uncertainty about whether ACP documented preferences and wishes that are sufficiently precise and directive will be treated as having the binding effect of a common law directive. Nevertheless, the uncertainties in interpretation and confidence in implementation by healthcare professionals that originally concerned the NMEC in its 1995 report appear, to some extent, to have been addressed by the development of ACP policies, documents and protocols at the institutional level. Information technology has also afforded the means to overcome barriers to access for common law advance directives that are produced as a result of ACP. What is needed is clearer professional guidance on the recognition and implementation of common law advance directives, otherwise any documented preferences may simply be overridden by professional medical judgement of the patient's best interests or family objection on similar grounds.

2.3 Assessing the Impact of Advance Directives in Singapore

If we look at absolute numbers, the take-up of AMDs in Singapore has thus far been very low. The Registry of AMDs does not publish statistics on AMD registrations and implementation, although the public is given periodic updates in the form of answers to questions filed in Parliament

[48] See Menon, note 45.

[49] See T.E. Chan, "Advance Care Planning: A Communitarian Approach?" (2019) 26(4) *Journal of Law & Medicine* 896, Appendix 2 – Preferred Care Plan, para. A.

[50] Ibid., Appendix 1 – Disease Specific Advance Care Plan (General), para. H.

[51] Ibid., Appendix 1 and 2.

[52] MCA 2008, s. 6(7)(a).

on AMDs. Between 1997 and 2008, a total of 10,100 AMDs were registered representing 0.4% of the resident population (three quarters of those between 2004–8), 19 were revoked and six were implemented.[53] By 2015, the last recorded disclosure on AMD statistics, 24,682 AMDs were registered and 10 AMDs were implemented, representing 0.7% of the resident population.[54] There are no apparent data on or research looking at common law advance directives, although in the parliamentary response in 2016 just mentioned, it was revealed that about 5,100 advance care plans had been completed between 2011 and 2015.

These numbers should not be surprising given the very restrictive ambit and formalities of the AMD. As mentioned previously, patients in a persistent vegetative state or other prolonged disorders of consciousness cannot depend on an AMD to refuse such treatment. Imminent death, as part of this definition, is also not defined in chronological terms but left to medical specialists to determine.[55] However, studies elsewhere and in Singapore reveal that it is very difficult to make a definitive prognosis of death even when it is very close.[56] Thus consensus between the required two or three medical practitioners certifying terminal illness will be less frequent. Extraordinary life-sustaining treatment hinges on terminal illness in order to be considered as merely prolonging the dying process. It further excludes palliative care, which includes the reasonable provision of food and water without specifying the means – commentators assume this exclusion will cover the reasonable provision of artificial nutrition and hydration.[57]

The sum effect of these restrictions means that AMDs only cover situations of undeniable medical futility, for which the existence of an AMD adds little deliberative value to the decision to withdraw life-sustaining treatment.[58] Thus, local medical practitioners familiar with its terms have observed that there was no practical point in executing an

53 Sing. Parl. Debates, vol. 85(1) col. 695 (17 November 2008), Minister Khaw – Oral Answers to Questions: Advance Medical Directive.

54 Sing. Parl. Debates, vol. 94(21) (11 July 2016), Minister Gan – Written Answers to Questions: Number of Singaporeans Who Have Signed Advance Medical Directives.

55 NMEC (note 1), p. 14; Select Committee Report, note 12, para. 36.

56 J. Lynn, "Living Long in Fragile Health: The New Demographics Shape End of Life Care" (2005) 35(6) *Hastings Center Special Report* S14;J. Tan and J. Chin, *What Doctors Say about Care of the Dying* (Singapore: Lien Foundation, 2011), p. 3, www.lienfoundation.org/sites/default/files/What_Doctors_Say_About_Care_of_the_Dying_0.pdf.

57 See Ter and Leong, note 36, p. 74.

58 A.E. Buchanan and D.W. Brock, *Deciding for Others: The Ethics of Surrogate Decision Making* (Cambridge University Press, 1989), 296–7, discussing the California *Natural*

AMD.[59] Part of the reason for this overly cautious legislative approach might have been the prevailing health policy zeitgeist at the time the idea of advance directives was first mooted by the NMEC in its position paper in August 1994.[60] This was not long after the Singapore Government had promulgated its White Paper on *Affordable Health Care*,[61] which emphasised cost containment and sustainability in healthcare expenditure, along with individual responsibility for one's health and to avoid overreliance on state welfare or medical insurance. This juxtaposition, along with the common misunderstanding that AMDs were a form of passive euthanasia because they involve the withdrawal of treatment leading to death,[62] may explain public concerns over neglect by medical practitioners once a patient had signed an AMD[63] or that the underlying motivation for recommending an AMD was healthcare cost containment.[64] These concerns led to stifling restrictions like making it a criminal offence for any doctor to ask if a patient had executed, or intended to execute, an AMD, thus making it that much harder for them to broach the issue as a legitimate part of end-of-life care. The NMEC has since clarified the ethics of communications in ACP, which may include the execution of an AMD or common law directive, thus providing a clearer path for physicians to raise these issues in clinical practice and, correspondingly, questioning the further need for such restrictions.[65]

Even if the AMD were not so restrictive, it is questionable if patient responses would have been markedly different. Health decision-making practices in Singapore tend to adopt family-centric decision-making models that run counter to the individualistic, transactional model that the AMD is based on. Under the former model, many patients prefer to leave decision-making to trusted family members, and do not see it as their responsibility to make decisions, much less execute an advance

Death Act (1976); Cal. Health & Safety Code, §7187(f) (1976), on which the definition of "terminal illness" in the AMDA is adapted: see NMEC (note 1) p. 14, para. 3.

59 See Tan and Chin, note 56, p. 41.

60 See Section 2.2.1.3 for the details of these statutory safeguards.

61 Ministry of Health, *Affordable Health Care: A White Paper*, Cmd. 16 of 1993; advance directives were first mentioned in Parliament in connection with this White Paper: K.H. Tee et al., "Advance Directive: A Study on the Knowledge and Attitudes among General Practitioners in Singapore" (1997) 38(4) *Singapore Medical Journal* 145.

62 See Tee et al., ibid., p. 147; see also Sing. Parl. Debates, vol. 65(4) col. 355, Health Minister George Yeo.

63 See Health Minister George Yeo, ibid., col. 356; Health Minister Khaw, note 53.

64 See Ter and Leong, note 36, p. 65.

65 NMEC Guide, note 14; AMDA, s. 15(2) respectively.

directive.[66] An additional challenge is the not uncommon practice of collusion between families and physicians to withhold diagnosis and poor prognosis from a vulnerable patient, which also prevents active participation and independent decision-making.[67] Amidst such practices, the need and ability to exercise individual moral authority to take responsibility for one's healthcare decisions do not arise at all. Others argue that in such a familial model of decision-making, advance directives are means of helping family members understand the patient's voice in order to arrive at a family decision, which should not be dictated by the literal meaning of the advance directive.[68] Therefore it is not necessary in this thinking to institutionalise individualistic expression of prior wishes strictly by laws and regulation.

Finally, even if we were to put aside cultural values and practices, human psychology imposes various challenges in making good anticipatory decisions about future health scenarios with incomplete information. The literature raises doubts about people's ability to accurately anticipate their reactions to serious illness, the stability of their life-sustaining treatment preferences even over short periods of up to two years (at least for a substantial minority) and their tendency to overestimate the stability of their attitudes and beliefs over time.[69] More recent psychological research on affective forecasting has led to better understanding of the systematic biases at play in making predictions about future preferences, apart from a lack of information about the future. One example is impact bias, which tends to predict greater intensity and longer lasting effects of future events than is actually the case. This is a result of the overweight of focus on the event itself, to the exclusion of the contribution of other factors to the predicted outcomes. Secondly, we also tend to underestimate our ability to adapt to negative events and habituate to positive ones.[70] As a result, individuals will often mis-predict

[66] See e.g. Tan and Chin, note 56, p. 12; K. Tay et al., "Cultural Influences upon Advance Care Planning in a Family-centric Society" (2017) 15 *Palliative & Supportive Care* 665.

[67] See Tan and Chin, note 56, pp. 13–5; S. Menon et al., "Some Unresolved Ethical Challenges in Healthcare Decision-Making: Navigating Family Involvement" (2020) 12 *Asian Bioethics Review* 27, 29.

[68] H.M. Chan, "Sharing Death and Dying: Advance Directives, Autonomy and the Family" (2004) 18(2) *Bioethics* 87, 96–7.

[69] P.H. Ditto et al., "Imagining the End of Life: On the Psychology of Advance Medical Decision Making" (2005) 29(4) *Motivation and Emotion* 475, 486–88; in respect of the last finding, see also J. Quoibach et al., "The End of History Illusion" (2013) 339 *Science* 96.

[70] Ditto et al., ibid., pp. 488–9.

their future preferences, and weigh relevant considerations differently depending on how far in the future a present decision is meant to apply. There is some correspondence between these findings and qualitative studies looking at the reasons why individuals do not see advance directives as useful,[71] and in the experience with ACP and patient preferences in Singapore.[72]

If we combine these insights based on history, culture, typical preferences for methods of medical decision-making and human psychology, we should question whether continued promotion of advance directives by improving the legal and supportive healthcare framework is the best way forward. Although there were discussions about amending the AMDA circa 2008, nothing came to bear on this.[73] Instead, in 2009, ACP was piloted in a Singapore tertiary hospital and subsequently scaled up to a national programme, "Living Matters".[74] This approach to advance healthcare decision-making seeks to emphasise a relational, patient-centred process supported by trained healthcare professionals and trusted family members. It seeks to move away from the earlier, legally focussed, transactional process[75] towards a more open, inclusive and iterative communications process directed towards the same goal of enabling patients to retain control over their care once they lose decision-making capacity.[76] Ideally, when properly engaged, ACP will prepare patients and their proxy decision makers to make better in-the-moment medical decisions with their physicians on the basis of these communications, instead of advance decisions with incomplete information.[77]

[71] See M. Spranzi and V. Fournier, "The Near-Failure of Advance Directives: Why They Should Not Be Abandoned Altogether, but Their Role Radically Reconsidered" (2016) 19 *Medicine, Health Care and Philosophy* 563.

[72] See Chung, note 46.

[73] See Health Minister Khaw, note 53; in particular, it was mentioned that the AMDA should be amended to simplify the process and do away with the requirement for a medical practitioner witness, and also remove restrictions on healthcare professionals raising the issue of executing an AMD with patients.

[74] See Chung, note 46, pp. 326–7. For a more detailed discussion of the issues related to ACP and Living Matters in Singapore, see Chan, note 49, pp. 897–8.

[75] T.J. Prendergast, "Advance Care Planning: Pitfalls, Progress, Promise" (2001) 29(Supp 2) *Critical Care Medicine* N34, N37–38.

[76] S.E. Hickman et al., "Hope for the Future: Achieving the Original Intent of Advance Directives" (2005) 35(6) *Hastings Center Report* S26, S30.

[77] R.L. Sudore and T.R. Fried, "Redefining the 'Planning' in Advance Care Planning: Preparing for End-of-Life Decision Making" (2010) 153(4) *Annals of Internal Medicine 256; see NMEC, Guide for Communication in ACP*, note 14, para. 16; see Chung, note 46, p. 330.

Even so, there will still be room for more flexible advance directives. Some patients have firmer preferences for end-of-life care, particularly when disease trajectories are relatively more predictable.[78] Family and social bonds may also be diminishing, with an increasing proportion of single adults and married persons without children.[79] This may result in a lack of adequate social support for effective proxy healthcare decision-making pursuant to an ACP programme. Differing social contexts suggest that the ACP model of decision-making may not suit all patients, some of whom may want more reliable means of ensuring respect for personal preferences in healthcare in the absence of trusted and willing proxy decision-makers. Studies elsewhere have revealed the existence of a stable minority of patients who want to retain control through the use of advance directives,[80] and the more informal ACP framework will need to be augmented to accommodate their preferred model of ACP.[81]

2.4 Conclusion

In summary, while Singapore was out of the gates very early as far as advance directives are concerned, AMDs have never really taken off in ACP and healthcare decision-making. For reasons that have to do with the social and policy climate at the time they were first introduced, prevailing cultural values and familial approaches to healthcare decision-making, and limitations on anticipatory decision-making in human psychology, the AMD initiative to jump start better respect for patient autonomy at the end of life has faltered. The current preferred Living Matters ACP programme seeks to learn from and avoid the difficulties experienced with AMDs, but it is argued that there remains a legitimate role for more flexible advance directives as the values, needs and expectations of the Singapore populace evolve.[82]

[78] See M. Ho et al., "The Physician-Patient Relationship in Treatment Decision Making at the End of Life: A Pilot Study of Cancer Patients in a Southeast Asian Society" (2013) 11 *Palliative & Supportive Care* 13.

[79] National Talent and Population Division, Prime Minister's Office, *Population in Brief 2020* (Singapore: September 2020); www.strategygroup.gov.sg/files/media-centre/publications/population-in-brief-2020.pdf.

[80] See Spranzi and Fournier, note 71, pp. 565–6.

[81] For more detailed discussion on this, see Chan, note 49, pp. 911–12.

[82] See Tay et al., note 66, p. 672.

3

South Korea's End-of-Life Care Decisions Act: Law for Better End-of-Life Care

ILHAK LEE

3.1 Introduction

On 8 January 2016, the National Assembly of the Republic of Korea passed the Act on Hospice and Palliative Care and Decisions on Life-Sustaining Treatment for Patients at the End of Life (ELDA). The Act's lengthy name arguably reflects the lengthy discussions in Korea about what constitutes acceptable end-of-life care. Although ELDA regulates end-of-life care in general, the legislators tried to narrow its potential application to the less-controversial condition of the "dying stage". This chapter begins with a description of end-of-life care, especially of those features of such care for which remedies are needed, and then moves on to a discussion of the law and ethics of end-of-life care in Korea. My focus is on end-of-life care decision-making rather than palliative care. The implications of ELDA are also discussed.

3.2 Background and History

3.2.1 End-of-Life Decisions in the Courts

Whilst ELDA 2016 represents the most significant legal development concerning end-of-life care in Korea, a full understanding of the trajectory of legal developments in this area requires that we first look at two landmark court cases that preceded the law and played an important role in motivating legal reform and changes to professional practice: the *Boramae Hospital* case (1998) and *Severance Hospital* case (2008). The latter was a civil lawsuit brought against the hospital concerned to force it to forgo life-sustaining treatment (LST), and the former was a criminal case against surgeons who had discharged a patient at his wife's request. The current legal regulation on end-of-life care decisions took its shape from the Supreme Court's decisions in these two cases. It is important to note that both cases pertained to the forgoing of LST, not to euthanasia.

3.2.1.1 Boramae Hospital Case

This case dealt with the legitimacy of surrogate decision-making when the withdrawal of LST and discharge would mean the death of the patient.[1] The issue contested at trial was how far the duty of care extends when a family insists upon a particular treatment. The physicians at Boramae Hospital had discharged the patient concerned, whose treatment was deemed to be LST, at the request of his wife. She had requested that her husband be discharged for economic reasons, that is, the financial burden of continued hospitalisation. The final verdict arrived on 24 June 2004. The Supreme Court found the surgeons guilty and sentenced them to one year and six months' imprisonment each. The court considered the surgeons to be guilty as accomplices to murder because they had (i) honoured the wife's request, which could not be regarded as an authoritative proxy decision and (ii) not taken proper measures to prevent an anticipated harm.

This judgment rang alarm bells amongst Korean doctors, who became concerned about the decision-making process at the end of life. The judgment confirmed that doctors' duty is this: treating a patient as an autonomous individual and considering his or her best interests under any circumstances.[2] However, confusion remained over whether every withdrawal of LST would result in liability or whether it was sufficient to consult all family members before any decision was made. Such confusion arose in part because there was no explicit written provision in Korean law. Further, most – but not all – decisions were made jointly by doctors and patients' family members on the assumption that the latter were conferred with the power to consider what is best for the patient, even though, as noted, there was no explicit legal provision for this.

Despite the serious ethical discussions on end-of-life care following the *Boramae Hospital* case, no formal mechanisms such as advance directives (ADs), durable power of attorney or clinical ethics consultation were implemented. Accordingly, many professional bodies were quick to develop guidelines to realise the spirit of the Supreme Court's decision. For example, the Korean Association of Medical Societies (KAMS) in 2002 developed guidelines on the forgoing of LST for dying patients that provide a clinical pathway resembling that of the American Medical

[1] K.H. Hahm and I. Lee, "Biomedical Ethics Policy in Korea: Characteristics and Historical Development" (2012) 27 *Journal of Korean Medical Science* S76.

[2] Korean Supreme Court Decision 2009 Do 995 delivered on 24 June 2004.

Association.[3] Although the KAMS guidelines were developed and modified to fit the Korean context, they did little to improve the practice of end-of-life care planning, primarily because they have little binding force: there is no duty for doctors to follow the KAMS guidelines. Accordingly, doctors wanted a secure legal basis for following a patient's wishes, such as a clear exemption from liability. That desire stemmed from fear of the heavy penalty imposed by the Supreme Court in the *Boramae Hospital* case, not least the cancellation of the guilty doctors' medical licences.

It was not only the medical community that was concerned by the case; there were also concerns amongst bioethics activists that this decision would lead to euthanasia being legislated. The controversy continued for several years until the *Severance Hospital* case in 2009, which triggered the start of the ELDA legislation process.

3.2.1.2 Severance Hospital Case

This case concerned a request made by the family of a patient, a woman in her late 70s who was in a persistent vegetative state, to discontinue the medical treatment she was receiving. The family filed a lawsuit against Severance Hospital, which had refused to stop the treatment. The trial process in the case was unusually quick, with the Supreme Court ruling in 2009 that the withdrawal of LST could proceed based on the patient's presumed intent. The patient had once made a similar decision for her husband, and her preferences concerning LST were thus deemed by the court to be recognisable from her life attitudes. Notably, the Supreme Court imposed a limitation on the withdrawal of LST, ruling that "when it is recognised that a patient who has reached an irreversible stage of death exercises her right to self-determination on the ground of the constitutional rights of human dignity and right to pursue happiness, it is permissible to withdraw life-sustaining treatment".[4]

The *Severance Hospital* case was important in the sense that it was the first case in which a Korean court recognised a patient's right to refuse futile LST. Whilst the Supreme Court's decision apparently recognised patients' right to self-determination with respect to LST, we must take care not to interpret it as confirmation of the right to refuse life-saving treatment in general. There is a condition that must be fulfilled before a patient's

[3] Committee on Reporting of Symposium on Euthanasia and Death with Dignity, Korean Association of Medical Societies, *KAMS Medical Ethics Guideline No. 1: On the Forgoing Life-Sustaining Treatment of the Dying Patient* (2002).

[4] Korean Supreme Court Decision 2009 Da 17417 delivered on 21 May 2009.

treatment preferences can be executed: "he/she (should) have reached an irreversible stage". This condition leaves little room for interpretation. Nevertheless, the spirit of the court's decision in this case is that a patient's right to refuse treatment should be institutionalised by legislation on end-of-life medical decision-making. Hence, the legislative process began.

3.2.2 Consensus Building Process (2009–2012)

The period prior to ELDA's passage saw the Government set up various consultation bodies to facilitate social consensus-building in relation to end-of-life decision-making issues.[5]

3.2.2.1 Ministry of Health and Welfare's Council on the Institutionalisation of Forgoing Life-Sustaining Treatments (2009–2010)

In 2009, the Ministry of Health and Welfare responded to the *Severance Hospital* case by organising the Council on the Institutionalisation of Forgoing Life-Sustaining Treatments. The council released its report in 2010. The minimal consensus the council members reached, which subsequently served as the starting block for a public engagement process, was as follows. The permissibility of LST withdrawal was to be restricted to "terminal patients" and to certain treatments. Nonetheless, the report recommended documenting end-of-life care preferences to make them explicit and establishing a review committee and conflict resolution mechanism. The consensus report can be summarised as follows:

(i) The forgoing of LST is permissible only for terminal patients; patients in a persistent vegetative state are excluded unless they are in the terminal stage.
(ii) The only treatments that can be withdrawn are extraordinary LSTs such as cardiopulmonary resuscitation (CPR) and artificial ventilation; hydration and nutrition should not be withdrawn.
(iii) An "Advance Medical Directive (or Advance Medical Intention Documents)" should be written if a patient in the terminal stage wishes to express his or her preferences. Notably, an adult can write such a document after consulting with the attending physician following two weeks of mature deliberation.

5 M. Tanaka et al., "Forgoing Life-Sustaining Treatment – A Comparative Analysis of Regulations in Japan, Korea, Taiwan, and England" (2020) 21 *BMC Medical Ethics* 99.

(iv) A National Terminal Care Review Committee under the Ministry of Health and Welfare and Hospital Ethics Committees in individual healthcare institutes should be established to facilitate the decision-making process in the end-of-life care context.

The council's 2010 report constituted baseline consensus amongst Koreans regardless of their attitudes towards the scope of end-of-life decisions. The National Bioethics Advisory Committee then joined the discussion by establishing a task force under the auspices of the National Bioethics Review Committee in 2013.

3.2.2.2 National Bioethics Review Committee's Task Force for Decision-Making about Futile LST and Recommendations of the National Bioethics Advisory Committee (2012)

In 2013, the National Bioethics Review Committee, established under the Korean Bioethics and Safety Act 2005, launched the Task Force for Decision-Making about Futile Life-Sustaining Treatment with the aim of giving the council's consensus concrete shape.[6] The task force's final report discussed six issues: basic principles, potential patients, medical interventions, identifying a patient's preferences, social engagement and methods of institutionalisation.[7] Although the National Bioethics Review Committee announced "agreed" recommendations for drafting an act, concerns remained over the potential abuse of end-of-life care decisions, and there were also demands for a more permissive law allowing patients to decide.

As for the basic principles of medical decision-making concerning LST, these were determined to be (i) a patient's right to an informed decision, (ii) respect for self-determination, and (iii) the provision of

[6] There was some controversy about what futile LST should be called in Korean society around this time. Whilst the term "futile LST" or 无意义的 延命治疗, meaning "LST without any purpose", had been used previously, an influential member of the National Bioethics Review Committee, as well as a leading member of the hospice and palliative care movement, argued that this term should be replaced with the term "LS procedure" or 延命施術. He felt that removing the term "futile" would better reflect the societal view that futility was implied in the term "life-sustaining" and that it was important to replace the word "treatment" because of its connotation of benefiting patients. (See further M. Kim, "Context and Issues of 'National Bioethics Advisory Committee's Recommendation on Decision on Life-Sustaining Treatment': Emphasis on the Procedures of Task Force for Institutionalisation of Decision on Life-Sustaining Treatment" (2013) 11(3) *Research Institute for Healthcare Policy* 8.)

[7] Y.S. Lee, "On the Life-Sustaining Treatment in Korea" (2012) 55(12) *Journal of Korean Medical Association* 1161.

hospice palliative care. The agreed recommendations limited the patients of concern to those in an irreversible condition with no hope of a cure and those with a rapidly aggravating condition that does not respond to treatment of the underlying disease. This narrow perspective can also be found in the treatments of concern, which are restricted to LSTs that require professional medical knowledge, skills and equipment, namely, extraordinary LST such as CPR, ventilator care, haemodialysis, anticancer chemotherapy and so forth. Patients can choose hospice palliative care. As for the method of identifying a patient's preferences, the recommendations prioritised a patient's explicit preferences over other means, such as a presumed will or surrogate decision-making. In the case of incompetency, documentation was recommended.

The task force's recommendations recognised the importance of the cultural and socioeconomic environments and the role of collaboration for improvement, although such recognition appeared to be largely symbolic, with very few follow-up actions apart from the establishment of a National End-of-Life Day and Ceremonial Day and social media and other campaigns promoting the concept of self-determination. The National Bioethics Review Committee's final recommendation was the institutionalisation of end-of-life care decisions through legislation.

3.2.3 Legislation

Before the successful legislative attempt in the 19th session of the National Assembly (2016), there had been seven bills drafted since 2006, namely, the Revision of the Medical Practice Act (2006), Hospice-Palliative Care Act (2008), Death with Dignity Act (2009), Law on the Right to a Natural Death at the End Stage of Life (2009) and three additional bills drafted during the 18th session and then again in the 19th. These draft bills, each of which had a different emphasis, were unsuccessful, perhaps because the public was unclear about the nature of futile treatment and there was insufficient societal pressure to engage with such issues more actively. It is noteworthy, however, that the Death with Dignity campaign subsequently took hold within Korean society.[8] Owing to newspaper coverage of the *Severance Hospital* case and to the "dying well" campaign, the broader population gradually began to understand the importance of the right to

[8] For more information, see Kakdang Social Welfare Foundation, www.kadec.or.kr/; see Korean Initiative for Advance Directive, www.sasilmo.net.These two organisations were representatives of these activities.

self-determination and the possibility of dying free of any unnecessary medical interventions.

In 2015, a National Assembly member submitted a bill based on the recommendations of the National Bioethics Review Committee, and three other competing bills were also submitted. At a later stage of the legislative process, the bill on end-of-life decision-making and the bill on hospice palliative care were merged. In a sense, palliative care and end-of-life decision-making are closely related, and both had hitherto received less attention than they deserved. The new law came into force in July 2017, and its executive orders – a presidential decree and enforcement regulation – were legislated thereafter.[9]

As noted at the outset of this chapter, ELDA was passed on 8 January 2016. The Supreme Court had in the *Severance Hospital* case recommended legislation on the issues concerned in 2009, and thus the Act took many years to execute. ELDA's goal is "to secure the patient's best interest and to protect ... human dignity and value by respecting self-determination" (Article 1 of ELDA). To achieve that goal, the Act is equipped with two mechanisms: the provision of hospice palliative care to terminal patients and clarification of the end-of-life care decision-making process. With respect to the former, ELDA declares the right of patients to hospice palliative care and the responsibility of healthcare providers and states to provide it. With respect to the latter, the legislation provides clinicians and patients with a decision-making framework, as well as the interpretation and application of relevant principles, which can potentially remove the confusion and settle the debate amongst Korean society.

3.3 Characteristics of ELDA[10]

3.3.1 Principles of End-of-Life Care and the State's Responsibilities

3.3.1.1 Principles of End-of-Life Care

ELDA emphasises three principles in end-of-life care: human dignity and value, patients' right to know and to self-determination and the duty of medical professionals to provide the best care and information and to

[9] M.H. Kim, "The Problems and the Improvement Plan of the Hospice/Palliative Care and Dying Patient's Decisions on Life-Sustaining Treatment Act" (2018) 21(1) *Korean Journal of Hospice and Palliative Care* 1.

[10] The English translation of ELDA can be found at: https://law.go.kr/LSW/lsInfoP.do?lsiSeq=180823&viewCls=engLsInfoR&urlMode=engLsInfoR#0000. Although this translation originates from a government website, it is not considered an official or legally

respect a patient's decision (Article 3 of ELDA). Whilst the language of the law has raised awareness of the concept of autonomy amongst patients and practitioners, the culture (and even the interpretation of the law) generally continues to place the best interests of the patient first. The tension between autonomy and best interests appears to have been dealt with by placing limits on autonomy and the scope of the right to refuse treatment.

3.3.1.2 State's Responsibility to Improve Quality of End-of-Life Care

There have long been concerns about the poor quality of death amongst Koreans, with most commentary suggesting palliative care as an alternative. However, palliative care had remained only an ideal, not everyday practice, for several reasons, not least the fear that recommending hospice care constituted a recognition of failure by physicians and the abandonment of patients.[11] What was notable for Korean legislation was that the opponents of ELDA argued that good hospice care should precede end-of-life decision legislation.[12] It was partly as a result of that argument that the legislative strategy of merging the hospice palliative care bill with ELDA surfaced in the last phase of parliamentary review.

ELDA provides a justification for the state to operate nationwide hospice palliative care (which had in fact been part of the state's responsibility since 2005, as defined by the National Cancer Control Act). It mandates that the state establish a discussion body (the National Hospice and Palliative Care Committee) and submit and implement a national plan (General Plan for Hospice and the Provision and Withdrawal of Life-Sustaining Treatment) (Article 8 of ELDA). The new legislation authorises the Ministry of Health and Welfare to plan and implement programmes. To a certain extent, ELDA can be seen as an extension of hospice palliative care to disease categories other than cancer, as well as a clarification of the Government's authority to set standards for and support hospice palliative care providers.

binding translation. The author has used terms from the translation in this chapter, although he does not agree with the choice of words in all cases.

11 D.H. Moon et al., "Doctor's Attitudes toward Hospice and Palliative Care for Terminal Cancer Patients" (2006) 9(2) *Korean Journal of Hospice and Palliative Care* 93.

12 Y.H. Ji, "The Catholic Church's Statement on the End of Life Decision Act Bill" (2014) 57 *Hospice* 2, www.koreascience.or.kr/article/JAKO201467958869374.page.

3.3.2 *Scope of the Application*

Article 2 of ELDA provides definitions and defines the subjects of application. Interestingly, the law distinguishes the *terminal* stage of disease from the *dying* stage and *terminal* patients from *dying* patients. A "terminal patient" is defined in Article 2 as

> a patient who has been diagnosed as expected to die within a few months [by] the doctor in charge and one medical specialist in the relevant field in accordance with the procedures and guidelines prescribed by Ordinance of the Ministry of Health and Welfare, because there is no possibility of a fundamental recovery, and the symptoms [will] gradually worsen despite proactive treatment.

He or she is also regarded as a potential hospice palliative care beneficiary, but one who is unable to elect the termination of LST. The article originally listed four diseases as terminal illnesses: cancer, AIDS, chronic obstructive pulmonary disease and chronic liver cirrhosis. However, other diseases were added by ordinance of the Ministry of Health and Welfare following the 2018 revision. Patients at the dying stage, or in the "end-of-life process", are defined as in "a state of imminent death, in which there is no possibility of revitalisation or recovery despite treatment, and [whose] symptoms [are] worsen[ing] rapidly" (Article 2 of ELDA).

Article 2 of ELDA also originally limited the potential LSTs that could be foregone to four specific medical interventions: CPR, haemodialysis, anticancer chemotherapy and artificial ventilation care. This narrow definition was designed as a safeguard against the possible hasty withdrawal of LST but was criticised for ignoring clinical realities. It was thus subsequently revised to include (i) extracorporeal life support, (ii) transfusions, (iii) the infusion of hypertensors and (iv) any procedures medically assessed by the physician to be withheld or withdrawn in the patient's best interests. It can thus be seen that the legislative approach moved away from narrow definitions towards leaving the determination of whether a given treatment constitutes a *futile* LST to clinical judgement. As for how such judgement should be exercised, there is published professional guidance that suggests, for example, how a patient's vital signs should be interpreted. This approach demonstrates an understanding that not everything can be specified by law, and hence that the application of the law should be left to professional guidelines.

3.3.3 *Institutionalisation of End-of-Life Care Decisions*

According to ELDA, the state can establish several institutions to support the making and executing of end-of-life decisions on LST. Three official institutions have accordingly been established: the National Agency for the Management of Life-Sustaining Treatment (established under Article 9), the Agency for the Registration of Advance Statements for Life-Sustaining Treatment (ARAS) (established under Article 11) and Institutional Ethics Committees (IECs) (established under Article 14).

The National Agency operates the national end-of-life infrastructure, provides certified education and handles public relations. It works as a national AD registry, identifying and confirming LST plans (LSTPs) and ADs, and is accountable for producing and managing databases of ADs for LST, which cover both AD and LSTP registries. The National Agency also provides research and statistical information on end-of-life decision-making and the execution thereof and is responsible for granting licences to institutions such as hospitals to become registering institutions.

ARAS oversees the private and public institutions that are the focal point of end-of-life decision-making services for the public. These institutions, which can be healthcare institutions, public health centres or qualified non-governmental organisations, provide information to patients (see Section 3.4.2 for further details) and transfer the documents that patients create.

Finally, IECs have similar functions to clinical ethics committees. Their various functions include (i) deliberation (including the review of consulting requests from patients and physicians and requests to change the attending physician) and the review of ADs (although they do not decide on them); (ii) the education of professionals; and (iii) reporting and referral to the National Agency. Physicians may also consult an IEC on a particular prognosis or to seek legal clarification. Whilst IEC recommendations carry some weight, they are not technically binding. In light of the IECs' wide range of functions, they are expected to become the focal point of reporting and communication with the National Agency.

3.4 Application of ELDA

ELDA provides for two processes relating to end-of-life decision-making, which will be referred to here as LSTPs and Advance Statements for LST

(ASLSTs). The Act requires that a patient be in the "dying stage" before his or her decision regarding LST under either an LSTP or ASLST can be executed. Although a patient's decision on LST under a physician's order for LST (Physician Order for Life-Sustaining Treatment, POLST) is binding, decisions under a valid ASLST represent only the patient's (explicit) preferences and are not binding until and unless the ASLST is verified. The two processes are discussed in further detail next.

3.4.1 *Life-Sustaining Treatment Plans*

According to Article 10 of ELDA, an end-of-life care plan takes the form of an LSTP. Under this regime, a doctor may supply the patient with the information required to prepare a plan to terminate LST or, at the patient's request, prepare an LST plan for a terminal patient at a medical institution. Although the process can be initiated by a patient or the doctor in charge, physicians are seen as playing the leading role.

The process of preparing an LSTP under ELDA is akin to advance care planning, but is limited to LST during a terminal patient's last days of life. The patient may in his or her LSTP specify matters relating to the termination of LST, as well as matters concerning the use of hospice care (Article 10(4) of ELDA). As safeguards, Article 10 of ELDA prescribes formalities for LSTPs and provides requirements for the registration of POLSTs at a medical institution, record-keeping and notification of the National Agency.

3.4.2 *Advance Statement for Life-Sustaining Treatment*

In Korea, an ASLST can be viewed only as evidence of a person's preferences regarding LST until and unless it has been verified, as discussed in further detaillater. At the point of verification, it becomes binding on the doctor. An ASLST is a document similar to a living will. It is written when a person is relatively healthy and independent. It contains the person's decisions regarding (i) the termination of LST and (ii) the use of hospice care where necessary (Article 12 of ELDA). There are no legal requirements in relation to either witnessing or how the person's mental capacity is to be assessed. ELDA does, however, mandate that personnel from the registering institution meet with the person to confirm that he or she understands the following matters before the ASLST can be considered valid.

i. Matters concerning the methods of implementing LST and making a decision to terminate such treatment.
ii. Matters concerning selecting and using hospice care.
iii. Matters concerning the validity and invalidity of ASLSTs.
iv. Matters concerning the preparation, registration, keeping and notification of ASLSTs.
v. Matters concerning amending and withdrawing ASLSTs and subsequent measures.
vi. Other matters prescribed by ordinance of the Ministry of Health and Welfare.

The definition of registering institutions is construed narrowly under Article 11(1) of ELDA as a safeguard, limiting them to regional healthcare institutions under the Regional Public Health Act; medical institutions; public institutions under the Act on the Management of Public Institutions; and non-profit corporations registered with the Government that have the proper qualifications and trained personnel to provide services related to ASLSTs. Although registering institutions must be licensed, their personnel need not be medically or legally trained and may be representatives of the medical institution concerned or even volunteers. As they may have only a basic understanding of ASLSTs, it is not uncommon for the assessment of whether a person is mentally capable of making an ASLST to be left to the institution's nurses or volunteers. After the ASLST is prepared, it has to be registered and kept at the registering institution (Article 12(4) of ELDA), and the National Agency must be notified of the registration (Article 12(5) of ELDA). Licensed healthcare professionals will then be able to access this ASLST when a decision regarding the use of LST or hospice care needs to be made.

As noted, although a registered ASLST is valid under ELDA, it can serve only as evidence regarding the patient's LST preferences. For an ASLST to be binding, the doctor must verify the patient's intentions with him or her when the ASLST is retrieved for use (Article 15 of ELDA). When the patient is in the "end-of-life process" but is still of sound mind, the requirement to verify the patient's intentions does not pose much of a hurdle. In situations where the patient becomes incapacitated and is unable to verify the ASLST, however, the doctor needs to obtain the agreement of a second doctor (Article 17 of ELDA), and during this confirmation the doctors typically have a discussion with the family about the authenticity of the document. An additional complexity arises when a patient in the "dying stage" becomes incapacitated and has no ASLST. The current law does not provide for the designation of a proxy for LST-related decision-making, although it is worded such that the patient's family members can bear witness to his or her LST preferences, which means that they are effectively able to make LST-related decisions on behalf of the patient in the event of incapacity. In such a situation, the doctor will consult with family members, and if they unanimously bear witness to a consistent expression of the patient's preference, then that preference will be regarded as the patient's will (in other words, his or her presumed will), and the doctor will need to follow it (Article 17, Clause 2 of ELDA).

3.4.3 LSTPs versus ASLSTs

There are thus two legal mechanisms by which individuals can indicate their preferences in relation to LST under ELDA, with LSTPs having priority over ASLSTs. That priority explains much of the confusion surrounding the force and application of ASLSTs. If an LSTP is made, any ASLST made prior to it becomes invalid. There are also many more hurdles to overcome before an ASLST can be made and/or implemented, including confirmation of the six matters listed previously and verification of the patient's intentions (where the patient is capacitous), which reflects a rather reserved attitude towards ASLSTs.

There have been attempts to give more weight to ASLSTs, but there seems to be no appeal in legislation. In fact, the original objective was for LSTPs to support the implementation of ASLSTs, with an AD being a small but important component of giving a patient full control over a key decision within the larger process of planning his or her end-of-life care. However, that objective appears to have been lost in the legislative process. ASLSTs have yet to move past being an overarching statement of patient preferences that assists physicians in deciding on the use of LST. We will likely have to wait for another legislative opportunity for ASLSTs to reach their full potential. In the meantime, it is likely that they will remain marginalised or perhaps become even further marginalised given the reality of decision-making by patients and families in the Korean context, as we will see in the following section.

3.5 End-of-Life Decision-Making in Practice

3.5.1 Low Utilisation Rate

Equipping patients with the power to decide what end-of-life care, LST in particular, best suits them is closely tied to the general well-being of the population. Such end-of-life decision-making mechanisms as LSTPs and ASLSTs enable patients to communicate their preferences regarding the use of LST and hospice care, allowing sufficient planning for a death with dignity and reducing the need for futile LST. However, as of January 2020, 85,076 LST decisions (LSTD) had been implemented, with the number of decisions made through family statements or agreements (55,775) nearly twice as high as the number made using an LSTP or ASLST (29,301). The LSTD system thus appears to be based on family decisions, which may or may not be based on patients' preferences or wishes, rather than on direct records of those preferences/wishes, and less than 20 per cent of dying people seem to be benefiting from the legislation. One potential reason is the age and health status of those who currently make an AD, and the situation should improve as awareness of AD use grows and more healthcare professionals gain experience and knowledge of using ADs for end-of-life decision-making. Other reasons for the low utilisation rate of LSTPs and ASLSTs may be linked to the sociocultural context of Korea, which is explored in further detail next.

3.5.2 Sociocultural Context

The two key sociocultural factors that play an important role in end-of-life decision-making in Korea are the role of the family and the role of Confucian values.

In relation to first factor, as in other Asian countries, the life of the individual in Korea is strongly tied to the family. Individuals live for the family and by its support. The dignity of the individual is seen to come from the family, especially from generational relations. Accordingly, decisions regarding end-of-life care tend to be taken collectively. A study of end-of-life communication amongst elderly Koreans found that less than 20 per cent of patients prefer making treatment decisions alone,[13] with over 90 per cent of cancer patients and their caregivers preferring family involvement in treatment decision-making.[14] Family members do not perceive their involvement as infringing the patient's autonomy, but rather as a means to show support and alleviate the

[13] D.W. Shin et al., "End-of-Life Communication in Korean Older Adults: With Focus on Advance Care Planning and Advance Directives" (2016) 16(4) *Geriatrics Gerontology International* 407, 412 (footnote 46).

[14] Ibid., footnote 45.

patient's burden.[15] There is thus less emphasis on the individual in end-of-life decision-making in Korea than in the West: patients generally do not express their preferences for a given treatment, and the family can be expected to take an active role[16] or even decide on the patient's behalf when it comes to life/death decisions.[17,18]

In relation to the second factor, the current underutilisation of LSTPs and ASLSTs reflects the ethos of a traditionally Confucian society such as Korea,[19] particularly with respect to the elderly. Confucian values dictate that the care of elderly parents is the duty of children,[20] and the elderly are, in turn, often dependent – financially and physically – on their children for healthcare and are expected to follow the decision of the family, particularly with respect to decisions pertaining to such value-laden issues as birth, marriage and death. The concept of *Hyo* (meaning filial piety) is also a cardinal Confucian virtue that plays a role in end-of-life decision-making. For example, it is common for children to feel obliged to continue LST for their family members because they equate providing medical treatment with being filial.[21] Furthermore, filial piety requires children to keep their parents comfortable for as long as possible. As many Koreans consider knowledge of a poor prognosis to be painful and even unbearable, information relating to their condition is often concealed from patients until the very end of their illness trajectory.[22]

15 D.W. Shin et al., "Preferences for and Experiences of Family Involvement in Cancer Treatment Decision-Making: Patient-Caregiver Dyads Study" (2013) 22 *Psycho-Oncology* 2624, 2628 (footnote 22).

16 Ibid., p. 2624 (footnotes 1, 2).

17 Ministry of Health and Welfare, "End of Life Care Consultation Guidelines for Healthcare Professionals" [in Korean] (2020), www.lst.go.kr/comm/referenceDetail.do?pgNo=1&cate=&searchOption=0&searchText=&bno=1970.

18 S.Y. Park et al., "A National Study of Life-Sustaining Treatments in South Korea: What Factors Affect Decision-Making?" (2021) 53(2) *Cancer Research and Treatment* 593.

19 I. Lee., "Filial Duty as the Moral Foundation of Caring for the Elderly: Its Possibility and Limitations", in R. Fan (ed.), *Family-Oriented Informed Consent: East Asian and American Perspectives* (Cham: Springer International Publishing, 2015), 137–47, https://doi.org/10.1007/978-3-319-12120-8_9.

20 Ibid.

21 S. H. Kim, "Family Surrogates' Decision Regret and Psychological Stress about End-of-Life Cancer Treatments: Path Analysis" (2018) 48(5) *Journal of Korean Academy of Nursing* 578, https://doi.org/10.4040/jkan.2018.48.5.578.

22 See, for example, S.Y. Park et al., "End-of-Life Care in ICUs in East Asia: A Comparison among China, Korea and Japan" (2018) 46(7) *Critical Care Medicine* 1114, 1121 (footnote 22), which discusses the concealing of information from terminally ill patients and the reasons for doing so, and D.Y. Oh et al., "Discrepancies among Patients, Family Members, and Physicians in Korea in Terms of Values Regarding the Withholding of

Given that research demonstrates a strong association between a patient's understanding of his or her condition and his or her preference for making an AD,[23] such concealment of information likely contributes to the low utilisation rate of LSTPs and ASLSTs.

3.6 The Way Forward

In considering the way forward for Korea, we need to address some of the concerns with the current legislation.

3.6.1 Limited Autonomy

Although patients have opportunities to express their preferences to the people who care for them, such as their doctors, family members and other caregivers, the current law may limit their ability to exercise their autonomy, for example, by viewing an ASLST only as evidence of a person's preferences rather than a binding statement and permitting surrogate decision-making by family members when the person is incapacitated. The result could well be too much emphasis on the family's opinion at the expense of the patient's. In addition to the risk of family members misinterpreting patients' preferences, there is also the possibility of family members putting forth statements contrary to the ASLST if they do not agree with it and the patient is incapacitated. Revising ELDA in such a way that a valid ASLST always trumps the family's decision-making authority would be one way to ensure that patients' autonomy is strengthened in incapacitation scenarios.

In addition, the scope of ELDA's application is overly narrow. For example, it applies only after a patient's condition has been confirmed by two physicians to be irreversible and not responsive to treatment. Moreover, there are just four types of LSTs that can be withdrawn, namely, CPR, haemodialysis, the administration of anticancer drugs and mechanical ventilation (Article 2 of ELDA). These restrictions leave little space for patients' preferences to be afforded much significance.

Treatment from Patients with Terminal Malignancies" (2004) 100(9) *Cancer* 1961, 1965, a study in which it was found that only 26 per cent of patients in the sample understood their disease progression and that less than half of cancer patients already in an advanced stage accurately understood their illness.

[23] S.H. Yoo et al., "Association of Illness Understanding with Advance Care Planning and End-of-Life Care Preferences for Advanced Cancer Patients and Their Family Members" (2020) 28 *Supportive Care in Cancer* 2959, 2961.

3.6.2 ELDA's Inability to Reflect Societal Changes

ELDA adopts a narrow definition of "family members", requiring them to be of the same bloodline (lineal ascendants, descendants and siblings) as the patient with the single exception of the patient's spouse. In reality, not only are unregistered partnerships on the rise in Korea, but indirect family members (e.g. nieces and nephews) are also increasingly becoming patients' primary or sole caregivers. As discussed previously, family members have a role in bearing witness to the patient's preferences regarding LST, and, under the current legislation, that role is limited to family members as narrowly defined in ELDA to the exclusion of other caregivers who might be better able to offer evidence of those preferences. Furthermore, recent studies have shown a decrease in the younger generation's perceived duty to take care of elderly parents.[24] This shift in perceived responsibility and levels of involvement may also affect the feasibility of verifying a patient's preferences through their family members. To adapt to Korea's changing needs, it is worth considering whether ASLSTs could be implemented without further verification, particularly given that there are already procedures in place to confirm a patient's understanding prior to the making of an ASLST.

In terms of the way forward, patient empowerment should be the first priority. The current legislative framework permits too large a role for the family in end-of-life decision-making. This is not to say that the family should not be engaged in the process at all, but rather that enabling patients to exercise their right to know and have their preferences respected should come first. From a legislative point of view, ELDA currently leaves many matters relating to ASLST validation open ended, and the legislative framework would thus benefit from a more systematic, well-planned validation process for ADs.[25]

[24] H.K. Kim, C.M. Park and K. Nakajima, "A Study on the Perception of Social Care for the Elderly: Comparison Analysis between College Students and their Parents Group" (2010) 30(1) *Health and Social Welfare Review* 170;Ministry of Health and Welfare, "Report of the Survey of Living Conditions and Welfare Needs of Korean Older Persons" (2020), www.mohw.go.kr/react/jb/sjb030301vw.jsp?PAR_MENU_ID=03&MENU_ID=032901&CONT_SEQ=366496, p. 254.

[25] Despite the lack of a systematic process, there is in fact little room for ambiguity in current ASLST implementation owing to the limited scope of ASLST application. As discussed previously, ASLSTs apply only in the patient's last days during the "end-of-life process". Where treatment is deemed futile at that stage, there is little left to be determined, and the patient will likely pass away soon after.

3.7 Conclusion

ELDA is the result of experience and a painstaking consensus-building process, although the law is narrow in application and areas for improvement remain. What Korean society has agreed is that every dying patient deserves respect and humane care and that such care is something that society should provide. As with other social institutions, however, ELDA and related social institutions need further improvement, particularly with regard to the scope and application of ADs. Accordingly, continued discussion of ELDA and the implementation of end-of-life decision-making tools is necessary. Respectful communication and collaboration amongst all relevant stakeholders will be necessary to balance the opinions of the public with empowering patients in the end-of-life decision-making process.

4

The Law and Practice of Advance Directives in Taiwan

DANIEL FU-CHANG TSAI

4.1 Introduction

Achieving a good death (善終) is regarded as one of the Five Blessings (五福) of life in traditional Chinese culture. The introduction of modern Western medicine and the practice of cardiopulmonary resuscitation (CPR) and other forms of life-sustaining treatment (LST), however, made a good death difficult to achieve for many of those accepting end-of-life care in hospital settings. Through three decades of effort to promote hospice and palliative care, Taiwan has developed comprehensive and pioneering legislative frameworks to govern advance directives (ADs) and end-of-life decision-making more generally. In 2015, Taiwan was ranked number six in the world and number one in Asia in terms of "quality of death" by *The Economist*. Despite these advances, however, the uptake of ADs in Taiwan remains low, which may be the result of insufficient understanding and awareness, as well as sociocultural factors such as an emphasis on the role of the family in medical decision-making. This chapter begins with an introduction to the legal regulation of ADs in Taiwan, followed by a discussion of the available data on the practice of ADs and an exploration of the possible reasons for their low uptake. The chapter concludes with several suggestions for the way forward.

4.2 The Legal Regulation of Advance Directives in Taiwan

The regulation of ADs in Taiwan is governed primarily by two legislative frameworks, the 2000 Hospice Palliative Care Act (HPCA) and the 2019 Patient Right to Autonomy Act (PRAA). No court decisions to date have independently recognised the right of terminally ill patients to withhold or withdraw LST because the use of court decisions to resolve end-of-life care disputes is inefficient under the continental law system of Taiwan, nor is it an acceptable practice in medicine.

4.2.1 *Legislative Background*

Although the first hospice (安寧病房, or palliative care ward) in Taiwan was established in 1990 in a Christian hospital (MacKay Memorial Hospital),[1] and many academic medical centres have begun to establish palliative medicine wards, only a small portion of terminally ill patients are able to receive hospice care owing to the limited service volume and such care being an unfamiliar concept. Because the "doctor's duty to rescue" was emphasised in the earlier version of the Medical Care Act[2], many terminally ill patients received painful and burdensome CPR and other forms of LST in their final days in hospital. There was no definitive regulation or protocol concerning the withholding or withdrawal of LST from terminally ill patients prior to the HPCA's enactment in 2000.

In response to the increasingly urgent need for Taiwan to establish clear legal procedures in relation to end-of-life care, a joint effort by healthcare professionals, social and religious leaders, legislators, and government officials was launched in 1993, with the HPCA finally being passed in 2000 after years of discussion and negotiation.[3]

4.2.2 *Hospice Palliative Care Act*[4]

The goal of the HPCA is to ensure that patients who are terminally ill have the freedom to choose hospice palliative care and refuse LST,[5] as demonstrated by Article 1, which states that the Act's aim is to respect the wishes of terminally ill patients in relation to medical treatment and to protect their rights. A terminally ill patient is defined in Article 3 of the HPCA as an individual (i) who suffers from serious injury or illness, (ii) who has been diagnosed by a physician as incurable and (iii) for whom

1 Hospice Foundation of Taiwan, "Hospice and Palliative Care Continues in Taiwan" (2020), www.hospice.org.tw/content/3010.

2 The 1986 version of the Medical Care Act, Article 42 of which states "Hospitals and clinics should immediately treat patients in critical condition with the equipment they have or take all necessary measures without undue delay." The 2004 version has made the description of "duty to rescue" more flexible.

3 S.Y. Tu [凃心怡], "The Companion of the Hospice Palliative Care Act and the Patient Right to Autonomy Act in the End of Life" [in Chinese], Hospice Foundation of Taiwan (2020), www.hospice.org.tw/content/3154.

4 Hospice Palliative Care Act (2021), https://law.moj.gov.tw/ENG/LawClass/LawAll.aspx?pcode=L0020066.

5 Hospice palliative care is defined in Article 3 of the HPCA as "mitigatory and supportive medical care given to relieve terminal illness patients from and rid of physical, mental and spiritual pain, to improve their quality of life".

there is medical evidence showing that the inevitable prognosis is death within the near future.

Whilst the term "advance directive" is not used in the HPCA, Article 4 establishes a mechanism called the "letter of intent" by which a terminally ill patient can make a decision about whether he or she wishes to receive hospice palliative care or LST. To make a letter of intent, an individual needs to be a capacitous adult (Article 5).[6] The letter, which should state the individual's wishes regarding the receipt of hospice palliative care or LST, should also contain his or her personal information and the date on which the letter was written (Article 4). The signing of the letter of intent should be witnessed by two individuals with full capacity. However, neither healthcare workers who are affiliated with medical institutions that provide hospice palliative care nor the individuals who will carry out the individual's wishes with respect to LST are permitted to act as witnesses to avoid conflicts of obligations or roles (Article 4). Individuals can withdraw their wishes in writing at any time, either on their own or via their medical surrogate agent (Article 6), who can be appointed as part of the letter of intent (Article 5).

Once the letter of intent has been signed, the relevant competent authority (as defined in the HPCA) will note the letter's existence in the individual's national health insurance certificate, and the letter will be stored as an electronic file in the central competent authority's database. If the contents of the letter of intent are inconsistent with the written wishes specified by the individual during the consent process prior to clinical treatment, the contemporaneous written consent, or refusal of consent, will prevail. In terms of application, where there is a signed letter of intent refusing consent to CPR or other forms of LST, these interventions cannot be administered as long as two physicians have confirmed that the patient is terminally ill (Article 7). If CPR or other LST has already begun, and the foregoing conditions have been satisfied, Article 7 (5) allows such treatment to be terminated or withdrawn.

Where there is no letter of intent, and the patient is unable to express his or her wishes clearly, Article 7(3) of the HPCA provides that consent can be given instead by his or her closest relative, or by the physician in the patient's medical best interests, although it is explicitly stated that neither of these decisions can contradict the patient's previously

[6] A minor can sign a letter of intent with the consent of his or her legal representative, and where a minor cannot express his or her will, the legal representative is to sign the letter of intent (see further Article 7 of the HPCA).

expressed wishes. Article 7(4) provides a list of "closest relatives", which are defined broadly to include third-degree relatives and first-degree relatives by marriage. In the event of disagreement between a patient's closest relatives, the order in which the relatives are listed in Article 7(4) determines their priority. Article 7 defines the essential elements and practice of ADs for the withdrawal/withholding of CPR/LST from terminally ill patients. It also indicates the priority ranking of decision types: first, the patient's personally signed AD/letter of intent; second, an AD/letter of intent signed by the patient's surrogate or closest relative; and, third, a doctor's medical order when the patient has no close relatives. In the third condition, the doctor's decision must be made in the best interests of the patient after consultation with a palliative care specialist. None of these surrogate decisions should be contrary to a patient's formerly expressed wishes.

The HPCA stipulates strict penalties for the violation of Article 7, which provides for the circumstances in which CPR or LST should be withheld. Article 10 states that physicians who violate Article 7 will be fined a sum between NT60,000 and NT300,000, and will either be suspended from practice for a period of between one month and one year or have their licence revoked completely. In terms of individuals who choose to end the lives of their family members without following the procedures laid down by the HPCA, court decisions suggest that such actions will be considered homicide.

4.2.3 Concerns with the HPCA

After the HPCA's passage in 2000, clinical practice relating to end-of-life care in Taiwan changed gradually but remarkably. Both patients and doctors began to embrace the concept of respecting patients' autonomous decisions at the end of life and to recognise that refusing CPR and LST was acceptable as long as the relevant procedures and documentation required by the HPCA were followed.

However, the HPCA has a number of limitations. First, it has been argued that the Act's protection of patient autonomy is insufficient. For example, Article 8 requires that physicians inform terminally ill patients *or* their family members of the patient's condition, hospice palliative care treatment and LST choices. Article 8 further stresses that patients are to be informed if they explicitly express the desire to be informed of their condition. Although this stipulation, on the one hand, protects a patient's legal right to know about his or her own diagnosis, on the other hand, it also seemingly permits the traditional practice of information (bad news) being shared only with a patient's family members but not the patient. Owing to such a vague zone of who can or should be informed of a diagnosis, some have argued that the individual's right to informed consent is not fully protected under the HPCA.[7] However, such criticism lacks understanding of the fact that medical practices must progress over time with the evolution of social conceptions of patient autonomy. In a family-oriented model of end-of-life care practice such as that which prevails traditionally in Taiwan, the patient's right to informed choices is made clear and affirmed through efforts to advance legal frameworks.

Second, the HPCA applies only to terminally ill patients. It does not cover individuals who cannot be described as having a terminal illness, such as those in a permanent vegetative state, those with severe dementia, those in an irreversible coma or those with motor neuron impairment arising from such rare diseases as amyotrophic lateral sclerosis. In response to this concern, representatives of rare disease patient groups and Legislator Yu-Shin Yang of the Legislative Yuan (the unicameral legislature of Taiwan) have launched efforts to meet the needs of these groups by advocating for a more fundamental solution through a legislative framework aimed at protecting a patient's right of self-determination.

4.2.4 Patient Right to Autonomy Act

The PRAA was passed in December 2015, announced in January 2016 and became effective in January 2019. Its aims, as stated in Article 1, are to respect patient autonomy in the healthcare context, to safeguard patients' right to a good death and to promote a harmonious physician-patient relationship.

The scope of the PRAA is wider than that of the HPCA. It no longer limits the withdrawal or withholding of CPR and LST to cases of terminal illness assessed by two specialist physicians. The LST category has also been broadened to include such interventions as artificial nutrition and hydration and antibiotics where they are being used to sustain life. Moreover, the PRAA expands the clinical conditions in which CPR and other forms of LST can be withdrawn or withheld beyond terminal

[7] C. Chen, "Legislating the Right-to-Die with Dignity in a Confucian Society – Taiwan's Patient Right to Autonomy Act" (2019) 42(2) *Hastings International and Comparative Law Review* 485.

illness: (1) irreversible coma; (2) a permanent vegetative state; (3) severe dementia; or (4) other disease conditions announced by the central competent authority (as defined in the PRAA) that meet the requirements that the condition or suffering is unbearable, the disease is incurable and no other appropriate treatment options are available given the medical standards at the time of the disease's occurrence. The patient's condition must also be diagnosed by two physicians in relevant specialties and confirmed through at least two consultations convened by the palliative care team (Article 14).

In terms of decision-making, the PRAA provides for an "advance medical decision" (預立醫療決定), defined as "a prior written and signed statement expressing the willingness of a person to accept or refuse life-sustaining treatment, artificial nutrition and hydration or other types of medical care, and their wishes relating to a good death, when they have been diagnosed with specific clinical conditions" (Article 3). As noted previously, the scope of this AD is wider than that of the letter of intent under the HPCA, which covers only decision-making with respect to hospice palliative care and LST.

The PRAA also provides more comprehensive protection for a patient's right to informed consent. Article 4 states that patients have a right to be informed of their diagnosis and treatment options, as well as the potential effectiveness and risks of those options, and the right to choose and make decisions regarding treatment options. Moreover, a patient's legal representative, spouse, relatives, healthcare agents and other closely related people (defined in the PRAA as "parties concerned") are not to prevent a medical institution or physician from acting on the patient's treatment decisions. This measure arguably provides patients with a rights-based form of resistance against the common phenomenon of family-based decision-making in Chinese culture, discussed further subsequently, and physicians with a way to preserve their authority to carry out a patient's decision free of family influence. Accordingly, there is much greater emphasis in the PRAA on both enhancing and protecting patients' autonomous decision-making, as expressed through an AD and other legislative requirements.

This is not to say that the PRAA does not envisage a role for the family in the end-of-life process, and indeed there are implicit tensions between the value of maximising respect for patient autonomy and the value of involving the family in identifying patients' best interests within some of the PRAA's articles. For instance, after specifying the list of items about which a medical institution or physician must inform the patient (in other words, the scope of the physician's "duty to inform"), Article 5 states that "in the absence of clear objections from the patient, the parties concerned may also be informed". Thus, unless the patient explicitly objects, his or her physician is permitted to share this information with his or her family. It is noteworthy that instead of requiring consent from the patient before such information is shared, the presumption is that the family is to be informed. Therefore, it is important to recognise that this requirement could be interpreted such that it does not mandate the physician to initiate a discussion with the patient about sharing information with his or her family during which the patient may or may not express an objection.

Another notable feature of the PRAA is the way in which it embeds the process of making an AD in a wider legal requirement to instigate advance care planning (ACP; 預立醫療照護諮商). The procedures for establishing an "advance decision" through ACP consultation must fulfil the following requirements: (i) a medical institution has provided consultation on ACP to the declarant and affixed its seal on his or her advance decision; (ii) the advance decision must be notarised by a notary public or witnessed by two or more persons with full disposing capacity; and (iii) the advance decision must be registered in the declarant's national health insurance IC card. Furthermore, ACP must take place with the participation of at least one relative of a first or second degree of affinity (Article 9).

The Taiwanese Government has not yet taken any steps to cover ACP through the national health insurance system, which means that ACP participants currently need to pay a small out-of-pocket fee, generally in the region of US$80–150, depending on the standard set by the individual hospital. Some have thus argued that financial incentives may be necessary to increase the public's willingness to embark on ACP consultation.[8] This author argues, however, that because ACP is resource-demanding and time consuming (as with any counsel of a psychologist or social worker), if the patient in question lacks motivation and understanding of the value and importance of ACP, then a fee-waiver policy would simply place an unnecessary burden on ACP consultants and waste scarce resources.

[8] Y.J. He et al., "Overview of the Motivation of Advance Care Planning: A Study from a Medical Center in Taiwan" (2021) 18 *International Journal of Environmental Research and Public Health* 417.

Other components of Article 9 are also worth noting. For example, it is expressly stated in Article 9(3) that at least one relative of a first or second degree of affinity must participate in the ACP process, which is in line with the emphasis on family-oriented decision-making in the Taiwanese context.[9] The rationale for such a legal design is that when tough end-of-life choices need to be made, family members must often act as patients' surrogate decision-makers. The purpose of requiring close relatives to participate in the procedures of ACP consultation and AD signing is to build understanding of and consensus on a patient's informed choices among family members to ensure that when the time comes to execute the AD there will be less disagreement and conflict.

4.2.5 Differences between the HPCA and PRAA

Whilst the HPCA and PRAA both concern a patient's advance expression of his or her wishes in relation to end-of-life care, there is a significant difference between them in terms of physician liability. As discussed previously, the HPCA includes strict penalties for physicians who violate end-of-life procedures. The PRAA, in contrast, contains no such punitive measures, which were removed during the legislative process. The Ministry of Health and Welfare has explained that "since patient autonomy involves ethics, professional judgement, personal belief and other variables, using penalty or compulsory means to force physicians, patients or families to comply with the law would be non-beneficial to the promotion of such legislation".[10]

One of the difficulties that arose during the legislative process concerned physicians' unwillingness or refusal to withhold or withdraw LST and/or artificial hydration or nutrition from non-terminally ill patients due to conscientious objection.[11] Indeed, Article 14 allows very wide space for professional autonomy in that it permits a physician to refuse to implement a patient's AD on the basis of his or her "professional expertise or wishes", a wider scope of opt-out for a professional than

[9] This is the case unless all of the patient's first- and second-degree relatives are deceased, missing or have specific reasons for exemption (Article 9(3) of the PRAA).

[10] Ministry of Health and Welfare, "Protecting the Autonomy of Patients, Passing the Third Reading of the Patient Right to Autonomy Act" [in Chinese] (18 December 2015), www.mohw.gov.tw/cp-2651-19687-1.html.

[11] D.F.C. Tsai and H.H. Kuo, "The Ethical Perspectives and Practical Challenge of the Patient Right to Autonomy Act" [in Chinese] (2017) 21(1) *Formosan Journal of Medicine* 62.

reliance on his or her personal values or beliefs. In such a case, the physician is required only to inform the patient or parties concerned (Article 14), and the patient may then turn to other healthcare professionals who are able to assist.

Article 14 further protects physicians from liability by stating that they will not be subject to criminal or administrative liability if they terminate, withdraw or withhold LST and/or artificial nutrition and hydration in accordance with the article and that they will bear no responsibility to compensate for any damage incurred unless intentional or grossly negligent conduct is involved and the action is in violation of the patient's AD. These detailed, comprehensive guarantees of protection from liability for physicians, which resulted from negotiation during the legislative process, are arguably a way to reduce the pressure and burden involved in forgoing LST and/or artificial nutrition and hydration and to provide reassurances to mitigate the tensions that may arise.

4.3 Professional Guidelines Relating to Advance Directives in Taiwan

Whilst the HPCA and PRAA have been promoted and endorsed by many professional associations in Taiwan,[12] unlike their Western counterparts few of these associations have issued professional guidelines concerning end-of-life care, although the Taiwan Academy of Hospice Palliative Medicine, whose members are primarily physicians practising in the field of palliative medicine, issued a position statement expressing a firm objection to euthanasia and physician-assisted suicide in 2017.[13] The National Health Research Institute also published a "White Paper for Palliative Care in Taiwan" in 2019[14] and a "Policy Statement and Action Plan for Palliative Care in Taiwan"[15] in 2020. However, although both

[12] For example, since the announcement of the PRAA in January 2016, professional societies, associations, medical centres and hospitals have devoted considerable time and effort to introductory programmes, training courses, seed teacher licensing workshops, conferences and continuing medical education classes about the PRAA.

[13] Taiwan Academy of Hospice Palliative Medicine, "Position Statement on Euthanasia and Physician-Assisted Suicide" (25 May 2017) www.hospicemed.org.tw/ehc-tahpm/s/w/Statement/article/096b75c16d004db0b950248398e7a30b.

[14] National Health Research Institutes, "White Paper for Palliative Care in Taiwan" (September 2019), tinyurl.com/2zaaadk9.

[15] National Health Research Institutes, "Policy Statement and Action Plan for Palliative Care in Taiwan" (March 2020), tinyurl.com/2p8p3npc.

relate to the future development and promulgation of a comprehensive national plan for advancing citizens' rights and dignity with high-quality end-of-life care, as well as the expansion of ACP within hospitals, neither make any mention of ADs. Thus, there is likely to remain much uncertainty in practice about how the basic legal provisions should be implemented and managed in professional healthcare settings.

4.4 The Practice and Sociocultural Context of Advance Directives in Taiwan

This section now considers the practice of ADs in Taiwan in light of the implementation of the aforementioned frameworks, as well as the sociocultural factors affecting such practice.

As of March 2022, of Taiwan's population of 23 million, approximately 800,000 people (3.4 per cent) had completed a letter of intent under the HPCA, and only 33,000 (0.14 per cent) had completed an AD under the PRAA.[16] It is understandable that the completion rate of ADs would be low, as the PRAA has been in force only since 2018. However, the reasons for the low uptake are still worth exploring, given the pioneering nature of this legislation. Two possible such reasons, namely, insufficient awareness and/or understanding of ADs and the sociocultural emphasis on family-based decision-making, are explored next.

4.4.1 Insufficient Awareness and/or Understanding

There are data suggesting that there is insufficient awareness and understanding of the concepts of ADs and palliative care among the general public. In 2016, Lin et al. reported that the majority of the elderly individuals and their family members whom they had surveyed in the intensive care unit of a medical centre in central Taiwan had an insufficient understanding of ADs.[17] In a more recent study conducted in 2021 that compared the differences in AD acceptance between millennials and baby boomers, Liang et al. found that, despite the Ministry of

[16] 安寧緩和醫療、器官捐贈及預立醫療決定整合資訊系統平台 [Integrated Information System Platform for Palliative Care, Organ Donation and Advance Medical Decisions] [in Chinese], https://hpcod.mohw.gov.tw/HospWeb/.

[17] H.C. Lin et al., "Exploring Understanding of Advance Directives among the Elderly ICU Residents and Their Families at a Medical Centre in Central Taiwan" [in Chinese] (2016) 11(1) *Taiwan Geriatrics & Gerontology* 50.

Health and Welfare of Taiwan announcing measures associated with the PRAA to assist the general public in understanding ADs, participants from both generations were still unfamiliar with ADs and who was able to accept palliative care.[18]

The data from these studies align with commentary suggesting that the general public has misconceptions concerning the nature of advance decisions to refuse LST such as CPR and of hospice care. Among the misconceptions are that signing up for either effectively means that they have "given up" or that they are giving up all treatment.[19] Liang et al. similarly found the low willingness among their participants to sign a letter of intent under the HPCA to be "associated with their erroneous perception that signing the intent [letter] means giving up all medical treatment".[20]

In relation to medical professionals, the data are slightly less clear. Preliminary data from Chen et al. suggest that the PRAA has had a significantly positive impact on the knowledge of healthcare practitioners, with concepts such as "informed consent" and "decision-making directives" becoming more widely accepted in 2018 (as compared with 2013).[21] In a study conducted among healthcare professionals in the field of nephrology, Chiu et al. found that when asked about their knowledge of laws related to ADs, there were three particular areas in which the respondents achieved relatively low scores: (i) understanding of the scope of the HPCA following its revision; (ii) understanding of the matters that one should be aware of when intervening with an AD; and (iii) the difference between an AD and a do-not-resuscitate order.[22] Whilst the latter study does not provide us with sufficient information to properly interpret its results,[23] taken together the findings of the two studies seem

[18] Y.W. Liang et al., "Differential Acceptance of Advance Directives between Millennials and Baby Boomer Generations: A Cross-Sectional Survey Study Among College Students and Their Relatives" (2021) *Journal of Palliative Care* 1.

[19] C.Y. Wu, "Hospice and Palliative Care and Do-Not-Resuscitate" [in Chinese] (2014) 34 (7) *Health News KMUH* 7.

[20] See note 18, p. 2.

[21] I.H. Chen et al., "Knowledge of and Barriers to Palliative Care Perceived by Healthcare Providers before and after Promotion of the Patient Autonomy Act: A Cross-Sectional Study" (30 March 2020), www.researchsquare.com/article/rs-19867/v1.

[22] T.C. Chiu et al., "An Investigation on the Cognition of Advance Directive and Willingness to Promote Advance Directive in Nephrology Staff" [in Chinese] (2019) 18 (2) *Journal of Taiwan Nephrology Nurses Association* 1.

[23] We do not know, for example, what is covered by each of these areas (in particular what the authors mean by matters that one needs to be aware of when intervening with an AD), how these questions were scored and how many of the sample population of 65 performed poorly on the questions.

to suggest that although efforts to promote the PRAA appear to have had a positive effect on healthcare professionals in Taiwan, there are still specific areas in which their knowledge and understanding remain weak and require further training.

4.4.2 Emphasis on the Role of the Family

In addition to insufficient awareness and understanding of ADs, particularly among the general public, the low uptake of ADs may also be explained by certain sociocultural characteristics of Taiwan. In addition to the taboo associated with death, which results in the avoidance of conversations about end-of-life care,[24] there is a significant emphasis on the role of the family in the medical decision-making context. Medical decisions in Taiwan are commonly seen as family decisions that should be made collectively between the family and the patient rather than decisions that patients should make on their own.[25] In extreme cases (which were not uncommon as recently as one or two decades ago), the family takes complete responsibility for medical decision-making, with patients denied any opportunity to participate. Presumably, however, this type of collusion between physician and family will be made much more difficult by the regulatory requirement to inform patients of their diagnosis, treatment options and right to make autonomous decisions, as enshrined in the PRAA.

In addition, because of the strong influence of the Confucian doctrine of filial piety, which results in adult children remaining subordinate to their parents and being expected to provide care without question, in some instances adult children in Taiwanese society do not proactively engage in discussions about ADs with their parents or other elders.[26]

[24] See note 11; S.Y. Cheng et al., "Advance Care Planning in Asian Culture" (2020) 50(9) *Japanese Journal of Clinical Oncology* 976, 982; H.T.S. Lee et al., "Cultural Perspectives of Older Nursing Home Residents Regarding Signing Their Own DNR Directives in Eastern Taiwan: A Qualitative Pilot Study" (2016) 15 *BMC Palliative Care* 45.

[25] H.H. Chou, "Exploring the Issues of Advance Directives in Patients with Mild Dementia in Taiwan" (2020) 74(3) *Acta Medica Okayama* 215; S.C. Lee, "Family Consent in Medical Decision-Making in Taiwan: The Implications of the New Revisions of the Hospice Palliative Care Act", in R. Fan (ed.), *Family-oriented Informed Consent* (Cham, Switzerland: Springer International Publishing, 2015), pp. 125–36; Lee et al., ibid.; X. Chen and R. Fan, "The Family and Harmonious Medical Decision Making: Cherishing an Appropriate Confucian Moral Balance" (2010) 35 *Journal of Medicine and Philosophy* 573; Cheng et al., ibid.

[26] Chou, ibid.

4.4.3 *The Way Forward*

What might be the way forward for Taiwan in light of these possible challenges to the acceptance and uptake of ADs? In terms of improving awareness and understanding, there are data suggesting that implementing ACP programmes containing education on palliative care and ADs has the potential to improve knowledge of and attitudes towards ADs in Taiwan.[27] The lack of focused good practice guidelines emanating from within the healthcare profession on how to translate basic legal requirements into a complex, skilled and multidisciplinary process of making advance care plans and advance decisions across different health and community care settings should also be addressed.

Additionally, the 2018 study of Chu et al. on the factors associated with the completion of ADs found that patients were more likely to complete them if social workers participated in the ACP meeting required by the PRAA.[28] The authors observed that social workers provide support in multiple ways, including offering patients more information about their rights, identifying the major decision-makers among family members and offering emotional support. Because of such support, they suggested that social workers have an important role to play in the ACP process. In light of these findings, the development and implementation of ACP programmes that provide education on ADs, as well as further research on the proper role of social workers in the ACP process, may be steps that can be taken to improve the uptake of ADs in Taiwan.

A thornier issue may be the cultural influences on the acceptance of ADs. For example, both the traditional emphasis on family-based decision-making in the medical context and the expectation that children will take care of their parents in their old age without question may make it difficult for families to support an individual-oriented form of decision-making through the practice of ADs. However, from the author's experience and observations in clinical practice and ethics consultation, such traditional

[27] C. Sung et al., "The Effects of the ACP Program on Knowledge and Attitude of Palliative Care and Advanced Directives among Elders in Long-Term Care Facilities" (2013) 11(3) *International Journal of Evidence-based Healthcare* 250. See D. Chu et al., "Factors Associated with Advance Directives Completion among Patients with Advance Care Planning Communication in Taipei, Taiwan" (2018) 13(7) *PLOS ONE* e0197552 for data suggesting that comprehensive palliative care training programmes targeted at healthcare providers may also help to facilitate the completion of ADs.

[28] Chu et al., ibid.

concepts and practices have changed gradually but remarkably in the past two decades, during which Taiwan has also undergone tremendous transformation in terms of political freedom and a democratic system.[29] The young and even middle-aged adults who have grown up in a rapidly developing democratic society that emphasises personal freedoms and individual rights are likely to have little difficulty embracing patients' right to autonomy in medical decision-making. The aforementioned cultural influences and traditional practices are increasingly being transformed into an endorsement of patient autonomy and self-determination, or at least "shared decision-making", as more desirable standards. Portrayals of Chinese culture as characterised by "family-determinism" rather than "individual-determinism" are imprecise, dichotomised, unfeasible and inapplicable to the current Taiwanese context.[30]

The AD approach in the PRAA is family oriented to some extent. As discussed previously, whilst the Act protects individuals' right to informed consent and to treatment in accordance with their wishes without familial interference, it also contains provisions that presume that information about a patient's condition should be shared with family members unless otherwise explicitly indicated and, more importantly, that *require* a family member to attend the ACP meeting in order for the individual to be able to make an AD.

Hence, the PRAA preserves key features of family-based decision-making while advocating for respect for individual autonomy, and should arguably be promoted as such to emphasise its alignment with certain traditional cultural elements. In this sense, describing the Act in terms of a basic requirement to protect a person's autonomy rights fails to do justice to the complex and multiple values that intersect within its regulatory requirements and that need to be negotiated by practitioners, patients and family members in practice. The Asian Delphi Taskforce for Advance Care Planning has done initial work on developing good practice in light of these tensions, in particular through its publication of the 2019 Taipei Declaration on Advance Care Planning, which recommends tasks for each role in ACP, taking into account Asian cultural

[29] According to the newly released "democratic index", Taiwan is categorised as a fully democratic regime. It ranks number 8 in the world and number 1 in Asia. Economist Intelligence Unit, "Democratic Index 2021" www.eiu.com/n/campaigns/democracy-index-2021/.

[30] R. Fan, "Self-Determination vs. Family-Determination: Two Incommensurable Principles of Autonomy" (1997) 11 *Bioethics* 309.

influences.[31] Of particular note here is (i) recognising that family members and other caregivers have needs that should be attended to as part of the patient's care; (ii) expecting family members to participate actively in ACP discussions; and (iii) co-opting family members in the ACP process to remind, help or accompany the patient in the process of sharing goals and preferences.

4.5 Conclusion

Over the past two decades, Taiwan has developed comprehensive legislative frameworks for ADs and end-of-life decision-making that have expanded over time. It is particularly notable that Taiwan's recent approach has been to embed ADs within a wider regulatory push towards introducing and improving ACP more broadly. The legislation now in place emphasises the importance of the fundamental ethical principle of respect for patient autonomy while simultaneously aiming to enable patients' family members to retain a central role in medical decision-making in ways that are likely to give rise to tensions in practice.

Despite the enactment of the two pieces of legislation discussed herein, however, AD uptake remains low in Taiwan. Further research needs to be conducted to learn more about the practice of ADs in Taiwan, but the existing data suggest that greater effort needs to be devoted to increasing the awareness and understanding of the general public (and healthcare professionals to a lesser extent) about ADs and end-of-life care. Whilst certain cultural factors may hinder the acceptance of ACP and ADs, efforts to implement them in a culturally sensitive manner, such as the PRAA provisions discussed here do, as well as the recommendations of the Asian Delphi Taskforce for Advance Care Planning in the 2019 Taipei Declaration on Advance Care Planning, are important steps towards aligning high-quality end-of-life care and decision-making in ways that endorse the conflicting ethical values that play out within the healthcare context in Taiwan.

31 C.P. Lin et al., "2019 Taipei Declaration on Advance Care Planning: A Cultural Adaptation of End-of-Life Care Discussion" (2019) 22(10) *Journal of Palliative Medicine* 1175.

5

Advance Directives: The Thai Context

THITINANT TENGAUMNUAY

Recognising the principle that an individual's autonomy and dignity are to be respected, the law of Thailand provides the right for patients to make advance decisions concerning their future medical treatment. Advance directives (AD) are used by terminally ill patients to specify their wishes in the event that life-saving medical interventions would be considered futile, merely prolong death, or cause unnecessary suffering. Thailand is among the growing number of countries globally to have enshrined within its laws a well-regulated framework for the use of ADs. However, there is no single template or concept of the format of an AD, an absence that has the potential to undermine the effective application of ADs in practice. Furthermore, within Thai culture, clear tensions exist between the principle of individual autonomy and the importance and influence of the family in determining the extent to which their relatives' wishes expressed within an AD are upheld. This chapter explores these tensions between competing desires and interests and how they complicate the effective implementation of ADs.

The chapter begins with an outline of the legal regulations guiding the use of ADs in Thailand (Section 5.1). Section 5.2 explores the challenges posed to medical professionals involved in the implementation of ADs, and considers sociocultural values such as familism, which enables the patient's family to exercise influence in the context of ADs. The discussion in Section 5.3 identifies some particular problems of ADs in Thailand and concludes that effective implementation requires more than legal backing; it requires the introduction and implementation of formal procedures such as a system for registering ADs. A registration system would help to ensure that the legal framework for ADs, implemented in response to the recognition of the right of terminally ill individuals to autonomy as they approach death, and to be enabled to die with their dignity intact, can be achieved in practice.

5.1 The Legal Framework: Background, Scope and Conditions of ADs in Thailand

5.1.1 Background of Thai Laws on ADs

Since 2003, the notion that individuals may aspire to achieving a 'good death', aligned with the principle of a patient's right to refuse medical treatment, has generated robust debate between medical professionals, legal scholars and practitioners. Before the introduction of Universal Health Coverage (UHC)[1] in 2002, the high costs of medical treatment imposed considerable financial burdens on most Thai people. The ability to access medical and health services was therefore regarded as a matter of "luck"[2]; few people therefore even considered the idea that in the event of a diagnosis of a terminal illness, they might wish to refuse medical treatment, or that such treatment might prolong the dying process and cause the terminally ill patient unnecessary pain and suffering. Unlike some other countries where health and human rights groups have been advocating for patients' rights – especially the right to refuse medical treatment – most Thai people are unfamiliar with the principle of the right of patients to self-determination. Thailand's Constitution recognises the principle of individual autonomy and the rights of human dignity, yet, the notion that some people might wish to refuse medical treatment has been characterised by some people – including some within the legal profession – of representing a threat to public order and morals; refusal of treatment was therefore void under Thai law.

The issue of patients' right to refuse life-saving medical treatment was explicitly raised in 2003, when the Ministry of Public Health submitted a legal question to the Office of the Council of the State (OCS), a body which functions as a legal consultant for state agencies.[3] The question concerned a case involving a member of the Jehovah's Witnesses faith community, who made an AD stipulating that they wished to refuse blood transfusions as part of any life-saving treatment. Medical

[1] The UHC was the public health scheme provided for all Thai citizens to get access to medical treatment with the fixed fee of thirty bahts. See National Health Security Office, "Philosophy and Background", http://eng.nhso.go.th/view/1/Philosophy_Background/EN-US.

[2] V. Ungprapan, "The Perspectives of Thai Lawyers on Refusal to Treatment and Good Death" in S. Boonchaleamvipas (ed.), *Understanding Article 12 of National Health Act 2007* (Bangkok: 3D Printing, 2016), p. 12.

[3] Office of the Council of State, "Council of State", www.krisdika.go.th/web/office-of-the-council-of-state/philosophy-mandate-and-organisation-chart.

professionals were undecided as to whether they should follow such a directive, or should prevail in providing the blood transfusion treatment to forestall any criminal liabilities. Responding to the concern of medical professionals, the OCS suggested that in cases where blood transfusion was a critical element of the life-saving treatment, doctors must provide the blood transfusion, even though doing so went against the patient's expressed will. Medical professionals are dutifully and legally bound to save a patient's life, so to follow the patient's will, and to therefore cease to provide life-saving treatment, would be construed as having breached Thai law, and hence, they might be criminally liable for failure to provide life-saving treatment.[4] The OCS argued that implementation of the patient's will – here specifically, allowing the patient to refuse treatment – could potentially ruin the existing positive relationships between doctors and patients. More so, to implement a patient's AD to withhold life-saving treatment would represent an act of non-compliance with medical ethics, which stipulate that doctors must act to save life. And finally, it was argued that for doctors to observe patients' right of autonomy would also conflict with the concept of the good Samaritan, a humanistic principle which holds that a person should help others – including strangers – who are in danger. Several doctors disagreed with the OCS' legal advice, arguing instead that allowing the implementation of a patient's AD in no way represented a threat to public order and morals, but should instead be respected as the exercise of a patient's right to autonomy.[5]

While not binding, the legal opinion of the OCS is the starting point for debates over which patients' rights require legal protection. This legal issue was of particular concern to a number of public health professionals,[6] presumably because of the serious implications for their possible criminal liabilities. The debate led to much discussion about, and the drafting of specific legislation on ADs, in 2004, one year after the OCS had rendered its legal opinion. Notably, the drafting committee included representatives of the medical professions.[7] The subsequent introduction of the National Health Act in 2007 incorporates ideas that

[4] Memorandum of Office of the Council of State 250/2546.

[5] Ungprapan, note 2, pp. 15–16.

[6] See N. Kamnuan, *Legal Problems regarding Physicians' Duties and Ethics upon Patients' Refusal of Treatment before Death*, LLM thesis, Dhurakij Pundit University (2015).

[7] Correspondence of the Secretariat of the Cabinet นร 0503/11888 dated 20 August 2004 to Office of the Council of the State.

emerged from the drafting process, and Article 12 explicitly gives recognition to a patient's right to self-determination in the context of ADs. The details of the AD regime were further clarified in a ministerial regulation of 2010.[8]

5.1.2 Scope and Conditions of ADs under Thai Laws

Article 12 of the National Health Act 2007 states that a person has the right to make an AD setting out their desire "*to refuse any futile health services which simply prolong death or cause suffering*". Public health professions are exempted from any liabilities arising from their actions taken in accordance with fulfilling the patient's expressed will. Article 12 seeks to preserve the human dignity of a patient, as enshrined in the Constitution's specific mandate for the protection of patient autonomy over their lives and bodies. It gives patients the right to refuse medical treatment and to have a "good death", rather than to accept life-prolonging treatment involving the use of medical technologies that would likely cause further pain and suffering but which would ultimately prove futile.[9] The scope of an AD is therefore limited to ensuring that a patient has some control over their dying and can experience a "good death".[10] In other words, an AD explicitly sets out the patient's refusal of medical treatment. An AD will only be implemented if (i) the patient is in a terminally ill stage; or (ii) the patient has an incurable disease for which medical treatment will merely prolong an inevitable death, including a persistent vegetative state.[11] In cases where the patient remains conscious and retains the capacity to communicate, the medical professional responsible for the treatment of such a patient must ask for the patient's confirmation of their wish as expressed within the AD, prior to implementing their will.[12] It must be noted that Article 12 does not allow for either "mercy" killing or active euthanasia, but is applicable solely within the context of a strictly defined "end-of-life" scenario.

[8] Ministerial Regulation on Conditions and Processes to Apply an Advance Directive to Refuse Futile Medical Treatment Which Merely Prolongs Death or Causes Suffering 2010.

[9] Y. Phoopradab, "Good Death: The Right that Everyone Deserves and the Practical Problems", www.krisdika.go.th/data/activity/act13459.pdf.

[10] The concept of a "good death" in the Thai context is discussed in further detail in Section 5.2.

[11] Section 2 of the ministerial regulation.

[12] Section 6(1) of the ministerial regulation.

Its use is limited to the right to refuse to accept treatment when the disease has progressed to the stage where treatment is futile and/or causes further suffering.

Thai legislation does not prescribe a specific formal format for an AD; Article 12 merely requires a written statement to be made while the individual is conscious, of sound mental capacity and has full understanding of their actions and the consequences. There is no requirement that medical or legal personnel should be involved or present; a person can make an AD, alone, without having to consult public health professionals. The practical difficulties involved in establishing whether an AD was made when its maker possessed the mental capacity to make such a momentous decision is an issue to be discussed in a later section, but in theory or practice, Thai laws do not require an assessment of mental capacity at the time of writing the AD. Ministerial regulations merely provide guidelines on the information to be included in an AD:[13]

- The personal biodata information of the person who makes the AD, namely name and surname, age, national identification number, and address or contact number.
- Date the AD was made.
- Name(s), surname(s), and national identification number(s) of a witness/witnesses, and their relationship to the person making the AD.
- The specific medical services or treatment that the patient does not wish to receive.
- In cases where individuals have requested another person to write or type the AD on their behalf, the surname and national identification number of that person should be stated.
- The signatures or fingerprints of the person who makes the AD and that of the witness/witnesses.

It must be noted that the ministerial regulations require only that the intentions of the patient making the AD are clearly stated; other requirements, such as stating the name of the witness and their signature, are solely intended as guidance on how to make a clear AD. It is an illustrative, rather than an exhaustive list, and as such, the AD is valid whether it provides less – or more – information than the AD guidance suggests. It stipulates only that the AD be in the form of a written statement and clearly indicates the individual's will.

[13] Section 3 of the ministerial regulation.

Since the clarity of intention of an AD is required, in order to ensure the precise understanding of their intention, a patient can specify the name of a person who is able to clarify their intention as stated in the AD. Generally, the patient chooses a family member with whom they share close relationship, and who has been (unofficially) informed by the patient of their will.[14] The option to enlist the help of a trusted and familiar person is particularly helpful in cases where there is some confusion or ambiguity, and the person who made the AD is no longer in a state where they are able to explain their will. As stated previously, it is imperative that a patient who makes an AD put their signature and national identification on the document,[15] so as to enable the later identification of such persons. In some cases, while the patient might believe that the terms used in the AD are unambiguous and clear, it is possible that the language or terms employed might be confusing to the reader. In such a situation, it is envisaged that the named person would be able to clearly and correctly articulate and explain the patient's will to the doctor. The inclusion of this named person therefore serves to ensure that the AD conforms with the requirement for clarity; the named person is not authorised to make any decisions on behalf of the patient, and they play no part in proving the validity of an AD, their sole purpose being to help clarify the patient's will.

The state does not require the registration of ADs with state officials; the ministerial regulation suggests only that a patient give their AD to public health professionals as soon as possible, when receiving medical treatment.[16] Article 12 exempts medical professionals from criminal liabilities for carrying out the patient's will as set out in an AD. However, neither Article 12 nor the ministerial regulation imposes sanctions for *non-compliance* with an AD. In other words, if a doctor does not follow the patient's request for termination or withholding of medical treatment, they will not face any particular liabilities under the laws regulating ADs. This then raises questions about the actual effectiveness of ADs in Thailand, as will be further discussed in Section 5.3.

In terms of implementation, practical problems can also result from the informality of the template of an AD. While the laws require the

[14] National Health Commission Office, *Manual Guidance on Advance Directive for Public Health Professions* (Bangkok: 3D Printing, 2019), www.thailivingwill.in.th/sites/default/files/Public_health_service_manual_9_12_2562.pdf .

[15] Section 3 of the ministerial regulation.

[16] Section 5 of the ministerial regulation. This causes a problem if the patient is unconscious or otherwise incapacitated, in which case the doctor may not realise that an AD exists.

clarity of an AD, the inclusion of some important information – albeit, limited – to support the validity of an AD, such as the identification and signature of a witness, is merely a recommendation, and not mandatory. Flexibility may facilitate and perhaps encourage more people to make ADs, but an AD that does not contain sufficient information to support its validity can be the source of problems that might inhibit its implementation. When identification of witnesses is not required, the possibility arises that some people might choose to simply forgo a witness, an issue to be further discussed in Section 5.3.

The provision of palliative care, however, must continue even if medical treatment is refused.[17] There is no definition of "palliative care" within Thai laws; instead, Thai healthcare services employ the definition provided by World Health Organisation (WHO) to clarify the particular healthcare provision and duties of health professions for patients.[18] The obligation for healthcare professions to provide palliative care against the patient's expressed will raises the question of how to balance the tensions between maintaining respect for individual autonomy and enabling the achievement of a good death. The concept of "patients' rights" is conventionally based on the notion of individuals having decision-making autonomy over their own lives, in accordance with their own values. These tensions have long been the subject of debate; what, if any, are the limits to patient autonomy, and how can this be squared with medical knowledge and judgement on the best course of action (or inaction) for a patient?[19] Thailand has grappled with these tensions after the patients' right to self-determination was recognised in Article 12 of the National Health Act, in a form of ADs. Some medical professionals were concerned about their possible criminal liability under this provision; it is they, after all, who generally shoulder responsibility for their patients' healthcare, and the decision on whether to continue or terminate medical treatment should, they reasoned, be made by physicians, rather than by patients.

[17] Section 2 of the ministerial regulation.

[18] WHO has revised the definition of palliative care in 1990, 2005 and, most recently, in 2018, adding details to make the definition more accurate and to prevent misinterpretation. See World Health Organization, *Integrating Palliative Care and Symptom Relief into Primary Health Care: A WHO Guide for Planners, Implementers and Managers* (Geneva: World Health Organization, 2018).

[19] See M.J. Wreen, "Autonomy, Religious Values, and Refusal of Lifesaving Medical Treatment" (1991) 17 *Journal of Medical Ethics* 124.

In 2011, a group of physicians brought a case to court, claiming that Thai legal regulations on ADs were against public order and morals, since such rules impose burdens on medical professionals who carried the weighty responsibility of deciding whether a patient had reached the terminal stage, before implementing an AD. They must also decide what forms and nature of treatment constitute palliative care. However, the law allows medical professionals to avoid any possibility of being held criminally liable if they are acting in accordance with the patients' advance decisions. An AD was hence alleged to enable a patient to reject the evidence-based knowledge, expertise and decisions of medical professionals. The court decided that the legal rules on ADs did not impose any significant burdens on medical professionals, for under Thai law, the right to the use of an AD was not to be construed as allowing active euthanasia or mercy killing; it was instead to be interpreted as the patient's right to refuse treatment in order to die a peaceful and dignified "good death"; medical professionals merely had to respect the patient's decisions. The Thai legal rules on ADs are thus lawful and constitutional.[20]

Superficially, the court's decision in this case appeared to emphasise the value of patient autonomy over medical judgement, by prioritising respect for the patient's decision rather than privileging the doctors' judgements of the best course of action and treatment for the patient. However, Article 12 does not leave all decision-making power with the patient. The mandatory provision of palliative care under the ministerial regulation demonstrates continued state intervention to a certain extent, in particular in relation to the imposing of normative values about what constitutes a good death. Moreover, this insistence on continued palliative care overrides the patient's will. In practice however, such state intervention might not be harmful to most patients; should a patient decide to refuse what they consider to be ultimately futile treatment,[21] the palliative care regime usually coheres with the patient's desire for less suffering.

5.1.3 *Further Development of the AD Regime*

Apart from establishing specific legal rules for ADs in the form of the National Health Act and the ministerial regulations, the National Health

[20] Decision of the Supreme Administrative Court 11/2557.

[21] See B.L. Miller, "Autonomy & the Refusal of Lifesaving Treatment" (1981) 11 *The Hastings Center Report* 22.

Commission Office (NHCO) has published a manual (generally referred to as the NHCO Guide) which provides guidance for health service providers on dealing with ADs. Despite its 2007 introduction in the provisions of the National Health Act, the concept of an AD is not well understood among health professionals. The aforementioned court case brought in 2011 provides a salient and instructive example of the limited knowledge of some public health professionals as to the proper scope of palliative care.[22] It also revealed their prominent anxieties about the possibility of facing criminal liability should they fail in their professional and ethical duty to provide medical treatment. The claimants in this case (whom it will be recalled were medical professionals) had misinterpreted the regulations and believed that an AD enabled a patient to request a "mercy killing". The basis of their claim indicates the paucity of their knowledge and understanding about ADs, as well as a degree of uncertainty about the correct meaning of some terms (such as palliative treatment and futile treatment that simply prolongs death) contained within the ministerial regulations. Acknowledging this problem, the NHCO responded with efforts to enhance understanding of ADs, including the publication of a web-based manual which provides clarity to the concept of an AD, the conditions framing their use and implementation, as well as clarifying the definition and processes of palliative care.[23]

The NHCO's guidance manual also suggests the proper practice of public health professionals when faced with a situation where a patient has written an AD. When informed of the AD, public health professionals must first observe and confirm the mental capability of the patient to ensure that they had created the document while fully conscious of its intended outcome and were of sound mental capacity at the time of writing. It must be noted that this action constitutes guidance rather than an actual directive mandating a public health professional to conduct a preliminary assessment of the patient's mental capabilities. Such an approach is inherently problematic, however, for the mental capability of a patient at the time they provide the AD to the doctor generally does *not* always equate to the patient's mental state at the time of crafting their AD. It is possible that while the AD was made when the patient was

[22] In particular, the claimants of the case thought that the termination of medical treatment would cause the patients to suffer, while in fact, provision of food and water and/or painkilling medicines is within the scope of palliative care which, as mentioned, cannot be refused via an AD.

[23] See note 14.

conscious and cognisant of their intentions, by the time the AD was submitted to the relevant medical professional, the patient no longer had capacity. Another possible scenario is where a patient did not have mental capacity when the AD was made, but subsequently regained their mental capacity at the time of submitting the AD. In such cases, the medical professional might face difficulty in verifying the patient's capability at the time of making the AD, and therefore not be able to implement the AD.

After the preliminary assessment of the patient's capacity, the patient's will as indicated in an AD must be noted in their medical record. The physician then makes a copy of the AD and returns the original AD to the patient. Should the patient be later moved to another public health facility, another copy of the AD should be made and sent with the patient to the new public health facility.[24] The NHCO also raises public awareness of ADs through the publication of information leaflets, guidance manuals, and samples of ADs, which can be easily found on an online website which provides specific information on ADs under the supervision of the NHCO.[25]

5.1.4 *Child ADs*

Does a minor have the autonomy to make an AD of their own? This troubling question has been the subject of much debate, since Article 12 does not specify any minimum age as one of the conditions of an AD. Some lawyers have referred to the Declaration of Patient's Rights[26] in seeking answers to this question. This declaration confirms parental rights to exercise a patient's rights on behalf of their minor children below eighteen years of age, thus leading some scholars to argue that parents are therefore empowered to write an AD for their child.[27]

24 Ibid, p. 21.

25 See National Health Commission Office's website on advance directives at www.thailivingwill.in.th.

26 The Medical Council of Thailand, the Thailand Nursing and Midwifery Council, The Pharmacy Council of Thailand, the Dental Council of Thailand, the Physical Therapy Council, the Medical Technology Council and the Committee of Medical License have collaborated to announce Declaration of Patient's Rights in 2015 to recognise and support patient's rights.

27 S. Somjai, "Minor Patients' Consents to Euthanasia: Comparative Study of the Netherlands, Belgium, and the United Kingdom [with Thailand]" (2019) 12 *Naresuan University Law Journal* 47, 59.

Meanwhile, the NHCO guidance mentioned previously states that a person below eighteen years of age can make an AD with the permission of their parents.[28] The difference between the declaration and the NHCO guidance matters, in that in the former, parents may make an AD on behalf of their child, while in the latter interpretation, a child patient has the right to make an AD, but only with parental permission. In other words, the former assumes the patient's will, while the latter directly reflects the patient's will.

The matter of children's capacity and right to make an AD remains undecided by the courts, and in fact, has not generated much debate, presumably because children are not usually expected to have fatal illnesses in their youth; it is rare indeed to find an AD made by or on behalf of a child patient. Nevertheless, it is still of theoretical interest that a minor might be interpreted as having the capability to make an AD, albeit with parental permission. Conventionally, Thai laws recognise the incapacity of a minor to make a juristic act, and prevents a minor from doing as such for the minor's own benefit, though there are some exceptions including some personal acts that a minor must decide their own, and in which no other persons are permitted to intervene, or to pre-empt such decision, such as certifying a child's birth.[29] A minor is allowed to make a will when they reach the age of fifteen years.[30] Any will made before that, even if it lasts until a minor becomes *sui juris*, are deemed void.[31] Parents cannot make a will on behalf of their child, nor can they give permission to a child below fifteen years of age to write their own will. An AD – usually called a living will – is comparable to a typical will. The limitations placed on the juristic acts a minor is able to make are justified on the grounds that they are intended to protect a minor's benefits, and to safeguard them from those who might seek to take advantage of their young age. While the law allows a minor of fifteen years of age to make an enforceable will, there is currently no minimum age for the same minor to make an AD (even if parental permission is required), which could disadvantage rather than benefit a minor. What a "good death" means to a person is considerably subjective and personal, and the idea that parents can make an AD on behalf of their child expands parental powers over a child, which is not coherent with other

[28] See note 14.
[29] Sections 21 and 23 of the Civil and Commercial Code of the Kingdom of Thailand.
[30] Section 25 of the Civil and Commercial Code of the Kingdom of Thailand.
[31] Section 1703 of the Civil and Commercial Code of the Kingdom of Thailand.

legal provisions that preserve some rights solely for the individual, rather than the entire family. Even the other interpretation that imposes no age minimum but instead allows a minor to themselves make an AD raises doubts about the appropriateness of allowing a child to make such a grave and consequential life-concerning decision. Although the family relationship is of great importance within Thai culture, some legal rights are nevertheless personal, and should be reserved for one's own decision. I explore further the tension between the principle of autonomy and the role of family in implementing an AD in Section 5.2.

5.2 Practice, Value, Commitments and Sociocultural Influences in Thailand

With an individual's autonomy as the normative foundation of an AD, Article 12 allows the patient to make an AD by themselves, without having to obtain consent from or to discuss with other family members. A medical professional does not have to ask the patient's family for permission before implementing an AD. Even where the patient is unconscious, the only duty of a medical professional towards the patient's family is to explain the current stage of their family member's illness, and the medical process for implementing the patient's AD.[32] In cases where a patient has not made an AD, or where there are ambiguities within their AD, but the patient has not specified a named individual able to clarify their intention, it is not possible to simply appoint family members to make an AD or to make decisions about palliative treatment and/or any futile treatment that simply prolongs death for the patient. If the patient's will as stated within the AD lacks clarity, it cannot then be implemented; the patient's right to refuse treatment cannot be given by proxy to any other person, even to a close family member. The right to make an AD is preserved solely for the individual,[33] and as such stands in stark contrast to traditional Thai values of collectivism and paternalism.

[32] Section 6(2) of the ministerial regulation.

[33] There is another observation that highlights the idea that an AD is personal. The ministerial regulation indicates that an AD cannot apply when the patient is pregnant; however, it can become applicable again after the pregnancy period (section 6(4) of the ministerial regulation). Since abortion is still illegal in Thailand, albeit with limited exceptions, the scope of an individual's autonomy under Thai laws does not cover any rights over a foetus. A woman cannot make any decisions that might affect the life of a foetus. This limitation on the implementation of an AD infers that the patient's will is considerably personal, to the extent that it cannot even extend to affect the potential life of a foetus.

Like many other Asian countries, Thai society embraces the concept of collectivism rather than individualism.[34] The closeness of familial relationships makes it possible for an individual's everyday decisions to be influenced by their family. That paternalism has been embedded within Thai culture for a long time[35] is demonstrated by the traditional convention that children should respect and accept the advice of seniors.[36] This value is so deeply entrenched that Thai people allow "elites" or experts whom they believe to possess greater knowledge to make personal decisions on their behalf.[37] In the case of ADs, this would suggest that Thai individuals would be discouraged from making ADs, but would instead be inclined or persuaded to defer the decision to specialist and expert medical professionals. The perceptions of the patient's family can also influence whether the patient will make an AD, and the terms of that directive. This part explores perceptions about the "good death" in the Thai context, and discusses the tension between the principle of autonomy and the role of family in implementing an AD.

Long before Thai laws adopted the concept of a "good death" and recognised a patient's right to refuse medical treatment, public opinion emphasised the duty of medical professionals to treat patients, despite the fact that an AD had been made stipulating the patient's refusal of futile treatment. A 1984 survey revealed that a majority of the public at that time considered a doctor who terminated life-saving treatment according to a patient request made in advance was guilty of *committing a crime*; 71.8% of those surveyed regarded termination of treatment as murder while 24.3% thought that the doctor should be held liable for having committed a minor offence; only 3.4% believed that the doctor should be free of any criminal liability.[38] The later public survey in 1995 indicates

[34] For more information about collectivism and individualism, see G.H. Hofstede, *Culture's Consequences: Comparing Values, Behaviours, Institutions, and Organizations across Nations* (Thousand Oaks, CA: Sage Publications, 2001).

[35] For further historical details on paternalism and Thailand's politics, see T. Chaloemtiarana, *Thailand: The Politics of Despotic Paternalism*. (New York: Cornell University Press, 2007). While this discussion is grounded in politics, the strong tradition of paternalism is observable across contexts.

[36] O.F. Von Feigenblatt, "The Thai Ethnocracy Unravels: A Critical Cultural Analysis of Thailand's Socio-political Unrest" (2009) 1 *Journal of Alternative Perspectives in the Social Sciences* 583.

[37] G. Buchenrieder et al., "Participatory Local Governance and Cultural Practices in Thailand" (2017) 3 *Cogent Social Sciences* 1, 6.

[38] V. Ungprapan, P. Pengpaiboon, and A. Boonkerd, "To Let Patients Die in Peace and Criminal Liabilities" (1986) 42 *Bot Bundit* 111.

the changing perspectives, as respondents indicated more positive responses towards a "good death" - the termination of treatment requested in advance by a patient was not considered a crime by the majority (67.4%) of respondents.[39]

Although both studies discussed previously were conducted well before the passing of the National Health Act, they show how substantively public opinion can change from one extreme to another within the course of a decade. With growing understanding that some medical treatment is futile and cannot cure the patient's illness but will merely prolong their death, and thus cause more suffering, the termination of treatment has become more acceptable to the Thai public. Apart from the concepts of collectivism and paternalism embedded in Thai society, Thai culture and norms also draw heavily from Buddhism,[40] which prompts adherents faced with the prospect of death, to always recall the uncertainty of life, and to learn to let go of the materiality of life. The concept of a "good death" is consonant with most Thai beliefs that in cases where no treatment can cure the particular illness, a person should die peacefully rather than be forced to undergo futile treatment that merely prolongs their suffering.[41] The concept of good death and the recognition of the patient's right to self-determination have their origins in Western countries, which generally rests on cultures of individualism, and which promote awareness of citizens' rights and freedoms. As discussed previously, Thai culture fosters paternalism: most people tend to believe in the superiority of expert knowledge and unquestioningly obey seniority, norms that conflict with the principle of individual autonomy, which supports an individual's right to make an advance decision concerning their medical treatment, especially where it leads to death. Buddhism's strong focus on the truth of impermanence and the contemplation of death, however, may have contributed to acceptance of the view that individuals should be permitted to plan ahead to enable them to achieve a "good death". It is thus the influence of Buddhism that led Thai laws to adopt Western ideas of the "good death" and ADs.

More recently, empirical studies conducted in 2017 and which explored patients' views of ADs found that only 1.4% of those surveyed

[39] V. Ungprapan and W. Chairattanamanokorn, "Right to Die in Cases of Patients with Hopeless Recovery" (1998) 4 *Journal of the Association of Researchers in Social Science* 27.

[40] P. Niffenegger, S. Kulviwat, and N. Engchanil, "Conflicting Cultural Imperatives in Modern Thailand: Global Perspectives" (2006) 12 *Asia Pacific Business Review* 403, 405.

[41] See note 9.

held negative perceptions of their use, although it was also found that most participants were unaware of their legal right to make an AD until they were informed about this during the study. Nearly half (42.9%) of participants had limited knowledge about ADs, while 38.6% had 'moderate' knowledge, and only 18.6% were highly knowledgeable.[42] Interestingly, after being informed of their right to do so,[43] over half (57.1%) of all participants decided to make an AD, suggesting that general attitudes towards ADs continue to be positive.

While Buddhism emphasises the recognition of a life cycle in the sense that death surely follows life, no human can avoid death, and should therefore be prepared to die peacefully, a philosophical approach that supports the concept of the "good death", Buddhists also enshrine some of the wider social conventions, such as the norm of gratitude towards their parents. That children should express gratitude to their parents is a deeply rooted norm in Thai society;[44] sons or daughters who hurt or kill their parents receive extremely severe public condemnation. This norm instils obedience to the parent, alongside gratitude, and can act as a restraint on some patients' children, who may refuse to allow medical professionals to terminate their parent's treatment, despite the presence of an AD. Even though the patients' families may fully understand the futility of treatment, some are afraid of attracting social condemnation for not having made every effort to keep their parents alive.[45] As noted before, Article 12 of the National Health Act enables a patient to make an AD and exempts medical professionals from criminal liability for any acts undertaken in implementing the AD. Yet, as also noted, this legal provision does not impose liabilities for acting *against* the patient's will where the patient's family decide that their family member should continue medical treatment. Medical professionals do not have legal standing to petition for the judicial enforcement of an AD. In practice,

[42] Ibid.

[43] P. Purithammachot, "Attitudes towards Living Wills and Factors Affecting Decisions to Make Living Wills of the Patients of Borabue Hospital" (2016–17) 1 *Academic Journal of Mahasarakham Provincial Public Health Office* 39.

[44] See M. Pinyuchon and L.A. Gray, "Understanding Thai Families: A Cultural Context for Therapists Using a Structural Approach" (1997) 19 *Contemporary Family Therapy* 209; C. Seefeldt and S.R. Keawkungwal, "Children's Attitudes toward the Elderly in Thailand" (1986) 12 *Educational Gerontology* 151, 151.

[45] A. Chantrawongpaisarn, "Interviewing Kitipong Urapeepatanapong: Planning the Death, Making a 'Living Will' for Good Death" (3 September 2017), www.matichon.co.th/prachachuen/interview/news_650989.

resistance from the patient's family can obstruct the implementation of an AD, as most medical professionals wish to avoid a suit brought by the patient's family.[46] To date, the laws have not been able to provide a satisfactory solution out of the impasse when there are conflicts between the desires of the patient's family and that of the patient as expressed in the AD.

This causes a fundamental practical difficulty in the implementation of ADs. As mentioned previously, the principle of individual autonomy provides the theoretical grounding for ADs, and the individual's will regarding their medical treatment is considered personal; there are absolutely no legal measures permitting family intervention. However, resistance from the patient's family can potentially induce hesitancy among some doctors, causing them to delay or abstain from implementing their patient's AD. This problem suggests that the concept of individual autonomy has not been adopted well in Thailand's legal framework for ADs. Further regulatory development is needed to ensure that ADs will be actually implemented, and that the patient's family cannot influence the physician to go against the wishes of their patient's AD. One possible solution is to adopt the ministerial regulation that proposes that individuals should identify an advocate to act on their behalf, in the event that there is a need for clarity about the patient's desire as expressed within their AD. Since the advocate will presumably share a close relationship with the patient, and is cognisant of, and understands the patient's rationale for choosing to refuse medical treatment, selecting a family member as advocate can be an interesting approach that facilitates mutual understanding between the patient and the family, and helps to diminish the family's resistance to the AD. Another possible solution is to mandate registration of ADs, as will be discussed in the following section.

5.3 Would a Flexible Format in the Design of ADs Support or Discourage Their Use in Practice?

Thai legal rules on ADs as embodied namely within Article 12 of the National Health Act and the ministerial regulations, do not require a strict format for ADs. Compared with other jurisdictions where specific

[46] MGR Online, "Fewer than 1% of Thai People Has Made an Advance Directive – Doctors Are Afraid of Legal Cases" (15 September 2014), https://mgronline.com/qol/detail/9570000105867.

legal rules set out mandatory requirements for ADs to be regarded as legally binding documents, the Thai state imposes few requirements, making the creation of ADs a more straightforward and uncomplicated task than demanded by neighbouring states. Singapore, for instance, requires that ADs assume a fixed format, while South Korea and Taiwan insist that ADs must be registered with national authorities. Thai laws do not require ADs to have a fixed template – a simple written statement will suffice. There is no mandate for ADs to be registered, and no involvement of national authorities or public health professions is required for an AD to be deemed valid under Thai laws. This flexibility in the making of ADs might appear to be supportive of patients' right to exercise self-determination in the matter of their death. However, fewer requirements do not always ensure fewer difficulties in implementation. The fact that Thai laws merely set out a few basic guidelines for an AD can, on one hand, benefit a patient in that they can easily make an AD, but on the other hand, medical professionals can face difficulties relying on an AD. Such challenges may reduce the effectiveness of ADs in actual application. Three problems can potentially undermine Thailand's flexible rules for ADs, which are (1) uncertainty about its validity, (2) unawareness of its existence, and (3) conflicts with the patient's family.

5.3.1 Uncertainty about the Validity of an AD

As we have seen, under Thai law, a written statement by a mentally capable individual is sufficient to confirm the validity of an AD. However, the laws do not indicate how the individual's capacity is to be assessed. The NHCO guidance simply suggests that health professionals should conduct preliminary assessments to confirm the consciousness and mental state of the patient at the time the physician is presented with an AD.[47] Although the ministerial regulations suggest that an AD should be witnessed, this is not a mandatory requirement, and leaves the possibility that a patient lacking full mental capacity could proceed without a witness. This flexibility can raise concerns for medical professionals, for example, in cases where a patient allows the family to give the AD to the physician on their behalf. In such cases, the physician cannot be certain that the AD was actually made by the patient, or whether the statement was made when the patient was fully conscious and aware of the

[47] See note 14.

implications of their decision. In addition, the NHCO's suggestion that the capacity of a patient be assessed when the AD is received poses yet another problem; as discussed previously, mental capability at the time the AD is produced does not necessarily mean that the patient was mentally capable at the time of the writing of the AD.

A comparable case with an AD is the 'last will' of an individual. There are five legal formats that the last will can assume in order to be enforceable under Thai laws.[48] One such format is a document wholly written and signed by the testator.[49] This format does not require witnesses or registration, and therefore can be compared with an AD. However, the application of this form of the last will does not cause the same concern as an AD, because in cases where there is any doubt surrounding its validity, a challenge can be brought to the court. In contrast, the physician's decision-making on whether to rely on an AD is shaped by the limited time in which the case may be brought to the court.[50] In other words, the physician has to make a nearly immediate judgement on the authenticity and validity of an AD. This difficult situation can worsen if there is conflict within the patient's family over the reliance on an AD.

The requirement that an individual must register their AD with national authorities might – to some extent – resolve these problems. Registration does not only address the issue of medical hesitation and prevent a family's objection to an AD, it also provides an opportunity for authorities to examine and validate (or otherwise) the AD. It is also possible for the law to require that a physician certify that an individual who makes an AD is capable of understanding and communicating their will *at the time* of making the AD. This examination or verification can prevent ambiguity or lack of clarity that might cause problems in its later application. Medical professionals can feel more confident of the validity of an AD and will be less likely to hesitate before implementing their patient's directive. The requirements for either registration or verification from a physician can also help to protect the enforceability of the patient's will, ensuring that the principle of the patient's autonomy is pragmatically secured.

[48] Section 1655 of the Civil and Commercial Code of the Kingdom of Thailand.
[49] Section 1657 of the Civil and Commercial Code of the Kingdom of Thailand.
[50] V. Fongsiripaiboon, "Living Will: Practical Point for Doing" (2015) 432 *The Medical News* 37, 39.

5.3.2 Unawareness of the Existence of an AD

In some circumstances, a patient will not have had the opportunity to inform others that they had made an AD. Since Thai laws do not require registration, there is no record of an AD unless the patient informs the physician or other health personnel. It is possible therefore for others to be unaware of the existence of an AD, in which case, the patient's exercise of their right to make an AD fails to achieve its purpose. In some jurisdictions such as Taiwan,[51] an AD is required to be registered and recorded in the data memory of an individual's national health insurance card; this can help to provide information immediately in the event the patient is admitted to a healthcare institution.

5.3.3 Conflicts with the Patient's Family

As already mentioned, the cultural norm that children express gratitude to their parents is deeply ingrained within Thai society. This can leave medical professions with a problem whereby the patient's family is unwilling to allow physicians to terminate their family member's treatment despite the declared wishes of the AD. Although reliance on an AD is not conditional on permission from the patient's family, most medical professionals would prefer not to have to act against the family's wishes. Article 12 exempts doctors from criminal liability arising from acting in accordance with an AD, but it cannot shield medical professionals from threats of legal actions from dissatisfied families. Most physicians do not wish to undergo the exhausting judicial process, and tend therefore to accede to the wishes of the patient's family, rather than observe the patient's desires as stated within the AD.[52]

Growing recognition of the notion of a "good death" and the changing perception of Thai society towards ADs can decrease resistance from the patient's family. Apart from relying on raising awareness via education, increasing the formalities associated with ADs can also demonstrate respect for patients' wishes. Introducing mandatory registration can signal formal recognition of an AD and help raise its significance above the views of the patient's family, which will, in turn, result in greater confidence among medical professionals to act in accordance with their patients' ADs. Selecting a family member who can act on behalf of the

[51] D.F. TSAI, Taiwan, in this volume.
[52] See note 50, p. 40.

patient and help to clarify any ambiguities of the AD may also reduce familial resistance to the AD.

5.4 Conclusion

With specific legal rules for ADs, namely Article 12 of the National Health Act and the ministerial regulation, the Thai government has legislated a formal legal framework for ADs. Empirical studies indicate the changing perceptions of Thai society towards the understanding and acceptance of the concept of a "good death", and of terminally ill patients' right to autonomy. Current positive responses towards ADs will likely lead to increased use of ADs in the future. However, the lack of formalities in relation to the making of ADs under Thai laws can obstruct the application of ADs in practice, as medical professions might encounter difficulties in relying on ADs, namely uncertainty about their validity, unawareness of their existence, and conflicts with the patients' family. This chapter suggests the requirement for registration as an approach to relieve such difficulties, and to ensure that the aim of an AD to protect the patient's right to self-determination and preserve human dignity can be achieved in practice.

6

Advance Directives in India: Seeking the Individual within the Community

KELLY AMAL DHRU & RAVINDRA B. GHOOI

पुनरपि जननं पुनरपि मरणं,
पुनरपि जननी जठरे शयनम्।
इह संसारे बहु दुस्तारे,
कृपयाऽपारे पाहि मुरारे।।

(Born again, dead again, born again to stay in the mother's womb. It is indeed hard to cross this boundless ocean of samsara. Oh Lord! Redeem me through thy mercy.)

– "*Bhaja Govindam*", Adi Sankara, Eighth Century

6.1 Introduction

The legal regime surrounding advance directives (ADs) and living wills in India took a long journey to reach where it is, and yet the journey remains incomplete. Legal recognition of end-of-life ADs in India is usually seen as closely tied to questions of the legalisation of passive euthanasia and decriminalisation of suicide attempts. Much of the literature has overemphasised the connection between euthanasia and ADs, particularly because they are conflated with do-not-resuscitate orders and enforcement of the right to refuse treatment that ADs may contain.[1] This chapter explores legal developments in relation to end-of-life care and ADs in India, with the aim of decoupling ADs from the euthanasia discourse and focusing on the former. We lay out the current guidelines on ADs laid down by the Supreme Court of India, followed by a

The authors would like to express their gratitude to Professor Werner Menski and the editors of the volume for the painstaking edits and valuable comments.

[1] The authors have themselves been guilty of such overemphasis in the past. See R.B. Ghooi, K. Dhru and S. Jaywant, "The Urgent Need for Advance Directives in India" (2016) 1(4) *Indian Journal of Medical Ethics*, 242.

consideration of ADs in the psychiatric context, and compare some of the crucial elements of each, including the role of the family and the consultation process.

An important thread connecting the legalisation of euthanasia with ADs is the role of individual autonomy. In the landmark case of *Common Cause (A Registered Society)* v. *Union of India*[2] in March 2018, which saw the legal sanction of passive euthanasia and legal recognition of ADs, as well as the creation of the aforementioned current guidelines on ADs, the judges explored the value of patient autonomy. In his judgment in the *Puttaswamy* v. *Union of India* decision, which was quoted in *Common Cause*, Justice Chandrachud said:

> Life is precious in itself. But life is worth living because of the freedoms, which enable each individual to live life as it should be lived. The best decisions on how life should be lived are entrusted to the individual. They are continuously shaped by the social milieu in which individuals exist. The duty of the State is to safeguard the ability to take decisions – the autonomy of the individual – and not to dictate those decisions.[3]

There remain in the background, however, concerns over the social and religious relevance of the notion of autonomy. Whilst the value of individual autonomy may be quite central to Western culture, the cultural context has often been neglected in discussions about ADs in India. For example, the family plays an important role in India's sociocultural context, with respect to decision-making in particular, but there is also a presumption by the courts that the patient has to be protected from the family. We argue in this chapter that the role of doctors and the courts can be seen as protecting patients from their families. The chapter also briefly addresses the questions surrounding autonomy in the religious and medico-cultural context.[4]

In terms of the practice of and attitudes towards ADs, there is very little understanding, although a survey we conducted on the level and

[2] *Common Cause (A Registered Society)* v. *Union of India* (2018) 5 SCC 1.

[3] See J. Chandrachud in *Puttaswamy* v. *Union of India* (2017) 10 SCC 1, para. 118 as quoted by C.J.I. Misra in *Common Cause (A Registered Society)* v. *Union of India* (2018) 5 SCC 1, para. 153.

[4] While the Indian social milieu is richly diverse, with members of its population belonging to a plethora of religions, this chapter will mainly focus on some of the common themes across Hinduism, Buddhism and Jainism. The authors have no intention of undermining the importance of Islamic, Christian, Sikh or any other faith-based and cultural interactions with the relevant legal developments, or the legal interpretation of the freedom of religion.

extent of knowledge about ADs amongst educated persons with and without a medical background provides some empirical data on the level of AD awareness in India. The last section of the chapter discusses this survey, highlighting that there is a need for greater awareness of ADs. We conclude with reflections on the problems with the current AD regime and recommendations for the way forward.

6.2 The Legal Background: *De Lege Lata*

6.2.1 The Legal Understanding of Life and Death

To understand the legalisation of ADs, one must first understand the Indian legal approach to life and death. Article 21 of the Constitution of India guarantees the right to life: "No person shall be deprived of his life or personal liberty except by a procedure established by law".[5] Following the case of *Maneka Gandhi* v. *Union of India*,[6] Article 21 of the Constitution of India has been given a very expansive interpretation by the Supreme Court of India to embody dignity[7] and a meaningful, complete life worth living. Since then, Article 21 of the Constitution of India has also been the anchor of many welfare rights.

In the context of patients suffering from terminal illness, the pertinent question is whether the right to life includes the right to die and to die with dignity. The legalisation of end-of-life ADs has been by extension of the right to self-determination involved in the refusal of treatment and withdrawal of life support in this context. As the legal situation currently stands, ADs are seen as a mechanism to ensure death with dignity, as they involve self-determination. What the situation thus demands is translation of the abstract right to death with dignity into concrete regulatory processes to ensure realisation of that right. Accordingly, it is important to understand, as part of the AD context, the journey that led to the legalisation of death with dignity in the form of passive euthanasia.

6.2.2 The Aruna Shanbaug Case (2011)

The battle surrounding the legalisation of euthanasia took centre stage and garnered nationwide attention with the *Aruna Ramchandra*

5 Constitution of India, Art. 21.

6 *Maneka Gandhi* v. *Union of India* (1978) SCC (1) 248.

7 Also found in the Preamble to the Constitution of India.

Shanbaug v. *Union of India* case.[8] The case concerned the brutal rape and assault of a nurse at KEM Hospital Mumbai by a ward boy, which left her in a persistent vegetative state. The Supreme Court held that passive euthanasia (understood here as the withdrawal of life-sustaining treatment) could be legalised only through an act of Parliament. The two-judge bench of the court made a distinction between active and passive, and voluntary and involuntary, euthanasia. The procedure it devised required that a high court be approached directly concerning every single case in which life-sustaining treatment was to be withdrawn.

Just as in the *Airedale National Health Service Trust* v. *Bland* case,[9] Aruna Shanbaug had made no express provision for an AD. In *Aruna Shanbaug*, a reference to ADs was made in the report submitted to the court by medical experts, who also stated that they had no information concerning the expressed views or wishes of Aruna Shanbaug.[10] The amicus curiae in the case also brought up the link between self-determination, used interchangeably with informed consent, and ADs.[11] The court laid down guidelines on the withdrawal of life support, which were to remain in force until Parliament enacted a law. Under those guidelines, the decision to withdraw life support should be taken in the best interests of the patient if she is unable to make a decision for herself.[12] Such a decision could be taken by a person or body of persons acting as "the next friend" and could also be taken by the patient's doctors. However, the decision required the approval of the high court concerned.[13] The Supreme Court in this case limited itself to acceptance that there had been no expression of wishes without going into the question of the legality of ADs per se.

6.2.3 *Law Commission of India Reports (2006 and 2012)*

The next milestone in the development of end-of-life AD legislation was two Law Commission of India reports, specifically the 196th report

[8] *Aruna Ramchandra Shanbaug* v. *Union of India* (2011) 4 SCC 454.

[9] *Airedale National Health Service Trust* v. *Bland* [1993] 1 All ER 821, a landmark House of Lords case in the United Kingdom dealing with the question of withdrawal of life-sustaining treatment.

[10] J. Katju in, *Aruna Ramchandra Shanbaug* v. *Union of India* (2011) 4 SCC 454, para. 9.

[11] Ibid, para. 24.

[12] Ibid., para. 126.

[13] Ibid., para. 126.

published in March 2006,[14] which discussed the withholding of life support measures from terminally ill patients, and the 241st report published in August 2012[15] after the *Aruna Shanbaug* decision.

The 196th report recommended allowing passive euthanasia for both competent and incompetent patients. However, despite acknowledging the recognition of ADs in other countries, the report resisted recognising their legal validity, citing "complex legal and factual issues", such as subsequent changes in circumstances, or changes in technology, and problems of proof in the event of a subsequent withdrawal.[16] The Law Commission, in the 196th report, seems to have been greatly influenced by Justice Munby's considerations in *HE* v. *Hospital NHS and Another*,[17] which centred on the efficacy of ADs (in this case in the context of blood transfusions) and a test of their applicability being a matter of proof.[18] The commission seems to have been concerned about the problems of proof in oral ADs, particularly given the level of illiteracy in India. For policy reasons, it thus recommended that ADs not be legalised in India, fearing the huge amount of litigation stemming from conflicting evidence, even if the ADs were in writing.[19]

The 241st report of the Law Commission upheld the findings of the previous report. Interestingly, some of the questions concerning the subsequent withdrawal of consent, for example, which are found in contemporary discussions of ADs, were cited as reasons for not accepting their validity. In light of these findings, Section 11 of the draft bill arising from the two reports (i.e. the 2016 draft Treatment of Terminally-Ill Patients (Protection of Patients and Medical Practitioners) Bill) considered ADs to be invalid.

6.2.4 *The Common Cause Decision (2018)*

The *Common Cause* case, which was referred to the Supreme Court with a request that it declare that the right to life includes the right to die with

[14] Law Commission of India, *196th Report – Medical Treatment to Terminally Ill Patients (Protection of Patients and Medical Practitioners)* (New Delhi: Law Commission of India, March 2006).

[15] Law Commission of India, *241st Report – Passive Euthanasia – A Relook* (New Delhi: Law Commission of India, August 2012).

[16] See note 14, pp. 319–28.

[17] *HE* v. *Hospital NHS and Another* [2003] EWHC 1017.

[18] See, for example, note 14, pp. 321–23.

[19] Ibid., p. 327.

dignity and legalise ADs, dealt more generally with the end-of-life context in India. The court also considered the question of legalising ADs in the case. In light of international developments, in India too there had been repeated requests for the legalisation of euthanasia, many of which ended up on the doorstep of the Supreme Court. Advocacy groups had been writing about euthanasia and ADs and recommending legal sanction for the latter.[20] Everything changed in March 2018, however, with the court's ruling in *Common Cause*, which was heard by a five-judge bench comprising Justices Dipak Misra Chief Justice of India (CJI), Khanwilkar, Sikri, Chandrachud and Bhushan.

In the *Common Cause* decision, the court upheld the arguably problematic distinction between active and passive euthanasia[21] and legalised passive euthanasia, which it understood as the withholding or withdrawal of life support, not as physician-assisted suicide. In relation to ADs, Justice Sikri stated that the fear of misuse cannot be grounds for a blanket ban on ADs.[22] The Court laid down a set of detailed guidelines, discussed later, which are the law in place until the Indian Parliament enacts legislation. The guidelines provide for a rather long procedure in the event that the executor of an AD develops a terminal or incurable illness.

In this case, we find at least a prima facie reiteration of the right to decisional autonomy in the five-judge bench decision, particularly Justice Chandrachud's judgment.[23] Even the CJI, just before giving the guidelines for ADs, quoted John Rawls from his book *Political Liberalism*, wherein he emphasises choice, holding that between best interests and decisional autonomy, it is decisional autonomy that triumphs.[24] It could be said that the legal milieu for the recognition of ADs was established by the Supreme Court's increasing focus on individual decisional autonomy,

[20] See Ghooi, Dhru and Jaywant, note 1, and R.K. Mani, S.N. Simha and R. Gursahani, "The Advance Directives and Foregoing of Life Support: Where Do We Stand Now?" (2018) 22(3) *Indian Journal of Critical Care Medicine*, 135.

[21] The distinction between active and passive euthanasia has been questioned in the literature on ADs and euthanasia in India. See, for example, S. Rao, "The Moral Basis for a Right to Die" (2011) 46(18) *Economic and Political Weekly*, 13.

[22] J. Sikri in *Common Cause (A Registered Society)* v. *Union of India* (2018) 5 SCC 1, para. 130–2.

[23] This is in contrast to the focus on best interests in *Aruna Ramchandra Shanbaug* v. *Union of India* (2011) 4 SCC 454, where in the entire decision the word "autonomy" appears only twice, and even then in quotations. The focus is clearly on best interests. See in particular para. 27.

[24] See J. Misra in *Common Cause (A Registered Society)* v. *Union of India* (2018) 5 SCC 1, para. 162.

as is highly visible in the recognition of the right to privacy in 2017 by a unanimous decision of a nine-judge bench of the Supreme Court in *Puttaswamy*.

There has also been acknowledgement of the role that the right to privacy played in the court's reasoning in the *Common Cause* case. Justice Sikri, for instance, when formulating the questions concerned states that "with [the] right to privacy now a fundamental right under Article 21 (right to life), the principle of self-determination in India stands on a higher footing than before".[25] In the *Puttaswamy* decision, which was quoted in *Common Cause*, Justice Chelameshwar said, "An individual's right to refuse the life-prolonging medical treatment or terminate life is another freedom which falls within the zone of the right to privacy".[26] Hence, the domain of privacy has been extended to include end-of-life decisions.

6.3 Current Legal Position on Advance Directives in India

The key guidelines pertaining to ADs[27] come from paragraphs 191–4 of the *Common Cause* decision, described previously, under the judgment of the CJI and Justice Khanwilkar, which was reiterated by the rest of the bench:[28]

(a) **The format:** Under the guidelines, an AD can be executed only by an adult of sound mind, who is in a position to understand and communicate the purpose and consequences of the directive. The Court decision does not specify how soundness of mind is to be assessed, although soundness of mind in Indian law is a presumption under the Indian Contract Act 1872.[29]

[25] See J. Sikri in ibid., para. 10.

[26] See J. Chelameshwar in *Puttaswamy* v. *Union of India* (2017) 10 SCC 1, at para 38, as quoted by J. Bhushan in *Common Cause (A Registered Society)* v. *Union of India* (2018) 5 SCC 1, para. 78.

[27] While these are the first legal guidelines on the topic of ADs in India, there is some evidence that ADs have already been considered previously as a part of professional guidelines on end-of-life care. See, for example, All India Institute of Medical Sciences, *Guidelines for End of Life Care* (New Delhi: All India Institute of Medical Sciences, 2020). While these guidelines do not refer to the term ADs, they refer to the documentation of a mentally capacitated patient's wishes for withholding life-sustaining support (see p. 4).

[28] *Common Cause (A Registered Society)* v. *Union of India* (2018) 5 SCC 1, at paras. 191–4.

[29] Indian Contract Act 1872, s. 12.

Reference is also made to "informed consent" given without any undue influence or constraint. The AD must be clear, unambiguous, with specific terms and instructions, and in writing. It can be withdrawn at any time, and the withdrawal must also be in writing. The format requirement is that the AD has to be signed by the executor (who is an adult of a sound and healthy state of mind) and two (independent) witnesses and counter-signed by a judicial magistrate first class (JMFC). It is unclear what exactly is meant by "independent", but it presumably means someone with no vested interest in the property of the person making the AD.

The JMFC is a post established under Section 11 of the Criminal Procedure Code 1973.[30] The JMFC's role is to preserve the document in both paper and digital form and send a copy to the Municipal Corporation or local Panchayat (local village council[31]) for the appointment of a custodian of the document. The JMFC also needs to inform the executor's family of the directive, which risks compromising the executor's autonomy. Finally, the JMFC is required to maintain a copy of the AD in his or her office, with another copy forwarded to the relevant district court. The amount of responsibility placed on the JMFC is concerning given the huge backlog of cases in the courts.

The signature of the JMFC is likely to constitute a major hurdle given that the number of judicial officers of this level is very small in any given city. For example, in the city of Pune, there are only 19 such officials for a population of six million. There is also a huge backlog of cases with the lower judiciary in India, a concern that does not seem to bother the Supreme Court.

(b) **When ADs apply:** Under the Supreme Court guidelines, an AD can be given effect only in the event that the executor becomes terminally ill and is undergoing prolonged medical treatment with no hope of recovery or cure of his or her ailment or is surviving on life support.

(c) **The process if there is an AD:** The physician, when made aware of the existence of an AD, must check its authenticity with the JMFC and then inform the hospital, which in turn will form a hospital medical board comprising the head of the treating department and at least three experts from the fields of general medicine, cardiology,

30 Code of Criminal Procedure 1973, s. 11.

31 These are not informal institutions, but hold constitutional status through the Constitution (73rd Amendment) Act 1992.

neurology, nephrology, psychiatry or oncology with good standing in the medical profession and at least 20 years' experience.

The experts visit the patient and form a preliminary opinion on whether to execute the directive. If it is to be executed, the JMFC is to be informed, and he or she in turn appoints a medical board consisting of the Chief District Medical Officer as chairperson and three expert doctors (who are not members of the hospital's medical board). If this board agrees with the hospital board that the instructions in the AD may be carried out, it will approach the JMFC, who will visit the patient and "after examining all aspects" authorise the implementation of the board's decision.

If the JMFC-appointed medical board refuses implementation, the executor of the AD, his or her family members, or even the treating doctor or hospital staff may approach the High Court. The two-judge bench of that Court can, if it wishes, form another committee with expert doctors (each again with at least 20 years' experience), although the High Court is to keep in mind "the best interest of the patient".

(d) **No AD:** In the case of no AD (or an ambiguous AD), the procedure to be followed is this: after consultation with the patient's family, which must give its consent in writing, the hospital's medical board is consulted for a primary opinion, and the JMFC-appointed medical board for a secondary opinion.

This is obviously a highly complex and rather bureaucratic procedure, with too many opinions required to be obtained before life support can be withdrawn. There is also no separate procedure for emergency situations. The power to interpret and give effect to an AD lies largely with the physician and the various boards. There is little or no representation of persons other than doctors in the expert committees. It is likely that in future cases,[32] the Supreme Court will clarify the procedure, as well as the convoluted nature of the existing guidelines. In the meantime, however, the value of self-determination that the *Common Cause* decision ostensibly serves is taken away by the lengthy procedure laid out in the

[32] For example, the Vidhi Centre for Legal Policy, an independent think-tank, has already filed a clarification application in the Supreme Court as this volume goes to print. See further D. Mehta and A. Agarwal, "End of Life Care in India: A Model Legal Framework", Vidhi Centre for Legal Policy (15 November 2019), https://vidhilegalpolicy.in/research/end-of-life-care-in-india-a-model-legal-framework/.

guidelines given by the Supreme Court, which remain the law of the land until the Indian Parliament enacts legislation concerning ADs.

Interestingly, in a different context, India has experienced much less controversy in enacting AD legislation. We now turn to the psychiatric advance directive (PAD) regime in India.

6.3.1 PADs under the Mental Healthcare Act 2017

The recognition of PADs under Section 5 of the Mental Healthcare Act 2017 provides analogical strength in favour of the legalisation of end-of-life ADs. For example, Justice Sikri uses PADs in arguing against the Law Commission's concerns that ADs might be misused, relying on the safeguards in the PAD regime as an example of the safeguards that could be implemented to prevent abuse.[33]

Under the procedure for PADs, the power to determine the manner of the directive's implementation is delegated to the Rules and Regulations of the Mental Healthcare Act 2017, of which Part II deals with the same. An AD format is given in Form CR-A of the Mental Healthcare Rules 2017, made under the Mental Healthcare Act 2017. The AD is to be signed by two witnesses, and is to be registered with the Mental Health Review Board of the jurisdiction in which the person resides. There is also an obligation to make the AD available online within 14 days. According to Form CR-A, a person can appoint two or more nominated representatives in order of precedence to make decisions about mental healthcare treatment in the event of incapacity. In some regards, this stipulation renders a PAD more akin to a power of attorney than to an AD. There is also a need for certification by a medical professional that the capacity to make decisions exists at the time the PAD is made.

Whilst there appears to be no apparent basis for distinguishing between end-of-life ADs and PADs on the issue of capacity, there is an established procedure for assessing capacity under the Mental Healthcare Rules 2017, unlike under the aforementioned guidelines laid down by *Common Cause*. The determination of the capacity to consent for patients with mental illness is to be made by the expert committee appointed by the Central Mental Health Authority under Section 81 of the Mental Healthcare Act 2017.[34]

[33] J. Sikri in *Common Cause (A Registered Society)* v. *Union of India* (2018) 5 SCC 1, para. 132.

[34] Mental Healthcare Rules 2017, Rule 16.

Although PADs were used to provide analogical support for the legalisation of end-of-life ADs in that decision, as discussed previously, there remain crucial differences between the procedures and powers concerning PADs and end-of-life ADs. For example, compared with an end-of-life AD, a PAD confers a duty upon the medical caregiver to follow the directive.[35] Less discretion thus lies with the medical practitioner. The AD format is also specified by the Mental Healthcare Rules 2017, which constitute a much more detailed legislative scheme.[36]

The media attention surrounding euthanasia and ADs has been greater than that surrounding PADs. Because the legalisation of PADs generated little controversy, discussion or resistance in India, they may well have been easier than ADs to legislate. The law under which they were legalised, the Mental Healthcare Act 2017, received cross-party support, as it recognised the legal right to mental healthcare.[37] There is also a greater role for the family under the PAD regime, which will be discussed in the next section.

It thus seems that whilst ADs in the psychiatric and end-of-life contexts both aim to provide individuals with the opportunity to exercise autonomy in relation to decisions about medical treatment if and when they lose capacity, the respective regimes are very different, although the differences (in relation to the assessment of mental capacity or enforceability, for example) do not appear to be based on principle.

6.4 Advance Directives in Context

6.4.1 The Role of the Family

Illness in India, scholars have argued, is a family matter, and hence the role of the family is the most crucial for healthcare decision-making.[38] The role of the family is central in the epics that scholars often cite as

[35] Mental Healthcare Act 2017, s.10.

[36] Mental Healthcare Rules 2017, Part II s. 1.

[37] See, for example, S. Pathare, "Mental Healthcare Act: A Paradigm Shift", *Mint* (27 December 2017), www.livemint.com/Opinion/BdVVXjyKWDhAAcU1ulHwSI/Mental-Healthcare-Act-A-paradigm-shift.html.

[38] See S. Chattopadhyay and A. Simon, "East Meets West: Cross-Cultural Perspective in End-of-Life Decision Making from Indian and German Viewpoints" (2008) 11(2) *Medicine, Health Care and Philosophy*, 165, 169. For a very insightful discussion on end-of-life concerns and the role of family in the Hindu and particularly the British Hindu population, see particularly chapters 4–13 of S. Firth, *Death, Dying and Bereavement in a British Hindu Community*, PhD thesis, School of Oriental and

creating the landscape for Indian ethics.[39] In an interaction between the Indian legal landscape through personal laws and Hindu religious-cultural practices, the law itself allows for the fictional unit of the "Hindu Undivided Family", particularly in the context of the ownership of family property and inheritance under the Hindu Succession Act 1956.[40] Under this system, the eldest male of the family, that is, the father, husband or eldest son, has traditionally been considered to be the *Karta* or "manager" (or, by extension, the decision-maker). The definition of *Karta* has now been extended to include females.[41] Family lies at the heart of Indian society, and yet the treatment that ADs afford it is bittersweet. Under the Supreme Court guidelines, doctors have a greater role to play than family members. Nevertheless, the JMFC is to inform the family of the person making the AD that such a document has been made. How is one to interpret this apparent discrepancy?

Given the country's huge young population and cultural norms against the abandonment of one's parents in their old age, one would expect the family to play a crucial part in this context in India. Yet, the legal battles around who gets to make a decision on behalf of the patient in the case of ADs have centred on the roles of the courts and doctors. In light of the importance of the family in other law and ethics contexts, as demonstrated in the way decisions are to be made by the head of the family, and legal recognition of the Hindu Undivided Family, one can only wonder at the lack of any role for the family in the end-of-life context.

It is possible that the situation arises from concerns over the potential for abuse in that context. Such concerns are apparent in court decisions pertaining to ADs, as well as in the aforementioned Law Commission reports. Hence, one can argue that the main reason for the resistance is the potential misuse of ADs by family members. In light of this

African Studies, University of London (1994), https://library.soas.ac.uk/Record/eprints-28921/Description#details.

39 Consider, for example, B.K. Matilal and J. Ganeri, *Ethics and Epics: Philosophy, Culture, and Religion* (New Delhi: Oxford University Press, 2002). See also G. Das, *The Difficulty of Being Good: On the Subtle Art of Dharma* (New York: Oxford University Press, 2010). Both of these authors build on the ethical dimensions within the characters and conflicts in *The Mahabharata*, which centres on a family feud over the rightful inheritance of a kingdom.

40 The Hindu Succession Act 1956, in turn, is based on the *Dayabhaga* and the *Mitakshara* systems.

41 The amendment to the Hindu Succession Act 1956 was brought about by the Hindu Succession (Amendment) Act 2005.

scepticism of the role of the family, the state or third-party agencies perceive themselves as having a crucial role in preventing such abuse and preserving the autonomy of the individual, even though that perception may be unwarranted given the lack of empirical evidence on such abuse.

Scepticism about the role of the family is also reflected in the *Aruna Shanbaug* decision. The hospital and her caretakers were considered to be the next of kin rather than Aruna Shanbaug's family or even Pinky Virani, the humanistically intentioned person who filed the case. It was because of the decision of the staff and nurses at KEM hospital who had looked after Aruna Shanbaug in a persistent vegetative state for 37 years that she was kept on life support.[42]

In the *Aruna Shanbaug* decision, the role of the family in giving consent on behalf of the patient was also resisted. Justice Katju, for instance, said the following:

> The question arises, as to who should give consent for withdrawal of life support. This is an extremely important question in India because of the unfortunate low level of ethical standards to which our society has descended, its raw and widespread commercialisation, and the rampant corruption, and hence, the Court has to be very cautious that unscrupulous persons who wish to inherit the property of someone may not get him eliminated by some crooked method.[43]

Justice Katju discussed the appointment of a guardian in the *Aruna Shanbaug* case. He cited chapter IV of the 196th Law Commission Report, which considers the family and relatives to be just one consideration, placing power with the High Court as *parens patriae*. As with the High Court's authority to make decisions regarding the withdrawal of life support, there is strong jurisprudence on the role of the state, particularly that of the High Court as *parens patriae*. Somehow, the Supreme Court under *Common Cause* and Law Commission of India under the reports seem to view themselves as the protectors of individual patients from their own families. Under the new procedure resulting from the *Common Cause* case, the focus seems to have shifted from the role of the High Court to that of medical practitioners and the JMFC, with the family still placed in a secondary position. The sentiment remains similar: to protect the individual from his or her family.

Interestingly, concern over the potential for abuse is less evident in the PAD context, in which there appears to be a larger role for the family. In

[42] J. Katju in *Aruna Ramchandra Shanbaug* v. *Union of India* (2011) 4 SCC 454, para. 126.
[43] Ibid., paras. 101–2.

the PAD regime, for example, a relative or the caregiver of the person concerned can make an application to the hospital board to review, alter, modify or cancel the AD.[44] The greater role for the family in this regime may be the result of dialogue with stakeholders, who expressed scepticism about PADs. The Standing Committee Report on the Mental Healthcare Bill, which resulted in the Mental Healthcare Act 2017, attributes PADs to the Convention on the Rights of Persons with Disabilities, to which India has been a signatory since 2007.[45] In the report,[46] which, as noted, resulted from dialogue with stakeholders, there is scepticism regarding the creation of PADs, as well as resistance on cultural grounds, namely, that they may be in conflict with the role of the family in decision-making in India.

Whilst there has been no similar dialogue with stakeholders in the end-of-life context, and it is therefore unclear whether a similar concern would be raised, the foregoing discussion of the importance of the family in Indian culture and other legal contexts suggests that despite court scepticism about that role, there may be cultural reasons for the family to be given a larger role in the context of end-of-life ADs.

6.4.2 *Autonomy, Pain and Desire: The Role of Religions*

Law operates in the context of its society, which, in the case of India, brings together the peculiarities of that society owing to its highly diverse, pluralistic nature. In fact, doubts have been expressed in the past concerning whether a unified "Hindu" bioethics can exist given the plurality of Indian culture. The management of patients at the end-of-life is also influenced by religious and cultural beliefs, although there appears to be little discussion of personal will and desire in the context of end-of-life treatment.[47]

44 See Mental Healthcare Act 2017, s. 11.

45 See Department-Related Standing Committee on Health and Family Welfare, *74th Report on the Mental Healthcare Bill 2013* (New Delhi: Rajya Sabha Secretariat, November 2013).

46 The inclusion of the PAD provision has an interesting history in the consultations, as described in the *74th Report on the Mental Healthcare Bill 2013* (ibid.).

47 This may be because there is no clear "individual" or "auto" in Hindu or Buddhist phenomenology, which may cause difficulties when attempting to use autonomy as a ground value (cf. Ganeri, who argues that there may be space for autonomy; see J. Ganeri, "Buddhism and Bioethics: A Theravada Defence of Individual Autonomy" in S. Grätzel and E. Guhe (eds.), *Life, Body Person, and Self: A Reconsideration of Core Concepts in Bioethics from an Intercultural Perspective* (Munich: Verlag Karl Alber, 2016), pp. 176–92).

For a significant number of people belonging to the Hindu, Buddhist and Jain faiths, amongst others, there is the concept of an ongoing cycle of birth, death and rebirth. In these traditions, societal existence, or *Samsara*, sees its outer boundaries in the pursuit of the attainment of *Moksha* or *Nirvana*. According to this view, death is not the end, and there are many ideas pertaining to renouncing all material desires, and eventually the body itself.

Interestingly, the judgment of the CJI and Justice Khanwilkar in *Common Cause* holds that although Buddhism, Jainism and Hinduism are against euthanasia in the strict sense, the concept of the "good death" in each of these religions can be seen as reflecting the concept of dying with dignity.[48] More broadly, death can be seen within Indian religious tradition and philosophy as a union with the Divine, the greater Self.[49] In the Hindu epic of *The Mahabharata*, Bhisma, who had decided to remain celibate owing to various circumstances, was given in return the boon of *Iccha-mrityu*, or "the death of desires", meaning that he could choose the time of his death "as per [his] desire". This example demonstrates that a good death is considered the highest of rewards.

What about alleviation of the suffering of the Self? As per the famous bhajan *Bhaja Govindam* quoted at the beginning of this chapter, whilst the individual is to embrace pain, it is left to God to save the individual from pain and suffering. In Hindu and Buddhist philosophy, suffering is considered to be an eternal truth about life, to the extent that it is one of the noble truths of Buddhism. Hence, the desire to avoid pain is not celebrated. Pain is to be embraced and may depend on past-life deterministic forces such as *karma*, and freeing oneself of pain is not sufficient justification for bringing about death. Accordingly, the rejection of life-sustaining treatment to alleviate pain

[48] See J. Sikri in *Common Cause (A Registered Society)* v. *Union of India* (2018) 5 SCC 1, para. 54. However, for the view that there is a more sympathetic view of sacrificing one's life in Hinduism, as well as the spiritual, religious and political significance of doing so, see P. Bilimoria, "The Debate on Euthanasia in India" in P. Bilimoria et al. (eds.), *Gender, Justice, and Ecology*. Vol. II of *Indian Ethics* (New Delhi: Oxford University Press, 2015).

[49] For an account of end-of-life spirituality in various branches of Indian philosophy, see H. Inbadas, "Indian Philosophical Foundations of Spirituality at the End of Life" (2018) 23(4) *Mortality* 320. For an account of the different religious attitudes of Hindus towards the end of life, see S. Firth, "End-of-Life: A Hindu View" (2005) *Lancet* 366, 682–6.

and suffering, which will in turn bring about the person's death, would not be seen as in line with these religious beliefs.[50]

6.4.3 *The Medico-cultural Context*

In ancient India, physicians took an oath after completion of their studies. One of the commitments they made was that they would not try to prolong life in end-of-life situations or resort to what is known today as futile treatment.[51] In the West, however, medicine evolved on different principles. The original Hippocratic oath placed two important conditions on the practice of medicine. The first was to disallow euthanasia, and the second was to never conduct an abortion, with no exceptions.[52] In India, the Indian medical tradition was replaced by an interpretation of the Hippocratic formulation of doctors' duties in ways that stress the need to act paternalistically towards patients. Doctors in India, who may even have been favourably inclined towards self-determination at the end-of-life, were taught that life has to be preserved, at all costs if necessary.

The greater role of doctors and medical paternalism also have roots in Ayurvedic systems, where great faith is reposed in the medical community despite the issues of medical malpractice and institutional problems concerning hospital infrastructure. One can see a reflection of Ayurvedic ideas in doctors being seen as a rebirth of Dhanvantari, the lord of medicine. In Ayurvedic systems, there were codes of ethics, which can be found in the *Sushruta Samhita* and *Charaka Samhita*. The *Charaka Samhita*, for example, makes reference to autonomy and consent, although preference is afforded the physician in the case of, for instance, withholding the truth from the patient in his or her best interests, as opposed to full disclosure in order for him or her to make an informed

50 In any event, the identification of a self with a body that is suffering is questionable. As the texts of the dominant *Advaita* (non-dual) tradition, which focus on the emancipation of the individual *Aatman* or "self" from the illusion of the duality of the self and the larger consciousness (*Brahman*), suggest, the self should not be conceived of as attached to the physical body.

51 I.A. Menon and H.F. Haberman, "The Medical Students' Oath of Ancient India" (1970) 14(3) *Medical History* 295.

52 M.A. Faria Jr., "Utilitarianism and the Perversion of the Ethics of Hippocrates" (2000) 172(4) *The Western Journal of Medicine* 224.

decision.[53] Although medical paternalism and a larger role for doctors may in some jurisdictions result in greater reluctance to accept ADs (as individuals would presumably expect to defer to doctors about decisions at the end of life), this has not been the case in India. Instead, preference for the role of the physician in overseeing and enacting a bureaucratic process of reviewing the place and applicability of an AD has interestingly been accepted as a key component of the AD regime laid down by the Supreme Court, wherein medical practitioners have the greatest say in decision-making. This situation may well result from the fear of abuse by family members, as discussed previously, but is also consistent with the Indian medico-cultural context.

6.5 Survey Mapping the Level of AD Awareness

Autonomy, if it is to be realised, presupposes the knowledge required for an informed decision. Despite the legal permissions given by the Supreme Court, the common person in India remains unsure about the implications of AD legislation and the *Common Cause* ruling.

The question we come to now is this: to what extent is there awareness of the law as it currently stands? One way to understand perceptions of ADs is to conduct a survey amongst a broad swathe of people. To the best of our knowledge, no such survey had previously been undertaken in India since the *Common Cause* decision.[54]

6.5.1 Demographics

We conducted an online survey using Google Forms. The survey collected information from individuals who were internet users and had obtained at least a graduate degree in any field. Our respondents do not represent the Indian population in any way; rather the population we selected was a highly educated, elite group of people.[55] Our final sample

[53] See K.A. Tawalare et al., "Contribution of Ayurveda in Foundation of Basic Tenets of Bioethics" (2014) 35(4) *Ayu* 366.

[54] There have been a very small number of surveys, however, on the effectiveness of PADs. See, for example, B. Tekkalaki et al., "How Do Our Patients Respond to the Concept of Psychiatric Advance Directives? An Exploratory Study from India" (2018) 40(4) *Indian Journal of Psychological Medicine* 305.

[55] Graduates and above account for only 6.92 per cent (92 million) of the total population; see further Ministry of Human Resource Development, *All India Survey on Higher Education (AISHE: 2018-19)* (New Delhi: Government of India, 2019).

of 411 responses reflected a healthy mix of male and female respondents from the fields of medicine, science, the arts, engineering and law, with a mean 18.16 years of work experience. The responses were sorted by gender, qualifications and field of education for detailed analysis using simple statistical measures.

6.5.2 *The Findings*

In relation to their awareness of ADs, only 115 (27.9 per cent) of the respondents reported having some knowledge of ADs, meaning that 296 (72.1 per cent) had no such knowledge. Further questions about ADs were therefore not directed towards those with no knowledge of the subject matter. Amongst those who knew about such directives, 100 reported having thought about making them, but only 21 (18.2 per cent) had actually done so. Taking all respondents as a whole, only 5.1 per cent had prepared an AD.

We analysed the knowledge of respondents from the medical profession separately. Of the 147 medical professionals, 92 (62.6 per cent) had heard of ADs, whereas 55 (37.4 per cent) had not, and only nine (7.8 per cent) had actually made one. One question that we asked all respondents was whether, if they were unable to voice their preference about medical treatment, they would like to nominate someone as their proxy. We received a response from 226 respondents. Most (133, or 58.8 per cent) said they would want their spouse to act as their proxy. Seventy-one (31.4 per cent) chose their parents, and 18 chose family or their children. Only three said they would like a doctor to make decisions on their behalf if they were unable to do so. It is alarming that the doctors in our sample were only slightly better informed about ADs than our other respondents; roughly half were clueless.

Several findings emerge from these data. First, despite all of the benefits of ADs, not all are inclined to make them. Second, considerable effort is required to make ADs acceptable. Our survey revealed that although most of our respondents wanted autonomy over their medical treatment and the way in which they were treated, very few had an understanding of ADs, their legality or the process of making them.

The inference that can be drawn from our survey is that the likelihood of a well-educated Indian making an AD is rather slim. An added worry is that there appears to be little knowledge of ADs amongst medical professionals. Thus, the likelihood of a patient who has prepared an AD being treated by a medical practitioner with knowledge of ADs is remote.

This situation, added to the fact that responsibility lies with the medical practitioner, makes AD implementation a challenge. There is thus an urgent need for a campaign by governmental and non-governmental organisations to spread awareness of ADs, their advantages and the need for them. The Indian courts seek legal grounding in other common law jurisdictions, and yet ground-level adoption is often neglected. Whilst the governments of other countries have put huge effort into popularising ADs, no such effort has been seen in India. Without knowledge of ADs, they will remain an unrealised right.

6.6 Conclusion

India has come a long way in jurisprudence concerning end-of-life care, culminating in the current guidelines on ADs laid down by the Supreme Court of India, which remain the law of the land. There remain, however, various concerns about this regime. The first is in relation to the lengthy, bureaucratic and unrealistic procedure that the court has laid down for the creation of an AD. Whilst at first glance, the court's decision in *Common Cause* seems to have furthered decisional autonomy, the complex procedures it put in place may actually serve to disempower patients, reducing their control over decisions about their care and discouraging them from undergoing the AD process.

The second concern relates to the institutional dimension surrounding the legalisation of ADs. The *Common Cause* decision, a result of India's activist judiciary, raises questions about the separation of powers by showering rights on people without any democratic dialogue. Implementation is also a challenge, especially when new legal requirements are introduced without careful consideration of what is practically feasible in a healthcare context. Because of the different workings of the legislature and the judiciary, the idealism of the judiciary seldom translates into ground-level practices. The Health Ministry, for instance, has yet to hold a consultation meeting with stakeholders concerning the procedure for ADs.[56]

A third concern relates to how the law sits uncomfortably with the social reality of India, which is communitarian and family-based. Interestingly, despite the importance of the family being recognised in the PAD context, the courts have expressed concerns about the potential

[56] We are grateful to Dr Dhvani Mehta for this point.

for abuse by family members in the end-of-life context. Such concerns have not, however, translated into an endorsement of the person-centric approach that ADs encapsulate. Instead, a key role for healthcare professionals is envisaged, and looks to have been generally accepted.

In terms of the way forward, our survey demonstrates a significant lack of awareness of ADs, which needs to be remedied. Concerns over the lack of AD knowledge have also been expressed in the context of PADs.[57] One of the potential solutions has been to set up legal aid centres to spread awareness and afford access to vulnerable populations.[58] Such centres may be a way to educate the public about ADs, although the bureaucratic procedures will need to be streamlined if such directives are to be widely taken up by the population. At the hospital level, ethics committees could be empowered to keep a check on futile treatments and even make decisions where necessary.

[57] See A. Sarin, P. Murthy and S. Chatterjee, "Psychiatric Advance Directives: Potential Challenges in India" (2012) 9(2) *Indian Journal of Medical Ethics* 104, 106.

[58] Ibid., p. 107.

PART II

Semi-regulated Jurisdictions

7

The Proposed New Law on Advance Directives in Hong Kong: A Piecemeal Attempt at Codification?

DAISY CHEUNG & REBECCA LEE

7.1 Introduction

The population of Hong Kong is ageing rapidly. Twenty per cent of the population was aged 65 or above in 2021, a percentage that is projected to reach 34% by 2066.[1] Hong Kong also has the highest average life expectancy in the world.[2] The increasing number of older people, coupled with rising life expectancy and the impact of chronic illness on physical, psychological and social well-being, suggests that the demand for high-quality end-of-life palliative care services will only continue to increase.

Despite the ever-escalating demand for long-term care, end-of-life care in Hong Kong remains underdeveloped. According to the Economist Intelligence Unit's Quality of Death Index, an instrument used to highlight advances in, the challenges of and gaps in end-of-life care policy and infrastructure in 80 countries worldwide, Hong Kong ranks relatively low at 22nd.[3] A good example of the policy and infrastructure gaps in end-of-life care in Hong Kong is the poor uptake of the advance directive (AD), or a statement in which a competent person makes an advance healthcare decision that is to be implemented in the event that the person loses capacity in the future. This is despite the generally accepted view internationally, which is that the use of an AD can encourage discussions about patients' care-related preferences and values, as well as provide

[1] Census and Statistics Department, Government of the HKSAR, Summary results of the 2021 Population Census, https://www.censtatd.gov.hk/en/web_table.html?id=1A. See also *Hong Kong Population Projections 2017–2066* (Kowloon: 2017), p. 7.

[2] At 83 and 88 years old for males and females respectively. See, further, M.Y. Ni et al., "Understanding Longevity in Hong Kong: A Comparative Study with Long-living, High Income Countries" (2021) 6 *The Lancet Public Health* e919.

[3] The Economist Intelligence Unit, *The 2015 Quality of Death Index: Ranking Palliative Care across the World* (London: The Economist Intelligence Unit, 2015), p. 15.

clear documentation and facilitate regular review of such preferences and values.

This chapter first outlines the historical and current developments of ADs in Hong Kong. It then examines a number of legal and practical challenges in promoting the wider use of ADs in Hong Kong, including deficiencies in mental capacity law and inadequate promotion. The remainder of the chapter is divided into five parts. Section 7.2 traces the development of ADs in Hong Kong, leading up to the latest government proposal which is detailed in Section 7.3. Section 7.4 provides commentary on the legal obstacles that must be overcome for AD legislation to be successfully introduced in Hong Kong. Section 7.5 explores the local practice of ADs, as well as the sociocultural values and influences that shape this practice.

7.2 The Legal Framework: Historical Developments

Hong Kong currently lacks both a statute and local case law clarifying the legal status of ADs, although a legislative framework (discussed later in the chapter) has recently been proposed by the government. The common law principles in relation to informed consent with respect to medical treatment are generally applicable in making valid ADs to refuse life-sustaining treatment legally binding,[4] although, given the lack of relevant case law, it is unclear how such principles will be applied in individual cases. This is not to say that efforts to specify legal rules and/or guidance for ADs have not been made over the years. What follows is an outline of AD-related discussions and policy developments in the past two decades, which can be broadly divided into three stages.

7.2.1 Stage 1, 2002–2009: HKLRC Consultation

In 2002, the Hospital Authority, a statutory body that manages all government hospitals and institutions in Hong Kong, issued the first edition of the *Hospital Authority Guidelines on Life-Sustaining Treatment in the Terminally Ill*. This was primarily written as an elaboration of the section on "care for the terminally ill" in the Professional Code and

[4] See, for example, the case of *Re T (Adult: Refusal of Medical Treatment)* [1992] All ER 649.

Conduct of the Medical Council of Hong Kong,[5] but as part of its guidance, there was a brief discussion of ADs. In particular, it was stated that reference was to be made to the practice in the United Kingdom,[6] as detailed in section 10 of the British Medical Association Guideline on Withholding and Withdrawing Life-prolonging Medical Treatment (1999).[7] Apart from stating that a valid AD refusing life-sustaining treatment must be respected, section 10 provided various principles as to how validity of ADs were to be determined, as well as their legal effect.

In 2004, the Hong Kong Law Reform Commission (HKLRC) issued a public consultation paper entitled *Substitute Decision-Making and Advance Directives in Relation to Medical Treatment*,[8] the results of which were published in a report in 2006.[9] In this report, the HKLRC recommended that the government promote the concept of ADs under the existing common law framework instead of by legislation, as it was considered premature to legislate while the concept of ADs was still new to the community.[10] The government was recommended to review its position and reconsider the appropriateness of legislation once the community had become more familiar with the concept.[11] While noting that the lack of an agreed form of AD would likely lead to difficulties and uncertainty for both patients and doctors,[12] the HKLRC rejected the option of legislating a statutory form due to the prematurity of legislation at that stage.

In response to the HKLRC's report, the Hong Kong Food and Health Bureau (FHB) issued a consultation paper in 2009 entitled *Introduction of the Concept of Advance Directives in Hong Kong*,[13] with stakeholders consulted on (i) the procedures for making, altering and revoking ADs, (ii) the content of the information package on ADs for the public, and

[5] Hong Kong Hospital Authority, *Hospital Authority Guidelines on Life-Sustaining Treatment in the Terminally Ill* (April 2002), p. 3 (hereafter 'HA 2002 Guidelines').

[6] See HA 2002 Guidelines (note 5), p. 13.

[7] Included as Appendix 3 of the HA 2002 Guidelines (note 5).

[8] Hong Kong Law Reform Commission, *Substitute Decision-Making and Advance Directives in Relation to Medical Treatment: Consultation Paper* (July 2004).

[9] Hong Kong Law Reform Commission, *Substitute Decision-Making and Advance Directives in Relation to Medical Treatment: Report* (August 2006).

[10] Ibid., paras. 8.35 and 8.36.

[11] Ibid., para. 8.40.

[12] Ibid., para. 8.38.

[13] Food and Health Bureau, Government of the HKSAR, *Introduction of the Concept of Advance Directives in Hong Kong* (December 2009).

(iii) the need to promulgate guidelines for handling ADs. The majority of views it received agreed that a non-legislative approach to AD promotion should be adopted in Hong Kong.

7.2.2 Stage 2, 2010–2019: Hospital Authority Initiatives

In 2010, the Hospital Authority issued *Guidance for Hospital Authority Clinicians on Advance Directives in Adults*[14] for the reference of clinicians working in Hospital Authority hospitals.[15] This contained a model AD form that was based on that of the HKLRC. The guidance was then updated in 2014. The changes introduced included (i) the provision of a shorter version of the AD form for terminally ill patients refusing CPR only and (ii) the extension of the scope of application of ADs such that, in addition to (a) terminally ill and (b) in a persistent vegetative state or a state of irreversible coma, a new category of 'other end-stage irreversible life-limiting condition[s]' was added.

In 2014, the Hospital Authority also issued *Guidelines on Do-Not-Attempt Cardiopulmonary Resuscitation* (DNACPR). Under these guidelines, the doctors in charge of non-hospitalised patients could sign a DNACPR form on their patients' behalf if there was a valid and applicable AD refusing cardiopulmonary resuscitation (CPR). The doctors signing this form would certify that the AD was valid, and that the patient was already in a condition in which the AD would apply.[16] This was designed to assist 'emergency rescue personnel' to respect the patient's advance decision,[17] but this approach was not accepted by the ambulance services in Hong Kong[18] due to concern over the 'duty to resuscitate' in the Fire Services Ordinance (FSO). This will be discussed further later in the chapter.

14 Hong Kong Hospital Authority, *Guidance for HA Clinicians on Advance Directives in Adults* (July 2010).

15 All public hospitals in Hong Kong fall under the jurisdiction of the Hospital Authority. Private hospitals are not regulated by the Hospital Authority, and therefore these guidance documents would not apply directly.

16 Hong Kong Hospital Authority, *Guidelines on Do-Not-Attempt Cardiopulmonary Resuscitation* (October 2014).

17 Food and Health Bureau, Government of the HKSAR, *End-of-Life Care: Legislative Proposals on Advance Directives and Dying in Place* (September 2019), para. 4.32. (hereafter 'End-of-Life Care Consultation Paper 2019').

18 C.Y. Tse, "Advance Directives in Hong Kong" (November 2018) *Hong Kong Society of Palliative Medicine Newsletter* 6, 8.

7.2.3 Stage 3, 2019–Present: Reforms

In 2019, the FHB issued a public consultation paper entitled *End-of-Life Care: Legislative Proposals on Advance Directives and Dying in Place*[19] to consult the public on several proposals, including (i) whether to codify the current common law position in respect of ADs and strengthen the safeguards attached to them and (ii) whether to remove the legislative impediments to AD implementation by emergency rescue personnel. In the consultation paper, the FHB acknowledged that the lack of AD legislation in Hong Kong had created practical difficulties in AD implementation and, in particular, posed two concerns.[20] First, as a result of the lack of legal guidance on ADs, healthcare professionals may be unwilling to initiate discussions with patients about ADs or implement their ADs owing to concerns that they may not have legal protection in doing so. Second, it is unclear whether an AD would supersede another statutory provision if the two were in conflict.[21] In July 2020, the FHB released a consultation report[22] mapping out the way forward. Significantly, according to the report, the government considered that it was now an appropriate time to consider AD legislation. Introducing a consistent legal framework for ADs could remove conflicts with other laws and policies and afford protection to treatment providers (including health care professionals and emergency rescue personnel) acting in good faith and with reasonable care.

7.3 The Legal Framework: Legislative Proposal

The legislative framework proposed by the government in its 2019 consultation paper is built on four fundamental principles:

(i) The patient's right to self-determination must prevail in the case of conflict between the wishes of the patient and those of his family members.

19 See End-of-Life Care Consultation Paper 2019 (note 17).

20 Ibid., para. 3.2.

21 The consultation paper gives two examples, namely conflicting provisions in the Fire Services Ordinance and the Mental Health Ordinance. See further, End-of-Life Care Consultation Paper 2019 (note 17), para. 3.2(b).

22 Food and Health Bureau, Government of the HKSAR, *End-of-Life Care: Legislative Proposals on Advance Directives and Dying in Place* (July 2020) (hereafter 'End-of-Life Care Consultation Report 2020').

(ii) A valid and applicable AD overrides treatment decisions based on a treatment provider's interpretation of the patient's best interests.
(iii) Individuals have primary responsibility for ensuring that the original copy of their AD is presented to treatment providers as proof of a valid AD.
(iv) Sufficient safeguards need to be provided to preserve lives – if any grounds for doubt about the validity or applicability of an AD, treatment providers must continue to provide clinically indicated emergency life-sustaining treatments.

The key features of the legislative proposal,[23] which for the most part track the guidance issued by the Hospital Authority, are as follows:

7.3.1 *Definition and Scope*

An AD must be made by a mentally competent person who is aged 18 or above.[24] Life-sustaining treatments (including artificial nutrition and hydration) are considered a type of medical treatment that can be withheld or withdrawn from a patient in accordance with his AD. The pre-specified conditions of an AD include (i) terminal illness; (ii) a persistent vegetative state or state of irreversible coma; and (iii) other end-stage irreversible life-limiting conditions. An AD cannot include (i) a refusal of basic and/or palliative care that is essential to keep a person comfortable, such as nursing care and pain relief; (ii) a refusal of the offer of food and drink by mouth; or (iii) anything that is against the law, such as euthanasia.

In terms of the form of the AD, the government is proposing to use a non-statutory model rather than a statutory prescribed form.[25] However, ADs not made in that form would still be accepted if they contained statements that are clearly written and unambiguous. A person may choose to adopt other AD forms to set out other (additional) pre-specified conditions.

[23] As laid out in the End-of-Life Care Consultation Paper 2019 (note 17) and the End-of-Life Care Consultation Report 2020 (note 22).

[24] Currently, the only patients permitted to sign ADs within the Hospital Authority are those with advanced illnesses. The government proposes making it permissible at any time as long as the person concerned is mentally capable and not subject to any undue influence. This is consistent with the practice in many jurisdictions overseas, which encourage individuals to make an AD when they are well and healthy.

[25] This is in contrast to the DNACPR form, which the government proposes to be in a statutory-prescribed form.

An AD will take effect when the person concerned no longer has the capacity to make healthcare decisions. An AD will not be applicable (i) if the patient has the capacity to make a decision at the time the treatment concerned is proposed; (ii) if the decision to be made concerns treatments or conditions not specified in the AD; or (iii) if there are reasonable grounds for believing that the patient did not anticipate the current circumstances and, if he had, he might have made a different decision.

7.3.2 Formalities

Turning to the formalities, the government proposes mandating that the making and modification of an AD must be in writing to be legally valid, which would also serve to reduce uncertainty and potential disputes concerning validity. In contrast, no unnecessary hurdles should be imposed upon those wishing to revoke an AD, and so it is proposed that both verbal and written revocations be considered valid.

As to witnessing, the government has proposed adopting the same arrangements as those currently practised by the Hospital Authority, of which there are two notable features. The first is that the making and modification of an AD requires two witnesses, one of whom must be a medical practitioner. As part of the witnessing requirement, a capacity test for the making of the AD is included, namely that the medical practitioner should be satisfied that the person has capability to make an AD, and has been informed of the nature and effect of the AD and the consequences of refusing the treatments specified in the AD.[26] The second is that revocation can be made verbally or in writing. No witness is required for written revocation, but at least one witness who has no interest in the estate of the person making the AD is required for verbal revocation, and a second witness is required for the report of verbal revocation made by a single family member or carer. A person can also revoke his own AD by tearing it up or otherwise destroying it or asking some other person to do so in his presence and by his direction.

There will not be any central registry for AD, but a flagging alert is currently set up within the Hospital Authority Clinical Management System (CMS) to facilitate communication, even though the information contained therein is used only as a reference. The government is currently considering the feasibility of leveraging the existing Electronic

[26] See End-of-Life Care Consultation Report 2020 (note 22), para. 4.7.

Health Record Sharing System (eHRSS) to store and allow access to AD records by designated healthcare professionals and of accepting certified true copies of ADs to ensure that a patient's trusted family members or carers can produce the AD in timely fashion. Original AD documents would still be required as proof because storing records in the eHRSS is voluntary and there might be the possibility of a time lag between the latest status of the AD and its record in the eHRSS. Further, given that it may not be practicable to require emergency rescue personnel to first find out the eHRSS record of an AD while carrying out resuscitation at the same time, the government is also proposing that emergency rescue personnel may rely on the production of an original AD document attached to a signed DNACPR form, and it would be the responsibility of the individual/family to draw the attention of emergency rescue personnel to the existence of the AD.

7.3.3 *Safeguards*

The following safeguards are required to be implemented to ensure the validity of an AD. First, in normal circumstances, the original copy of the AD should be presented. If a valid AD is said to exist, but the original copy is not immediately available, the treatment provider should continue to provide emergency life-sustaining treatment while waiting for clarification. However, if the treatment provider (e.g. a clinical team) knows that a valid and applicable AD exists and the patient's family members agree, then the patient's advance refusal of such treatment should be respected.[27]

Second, the AD should be sufficiently clear and not under challenge, for example on the grounds of undue influence or lack of capacity. If an AD is challenged at the scene, its validity must be regarded as in doubt, and the treatment provider should continue to provide emergency life-sustaining treatment while waiting for clarification. Third, the AD must not have been withdrawn. Finally, the person must not have done something that clearly goes against the AD, thereby suggesting that he has changed his mind.

Safeguards should also be afforded to treatment providers. They should not incur any civil or criminal liability (i) for carrying out or continuing a treatment if, at the time, they reasonably believe that a valid

[27] This arrangement, while retaining flexibility, is likely to cause confusion and variation in implementation.

and applicable AD does not exist or (ii) for the consequences of withholding or withdrawing a treatment from an individual if, at the time, they reasonably believe that a valid and applicable AD exists. The same applies to CPR emergency rescue with/without a DNACPR form.

7.3.4 *Non-hospital Settings*

In an emergency situation, when an unconscious patient with impending cardiac arrest is seen by emergency rescue personnel, it can be difficult for them to tell whether the patient is in a condition specified in his AD. Accordingly, the Hospital Authority developed guidelines and a DNACPR form (specifying that CPR not be performed on a person when cardiac arrest is anticipated) for non-hospitalised patients in 2014. Doctors who sign the DNACPR form certify that the AD is valid and applicable. The government is now proposing the following: (i) that after ADs are legislated, emergency rescue personnel should respect a valid and applicable AD presented to them; (ii) to amend the FSO accordingly to enable such personnel to accept DNACPR forms (with or without an AD);[28] and (iii) to use a statutory prescribed DNACPR form for the sake of simplicity, instead of a non-statutory prescribed form.

7.4 Discussion

While the move to legislate on ADs is a welcome one, there remain legal obstacles to overcome. The government has stated that it is not prepared to enact all-encompassing legislation on mental incapacity, which would impact upon such areas as ADs, healthcare decision-making by attorneys and guardianship.[29] It is also unlikely for the government to overhaul the outdated mental health legal regime in Hong Kong. Consequently, the piecemeal attempt of the government at codifying the law on ADs is inadequate for two reasons. The first relates to inconsistencies or ambiguities in existing law. In addition to proposing separate legislation on ADs, the HK government is also currently proposing new legislation on

[28] It is not proposing, however, that ambulance or fire personnel accept ADs per se, as it may not be within their expertise to determine the applicability of an AD (which requires confirmation that a pre-specified medical condition has arisen).

[29] See End-of-Life Care Consultation Report 2020 (note 22), para. 5.8.

continuing powers of attorney, which will cover health, welfare and other personal matters. These new laws will add to existing decision-making tools, such as enduring powers of attorney. Such a piecemeal approach to legal regulation fails to take into account the fact that these are all components in the overall promotion of autonomy of the individual concerned, and need to be viewed in this larger context. Without an overhaul of mental health law in Hong Kong that considers all of these tools in a holistic manner, there may be ambiguities in the definitions of legal terminology and unclear overlapping boundaries or even inconsistencies between different legal tools.[30]

The second reason is that the lack of an overarching mental capacity test results in ambiguity as to what the test for mental capacity in relation to the making of ADs in Hong Kong should be. As discussed previously, the proposed formulation is that the medical practitioner must be satisfied that the person has the capability to make an AD, but what this capability entails is not further elaborated upon. There are several formulations of the capacity test that may apply, as detailed next.

Common law. The common law test for capacity that applies in Hong Kong is the test as developed by case law in the United Kingdom prior to the enactment of the Mental Capacity Act 2005. The steps of this test are generally taken to be the three steps as described in the foundational case of *Re C*[31], namely: (i) whether the patient is capable of understanding and retaining the treatment information; (ii) whether the patient believes it; and (iii) whether the patient is capable of weighing that information, balancing risks and needs. In the context of ADs, further principles as to the scope of anticipatory refusals can be found from the cases of *Re T* and *Bland*[32]. Taken together, these cases and principles demonstrate how one's capacity to make an AD should be assessed, looking at both (i) the individual's ability to refuse a particular medical treatment and (ii) whether or not the individual intended for the anticipatory refusal to apply to the future circumstances in question.

[30] These piecemeal attempts are also unlikely to satisfy the requirements of article 12 of United Nations Convention on the Rights of Persons with Disabilities, which require states parties to take appropriate measures to provide access by persons with disabilities to the support they may require in exercising their legal capacity (article 12.3).

[31] *Re C (Adult: Refusal of Medical Treatment)* [1994] 1 All ER 819.

[32] *Airedale NHS Trust* v. *Bland* [1993] AC 789.

Mental Health Ordinance. The MHO contains a different capacity test for the consent to treatment of mentally incapacitated persons, which, for this part of the MHO, is defined as either (i) a 'patient', or a person suffering or appearing to be suffering from mental disorder or (ii) a 'mentally handicapped person', or a person with sub-average general intellectual functioning with deficiencies in adaptive behaviour.[33,34] The test, as contained in section 59ZB(2) of the MHO, is whether the person is capable of understanding the general nature and effect of the treatment or special treatment. Putting the flaws of this test to one side,[35] this is a *different* test for capacity to the consent of treatment that only applies to individuals defined as mentally incapacitated in the MHO, suggesting that, for such individuals, the section 59ZB(2) test should be used instead of the common law *Re C* test to assess the individual's ability to refuse that treatment. If this is to be the correct approach, how do we justify and reconcile the fact that two different tests are being used in the same context?

Hospital Authority guidelines. In addition to the two legal tests described previously, other relevant capacity tests have been laid out in various guidelines issued by the Hospital Authority. While these tests are not legally binding, they constitute the practice guidance that doctors in the public sector follow when implementing the law, and thus are worthy of consideration. Two formulations of the test for capacity are laid out here:

(i) 'A competent adult is defined as one with decision-making capacity, which consists of the elements of (i) the ability to understand the medical information presented; (ii) the ability to reason and consider this information in relation to his own personal values and goals; and (iii) the ability to communicate meaningfully.' (from the *Hospital Authority's Guidelines on In-Hospital Resuscitation Decisions*, issued in 1998).

(ii) 'To demonstrate capacity to refuse treatment, individuals should be able to:

33 There is another definition that applies for the purposes of Part II of the MHO, which deals with the management of the property and affairs of mentally incapacitated persons (as defined in the MHO).

34 While a very problematic definition of incapacity, a discussion of why this is the case is beyond the scope of this chapter. See further D. Cheung, "Mental Health Law in Hong Kong: The Civil Context" (2018) 48 *Hong Kong Law Journal* 461.

35 See further Cheung, ibid.

a. Understand in simple language what the medical treatment is, its purpose and nature and why it is being proposed;
b. Understand its principal benefits, risks and alternatives;
c. Understand in broad terms what will be the consequences of not receiving the proposed treatment;
d. Retain the information for long enough to make an effective decision;
e. Use the information and weigh it in the balance as part of the decision-making process;
f. Make a free choice (i.e. free from pressure).' (Adopted from the British Medical Association in the Hospital Authority's most recent *Guidelines on Life-sustaining Treatment in the Terminally Ill* (2020)).

Both of these formulations are notably different from the two legal tests described previously, with the 1998 and 2020 formulations additionally requiring a higher level of reflection and a voluntariness requirement, respectively, which are not generally required for decisional capacity as defined by the law. In addition to contributing to the chaos that is the definition of mental capacity in this context in Hong Kong, the fact that the Hospital Authority saw it necessary to lay out its own tests for capacity suggests that they felt that the current position was inadequate, or at least not clear enough.

Thus, while the legislative initiative for ADs is no doubt welcome, the importance of legislating a unified, statutory capacity test cannot be understated. The unwillingness of the government to deal with this issue may cause ambiguity and difficulty in the implementation of ADs by medical practitioners in the long run.

7.5 Local Practice, Value Commitments and Sociocultural Influences

Turning to the practice of ADs in Hong Kong, the number of ADs signed in recent years has been on the rise. The number of ADs signed by Hospital Authority patients between the years of 2012–18 is as follows:[36]

[36] Government of the HKSAR, "LCQ15: Advance Directives in relation to Medical Treatment", 22 May 2019. These figures do not include, however, (i) the number of valid ADs received, (ii) the number of ADs that were implemented, and (iii) the number of ADs produced that were not made in accordance with the Hospital Authority's model form.

Year	Month	Number of ADs signed
2012	From August 21 to December 31	150
2013	From January 1 to December 31	325
2014	From January 1 to December 31	491
2015	From January 1 to December 31	706
2016	From January 1 to December 31	937
2017	From January 1 to December 31	1395
2018	From January 1 to December 31	1557
Total number of ADs signed		5561

There has been some suggestion that this tenfold increase in the number of signed ADs is not indicative of an increase in awareness or acceptance of ADs generally, but rather a result of the changing demographic of service users of the Hospital Authority, who take care of a disproportionately high percentage of persons with life-limiting illnesses.[37] This is consistent with empirical research that has demonstrated both a low level of awareness and a low uptake of ADs in Hong Kong.[38]

While the general lack of awareness about ADs may be readily explainable by inadequate promotion and education,[39] an interesting phenomenon that warrants further investigation is what appears to be a discrepancy between positive attitudes towards ADs and the actual making of ADs. For example, Chan et al.'s study (2019) found that, while only 368 of their participants (18.4%) had heard of ADs, the vast majority of those (80.2%, or 295 people) said they had made or intended

[37] Service utilisation of Hospital Authority hospitals is increasingly being taken up by these patients, particularly in their last year of life. This is further demonstrated by the fact that 90% of deaths occur in Hospital Authority hospitals. See further J. Yuen, "Advance Directives and End-of-Life Decision-Making in Hong Kong: A Medical Perspective", presentation given at the "Living Will, Living Well: Advance Directives across Asia" webinar on 2 October 2020.

[38] In relation to lack of awareness, see, for example, C.W.H. Chan et al., "Prevalence, Perception, and Predictors of Advance Directives among Hong Kong Chinese: A Population-Based Survey" (2019) 16 *International Journal of Environmental Research and Public Health* 365; F.H. Ting and E. Mok, "Advance Directives and Life-sustaining Treatment: Attitudes of Hong Kong Chinese Elders with Chronic Disease" (2011) 17 *Hong Kong Medical Journal* 105; and E.C. Hui et al., "Medical Information, Decision-Making and Use of Advance Directives by Chinese Cancer Patients in Hong Kong" (2016) 8 *Asian Bioethics Review* 109. In relation to low uptake, see Chan et al., Prevalence, Perception and Predictors (see earlier citation in this footnote).

[39] See also Chan et al., Prevalence, Perception and Predictors, ibid., where 72.7% of their 2002 participants expressed the view that ADs were inadequately promoted in the community.

to make an AD.[40] Out of these 295 people, however, only 11 of them had actually made an AD (i.e. only 3.7%). While not all studies have been able to demonstrate such a high level of positivity in attitude towards ADs,[41] there remains a significant discrepancy between reported attitudes towards ADs and actual uptake of ADs.

Although the reason for this discrepancy requires further study, some preliminary comments may be offered. There is of course the question of whether such positive attitudes towards ADs as reported by patients are reflective of their true preferences, but, assuming that they are, there appears to be some difficulty in the translation of that preference into action. This could be due to several reasons, two of which are briefly explored here. The first is resistance from family members and/or caregivers. Studies have shown that family members often feel compelled to maintain the patient's life, and are unwilling to forgo life-sustaining treatment. This stems from a strong belief in Confucian filial piety, according to which 'everything must be done' to save the patient, even if this may not be in line with the patient's own preferences.[42] This resistance from close family members can be a crucial factor contributing to the failure of the person to make an AD, because the unit of decision-making in Chinese culture, and in particular medical decision-making, is generally seen as the family.[43] As Fan and Li

40 See Chan et al, Prevalence, Perception and Predictors (note 38). This level of positivity towards ADs is consistent with L.W. Chu et al., "Advance Directive and End-of-Life Care Preferences among Chinese Nursing Home Residents in Hong Kong" (2011) 12 *Journal of the American Medical Directors Association* 143, where it was found that 88% of a sample of 1600 older Chinese adults residing in nursing homes in Hong Kong expressed a preference for having an AD concerning their medical treatment in the future.

41 See, for example, Ting and Mok, Advance Directives and Life-sustaining Treatment (note 38), which found that 49% of their 219 participants would sign an AD after they had been informed about the concept and Hui et al., Medical Information (note 38), which found that 33% of their 288 participants would sign an AD after they were informed about the concept.

42 R.Y.N. Chung et al., "Examining the Gaps and Issues of End-of-Life Care among Older Population through the Lens of Socioecological Model – A Multi-Method Qualitative Study of Hong Kong" (2020) 17 *International Journal of Environmental Research and Public Health* 5072, 5077. See also T. Kwok, S. Twinn and E. Yan, "The Attitudes of Chinese Family Caregivers of Older People with Dementia towards Life Sustaining Treatments" (2007) 58 *Journal of Advanced Nursing* 256, where it is argued that filial piety contributes to the difficulties in making decisions related to life-sustaining treatment, particularly if the decision to forgo such treatment is seen as incompatible with one's filial duties.

43 See, for example, Y. Cong, "Doctor–Family–Patient Relationship: The Chinese Paradigm of Informed Consent" (2004) 29 *Journal of Medicine and Philosophy* 149 and H.M. Chan, "Informed Consent Hong Kong Style: An Instance of Moderate Familism" (2004) 29

have argued, families are autonomous entities that are themselves the source of legitimating authority.[44] Because the family is the autonomous unit, medical decisions need to be made by the family as a whole, and not by the person herself.[45] This means that where there is strong objection from the family, the person will not likely proceed with an AD even if that is her preference. There is thus a need to encourage not only education and promotion targeted towards individuals who might wish to make ADs, but also their family members, such that open discussions between family members about one's end-of-life preferences can be encouraged. This, in turn, will make it more likely that family support for a decision to make an AD can be obtained, making the individual more likely to proceed with the AD.

The second reason is the lack of effective communication and coordination on the part of healthcare and other professionals regarding the making of ADs. While a person may be inclined to make an AD, a number of institutional factors may have a large effect on whether this is put into action. Cheung et al., for example, present a compelling case of "unprepared healthcare professionals and healthcare system" as one of the barriers to advance care planning more generally.[46] One of the various examples of this was a patient's experience with an oncologist, who kept persuading him to receive treatment despite an expressed reluctance to receive futile life-sustaining treatment. Chan et al.'s study also sheds some light on the importance of the role of healthcare professionals. When asked, the majority of their participants expressed that they would agree to making ADs (to varying degrees) in the following scenarios: (i) if healthcare professionals can provide a clear explanation and recommendation on ADs, (ii) if there is effective communication and coordination among healthcare professionals at different institutes to execute their decisions, and (iii) if they could have a thorough discussion

Journal of Medicine and Philosophy 195. More recently, see J.T.K. Cheung et al., "Barriers to Advance Care Planning: a Qualitative Study of Seriously Ill Chinese Patients and Their Families" (2020) 19 *BMC Palliative Care* 80. There is, however, evidence suggesting that this is not such a straightforward picture. See, for example, Hui et al., Medical Information (note 38), where the number of patients who preferred to make decisions alone exceeded those who invited family members to be decision-making partners.

44 R. Fan and B. Li, "Truth-Telling in Medicine: The Confucian View" (2004) 29 *Journal of Medicine and Philosophy* 179, 188.

45 C.Y. Tse and J. Tao, "Strategic Ambiguities in the Process of Consent: Role of the Family in Decisions to Forgo Life-Sustaining Treatment for Incompetent Elderly Patients" (2004) 29 *Journal of Medicine and Philosophy* 207, 212.

46 Cheung et al., Barriers to Advance Care Planning (note 43).

and follow-up with health professionals about ADs. This demonstrates the importance of healthcare professionals in facilitating the process of making an AD, and is consistent with the significant trust that is placed in medical practitioners by patients in Chinese culture.[47]

7.6 Conclusion

In light of Hong Kong's rapidly ageing population, and the resulting, inevitable increase in the demand for high-quality end-of-life palliative care services, there is a crucial need to identify and examine policy and infrastructure gaps in end-of-life care in Hong Kong. One key area that needs to be addressed is the regulation and implementation of the AD, an important tool that encourages discussions about end-of-life care and allows for an individual's wishes to be clearly documented and carried out. This chapter has first examined the legal and institutional framework of ADs in Hong Kong, in particular the government's latest proposal in legislating ADs which is a positive step in the right direction despite some remaining legal obstacles to overcome. The chapter then highlighted the socio-familial influences that may hinder the government's attempt to expand the take up of ADs. In a society where the family is often seen as the unit for healthcare decision-making, and Confucian doctrines like filial piety are a driving force behind the behaviour of family members at the end of life, the AD is perhaps even more important as a way to initiate end-of-life care discussions with one's family, so as to make clear one's wishes to the family and engender support from the family for one's end-of-life care preferences.

Hong Kong has come a long way since the Hospital Authority first included a discussion of ADs in its 2002 *Guidelines for Life-sustaining Treatment in the Terminally Ill.* While the government's proposal for AD legislation is a significant step towards facilitating large-scale uptake of ADs across Hong Kong, there remain both legal and practical obstacles that need to be confronted. In relation to the former, the validity and application of an AD rely heavily on a workable and consistent definition of mental capacity, which is something that Hong Kong does not currently have and will not likely have in the near future. In relation to the latter, the inadequacy of promotion and education about ADs needs to be tackled on a systematic basis, to address the clear gaps in awareness

[47] See, for example, K.W. Bowman and P.A. Singer, "Chinese Seniors' Perspectives on End-of-Life Decisions" (2001) 53 *Social Science & Medicine* 455.

across Hong Kong society. This promotion and education needs to target not only individuals who may make ADs, but also family members and caregivers, whose insufficient understanding of ADs may currently prevent them from supporting the making of ADs by their family members.[48] Improvement of support from healthcare professionals at the institutional level is another key area that needs to be urgently addressed. Finally, because empirical research in this area in Hong Kong has mostly focused on the making of ADs, there is little to no information about the interpretation and implementation of ADs by healthcare professionals. This is a gap that needs to be addressed – a better grasp of how ADs are implemented after they are signed is crucial to our understanding of ADs in the Hong Kong context.

[48] See also Kwok, Twinn and Yan, Attitudes of Chinese Family Caregivers (note 42), for a discussion regarding how the lack of knowledge about life-sustaining treatment may compound the cultural bias of family members and caregivers in refusing to forgo life-sustaining treatment even in critical illness.

8

The Law and Practice of Advance Directives in the Islamic Republic of Iran

ZAIN ABBAS SYED, EHSAN SHAMSI-GOOSHKI & ALIREZA PARSAPOOR

8.1 Introduction

Unlike other patient populations, end-of-life patients suffering a terminal illness often lose the capacity to make healthcare decisions. Advance directives (ADs) are one method for addressing such loss of capacity. They permit the decisions of competent patients about future treatments to be recorded for enactment if/when they lose mental capacity.

At present, physicians in the Islamic Republic of Iran tend to expend, often reluctantly, numerous resources caring for patients approaching the end of life. In fact, in a 2015 *JAMA* study comparing 16 Asian countries, Iranian physicians were among the least likely to withhold or withdraw treatment when presented with two scenarios of patients with no real chance of recovering a meaningful life.[1] Their response may have been influenced by the absence of ADs allowing the refusal of futile life-sustaining interventions in end-of-life patients, which are often demanded by relatives, as well as the lack of legislative and regulatory support for an alternative approach. A lack of hospice and in-patient/community palliative care services also provides Iranian physicians with few alternatives. The current situation imposes a significant financial burden on Iran's predominantly publicly funded national healthcare system, as well as on patients and their relatives, and results in suboptimal patient-centred outcomes during terminal illness.

There is therefore reason to believe that ADs could play a useful role in reducing futile healthcare expenditure on and interventions for end-of-life patients, alleviating guilt among relatives for taking decisions to withdraw/avoid futile treatments and promoting patient autonomy in a

[1] J. Phua et al., "Withholding and Withdrawal of Life-Sustaining Treatments in Intensive Care Units in Asia" (2015) 175(3) *JAMA Internal Medicine* 363.

healthcare culture that is largely family centric. AD implementation must, however, be sensitive to Iranian culture and social norms, including respect for the Islamic doctrine to which the nation and its infrastructure subscribe. Unfortunately, Islamic discourse on end-of-life healthcare ethics is rife with controversy, including on such issues as defining and determining death, the limits of personal autonomy and the freedom to refuse life-sustaining medical interventions even as a competent patient let alone once capacity has been lost. Therefore, the typical paradigm of honouring patient wishes, as expressed in an AD, to optimise patient-centred outcomes is not easily translatable in Iran.

Our discussion begins with a brief introduction to the history/culture of medical ethics and law in Iran. We then discuss the current legal status of ADs in Iran, including the criteria for their validity and their reliance on a surrogate decision-maker. We next reflect on the multitude of factors affecting the current (lack of) AD implementation in Iranian hospitals and community healthcare settings, including a critical-normative reflection on cultural, Islamic, legislative and infrastructural factors. We conclude by recommending a model for advance end-of-life decision-making in Iran. Although ADs can apply to a vast range of end-of-life treatment decisions such as artificial nutrition/hydration, resuscitation and hospital admission, our main example of AD application pertains to the withholding of life-sustaining treatment from terminally ill, mentally incapacitated patients. We also focus on ADs in the medical as opposed to psychiatric setting.

8.2 A History of Medical Ethics and Law in the Islamic Republic of Iran

Historically, the Iranian Zoroastrian medical tradition featured several commonalities with the Hippocratic tradition, although the latter's influence took hold during the Hellenistic period following Alexander III of Macedon's invasion of Iran and the subsequent migration of Nestorian Christians and Neo-Platonists to the interdisciplinary school of Gondhishapour in the then capital of the Iranian kingdom. Islam then entered the Iranian establishment in the seventh-century Sassanid period. The subsequent Golden Era of Iranian-Islamic medicine inspired the expansion of Hippocratic/Galenic medical ethical discourse, as seen in books such as *Ādāb al-Ṫabīb* (*Practical Ethics of the Physician*) by Al-Ruhawi, as well as Islamic medical theo-legal doctrine surrounding abortion, physician liability, patient consent and surrogate decision-making. However, owing to the prevalence of *Ash'ariy* thinking, which opposed the use of philosophical reasoning in the derivation of ethics, most Islamic works on medical ethics followed a virtue ethics-based approach without reference to theoretical/religious reasoning. That approach continued until the establishment of modern medical schools in Iran in the twentieth century. However, the Islamic Revolution of 1979 gave rise to a novel bioethical movement in Iran, with the [Shia] *Mu'tazali* approach demonstrating that a reason-based juristic methodology was effective in responding to sensitive, modern bioethical issues, cementing the role of religious reasoning and derivation (through theology, law and ethics) as a tangible objective and standard of medical practice.[2]

In 1979, Ayatollah Ruhollah Khomeini, a jurisprudent-cleric from the Holy City of Qom, spearheaded a popular revolution to depose the Pahlavi monarchy in Iran. Widespread public discontent led the nation to reject the monarchy and vote in favour of an Islamic theocratic democracy, at the heart of which lay the doctrine of the Guardianship of the Jurist,[3] granting divine authority to said Islamic Jurist to establish a government serving the interests of the Muslim nation, including the protection and propagation of its religious identity and infusion of Islamic doctrine into its state and public institutions. In the years since, Iran has experienced major academic and technological advances, including multidisciplinary engagement in the rapidly expanding field of Islamic bioethics/law, which has led to the ratification and implementation of several medical laws, including laws on the therapeutic termination of pregnancy, assisted reproductive technology, organ donation and brain death, as well as the integration of bioethics teaching into undergraduate medical syllabi and establishment of hospital ethics committees and national bioethics research centres. Thus, medical ethics is now among the most rapidly expanding, topical and translational academic fields in Iran.

8.3 The Regulation of Biomedical Ethics in Iran

To appreciate the legal position of ADs in Iran, one must first appreciate the basic structure of the Iranian Government and legislative apparatus.

[2] E. Shamsi-Gooshki, *Ethical, Legal and Jurisprudential Aspects of Do-Not-Resuscitate Orders in the Health System of Islamic Republic of Iran, in School of Traditional Medicine* (Tehran: Shahid Beheshti University of Medical Sciences, 2013).

[3] M.T.M. Yazdi, *A Cursory Glance at the Theory of Wilayat alFaqih* (Qom: Ahlulbayt World Assembly, 2003).

Essentially, the public elects the President, Members of Parliament and the Assembly of Experts. The latter consists of a chamber of religious jurists tasked with appointing the country's Supreme Leader (*Waliy-i-Faqih*), who must be a religious jurist. The Supreme Leader and Parliament together appoint the Guardian Council consisting of six lawyers and six Islamic jurists, whose tasks include the ratification (or rejection) of laws passed by Parliament based on whether they are in keeping with *Shariah* (Islamic law) and the Constitution. In the event of disagreement between the Guardian Council and Parliament, an Expediency Council appointed by the Supreme Leader mediates a resolution. Importantly, Iran has a Romano-civil legal system, although, unlike in other civil law countries such as France, Iran recognises the legally binding nature of a *fatwa* (edict/judgment) issued by an Islamic jurist in areas for which there is no statute or by-law (Article 167, the Constitution).[4]

Today, medical practice in Iran is governed at three levels: by statute laws, executive by-laws and official regulations/guidelines. The latter two gain legal standing through acts of legislation that empower state ministries/councils to implement by-laws or official regulations, as per Article 138 of the Constitution,[5] which grants individual ministers the right to "frame regulations and issue circulars in matters within their jurisdiction". This three-level hierarchy is demonstrated in the legal regulation of organ donation in Iran:

- Statute law: The Law on Organ Transplantation of Dead Patients or Patients in Whom Brain Death Has Been Confirmed (2000) - Parliament of the Islamic Republic of Iran-.[6]
- Executive by-law: Ratified by the Council of Ministers as per the recommendation of the Ministry of Health and Medical Education (MOHME), including particulars of the Statute's implementation and standards.[7]
- Official regulation: Published by the National Clinical Ethics Committee (and ratified by MOHME) on the necessity to confirm

[4] The Constitution of the Islamic Republic of Iran. Last reviewed in 1989.

[5] Ibid.

[6] Parliament of the Islamic Republic of Iran, "قانون پیوند اعضای بیماران فوت شده یا بیمارانی که مرگ مغزی آنان مسلم است" [The Law on Organ Transplantation of Dead Patients or Patients in Whom Brain Death Has Been Confirmed] (1379 [AD 2000]).

[7] Council of Ministers, "Executive By-law of the Law on Organ Transplantation of Dead Patients or Patient in Whom Brain Death Has Been Confirmed" (1381 [AD 2002]).

brain death and implement do-not-resuscitate (DNR) orders for such patients regardless of organ donor status.[8]

Iran has several national ethics policymaking bodies responsible for composing guidelines and regulations at the tertiary level. The Supreme Council on Medical Ethics (SCME) is the highest such body and participates in approving MOHME frameworks. It is chaired by the Minister for Health and Medical Education and includes representatives of the Iranian Legal Medical Organisation (medical forensics, including regulation of pregnancy termination), the Islamic Republic of Iran Medical Council (IRIMC) (a physician licensing body) and other important health institutions/stakeholders. The SCME reviews and provides final approval for ethical guidelines produced by second-tier policymaking bodies, including the National Clinical Ethics Committee (NCEC), National Committee for Ethics in Biomedical Research (NCEBR) and National Committee for Ethics and Medical Education (NCEME). The NCEC was established for policymaking, supervisory and decision-making activity in the field of clinical ethics, whilst the NCEBR and NCEME are responsible for research ethics and medical education ethics, respectively.

8.4 Advance Directives in the Legal System of Iran

Although ADs are essentially unutilised in the Iranian healthcare system (see next section), the law provides for their *potential* use, albeit only as a guide to decision-making (an advance *recommendation*) rather than a binding advance *directive*. As there is no statute law regulating ADs, AD implementation is primarily governed at the tertiary level of official regulations under the SCME Iran Charter of Patient Rights (2009) and IRIMC General Guidelines of Professional Ethics (2020).

The Iran Charter of Patient Rights (2003, revised 2009) was composed to elaborate on Article 29 of the Constitution, which recognises health/treatment services and medical care as a "universal right". The first version (2003) of the charter commented on classical issues such as the right to the best possible treatment, confidentiality and the consent/refusal of treatment except in emergencies. However, owing to its

[8] Q. Janbaba'iy, "افراد دچار مرگ مغزی با شرایط غیر کاندید اهداء عضو" [Brain Death Patients Who Do Not Possess the Criteria for Organ Donation], Ministry of Health & Medical Education of the Islamic Republic of Iran (1397 [AD 2019]).

wording and lack of auditing and stakeholder consultation, it lacked effective implementation.[9] Therefore, a revised version was spearheaded by Parsapoor et al. at the Medical Ethics & History of Medicine Research Centre at Tehran University of Medical Sciences.[10] The 2009 version followed extensive stakeholder consultation, was developed with special attention to the cultural issues of Iran and avoided contradiction with Islamic law. It is also patient centric, and, in chapter 3, elaborates on the issues surrounding autonomy, decision-making, ADs and surrogate decision-making.

In addition, in 2020 Shamsi-Gooshki et al., under the auspices of the IRIMC, composed the General Guidelines of Professional Ethics to act as a subsidiary to the disciplinary by-law.[11] Currently, the IRIMC Disciplinary By-Law is a general document, which, in Article 6, instructs the IRIMC to develop professional ethics guidance, thereby explicitly stating the ethical obligations and standards of medical professionals, including extensive elaboration in areas such as respect for patient autonomy.

Importantly, both documents are legally enforceable, not just "best practice guidelines" unless retracted by the Court of Administrative Justice. The charter gains its status by merit of its endorsement by MOHME and Article 138 of the Constitution. In the case of the Professional Ethics Guidelines, the statute establishing the IRIMC grants it the authority to take disciplinary action against its members (licensed physicians) for noncompliance with its professional guidelines. Thus, noncompliance with these codes of practice is a matter of both professional and legal compliance. In fact, they have recently been referred to in official court rulings on physician liability/negligence.[12]

9 F. Rangraz Jeddi and R. Rabii, "Level of Observance of Patients' Rights Charter in Kashan Public Hospitals" (2007) 10(1) *Behbood* 62 [in Farsi]; S.H.E. Razavi et al., "An Evaluation of Adherence to the Patient's Rights Charter among Patients and Physicians at the Emergency Department of Imam Khomeini Hospital, Tehran" (2006) *DARU Journal of Pharmaceutical Sciences* 17 [in Farsi]; S. Joolaee, "The Introduction of Patients' Rights Charter and the Approaches to Promote Observing Them in Iran" (2008) *Abstracts of Nursing Section of the Second International Conference of Iranian Medical Ethics, Tehran University of Medical Sciences*, pp. 8–9, http://fnm.tums.ac.ir/userfiles/NursingEthics/AbstractsOfThe2thInternationalConferenceOfIranianMedicalEthics-NursingSection.pdf.

10 A. Parsapoor et al., "Patient's Rights Charter in Iran" (2014) 52(1) *Acta Medica Iranica* 24.

11 E. Shamsi-Gooshki et al., "Developing 'Code of Ethics for Medical Professionals, Medical Council of Islamic Republic of Iran'" (2020) 23(10) *Archives of Iranian Medicine* 658.

12 See Rangraz Jeddi and Rabii, note 9.

Chapter 3 of the charter specifies that "every individual has the right to a free choice and decision about receiving healthcare services", including the right to "reject proposed treatments after being informed of the medical consequences of their decision except in cases of suicide or harm to others". The charter also emphasises optimising capacity to make autonomous decisions: "[I]f the patient lacks sufficient capacity to make decisions, but can participate in some parts of decision making reasonably, their decision must be respected".

Section 3-1-5 of the (original Persian language)[13] charter stipulates that the scope of individual choice in healthcare decision-making includes "[a] patient's **registered** advance directive made at a time when the patient retained capacity for decision making to be used to **guide** medical treatment when the patient lacks capacity for decision making, provided it is **in keeping with the legal requirements of the healthcare team** and the **surrogate decision-maker [SDM]**" (emphasis added). The first point to note is the essential loss of (legal) autonomy that is incurred upon a patient's loss of mental capacity in Iran. In fact, the (legal) decision-making rights of an incompetent patient are passed in full to their SDM when they lose capacity (elaborated upon later). Therefore, the SDM is obliged to use a registered AD, if it exists, only to *guide* their decision on the patient's behalf. The second point is that, in addition to the basic criteria for informed consent/refusal, the criteria for a valid AD include the following:

8.4.1 Registered

There is currently no national/regional registry for ADs in Iran, and therefore no clear mechanism for healthy patients to register their wishes in advance. Thus, the mechanism for potential AD registration envisaged by the charter is currently limited to an inpatient environment in which an unwell patient is consulted regarding their prognosis and future treatment decisions, and their wishes are documented in the patient's notes. This constitutes "registration", that is, documentation. The charter does not elaborate on any procedural requirements for such documentation, such as the necessity for witnesses or multidisciplinary team involvement.

[13] A. Parsapoor, A. Bagheri and B. Larijani, منشور حقوق بیمار در ایران [Iran Patient Rights Charter] (1388 [AD 2009) تاریخ و اخلاق پزشکی، زمستان [*Medical History & Ethics*] Winter issue.

8.4.2 *In Keeping with the Legal Requirements of the Healthcare Team*

In broad terms, an AD is invalid if it requests a physician to carry out a treatment that contradicts their professional obligations or expected standards of practice, as outlined in the Professional Ethics Guidelines. Thus, ADs are void if they request illegal procedures or those deemed negligent/liable, including euthanasia. By extension, ADs must also respect the usual standards of consent in competent patients, including not requesting treatments/procedures outside "options deemed scientifically/technically reasonable/authentic" (Chapter VII Article 67, the Professional Ethics Guidelines). Importantly, the charter obliges physicians to deliver "appropriate healthcare", which includes consideration of the justice of healthcare resource allocation, respect for patient dignity, the avoidance of unnecessary pain and palliation approaches.

Currently, there are no clear guidelines on how to address situations in which patients express their wish, via an AD, to refuse an intervention but are likely to die or suffer serious harm due to the refusal. Interestingly, however, the Professional Ethics Guidelines, in the case of patients possessing capacity, oblige doctors to make their "best effort to convince the patient" and, if unsuccessful, to "refer the case to the hospital ethics committee". As ADs are not currently practised in Iran, it is unclear whether the same approach, attempting to convince the patient and referring him/her directly to the hospital ethics committee, applies to the patient's SDM. What is clear, however, is that patient autonomy does not by default trump the preservation of life in the current Iranian-Islamic legal system, and the issue remains controversial in Islamic legal discourse.

8.4.3 *In Keeping with the Legal Requirements of the Surrogate Decision-Maker*

According to the charter, "[i]f the patient is not able to make decisions for any reason, all patient rights mentioned in this charter apply to the [SDM]", irrespective of whether an AD exists. The SDM (the *valiy or* "guardian") is a phenomenon rooted in the Islamic Guardianship Law.[14]

[14] The Civil Code of the Islamic Republic of Iran, Book 8 On Children, Chapter 3 On the Natural Guardianship of the Father and Paternal Grandfather over the Child. (1307 [AD 1982]).

Essentially, the legal guardian (and SDM) of a child (defined in Islamic law as a person below the age of puberty) is the child's father or paternal grandfather. After puberty (and "mental maturity"), a person becomes their own legal guardian. If during adulthood, a patient loses decision-making capacity, Iranian law recognises the patient's father or paternal grandfather as their guardian. In the absence of a father/paternal grandfather (which is the case with the majority of elderly patients admitted to hospital), the Islamic Jurist becomes the default guardian (and SDM) tasked with making best-interest decisions on the patient's behalf in all walks of life, including health. In theory, the Islamic Jurist in question is the Supreme Leader, although in practice such authority is indirectly transferred to a regional/local judge in a Court of Islamic Governance. The judge should then vet and appoint an individual (usually a family member) to act as an SDM/guardian on his behalf. However, if an adult has never possessed "mental maturity", owing, for example, to a syndrome/disability since childhood, then the guardianship of their father/paternal grandfather continues by default into the person's adulthood without intervention from the Islamic Jurist. If the father/paternal grandfather passes away, then guardianship (and SDM) rights pass to the Islamic Jurist (i.e. the courts) and follow the process outlined previously for appointing a relative as SDM.

SDMs are a necessary part of the healthcare system in Iran, as a legal decision-maker is required for an incapacitated patient. The Islamic Jurist is obliged to appoint the party who is best placed to protect the patient's best interests and make decisions on their behalf (usually a close relative). An AD is not a legally binding decision in this context because there is no recognition of precedent autonomy in Iranian-Islamic law. Thus, it can at most serve as a **guide** for the SDM's decisions.

There is currently no official guidance on the procedure for an SDM who wishes to act in opposition to a registered AD. However, according to the charter, where "the surrogate decision-maker is opposed to treatment, against the physician's advice, the physician can refer to related authorities [e.g. the hospital ethics committee] for reconsideration". This clause essentially exists to safeguard patients when there is suspicion that an SDM is making decisions that are not in the patient's best interests or when there is a conflict of interest (e.g. avoiding treatment costs to maximise personal inheritance). However, the more likely situation is that of an SDM requesting a futile intervention, such as continuing antibiotics for a dying patient, in opposition to that deemed appropriate by the treating physician. In this situation, the physician would be advised to consult the hospital ethics committee if efforts to negotiate the issue on the ward were unsuccessful.

8.5 Advance Directives in Practice

Whilst Iranian law provides for the potential use of ADs, in our experience they are essentially non-existent in Iranian hospitals and community healthcare settings. That said, there is some evidence that Iranian doctors and nurses support the use of ADs for decisions about resuscitation,[15] with one study demonstrating nurses' explicit support for honouring the previously declared wishes of patients, including the wish not to receive life-prolonging treatment.[16] However, the authors are unaware of any other studies in either English or Persian on AD usage rates or the implementation of or barriers to ADs in Iran. We are also unaware of any best-practice/clinical guidelines specifically on AD implementation from Iranian medical associations or hospital ethics committees.

Nonetheless, efforts are being made to develop the practice of appropriate end-of-life decision-making in Iran. For example, many cancer patients with progressive/terminal prognoses benefit from advance care plans (ACPs) to limit futile interventions such as cardiopulmonary resuscitation (CPR).[17] The Shahid Beheshti University of Medical Sciences, Tehran, also recently published detailed clinical practice guidelines on palliative care for end-stage cancer patients, including recommendations for ACPs and the avoidance of futile interventions such as CPR.[18] It would be fair to say, however, that the practice of avoiding CPR is not in widespread use nationally. Also, although ACPs constitute a beneficial approach for cancer patients, ADs aim to capture a much wider population, including those admitted to hospital without a known terminal diagnosis. In this context, the authors believe there is value in

15 M. Fallahi et al., "Nurses and Physicians' Viewpoints about Decision Making of Do Not Attempt Resuscitation (DNAR)" (2018) 13 *Multidisciplinary Respiratory Medicine* 20.

16 F. Razban et al., "Critical Care Nurses' Attitude towards Life-Sustaining Treatments in South East Iran" (2016) 7(1) *World Journal of Emergency Medicine* 59.

17 M. Ghajarzadeh et al., "Perspectives of Iranian Medical Students about Do-Not-Resuscitate Orders" (2013) 8(3) *Maedica* 261.

18 Department of Health, Shahid Beheshti University of Medical Sciences, راهنمایی طباطت بالینی: ارائه ی مراقبت ها ی تسکینی به بیماران مبتلا به سرطان در مراحل انتهایی در بخش طب تسکینی. [Clinical Practice Guideline: Delivering Palliative Care to End-stage Cancer Patients on Palliative Care Wards] (1399 [AD 2020]).

reflecting on current literature on the landscape of end-of-life decision-making in Iranian healthcare to better understand the context in which ADs could be practised. We draw in particular on the literature on DNR orders, of which there is a good amount, as a type of life-sustaining intervention withheld from end-of-life patients on the basis of practitioner-determined medical futility.

It is evident from the literature that there is support from both society and healthcare professionals in Iran for an approach that limits the use of futile, life-sustaining interventions in patients approaching the end of life. For example, studies show the practice of DNR orders to be present to some degree in Iranian hospitals,[19] with the majority of doctors,[20] nurses,[21] relatives[22] and even patients supporting the practice.[23] The common reasons offered for such support include protecting the dignity of the patient,[24] reducing futile interventions,[25] economic costs and pain/suffering,[26] and relatives sacrificing their own use of health resources for others.[27] Most of the participants in these studies agreed that DNR decisions should be led by physicians[28] with the consent of the patient/relatives[29] and in conjunction with the wider healthcare team. Interestingly, physicians were found not to support DNR orders for those not at risk of imminent death (i.e. those with a 6–12 month prognosis),[30] a stance mirrored in one hospital's palliative care guidelines.[31]

[19] See note 17.

[20] See note 17; M. Fallahi et al., "The Iranian Physicians Attitude toward the Do-Not-Resuscitate Order" (2016) 9 *Journal of Multidisciplinary Healthcare* 279.

[21] S. Mogadasian et al., "The Attitude of Iranian Nurses about Do-Not-Resuscitate Orders" (2014) 20 *Indian Journal of Palliative Care* 21.

[22] M. Tajari et al., "Attitudes of Patients' Relatives in the End Stage of Life about Do-Not-Resuscitate Order" (2018) 7(5) *Journal of Family Medicine & Primary Care* 916.

[23] M.R.F. Bordbar et al., "Investigating the Attitude of Healthcare Providers, Patients, and Their Families toward 'Do-Not-Resuscitate' Orders in an Iranian Oncology Hospital" (2019) 25(3) *Indian Journal of Palliative Care* 440.

[24] F. Bahramnezhad et al., "Iranian Nurses' Perspective on Non-Resuscitation: Content Analysis" (2016) 5(6) *International Journal of Medical Research & Health Sciences* 136.

[25] M. Cheraghi et al., "Experiences of Iranian Physicians regarding Do-Not-Resuscitate: A Directed-Content Analysis" (2016) 9 *Journal of Medical Ethics and History of Medicine*.

[26] See note 22; A. Assarroudi et al., "Do-Not-Resuscitate Order: The Experiences of Iranian Cardiopulmonary Resuscitation Team Members" (2017) 23(1) *Indian Journal of Palliative Care* 88.

[27] See note 24.

[28] See note 21.

[29] See note 17.

[30] See Fallahi et al., note 20.

[31] See note 18.

Whilst the relatives involved in the studies discussed here generally supported DNR orders, relatives can still play a key part in preventing their implementation. In contrast to the perception of healthcare professionals, patients' relatives disagree that resuscitation is "undignified".[32] It is also a matter of conscience for Iranian families to feel that they have done their utmost for the patient to avoid guilt.[33] It may also be the case that families disagree with physicians' suggestions for palliation and apply pressure for maximal intervention owing to poor communication on the latter's part regarding patients' poor prognosis.[34] Such poor communication may be related to the difficulties perceived by healthcare professionals of discussing dying/DNRs with patients/relatives,[35] as well as their expected role in prolonging life[36] and even providing hope to patients despite their imminent death.[37] It may also reflect a general weakness in communication skills and in the physician–patient relationship in Iranian healthcare culture. We will explore these issues further in the next section.

In sum, we can see that there is societal and professional support in Iran for restricting the use of futile interventions in terminally ill/end-of-life patients, as well as for the necessity of patients' advance participation in such decisions. It is unlikely, however, that ADs could function outside the terminal illness/end-of-life context. AD implementation clearly requires management of the emotional and cultural dynamic of relatives' perceived role in patient care, as well as of their expectation to receive comfort/hope from physicians in addition to physicians' duty to deliver candid and honest information on prognoses.

8.6 Critical Analysis of the Reasons for the Lack of AD Use in Iran

In this section, we distil the literature to answer a simple question: What are the factors currently preventing the utilisation of ADs in the Islamic Republic of Iran?

32 See note 22.
33 See note 25.
34 Ibid.
35 See note 21.
36 See note 17; note 21; K. Mirzaei et al., "Patients' Perspectives of the Substitute Decision-Maker: Who Makes Better Decisions?" (2011) 37(9) *Journal of Medical Ethics* 523.
37 See note 21.

8.6.1 Legal

Clause 295 of the Islamic Penal Code specifies that when a duty (e.g. of care) is neglected, a penalty is applicable to the person entrusted with that duty. This means that, by default, medical practice in Iran is often defensive, with the objective of avoiding liability by favouring life-prolonging interventions. Despite evidence of support for DNR orders among healthcare professionals, there is also evidence of ignorance and fear of legal retribution among physicians/nurses regarding commencing, signing or implementing DNR orders.[38] As mentioned previously, the fact that Iran has a civil legal system means that physicians look to and expect written guidelines at the least and executive by-laws or parliamentary statutes at best to govern the practice of ADs and DNRs. In the absence of clear statute law governing this area, it is difficult for Iranian healthcare professionals to abandon their defensive stance, particularly when faced with pressure from relatives to engage in maximal intervention. At the same time, the Professional Ethics Guidelines (Article 27, Chapter IV) forbid futile intervention for fear of litigation, although they fail to clarify the exemption from litigation in the case of ADs to refuse life-sustaining interventions. This creates a dilemma for Iranian physicians. For the sake of brevity, the authors refer readers to the PhD thesis of Shamsi-Gooshki,[39] who concluded that according to Islamic, civil, criminal, and professional liability standards and laws, DNR orders can be considered legal and judges may not hold a physician liable for implementing such an order.

Furthermore, the practice of surrogate decision-making in Iran has not taken place in the way envisaged by the charter, largely because it requires a lengthy legal process that conflicts with the obligation to provide timely care. Therefore, physicians usually consult the relatives/next of kin present at the bedside, which constitutes accepted practice in Iranian culture. This, despite being unlawful, has received little known opposition from the legal authorities. Nevertheless, Mirzaei et al. reported that "the people we usually consult for decisions concerning patient treatment are significantly different from the patients' preferred substitute decision-maker".[40] They also showed that there is no clear demographic predictor in Iranian society

[38] See note 21; note 24; note 25.

[39] E. Shamsi-Gooshki, *Ethical, Legal and Jurisprudential Aspects of Do-Not-Resuscitate Orders in the Health System of Islamic Republic of Iran*, PhD thesis, Shahid Beheshti University of Medical Sciences (2013).

[40] See Mirzaei et al., note 36.

regarding preferred SDMs, for example, a wife choosing her husband, parents choosing their eldest son, and that the preference is highly subjective and based on the individual patient's circumstances. That said, the lack of an official, legally appointed SDM would not be a reason to invalidate or devalue a registered AD, which would retain its place as a useful guide to patient preferences for whoever assumes the decision-making role, even if such decision-makers do not currently have authority according to the letter of the law.

8.6.2 *Islamic*

The three levels of the legal regulation of bioethics in Iran are all subject to the "sieve" of Islamic law, meaning that any laws, by-laws or official regulations/guidelines must be consistent with Shariah or face rejection by the Guardian Council (in the case of statutes) or the Court of Administrative Justice (in the case of by-laws and official regulations/guidelines). Thus, the Islamic legal stance on the issue of ADs is extremely important.

(Shia) Islamic law is derived from four canonical sources: the Koran, *Hadith* (verbal narrations from the Holy Prophet and his family, peace be upon them), *ʿAql* (logic) and *Ijmāʾ* (consensus of jurists). Shia Islamic jurists, referred to as Mujtahids or colloquially as Ayatollahs, receive several decades of vigorous training in religious seminaries in the traditional Islamic sciences, including Arabic grammar, logic, theology, philosophy, jurisprudence, history, *Hadith*, exegesis and many more in order to be able to independently derive law from primary canonical sources. Normative Islamic laws are divided into five types: *Wajib* (obligatory), *Mustahab* (recommended), *Mubah* (permissible), *Makruh* (not recommended) and *Haram* (impermissible). The avoidance of a *wajib* action or committing of a *haram* action warrants divine punishment; hence, much of an Islamic jurist's work involves trying to understand these "red lines" of the Shariah and feeding such understanding into a practical legal system such as that functioning in Iran. The final edict of a Mujtahid is known as his *fatwa*, or ruling, on a specific topic; for example, the *fatwa* for abortion is impermissibility unless certain conditions are met. Importantly, within the Shia clerical institution, Mujtahids are arranged in a hierarchy. A Faqih is a higher level Mujtahid who has broad understanding of various Islamic legal disciplines and teaches others to become Mujtahids. Higher on the hierarchy is a Marjaʾ (colloquially known as a "Grand Ayatollah") who is recognised as the most knowledgeable among the Fuqaha (pl. Faqih) and publishes a book of Islamic Edicts (*Risalah ʿAmaliyyah*) on day-to-day issues faced by Muslims in, for example, the areas of cleanliness, prayer, fasting, transactions/economics, marriage, divorce and medical issues. It is these Marajiʾ (pl. Marjaʾ) whom lay Shia Muslims are obliged to follow on day-to-day issues, including normative healthcare decision-making. There are currently several recognised Marajiʾ in the Holy City of Qom (Iran) and the Holy City of Najaf (Iraq), which are the two main religious seminaries of the Shia world. Naturally, having numerous Marajiʾ creates a diversity of opinion, which can create challenges for the Iranian legal system when deciding whether to accept or reject a parliamentary statute. However, the current practice of the Guardian Council and Court of Administrative Justice is to respect the viewpoint of the Supreme Leader (who is also a Grand Ayatollah) or, in areas where he has not issued a *fatwa*, to choose among the viewpoints of other Grand Ayatollahs.

Importantly, the accurate derivation of Islamic law requires not only mastery of traditional Islamic sciences but also an accurate conception of the subject matter for which the divine law needs to be derived. On this, there sometimes exist fundamental infrastructural limitations on obtaining reliable and accurate *fatawa* (pl. of *fatwa*) on medical issues from Grand Ayatollahs. For example, the *fatawa* on some medical issues lack reliability owing to the incorrect/lack of communication of facts by those who submit questions on the websites of the Marajiʾ. There is also often a lack of application of secondary laws/principles (*al-ahkam al-thanawiyyah*), which function to abrogate primary impermissibility. An example of a secondary law would be the permissibility of examining the private parts of a patient owing to the secondary principle of *avoiding hardship*, thereby abrogating the primary impermissibility of looking at this part of the body owing to the necessity of treatment for a physical ailment that is causing/could cause *hardship*. Many other opportunities exist in the medical arena for the application of secondary principles. Furthermore, there is often an inherent neglect of the role of a given medical issue in Muslim society (involving considerations of justice, economic factors and the public good), which could in turn affect a *fatwa* on it were these considerations taken into account.[41] Much of this

[41] Z.A. Syed, "On the Need for a Pragmatic, Multi-disciplinary, Evidence-Based Approach to Seeking a Fatwa on the Issue of Organ Donation after Death", in M. Abdul-Hussain et al. (eds.), *Organ Donation in Islam: The Interplay of Jurisprudence, Ethics and Society*, (Lanham, MD: Lexington Books, in press).

unreliability may result from the *unilateral* process by which *fatawa* are sought, as well as from a lack of stakeholder consultation or multidisciplinary input. The derivative reasoning for medical *fatawa* is also seldom published, resulting in the inability of ethicists, lawyers or clinical academics to analyse them. Admittedly, there are also tensions within some Islamic academic circles about the influence of "bioethics" (perceived as a Western secular movement) on the traditional Islamic legal approach to contemporary medicine, perhaps hampering engagement. The issue of ADs is also not immune from the consequences of this infrastructural limitation, as demonstrated later.

Furthermore, it is important to note that, in our view, "Islamic medical ethics" is not an accurate phrase, as in reality the only normative source in Islam is Islamic law (*fiqh*). However, within the field of Islamic medical law, traditional legal precepts have in recent times been organised into a system resembling something like the four-principle approach of Western clinical ethics.[42] We therefore apply and critically analyse the application of these principles to the issue of ADs in the following:

8.6.2.1 Principles that May Negate Respecting an AD to Limit Life-Sustaining interventions

- The Rule of the Preservation of Life:[43] Islamic law grants fundamental importance to the preservation of life, as per the Koran 5:32, numerous *hadith* and *ʿAql* (logic), which is why decisions about forgoing life-sustaining interventions are treated with caution. However, it could be argued that the current conceptualisation of life and death as a two-paradigm phenomenon results in the misapplication of this rule to dying patients. Reality is in fact closer to a three-paradigm concept involving (i) life, (ii) *al-ihtiḍār* (dying) and (iii) death. *Al-ihtiḍār* is a noun that refers to a person who is approaching death, that is, for whom the dying process has begun. Implicit within it is the recognition that death (i.e. separation of the soul from the body) is a gradual process rather than a single event. It can be appreciated from the Islamic acts of worship associated with *al-ihtiḍār* (such as turning the patient's feet towards Mecca, the recommendation to recite certain verses of the Koran, the recommendation to moisten the patient's lips and avoiding placing heavy objects on the patient's chest) that there is

[42] M. Muhaqiq-Damad, فقه پزشکی [*Medical Fiqh*]. Tehran: انتشارات حقوقی [Intishārāt-i-ḥuqūqī (publisher)], 1391 [AD 2012].

[43] See note 39.

an acceptance that the time of death is approaching. From such appreciation, many legal precepts such as the obligation to "save life" can be dissolved, as it can be argued that the patient is approaching (destined) death and therefore is not the intended subject of the obligation to preserve life. Of course, not all patients to whom ADs can be applied are in a state of dying, thus limiting the utility of this solution.

- The Rule of No Harm (*La Darar wa La Dirar fi al-Islam*):[44] Based on a widely narrated *hadith*, this rule can be translated broadly as "non-maleficence" to the self/others. It could be argued that accepting a patient's AD to withhold life-sustaining interventions would (whilst having established a duty of care) makes one complicit in harming the patient by not providing treatment. It also calls into question the original validity of such an AD, as the rule could be used to limit the scope of personal autonomy to instances of self-harm. However, one could also argue the opposite, as many life-sustaining interventions such as CPR are in fact futile for terminally ill patients and constitute harm without benefit.
- The Rule of Destruction and Causation (*Itlaf wa Tasbib*):[45] Derived from numerous *hadith*, this rule creates liability for a physician who either directly harms a patient or plays a role in the causality of that harm, for example, by ordering a DNR or even respecting an AD to refuse life-sustaining intervention where a duty of care exists. However, in our view, the rule is unlikely to cause liability, as the major potential application of ADs in Iran is to *futile* life-sustaining interventions, where a role in causing harm is difficult to prove.

8.6.2.2 Principles that May Favour Respecting an AD to Limit Life-Sustaining Interventions[46]

- The Rule of Consent (*Idn*): It is generally accepted among Shia jurists that consent is required for medical intervention, and that not obtaining it can incur liability. Thus, if a patient has refused certain interventions via an AD, it would be unlawful to deliver them in opposition to said directive. That said, whether such a right extends to refusing life-sustaining treatment without contradicting the Rule of No Harm remains a matter of controversy among Islamic jurists. Some

[44] See note 42.
[45] Ibid.
[46] Ibid.

scholars are of the opinion that the duty of stewardship (and of not doing harm) to oneself is an *act of worship* as opposed to a *transaction* or *law*, and thus does not fall under the authority of state enforcement, just as the state has no right to enforce prayer or fasting upon Muslims, as these are acts of worship between each person and God. Thus, whilst it might be considered a "sin" to refuse consent via an AD for life-sustaining treatment (due to neglecting a *wajib* act of worship), a physician cannot act in opposition to such refusal owing to insufficient argument to abrogate the right of consent. However, this approach is not accepted by all scholars.

- The Rule of Acquittal (*al-bara'at*): Derived from numerous *hadith*, a physician can avoid liability when a patient has agreed to the risks of intervention, provided that the physician has not been negligent in their duty. Thus, if a patient provides both consent and acquittal, they are removing liability from the physician even if harm occurs (e.g. by not conducting CPR, where that is considered the standard). However, some jurists disagree with the exculpation of a murderer by their victim before the victim's death, which could be applied to oppose the application of the Rule of Acquittal to life-sustaining interventions via an AD.
- The Rule of Beneficence (*Ihsan*): Based on the Koran 9:91, this rule broadly compares to "beneficence" and could be used to remove a physician's liability for respecting an AD to avoid life-sustaining treatment such as CPR, provided that the *intention* behind such avoidance is to do good to the patient and that no financial reward is involved.
- The Rule of Respecting Persons (*hurmat al-nufus*): This rule, based on *hadith*, instructs respect for persons and could be applied to remove a physician's liability for respecting an AD to refuse undignified interventions, such as intensive care unit admission or CPR. The rule would gain particular traction if it were also proven that such interventions would be futile for the patient in question.
- The Rule of No Hardship (*La Haraj*): Based on the Koran 22:78, the essence of this rule is to remove/avoid intolerable hardship when a Muslim is trying to follow the Shariah, as per the standard of acceptable hardship for the common layperson. If accepting life-sustaining interventions (as per one's perceived religious obligation to preserve their life) in a terminal illness setting would create physical hardship (e.g. owing to the side effects of chemotherapy), then one is not obliged to do so, and an AD to refuse such treatment might be considered valid, although this remains a controversial viewpoint.

- The Rule of *Iztirar* (Difficulty/Desperation): Similar to the previous rule, this rule, based on the Koran 2:173, negates an obligation when fulfilling it would cause severe difficulty. It could be used, for example, to validate an AD to refuse a life-sustaining intervention if the case were made that accepting the intervention would, by prolonging life, subject the patient to intolerable difficulty.
- The Rule of Public Good (*Maslaha*):[47] When there is sufficient ambiguity among canonical sources on an issue, an Islamic jurist can resort to the Rule of Public Good, reasoning, for example, on the basis of considerations surrounding the just allocation of limited public health resources and/or the need to avoid wastage or futile expenditure on patients with a poor prognosis. The rule could aid the acceptability of ADs to refuse futile, life-sustaining interventions from an Islamic jurisprudential perspective.

In summary, there is currently no clear or authoritative *fatwa* on the validity of an AD to refuse life-sustaining interventions.[48] It remains the duty of Islamic jurists to weigh up the foregoing principles against one another, while also considering other evidence from the canonical sources, to come to an accurate conclusion.

8.6.3 Social

For many, the non-binding nature of an AD on a patient's SDM could be viewed as undermining autonomy. However, it is worth considering how this approach, in our opinion, functions relatively comfortably within the family-centric patient autonomous healthcare culture of Iran. Here, "family-centric patient autonomous" is used in opposition to "patient-centric patient autonomous", the latter being a more representative construct for Western cultures. In our experience in Iran, the family is an integral part of a patient's healthcare decisions, and is what most patients autonomously want/prefer, as their decisions affect not only themselves but also their family, emotionally, spiritually, financially and practically. This is not to say that healthcare professionals should put the interests of family members on par with the interests of patients when making decisions (which would contradict the Professional Ethics Guidelines); rather, it is acceptance of the fact that Iranian patients

[47] See note 39.
[48] See note 25.

intentionally wish to consider their family's interests and seek their active involvement in healthcare decision-making, particularly at the end of life. Therefore, respect for patient autonomy requires the inclusion of family members in the discussion. The complete exclusion of the patient at the expense of their SDM in healthcare decision-making, however, is obviously problematic. Hence, ADs can arguably play an essential role in Iran for the purpose of optimising the delivery of appropriate medical interventions at the end of life. It would be fair to say then that ADs in Iran would not function as an opportunity to defend an extreme liberal individualistic right of autonomy,[49] but rather as a way to provide appropriate, patient-centric healthcare in a culture that currently functions using a family-centric patient autonomous model. Furthermore, the current system almost always "works" by merit of the fact that the family members who could take legal action against a physician are involved in the decisions being made for the incapacitated patient. Obviously, this does not necessarily translate into the best outcomes for the patient, and it also cannot be assumed that all patients want to include their family members, as will be mirrored in our recommendations at the end of the chapter.

On a separate issue, much of the motivation for end-of-life care planning is a direct product of each individual patient's health reflexiveness and of society's need to plan for death. The broader inclusion of the public within healthcare discourse is also required to normalise such planning and address the anxieties associated with it.

8.6.4 *Cultural*

It is not uncommon in Iran for cultural beliefs to be expressed using the language of religion even when not necessarily endorsed by Islam. For example, whilst it is the case that Islamic doctrine exerts a significant influence on the beliefs of healthcare professionals,[50] relatives[51] and patients[52] about DNR orders, such beliefs are in fact cultural (non-religiously substantiated) beliefs about not intervening in divine fate[53]

[49] N. Yavari and A. Parsapoor, "The Domain of Autonomy, Limitations and Solutions" (2017) 10(1) *Iranian Journal of Medical Ethics and History of Medicine* 182.

[50] See note 21.

[51] See note 22.

[52] See note 23.

[53] See note 24 and note 25; F. Bahramnezhad et al., "Do-Not-Resuscitate in Iranian Muslim Families: A Conventional Content Analysis" (2018) 32(5) *Holistic Nursing Practice* 240.

by trying to plan for/give in to what might be an end-of-life event or expectations that God will perform a miracle for end-of-life patients (*shafa*). Families often interpret this to mean "doing everything possible" until the patient's heart stops, an approach that makes it difficult for both Iranian healthcare professionals and families to engage proactively in future end-of-life planning. In addition, theological beliefs about illness being a source of forgiveness for sins are sometimes misapplied, resulting in a contradiction in the case of interventions that reduce suffering (which God had destined) at the end of life for the person's salvation. In Iranian culture, when someone suffers from illness at the end of life, it sometimes provides their families with solace, knowing that their loved one's sins may have been forgiven and that they may enjoy a peaceful life in the grave, on the Day of Judgement and thereafter. Despite the relatively institutionalised nature of the Shia Islamic clergy in Iran, the aforementioned beliefs remain prominent in society, implying a lack of adequate intervention by the clerical establishment, despite relatives often expressing a need for help from clergymen in healthcare decisions.[54]

8.6.5 Infrastructural

The current literature reveals evidence of concern regarding the association between DNR orders and reduced quality of care.[55] Given the underdevelopment of palliative care services outside the cancer arena in Iran, it may feel uncompassionate for doctors to implement DNR orders without a viable alternative treatment approach using palliative services. If one is not to resuscitate a dying patient without a clear plan for symptom control, for example, sedation, antipsychotics, anti-emetics and pain relief, then it may seem more uncompassionate to abandon the patient (at home or in hospital) without some intervention, even if futile, which reflects broader cultural issues. Furthermore, relatives may not expect maximal intervention for a patient being cared for in a hospice but may expect it while the patient is still in a hospital, where the predominant approach is to provide active treatment.

In addition, the current system of documentation in Iran is inadequate for advance end-of-life decision-making. For example, although nurses and doctors prefer a written DNR or DNR sheet/card, DNR orders often

[54] See Bahramnezhad et al., ibid.
[55] See note 22.

take the form of informal or verbal orders, creating operational challenges,[56] and are often not considered. The end result is often futile or "slow-code"/tokenistic resuscitation for the benefit of relatives. However, Iranian doctors and nurses generally agree that DNR orders should ideally be signed before admission.[57]

8.6.6 *Medical Education*

It has been suggested that the culture of healthcare delivery in Iran is in some areas "stereotyped", with physicians not encouraged to think critically and analytically about their treatment decisions, leading them to adopt a one-size-fits-all approach for their patients.[58] This situation results in a lack of thought regarding the appropriateness of resuscitation for patients with extreme frailty suffering from multiple comorbidities compared to healthier, functionally independent patients. In fact, there are currently no clinical practice guidelines that explicitly pertain to the practice of DNR orders in Iran, which prevents healthcare professionals from proactively inculcating them into their specialist training and practice.

8.6.7 *Professional Considerations*

The issue of defensive medical practice in Iran remains a prominent barrier to ADs, as in many countries debating appropriate end-of-life care. Therefore, considering a shift towards the avoidance of harm to patients through futile interventions may optimise the provision of more appropriate healthcare. Much of the aforementioned paradigm of defensive practice is a result of the inappropriate application of the beneficence used in living patients to the context of dying patients, whereas a greater focus on autonomy, the avoidance of harm and justice would be more appropriate for the latter patient group.

Ways of developing and strengthening the physician–patient relationship in contemporary Iranian healthcare are also needed. Patients need to feel empowered to request information on their prognoses and be able to understand that information to play their essential role in the process of shared decision-making. Similarly, Iranian physicians need to recognise

[56] See Assarroudi et al., note 26.
[57] See note 15.
[58] See note 25.

that seeking greater patient involvement is in no way a demotion of their experience or insight into optimal treatment, but in fact represents an approach towards optimising the delivery of patient-centric care.

8.7 Future Directions

In summary, it can be said that according to contemporary interpretation, the law in Iran recognises "advance recommendations" as opposed to "advance directives". The limits on personal autonomy also remain hotly debated in Islamic and legal circles. Whilst ADs have the potential to play an important role in improving end-of-life healthcare decision-making in Iran, several factors must be addressed to improve their implementation, including the following.

- A clear *fatwa* on the issue of ADs, including clarification of the scope of personal autonomy to refuse life-sustaining medical interventions that may be futile or otherwise: as with the majority of contemporary biomedical ethical issues in Iran, legislative/regulatory change often starts with an authoritative *fatwa* from a Grand Jurist, particularly the Supreme Leader, creating momentum within the governmental apparatus to address the issue as a priority. As the phenomena of precedent autonomy and ADs are new to Islamic law, an innovative approach may be required to provide an appropriate solution. Such a *fatwa* must also seek multidisciplinary input, be based on the best available evidence and appreciate the role of ADs in the broader healthcare system, including considerations of optimising patient outcomes and the just distribution of limited healthcare resources.
- Legal documents or official guidelines on ADs: although the charter mentions the role of ADs, more elaboration is required in the form of a focused, comprehensive law or official guidelines with legal standing ratified by the Iranian parliament or MOHME/SCME of IRIMC to provide clarity for physicians who wish to incorporate ADs into their practice and to help service providers to create the necessary infrastructure to support their implementation. Such guidelines should also include recommendations on best practice, as well as multidisciplinary team and family involvement.
- Reform of the SDM system in Iran: current practice does not reflect the law (and vice versa), including the lack of an officially appointed SDM, the impracticality of seeking a court-appointed SDM, the lack of patient participation in the appointment of SDMs and the limitation

of SDM status to fathers/paternal grandfathers, where they are still alive.

- Statute legislation to clarify a physician's liability when limiting futile life-sustaining interventions, including DNR orders, which could also incorporate articles on ADs.
- Development/empowerment of local hospital ethics committees to oversee the implementation and regulation of ADs in Iranian hospitals and community healthcare settings via clear official guidance and protocols for dispute resolution between relatives and healthcare professionals.

These recommendations constitute a set of first steps that the authors believe have the potential to stimulate legal, cultural, educational and social change in end-of-life decision-making in Iran, which, as per the foregoing discussions, is essential to improve patient outcomes while respecting the nation's Islamic doctrine and family-centric healthcare. Without such change, ADs will remain an underutilised tool with neglected potential.

9

The Law and Practice of Advance Directives and End-of-Life Care in Malaysia

SHARON KAUR, THOMAS TAN HOOI WANG, JENNY KA YAN YAU & RICHARD BOON LEONG LIM

9.1 Introduction

Malaysia is a multicultural and multifaith society. Although Islam is recognised[1] as the religion of the Federation of Malaysia, the country's legal system is most accurately described as a hybrid system comprising both secular and Islamic laws. Islamic law is primarily limited to family law matters,[2] whereas most areas relating to the provision and regulation of healthcare are governed by secular laws. In general, there is little tension or overlap between the two legal systems. However, in a number of situations,[3] the courts have had to navigate a difficult path between the two, a task made all the more difficult by social, political and religious forces. Whilst there have to date been no legally contested cases involving advance directives (ADs) or end-of-life decisions in Malaysia, it is probably only a matter of time before cases involving these issues are raised.

At present, there is no specific legal regulation that addresses ADs or care at the end of life in Malaysia. However, in 2019, the Ministry of Health (MOH) published the National Palliative Care and Care Policy and Strategy Plan 2019–30,[4] which is meant to serve as a road map towards the achievement of good palliative care nationwide and the integration of palliative care into the national healthcare system. It has been estimated that 100,034 of the Malaysians who died in 2014 required

[1] Federal Constitution of Malaya 1957, Art. 5.

[2] S.S. Faruqi, *Our Constitution* (Subang Jaya: Sweet & Maxwell, 2019), p. 44.

[3] For instance, the unilateral conversion of children to a different faith after a divorce or the right of transgender Muslims to cross-dress.

[4] Ministry of Health Malaysia, *National Palliative Care Policy and Strategic Plan 2019–2030* (October 2019), www.moh.gov.my/moh/resources/Polisi/BUKU_NATIONAL_PALLIATIVE_CARE_POLICY_AND_STRATEGY_PLAN_2019-2030.pdf.

palliative care, with that number slated to rise to approximately 230,000 by 2030.[5] Although the policy does not address the issue of ADs specifically, strategy 2 focuses on ensuring that all people should have "their needs recognised within the healthcare system and community they live in",[6] forming the basis for incorporating individual interests and values into palliative care. The implementation of training in advance care planning (ACP) as part of Malaysia's national palliative care strategy also constitutes a positive development, as advance care plans (ACPs) are commonly viewed as an important element of end-of-life care as a means of respecting the wishes of patients even once they have become incapacitated. Of course, the effective and meaningful implementation of ACPs depends on how well such plans are drawn up and the extent to which they are honoured. An important aspect of both is the development of good governance mechanisms. With respect to ADs in particular, both the Malaysian Medical Council (MMC) and MOH have published guidance documents in recent years.

Given the lack of formal legal recognition of ADs and ACPs and moves to embed the latter into palliative care practice in Malaysia, it is worth considering how the law potentially applies in situations in which particular decisions need to be made at the end of life and when the individual in question no longer has the capacity to decide.

This chapter considers the role of ADs in Malaysia, beginning with a discussion of the legal principles that are likely to apply in the end-of-life decision-making context. Section 9.2 then examines the professional guidance that has thus far been issued on ADs and highlights points of concern that such guidance has failed to address. Section 9.3 turns to consideration of the limited empirical data on AD awareness in Malaysia, followed by a discussion in Section 9.4 of the various sociocultural factors that may influence the acceptance of ADs, with a particular focus on the significant roles played by the family and physicians. Religion as a key influence is also explored in relation to Malaysian attitudes towards ADs.

9.1.1 Relevant Legal Principles in End-of-Life Decision-Making

Malaysia's legal system is made up of the Federal Constitution, or the "supreme law" of Malaysia,[7] acts enacted by Parliament and case law.

[5] Ibid., p. 24.
[6] Ibid., p. 26.
[7] Federal Constitution of Malaysia 1957, Art. 4(1).

In some circumstances, English common law and equity principles may also apply. More specifically, the Civil Law Act of 1956 provides that common law principles may apply in cases "as the Circumstances of the States permit", with attention paid to the necessity of applying such principles in "local circumstances".[8] It is important to note, however, that the Civil Law Act stipulates that common law developments after 7 April 1956 cannot be considered by the Malaysian courts.[9] The language used in the Civil Law Act also indicates that "common law" refers to principles developed and followed in common law cases, not to common law statutes.[10] Thus, the only way in which such principles can be directly incorporated into Malaysian law and applied by the courts is for Parliament to enact laws that take into account common law developments subsequent to the aforementioned cut-off date.[11] However, the courts have allowed for the consideration of current common law principles in certain cases as being of persuasive authority, which suggests that Malaysian judges have the discretion to apply the common law principles of other Commonwealth jurisdictions to local cases if deemed necessary, even if said principles were developed after 1956.

Given that there are currently no statutes or regulations in Malaysia that specifically address the issue of ADs, it is possible that common law principles, particularly those on advance refusals and the right to refuse treatment more generally,[12] may be applied in cases concerning ADs.

In cases in which there is no evidence of advance decision-making, there is also no specific law in Malaysia that deals with the issues of incapacity and surrogate health decision-making. The only statute that makes some provision for surrogate decision-making is the Mental Health Act 2001 (MHA). The main purpose of the MHA is to provide for the compulsory detention and treatment of mentally ill persons who are deemed to pose a risk to others or to themselves.[13] Accordingly, in situations involving surrogate healthcare decisions, the Act is limited in

[8] S.S.S. Ahmad, "Update: Introduction to the Malaysian Legal System and Sources of Law", GlobaLex (2014) , www.nyulawglobal.org/globalex/Sources_Law_Malaysia1.html.

[9] Ibid.

[10] Ibid.

[11] Ibid.

[12] *Re T (Adult: Refusal of Medical Treatment)* [1992] 3 WLR 782, [1992] 3 Med LR 306, [1992] 4 All ER 649 as an example.

[13] Mental Health Act 2001.

its application[14] and is usually considered a blunt instrument that does not engage with the challenges of trying to meet the needs of incapacitated individuals in a meaningful way.

Two additional points are worthy of note. The first is that individuals are not permitted to choose their own health proxies under the MHA because surrogate decision-makers are prescribed under section 77 of the Act and the courts are responsible for appointing a committee of the person under section 58.[15] Whilst the mental health context admittedly differs from the end-of-life decision-making context, the inability to choose one's own health proxy is in direct opposition to the philosophy of the AD, wherein individuals are afforded the freedom to choose healthcare proxies who are likely to share their values and interests.

The second point is that there is no oversight of surrogate decision-making under the MHA, and it appears that surrogates have unfettered discretion in making decisions on behalf of incapacitated individuals. There is nothing in the MHA that requires either the relatives or physicians of persons declared incompetent to make any sort of inquiry regarding those persons' interests. The only protection afforded a mentally disordered person is found in section 86,[16] which renders it an offence to ill-treat or wilfully neglect a patient. The section fails to recognise that it is possible to make a decision against the interests of a person, that is, to fail to respect his or her wishes and interests without being considered to have ill-treated or wilfully neglected him or her. The ethos of the MHA thus again appears to run contrary to the underlying tenets of ADs and ACP more generally, that is, to allow individuals to take control of decisions that affect their care and to promote patient autonomy.

9.2 Advance Directives: Professional Guidance

Although ADs are not subject to legal regulation in Malaysia, and whether common law principles apply remains unclear, there are professional guidelines in the country that touch upon ADs. This section discusses the professional guidance issued by the MMC and MOH.

[14] For example, situations in which proxies are appointed are limited to specific interventions under section 77 and to instances in which a person is a danger to him or herself, wherein a committee is appointed under section 58.

[15] Mental Health Act 2001, ss. 77, 85.

[16] Mental Health Act 2001, s. 86.

9.2.1 *Guidance from the Malaysian Medical Council*

The MMC is constituted under the Medical Act 1971 as the regulator of physicians in Malaysia, and therefore has disciplinary jurisdiction over all registered physicians in the country.[17] Whilst guidelines issued by the MMC are not legally binding, a physician who fails to comply with them may be subject to the council's disciplinary jurisdiction.[18] The Medical Act provides the MMC with wide disciplinary powers that range from reprimanding practitioners to striking their names off the Malaysian Medical Register.[19] The MMC may also refuse to renew physicians' annual practising certificates.[20] Two of the guidance documents issued by the MMC touch upon ADs: (i) the Guidelines on Consent for Treatment of Patients by Registered Medical Practitioners 2017[21] and (ii) the Code of Professional Conduct 2019.[22]

9.2.1.1 Guidelines on Consent for Treatment of Patients by Registered Medical Practitioners (2017)

Clause 18 of the 2017 Guidelines states that doctors "should refrain from providing treatment or performing any procedure where there is an unequivocal written directive by the patient that such treatment or procedure is not to be provided in the circumstances which now apply to the patient (Advance Care Directive)".[23] However, the clause does not apply when the directive contains instructions for such illegal activities as euthanasia or the termination of a pregnancy. In addition, medical practitioners are advised to consider the following:

(i) Whether the directive is sufficiently clear and specific to the circumstances that have arisen;
(ii) Whether the directive was made in contemplation of the current situation; and
(iii) Whether there is any reason to doubt the patient's competence or voluntariness at the time of making the directive (in terms of being subject to undue pressure).[24]

17 Medical Act 1971, s. 4.
18 Medical Act 1971, s. 29(2)(b).
19 Medical Act 1971, s. 30, 19.
20 M.K.M. Tan, "Considerations for Introducing Legislation on Advance Decisions in Malaysia" (2018) 10 *Asian Bioethics Review* 87, 87.
21 Malaysia Medical Council, *Guidelines on Consent for Treatment of Patients by Registered Medical Practitioners* (2017).
22 Malaysia Medical Council, *Code of Professional Conduct* (2019).
23 See note 21, para. 18.
24 Ibid.

Clause 18 also goes on to provide the following:

> In an emergency, the medical practitioner can treat the patient in accordance with his or her professional judgment of the patient's best interests, until legal advice can be obtained on the validity or ambit of any Advance Care Directive that may have been given by the patient. Where there are concerns about the validity or ambit of an Advance Care Directive in a non-emergency situation, the medical practitioner should consult the patient's spouse or next of kin or legal guardian and the medical practitioner should also consider the need to seek legal advice and to discuss the issue with his or her Colleagues, or other clinicians involved in the patient's care. Such discussions should be documented in the patient's medical case notes.[25]

9.2.1.2 Code of Professional Conduct 2019

Clause 1.14 of the 2019 Code of Professional Conduct states that a practitioner may be confronted with a living will (or advance medical directive (AMD)[26]), which is a written statement detailing a person's desires regarding future medical treatment in circumstances in which he or she is no longer able to express informed consent.[27] Such circumstances may be imminent death, terminal illness or severe and irreversible conditions.[28] Any decision made by the practitioner to comply or not comply with the AMD must be made in consultation with the patient's relatives and next-of-kin.[29]

9.2.2 *Guidance from the Ministry of Health*

9.2.2.1 Guidelines for Resuscitation Training for Ministry of Health, National Committee on Resuscitation Training 2016 (NCORT Guidelines)

Part 6.4 of the NCORT Guidelines[30] contains a discussion on the ethics of resuscitation and end-of-life issues. Notably, in relation to resuscitation, the NCORT Guidelines recognise that there has been a shift in

25 Ibid.

26 It is interesting to note that despite these documents being issued by the same entity, the words used to describe ADs are slightly different.

27 See note 22, cl. 1.14.

28 Ibid.

29 Ibid.

30 Ministry of Health Malaysia, *Guidelines for Resuscitation Training for Ministry of Health* (2016).

emphasis from a doctor-centred (beneficence) approach to a patient-centred (autonomy) approach.[31] Furthermore, they place the onus on healthcare providers to "equip themselves with sound knowledge in resuscitation and ethical issues pertaining to it in making end of life decisions".[32]

Paragraph 6.4.2, entitled "Advanced directives", specifically addresses the issue of ADs, stating that "Advanced medical plan and directives when made, should be clearly documented and visible in [the] patient's notes for other healthcare personnel to recognize on the spot. However, over time the situation or perspectives of [the] patient might change and do not attempt resuscitation (DNAR) orders should be revised accordingly. Exemption from DNAR should also be clearly specified".[33]

9.2.3 Discussion

The fact that the foregoing professional guidance exists despite the lack of a clear legal framework for ADs in Malaysia suggests that there is acknowledgment that ADs are being practised on the ground and that practice guidelines need to reflect that reality, as well as offer guidance on how healthcare professionals should deal with ADs even if the law does not do so. Thus, whilst the guidance documents discussed here are not legally binding, they can arguably play an important role in establishing the professional requirements of health professionals in practical settings even if those requirements are not underpinned by a formal regulatory framework. It is worthy of note, however, that none of the guidelines require healthcare professionals to take a proactive approach in encouraging patients to make an AD, or supporting them in doing so, as part of their responsibility to fulfil quality end-of-life

[31] Ibid., para. 6.4.1.

[32] Ibid.

[33] Ibid., para. 6.4.2. Whilst the term "DNAR order" is used, it is unlikely that this paragraph refers to the type of order that is based on a doctor's clinical judgement of futility; rather, it likely refers to the type of AD that is patient led and that lays out the person's personal wishes concerning how he or she does not want to be treated. This is the case because in the following paragraph, which covers the withdrawal and withholding of therapy, the existence of an "advanced medical directive" is listed separately from other clinical considerations that might point to medical futility, and the existence of the "advanced medical directive" is in itself one of the situations in which a healthcare provider is expected to consider withholding or withdrawing cardiopulmonary resuscitation.

care requirements. Instead, the guidelines appear to be entirely reactive, focusing only on what healthcare professionals should do if they encounter an AD in their practice.[34]

Of the three guidance documents, the 2017 Guidelines provide the most detail on what medical practitioners should do when provided with an AD. They highlight several important factors that medical practitioners should consider, namely, clarity, applicability and whether there was voluntary consent, although there are no definitions of the terms "competence", "voluntariness" or "undue pressure".[35] The absence of such definitions is likely to render the operationalisation of the guidelines more difficult given the lack of guidance on how the aforementioned factors should be properly assessed. The need for clarity is emphasised by the requirement that any AD be "unequivocal",[36] although no such requirement is explicitly stated in the 2019 Code of Conduct. Both that document and the 2017 Guidelines indicate that doctors should implement an AD only when it is in a written format,[37] and the NCORT Guidelines suggest that ADs should be clearly documented in patients' medical records.

Both the 2017 Guidelines and the 2019 Code of Conduct also emphasise the importance of family involvement when it comes to the acceptance and implementation of a patient's AD. The former requires that a medical practitioner "consult the patient's spouse or next of kin" in a non-emergency situation, and the latter requires that the decision to implement an AD be made in consultation with the patient's family.[38,39] Whilst these requirements reflect the family-oriented approach in medical decision-making that is still very much followed in Malaysia, as further discussed in Section 9.4 of this chapter, none of the guidelines make reference to persons who may be nominated by patients as their

[34] This claim is also supported by the fact that Hospis Malaysia, the largest hospice facility in Malaysia, notes in its brochure on "decision making for the end of life" that those who want to write an advance care plan should consult doctors about their wishes, suggesting that the initiative to draw up an AD is expected to be taken by patients themselves. See Hospis Malaysia, "Patient and Caregiver Resources" (2018), www.hospismalaysia.org/resources/.

[35] See note 21, para. 18.

[36] Ibid.

[37] In this vein, Tan notes that verbal requests are more common in the Malaysian setting, and it is therefore a concern that no mention is made of them in the 2017 Guidelines (see note 20).

[38] See note 21, para. 18.

[39] See note 22, cl. 1.14.

healthcare proxies. Individuals who are estranged from their families or who are in same-sex partnerships (which are not legally permitted in Malaysia) may prefer not to have their relatives involved in decisions about their care, which renders the requirement to consult family members problematic.

It is also notable that although the 2017 Guidelines ask medical practitioners to respect unequivocal written directives provided by patients, practitioners are also given a wide scope of discretion in the case of an emergency to treat the patient as they see fit until they can obtain legal advice on any directive in place.[40] Given the lack of clear legal rules on ADs, it is unclear how the validity of an AD could be demonstrated, although it is conceivable that common law principles on advance refusals would be relied upon in legal advice. More importantly, whilst obtaining legal advice may be feasible in non-emergency cases, permitting medical practitioners to treat patients as they see fit until such advice can be obtained in emergency cases in effect allows them to override what may be the unequivocal, written wishes of the patient. Tan further argues that a patient's wishes may be disregarded not only in emergency cases but also in non-emergency cases given that the wording of clause 18 states that medical practitioners "should" refrain from providing treatment contrary to an AD,[41] which suggests some flexibility in the requirement. The same can also be said of the 2019 Code of Conduct. The last line of clause 1.14, which states that "any decision by the practitioner, to comply with or not to comply with the AMD, must be made in consultation with relatives and next-of-kin of the patient",[42] suggests that medical practitioners have the flexibility not to comply with the explicit wishes of a patient, as written in his or her AD, as long as that decision is made in consultation with family members.

Tan additionally points out that, contrary to usual practice, the 2017 Guidelines unrealistically assume that the physician treating the patient will be aware of the existence of his or her AD and that the content thereof will be available to the physician at the relevant time, including during an emergency.[43] Furthermore, the 2017 Guidelines do not consider care in non-hospital settings, such as care homes or hospice

[40] See note 21, para. 18.
[41] Tan, note 20, 91.
[42] See note 22, cl. 1.14.
[43] Tan, note 20, 91.

facilities, which is problematic given that both the number of elderly people and the number of care homes are increasing in Malaysia.[44]

Thus, whilst the professional guidelines discussed previously provide some level of guidance for medical practitioners who may encounter ADs in their practice, there remain a number of concerns that need to be addressed. In particular, the phrasing of the guidelines suggests that the explicit wishes of the patient, even if clearly documented in a written format, are not necessarily given priority. Hence, the views of the physician, in consultation with family members, are still likely to take precedence, which is contrary to the principle of respect for patient autonomy.

9.3 The Practice of Advance Directives in Malaysia

There are no official statistics on the number of ADs in Malaysia, and there is a lack of empirical data on AD implementation in the country. However, a number of studies have demonstrated a very low level of awareness of ADs amongst the elderly. For example, a study conducted in 2007 by Htut et al. involving 15 elderly patients representing different ethnic and religious groups in Malaysia discovered that none of the respondents had heard of ADs or ACPs, although most agreed after discussion that plans for future medical management were something they should consider, with 5 expressing eagerness to make an AD for themselves.[45] Ten years later, a similar study carried out with a larger pool of respondents reported that only 8 out of 70 had heard of ADs, with none having drawn one up.[46] In this 2017 study, 70 per cent of the respondents (49 out of 70) said that they were open to the concept of using ADs.[47]

A recent study on end-of-life care in nursing homes found that none of the respondents had any ideas about or had discussed their end-of-life preferences with anyone.[48] After being afforded an opportunity to discuss their end-of-life plans and the AD concept for the first time with the researcher, nine respondents expressed positive feelings about the

44 Ibid.

45 Y. Htut et al., "The Views of Older Malaysians on Advanced Directive and Advanced Care Planning: A Qualitative Study" (2007) 19(3) *Asia-Pacific Journal of Public Health* 58.

46 T.L. Koh et al., "Advance Directives among Elderly Population: A Malaysian Experience" (2017) 13 *Journal of the Indian Academy of Geriatrics* 62.

47 Ibid., p. 65.

48 N.X. Jiao and N.A.M. Hussin, "End-of-Life Communication among Chinese Elderly in a Malaysian Nursing Home" (2020) 7(1) *Journal of Patient Experience* 62, 65.

experience and reported being motivated to initiate such a discussion with family members.[49]

Although empirical data remain limited, the data from these studies suggest that Malaysians previously unfamiliar with the concept of ADs may still be open to their use once informed of them. Additionally, although the studies sampled only a small pool of elderly individuals, they suggest a continuing lack of awareness in Malaysia about the existence of ADs and how they might be implemented. Knowledge deficiency concerning the purpose and use of ADs in Malaysia appears to constitute a very strong barrier, one that needs to be overcome if they are to be encouraged. This lack of knowledge and awareness is further discussed in Section 9.4 in the context of the physician's advisory role in ADs.

Taken together, the preliminary data presented in this section suggest that if more Malaysians were made aware of the AD concept and the use of ADs was encouraged to a greater extent, by the medical community for example, then a greater number of Malaysians would be likely to make ADs. Nevertheless, there are a number of factors related to Malaysia's sociocultural context that may exert an adverse impact on AD acceptance in the country. These factors are explored in Section 9.4.

9.4 Sociocultural Factors Influencing the Acceptance of Advance Directives in Malaysia

9.4.1 Influence of Family Members in Decision-Making

Much that has been written on the regulation and use of ADs in Malaysia highlights the key role that the family plays in medical decision-making. Malek et al. describe the family as an important aspect of a patient's attitudes towards making an AD, similarly to other Asian countries with a family-centred culture.[50] The concept of ADs is based on the principle of patient autonomy, a type of autonomy that is considered to still be in a "nascent stage" in Malaysia given the prioritisation of family-based, collective decision-making and deference to physician expertise.[51]

[49] Ibid., 67.

[50] M.M. Malek et al., "Honouring Wishes of Patients: An Islamic View on the Implementation of the Advance Medical Directive in Malaysia" (2021) 28(2) *Malaysian Journal of Medical Sciences* 28, 32.

[51] H.Y. Chan, "Regulating Advance Decision-Making: Potential and Challenges for Malaysia" (2019) 11 *Asian Bioethics Review* 111, 115.

According to Malek et al., the idea of patient autonomy "seems to clash with local practice" because most patients are heavily influenced by their families and doctors,[52] especially in situations involving end-of-life care. Patient autonomy is usually considered in conjunction with family-centred decision-making and professional medical expertise in this context.

The aforementioned studies conducted on ADs in Malaysia also support the claim that the family plays a significant role in the context of medical decision-making. For example, the majority of participants in the 2007 study by Htut et al. had nominated family members as their surrogate decision-makers, and even those participants who expressed an interest in ADs indicated that they would discuss the matter with their families.[53] A 2016 study on ACP conducted by Lai et al. found 87 per cent of participants preferred a "family-based decision-making process" pertaining to end-of-life care.[54] The authors argued that such a preference was likely the result of Malaysia's collectivist society, which "reverses the role of the individual" and "places more importance [on] family" for decisions, indicating that the opinions of family are far more influential for most patients than their own wishes.[55]

The aforementioned 2020 study on end-of-life care in nursing homes echoes this argument, with its authors stating: "Malaysia is very much a collectivist society. As such, most decisions related to elderly nursing home residents are influenced by the residents' family and friends".[56]

Whilst this emphasis on a family-oriented decision-making model may seem problematic for the acceptance and implementation of ADs, which tend to be conceived of as an individual expression of preference, that does not appear to be straightforwardly the case for at least two reasons. The first is that there are cases in which individuals wish to make an AD precisely *because* of their strong family ties, as demonstrated in

52 M.M. Malek et al., "Islamic Considerations on the Application of Patient's Autonomy in End-of-Life Decision" (2018) 57 *Journal of Religion and Health* 1524, 1528.

53 See note 45, 62.

54 P.S.M. Lai et al., "The Development and Validation of the Advance Care Planning Questionnaire in Malaysia" (2016) 17 *BMC Medical Ethics* 61, 69.

55 Ibid.

56 Jiao and Hussin, note 48, 67: citing the work of T. Oka et al., "The Diversity of Indigenous Wisdom on Grief: Exploring Social Work Approaches to Bereavement", in *The IAFOR International Conference on the Social Sciences: Hawaii 2017 Official Conference Proceedings* (Honolulu: IAFOR, 2017) on the determination that Malaysia is a collectivist society.

the 2007 study conducted by Htut et al.,[57] wherein some respondents indicated that their interest in pursuing an AD stemmed from a desire not to be a burden on their families. The second reason is that even when a family-based decision-making approach is adopted, that approach does not automatically exclude ADs. For example, in the 2017 Koh et al. study,[58] only 6 of the 70 participants stated that they opposed ADs because they preferred to leave medical decision-making to their families. Furthermore, 26.5 per cent of the participants stated that they preferred to have a family member act as a power of attorney to execute their ADs,[59] suggesting that the family may still have a role to play even if an individual wishes to make an AD and, further, that in a sociocultural context that emphasises the role of the family, the two can in fact be complementary.

Thus, whilst it is clear that the family plays a significant role in the context of end-of-life decision-making, the ways in which that role affects an individual's desire to make an AD may differ. On the one hand, those who wish their family members to make decisions on their behalf may be less likely to consider it necessary to make an AD. On the other, data suggest that others may not perceive a family role in decision-making to exclude the making of an AD, with some even likely to view family members as having a role in the making thereof.

9.4.2 The Role of Physicians

9.4.2.1 Important Advisory Role

Medical professionals play an important advisory role in the process of end-of-care decision-making in Malaysia because discussions about end-of-life decisions often involve complex medical issues on which medical professionals are considered best placed to provide advice. Additionally, some evidence suggests that patients prefer to have such discussions with their treating physicians. In their 2007 study, Htut et al. found that when respondents were asked who they should discuss ACP with, the majority cited their attending doctors. Interestingly, they

[57] See note 45, 62.

[58] See note 46, 65.

[59] It is not made clear in the study what the authors mean by a "power of attorney to execute an AD". Presumably, given the lack of clear legal guidelines on the format and requirements of an AD, it refers to the possibility of a family member executing an AD on a patient's behalf.

preferred hospital-based specialists to regular general practitioners. They expressed confidence in hospital specialists because "they know me better", "they have more experience" and "they are more appropriate to discuss this [issue] with".[60]

The key advisory role played by physicians can have an adverse effect on the acceptance and implementation of ADs in two ways. The first relates to whether physicians provide information on and encourage their patients to make ADs as part of their advisory role. Limited data from the 2016 Lai et al. study suggest that they do not. Lai et al. found that 89 per cent of their respondents who were against ACP stated that they had not been given enough information to make an informed choice and that that lack of information had influenced their objections.[61] The respondents also stated that if doctors were to provide sufficient information to patients regarding ACP, that would facilitate their acceptance of both ACP and ADs.[62] This finding is supported by the aforementioned fact that the professional guidelines issued by the MMC and MOH do not in fact require or even encourage physicians to initiate conversations about ADs or ACP more generally.

The second way in which physicians' key advisory role could potentially have an adverse effect is that individuals may prefer to rely on their treating physicians for medical decision-making rather than make their own ADs. There are limited empirical data supporting this possibility: in the 2020 study on end-of-life care in nursing homes, over half of the 13 respondents indicated that they would prefer to let their doctors handle decision-making for them and communicate with their families regarding end-of-life care.[63]

9.4.2.2 Public Interest versus Private Interests and the Important Role of Experts in the Islamic Context

It would appear that the key role of the physician is even more significant in the context of Islam, which can be attributed to the Islamic emphasis on the public interest rather than the interests of individuals. Salleh argues that physicians who possess the requisite training and are charged with saving lives may be deemed to be in a better position than the patient to ascertain the right choice, which he explains as follows:

[60] See note 45, 63.
[61] Lai et al., note 54, 69.
[62] Lai et al., note 54, 69.
[63] Jiao and Hussin, note 48, 68.

> Generally, Muslim scholars view that there is a limit to [a] patient's autonomy in choosing the forms of medical treatment and care, as [a] doctor's professional advice should also be considered. This is because choices made to satisfy personal interests and satisfaction are contrary to Islamic values. The emphasis in Islam is more on public interest compared to personal interest. Furthermore, Islam puts the emphasis on doctor[s'] efforts in saving lives. However, Islam also recognises the limitation of human endeavour, and as such all efforts must be followed by tawakkal. Having said that, doctors should exhaust all possible avenues in order to save a patient's life.[64]

In the specific context of ADs, Malek argues in a similar vein:

> In general terms, Islam does not disapprove [of] the application of AMD [s] [advance medical directives] in end-of-life decision-making. However, the application of [an] AMD may have certain limitations that must be addressed... Besides that, respecting autonomy via AMD[s] should not diminish the physician's role in decision-making as an expert in the medical field. Many Islamic views stress the necessity of taking the judgment of experts into account. Before any medical procedure is executed, it must undergo thorough medical evaluation and [the] judgment of experts. Therefore, patients must consult doctors before they can carry out their right to self-determination.[65]

Thus, whilst Malek is supportive of the right to autonomy and self-determination, he argues that patient autonomy should be "contextualised" according to Islamic values.[66] This contextualisation includes the prioritisation of the physician's views, as physicians are generally regarded as the "decision-making authority for patient care" in Malaysian society.[67] Malek further suggests that such deference to physicians confirms the influence of medical paternalism in healthcare decisions within the context of Islam.[68] Physicians must use their experience to judge whether a patient's choice "would bring more harm than good",[69] demonstrating that they have the authority to override any decisions made by their patients in order to follow Islamic principles. According to this reasoning,

64 S.M.S.S.M. Salleh, "Advance Medical Directive: How Prepared Are We?" *The Star* (2015), www.ikim.gov.my/index.php/2015/09/08/advance-medical-directive-how-prepared-are-we/.

65 M.M. Malek, "Applying Advance Medical Directive" (2017) *The Star*, www.thestar.com.my/opinion/columnists/ikim-views/2017/08/01/applying-advanced-medical-directive-islam-allows-its-application-in-endoflife-decisionmaking-but-the.

66 Malek et al., note 52, 1529.

67 Ibid.

68 Malek et al., note 52, 1533.

69 Ibid.

physicians should have the final say as to whether a patient's choice is implemented even when the patient has made an AD.

9.4.3 *The Role of Religion*

In addition to the significance of Islam in providing a context for the prioritisation of medical expertise, studies also indicate that religion is an important factor that comes into play when individuals are deciding whether or not to make an AD. The 2007 study of Htut et al., for example, reported that "the majority of respondents believed that their views on ADs were influenced by their religion", especially those of Islamic faith.[70] Most of them thought that it was best to leave matters pertaining to end-of-life care to either God or fate. Similarly, in their 2016 study, Lai et al. also identified fate and religion as two of the main justifications against ACP for participants who disapproved of it, with the majority of participants choosing fate and religion as reasons for not making an AD.[71]

Not all of the reported data are consistent. For example, in the 2017 study conducted by Koh et al., only 7.4 per cent of respondents (5 out of 70) said they would leave the decision-making process up to God or fate,[72] whereas 3 of the 13 respondents in the 2020 study on end-of-life care in nursing homes cited religion as playing the most important role in end-of-life care.[73] This evidence does not necessarily contradict the significance of religion, although it does suggest that even when religion is a factor that is taken into account, or a perspective through which many view the end-of-life process, it may not necessarily have an adverse effect on the use and acceptance of ADs.

9.5 Conclusion

ADs and end-of-life planning are not specifically regulated in Malaysia. This lack of regulation and what appears to be a low prevalence of ADs are influenced by many factors, including low levels of public awareness of ADs, dependence on family and physicians to make end-of-life decisions collectively (or in some cases on patients' behalf) and religious

70 See note 45, 63.

71 Lai et al., note 54, 68.

72 See note 46, 65.

73 Jiao and Hussin, note 48.

factors. Studies show, however, that patients are willing to consider ADs once they have been informed of them, suggesting that higher levels of awareness may lead to more people using ADs. The National Palliative Care and Care Policy and Strategy Plan 2019–30 has established a well-designed road map for embedding ACP services in hospitals and the community by training palliative care professionals and creating greater awareness within the profession and society, which is the first step towards recognising the value of ADs and ACP more generally in Malaysia. Well thought out governance mechanisms and legal regulations should also be put in place to ensure that the rights of patients are preserved, and patient autonomy is promoted.

10

Advance Directives in the Philippines: In Search of a Legal Framework

LEONARDO D. DE CASTRO, RENATO B. MANALOTO & ALEXANDER ATRIO L. LOPEZ

10.1 Introduction

The Philippines is a country located in Southeast Asia with a land area of around 300,000 square kilometres distributed across more than 7,000 islands in the western Pacific Ocean. Its population of 110 million is the second largest in the region and the 13th largest in the world. The country's archipelagic layout partly accounts for the inequitable distribution of healthcare resources across the population and for the concentration of large populations in under-resourced centres.

Many situations have arisen in the Philippines that suggest a possible role for advance directives (ADs) or similar instruments in that they give healthcare professionals and relatives the confidence to withdraw or withhold life-saving interventions from incompetent patients. The mounting cost of healthcare for people with chronic diseases and conditions associated with advancing age puts pressure on the resources that can be allocated for the care of all people in general. At the individual level, increasing healthcare expenses put pressure on ailing persons and their families to reconsider their "treat-at-any-cost" stance and explore ways of coping that are consistent with autonomous decision-making in anticipation of the point at which a person has lost mental competence.

Nevertheless, previous attempts to pass AD legislation have met with little success in the Philippines owing to religious and sociocultural influences. Given the practical need for ADs, as discussed previously, and highlighted by the pressures of the ongoing COVID-19 pandemic, hospitals have stepped in with their own institutional guidelines.

This chapter begins with an exploration of the religious and sociocultural factors that may account for the limited success of AD legislation in the Philippines. It then considers the specific context in which the country does have such legislation, namely, psychiatric ADs, and the difficulties that legislation faces. Lastly, the chapter examines the ways in which healthcare professionals have adopted alternative ways to offer greater legal certainty, such as the creation of specific guidelines at the institutional level, to avoid the pitfalls created by the gaps in AD legislation.

10.2 Religious and Sociocultural Influences

Religion and culture exert significant influences on the conception and practice of ADs in the Philippines. The country has long been known for its status as the only predominantly Christian country in Asia, and Christian values are enshrined in the Constitution of the Republic of the Philippines, the basic law of the land.[1] In addition to Christianity, Filipinos are also strongly influenced by cultural attitudes in relation to disease causation and family. The influence of religion and culture on ADs in the Philippines can be seen in two ways: through the Filipino understanding of what Christian values mean for ADs and what Filipinos' cultural attitudes towards disease, such as *bahala na* (what will be will be), and family mean for the end-of-life context.

The Christian faith frequently exerts an impact on legal developments in the Philippines, with the heated debates surrounding legal proposals often resulting in the upholding of Christian (often specifically Catholic) values to the point of violating human rights or disregarding essential human interests. Whilst there have been no significant public debates over ADs in the country, and there is a lack of high-quality empirical research on attitudes towards ADs or on how they are practised on the ground, there appears to be a general lack of sympathy for a legal framework for ADs. This lack of sympathy is likely due to ADs being seen – rightly or wrongly – as a rejection of the Christian commitment to upholding the value of a life that God has given and that only God can therefore take away.

With regard to cultural attitudes, the key theme in the characterisation of Filipino psychology concerning diseases and their causation has been the idea that people do not find it necessary – or useful – to prepare documents indicating their future treatment preferences because uncertainty generally does not worry them. It has been posited that Filipinos attribute unexpected negative or positive events in their lives to the grace

[1] Constitution of the Republic of the Philippines 1987.

of God, as doing so enables families to cope with challenges and accept their life experiences.[2] As well as being a coping mechanism, such an attitude also brings hope to families. It allows Filipinos to feel able to surrender their problems to a higher being who is all knowing and almighty, and exercises sovereign will, thus rendering ADs redundant for situations in which a patient is mentally incompetent. Rather than manifesting weakness on the part of the patient, readiness to offer his or her predicament to God allows the patient to experience a level of personal empowerment that reflects spirituality and is not incompatible with the concept of self-determination.

The phenomenon can also be explained in terms of the Filipino attitude of *bahala na*, which involves resignation to whatever may happen without any active participation in making it happen.[3] A person does not have to document treatment preferences for future contingencies through an AD because there is nothing to fear about a situation to which one is resigned. Recognising that human skills are not sufficient to overcome difficulties, the Filipino patient seeks the intercession of a higher being and resolves to accept whatever happens.

Many academics see the situation as a historical given, something that is especially highlighted, for example, by Filipino migrants in a country like the United States, where they have "built 'bonds' and 'bridges' with religious, civic, governmental, business and social institutions by means of... (1) transnational influence, (2) adaptive spirit, and (3) intergenerational cohesion...as they Filipinize elements of the cultural, political and economic arenas within the San Francisco Bay Area ... in which they have settled ... Because of the prevalence of religious practices in everyday life, daily discourse, verbal and written, is also influenced by religion".[4] The expression *bahala na* captures something essential about the cultural values that influence the way in which Filipino Catholics perceive and interact with society.[5] In addition to helping to explain the importance of religiosity and spirituality in the way that many Filipinos

[2] P.J.B. Abad et al., "Cultural Beliefs on Disease Causation in the Philippines: Challenge and Implications in Genetic Counselling" (2014) 5(4) *Journal of Community Genetics* 399.

[3] M.L. Tan, *Revisiting usog, pasma, kulam* (Quezon City: The University of the Philippines Press, 2008), 45–6.

[4] J.J. Gonzalez, *Filipino American Faith in Action: Immigration, Religion, and Civic Engagement* (New York: New York University Press; 2009), 2, 16.

[5] R.A. Lagman et al., "'Leaving It to God' Religion and Spirituality among Filipina Immigrant Breast Cancer Survivors" (2014) 53(2) *Journal of Religion and Health* 449.

approach decisions about health and healing,[6] the expression also helps us to understand why it is often difficult to convince a Filipino patient of the utility of ADs.

An example of such difficulty can be found in studies of Filipinos who have migrated to other countries, as the multicultural context allows observations of cultural differences. In a study of Filipino American patients in the United States, for instance, it was reported that "Filipino Americans who believe that the future is in God's hands may refuse to sign advance directives, even though they may recognise the need for hospice support. That is because signing advance directives would take the decision out of God's hands and would not be acceptable in their belief system".[7]

In addition to disease causation, Filipino cultural attitudes towards the role of the family are also relevant, as can be observed in the way that Filipinos prefer palliative care to be administered. Some academics have observed that "when the patient's condition becomes terminal, the home is usually the preferred place of care [and] ... many Filipinos take a passive role when they become ill and expect the family to care for them".[8] In fact, decision-making tends to fall upon the eldest male in the family as a matter of responsibility,[9] and it may even be considered irresponsible for the family to allow a vulnerable patient to make acute treatment decisions even when he or she still has decisional capacity. Self-care is generally frowned upon for being contrary to the best interests of the patient.

Thus, we can see that there are pervasive religious and cultural traits that are incompatible with Western notions of individual patient autonomy. In Filipino society, families decide as a unit on matters of healthcare, with the eldest male taking the key responsibility, rather than leaving such decision-making to the individual alone. In addition, decision-making takes place within a context characterised by acceptance of an unforeseen fate (*bahala na*), and people choose to surrender their

6 Ibid.

7 P.W. Nishimoto and J. Foley, "Cultural Beliefs of Asian Americans Associated with Terminal Illness and Death" (2001) 17(3) *Seminars in Oncology Nursing* 179.

8 A.D. Cantos and E. Rivera, "Filipinos" in J.G. Lipson et al. (eds.), *Culture and Nursing Care: A Pocket Guide* (San Francisco: UCSF Nursing Press, 1996).

9 J.L. McAdam et al., "Attitudes of Critically Ill Filipino Patients and Their Families toward Advance Directives" (2005) 14(1) *American Journal of Critical Care* 17. Although this study is based on Filipino Americans, the phenomenon is representative of Filipino medical decision-making more generally.

future to God's will when faced with difficult healthcare decisions. Reliance on these traits provides an explanation for the historically minimal discourse on ADs in the Philippines. Whilst the absence of a specific legal framework for ADs may be seen by the broader healthcare community as a deviation from the ideal scenario wherein individual patients' rights are protected, what is being manifested is in fact partiality towards an approach that is family rather than individual oriented and that is informed by religious and cultural sensitivities.

In the next section, we turn to an examination of laws that may be relevant to this discussion, with a brief consideration of ADs in the psychiatric context, which, unlike end-of-life ADs, have been legislated in the Philippines.

10.3 Philippine Legislation on Advance Directives

10.3.1 Advance Directives at the End of Life

Since the current constitution was ratified in 1987, numerous attempts to pass end-of-life AD legislation in both houses of the Philippine Congress have ended up in the archives. In a highly positivistic legal system like that of the Philippines, if there is no explicit law on end-of-life ADs (whether in the form of a statute, case law/jurisprudence or executive issuance), no such law can be considered to exist.[10] However, in situations in which an end-of-life AD is said to exist and needs to be ruled upon, the courts may invoke the following in their decision-making.

1. Cases in foreign legal jurisdictions (particularly those in the United States because of the Philippines' colonial history)
2. Philippine medical societies' codes of ethics
3. International documents to which the Philippines is explicitly or implicitly a signatory

Owing to the influence of the US legal system (its common-law tradition in particular) on the history and development of the Philippine legal system, US court decisions have a persuasive (as opposed to mandatory or binding) effect on legal decisions in the Philippines. In the absence of the country's own court decisions in cases involving ADs,

[10] Although ADs in the end-of-life care context are provided for in a number of professional guidance documents (which are further described in Section 10.4).

the Philippine courts may borrow US court decisions in interpreting or applying a provision, especially an unclear one.

Whilst the lack of legislative success with end-of-life ADs paints a murky picture concerning whether such instruments are effective, there are certain situations in which an end-of-life AD may be able to apply. In order for an end-of-life AD to be effective, there will likely need to be a finding of medical futility, as determined by a healthcare professional. However, two further conditions likely also need to be confirmed before an end-of-life AD can become operative: (1) the patient lacks decisional capacity and (2) the patient is unlikely to regain such capacity in the near future (i.e. the loss of decisional capacity is associated with the patient's underlying medical condition and will persist along with it).

10.3.2 Advance Directives in the Psychiatric Context

The closest the Philippines has come to legislative success in relation to ADs is a number of provisions in the National Mental Health Act (NMHA) 2018 (Republic Act No. 11036),[11] which defines ADs and the general conditions under which they may be expressed and implemented. The NMHA was signed into law on 20 June 2018 and took effect on 5 July 2020 after publication of its Implementing Rules and Regulations (IRR). In the chapter on treatment and consent, Section 9 makes specific reference to psychiatric ADs, stating: "A service user may set out his or her preference in relation to treatment through a signed, dated, and notarised advance directive executed for the purpose. An advance directive may be revoked by a new advance directive or by a notarised revocation".[12] The same wording is found in the IRR, where a psychiatric AD is held to be important for establishing the service user's or patient's consent, legal representative and supporters.[13]

With regard to consent, a psychiatric AD is important for documenting the authentic preferences of the patient. In Chapter III, Section 9 of the NMHA, it is indicated that the patient's expressed consent in an AD will also guide the healthcare team on what treatment options can be applied to the patient when he or she suffers a temporary impairment of decision-making capacity, such as in a neurologic or psychiatric emergency.

[11] Mental Health Act 2018.
[12] Ibid., s. 9.
[13] Implementing Rules and Regulations of the Mental Health Act 2018, s. 10.

With regard to legal representatives, Chapter I, Section 4 states that a representative of legal age may be appointed by a patient in his or her AD. Some of the functions of a legal representative specified in Chapter III, Section 11 are to be consulted on the patient's therapy, to assist the patient in various capacities and to act on the patient's behalf, especially when decision-making is impaired. If the patient fails to appoint a legal representative, the following people shall act as one in the specified order: spouse, children of legal age, parent, a medical director of the mental healthcare facility or someone appointed by the courts.

Finally, with respect to supporters, the patient can appoint up to three people in addition to his or her legal representative, as stipulated in chapter III, section 12 of the NMHA. Supporters may access the patient's medical information, consult the patient regarding treatment and be present during the patient's medical appointments. Appointing supporters can be seen as a way of keeping family members involved in the AD process.

Despite the aforementioned provisions in the NMHA, there is little clarity on how the psychiatric AD regime operates in practice. In a way, what has happened in the Philippines is a case of putting the cart before the horse: the NMHA[14] mentions ADs without the benefit of prior legislation specifically defining and describing the procedures for ADs. For this reason, many challenges can arise from disagreements in interpretations of when ADs are due for implementation after a patient loses mental competence. We explore some of these challenges next.

In situations in which patients appoint (in their written psychiatric AD) someone other than their next-of-kin as their legal representative, the NMHA may come into conflict with next-of-kin laws. Under the Philippine next-of-kin regime, the relative nearest in degree is usually the next of kin, with more distant relatives excluded. The Supreme Court of the Philippines describes this determination of the next of kin in the absence of a spouse as "[F]irst descends, then ascends, and finally, spreads sideways. Thus, the law first calls the descendants, then the ascendants and, finally, the collaterals, always preferring those closer in degree to those of remoter degrees".[15]

The next of kin may decide on the patient's behalf in any kind of case, psychiatric or not. By not observing the Philippine next-of kin laws, the

14 Mental Health Act 2018, s. 9.

15 *In the Matter of the Intestate Estate of Cristina Aguinaldo-Suntay* v. *Isabel Cojuangco-Suntay* [G.R. No. 183053: June 15, 2010].

decision-making granted by a patient to a legal representative who is not his or her next of kin may be held invalid. Accordingly, the legal representative and anyone else who implements the AD may be sued criminally (for physical injuries, assistance of suicide, homicide or murder) or civilly (torts and damages).

In the event that no next-of-kin is appointed, the appointment of a legal representative may still be questioned because of next-of-kin laws,[16] even in psychiatric cases, and the court will, after a trial, appoint a guardian for the patient. In all cases, regardless of whether any next of kin is appointed and who holds the decision-making power, the court has the power to veto choices made by physicians, parents, legal representatives, agents or guardians. The absence of pertinent jurisprudence regarding whether and how legal representatives trump next of kin in ADs makes it unclear whether the provisions in the IRR allow the appointment of legal representatives to make decisions on patients' behalf.[17]

Despite the potential legal complications, health practitioners and institutions have formulated legal instruments and procedures in the hope of providing themselves with legal protection while offering guidance to all, including patients and their families. Such a hope led to the formulation of guidelines relating to ADs by various Filipino hospitals, as well as guidance points pertinent to emergency healthcare practice during the current pandemic, both of which will be explored in the following section.

10.4 Advance Directives in Hospital Practice

Many hospitals in the Philippines have formulated their own guidelines for allowing, documenting and implementing patient preferences as part of a broader advance care planning process in scenarios that would ideally require ADs owing to patients' loss of decision-making abilities. Although these guidelines are not explicitly supported by AD legislation, they are considered part of good professional practice and are taught to

[16] The courts may invalidate the authority to decide granted by a patient to a legal representative (strictly speaking, a representative designated by the patient in a document, but where the designation is not consistent with next-of-kin laws) if that authority conflicts with an existing law or custom, morality or is contrary to the patient's frame of thought as noticed/known of him or her when he or she still had decisional capacity.

[17] Generally, in ruling on the validity of an AD in the context of the NMHA, the court will rely on other relevant laws (e.g. agency, notarial, contract and wills) owing to the lack of any explicit law providing for the procedures and policies for using ADs.

medical practitioners and students who work or rotate in clinical settings. There is also long-standing government recognition of professional self-regulation, and the medical community has codified its respect for a patient's right to refuse medical treatment in advance. Professional guidelines are also consistent with the contention that whatever their legal status may be, "advance directives are ethically valuable because they give a voice to patients at a time when their decision-making capacity has been lost" and that "such a voice is essential"[18] in the face of a proliferation of medical technologies that can prolong the process of dying almost indefinitely.

Because the practice of ADs has taken place in the absence of a clear legal framework, it is understood that the instruments are being used without the stakeholders being legally protected from any controversies or liabilities that may arise.[19] However, the guidelines could still have the effect of giving patients and their families confidence in the decision-making process, thereby forestalling legal suits. Thus, they continue to be offered routinely to patients. In the next part, we explore some of the AD guidelines and instruments implemented by various Filipino hospitals.

It is important to note briefly here that the concept of an AD is predicated on the idea that a patient has the right to refuse medical treatment or have it withdrawn by the doctor. Although that right is generally recognised, some hospitals impose conditions and limitations. For example, some imply that the right to refuse treatment is possessed by competent individuals alone,[20] and some explicitly stipulate that the refusal of treatment is permitted only to the extent allowed by law.[21] Such a stipulation is obviously problematic because, as already highlighted in

[18] N. Biller-Andorno et al., "Concluding Remarks" in P. Lack et al. (eds.), *Advance Directives* (New York: Springer, 2014), 204.

[19] In the event of a lawsuit, healthcare professionals still have to be able to show that they were acting on the basis of accepted standards of what is medically useful or what is medically futile in the specific circumstances pertinent to the particular patient. This is the standard by which healthcare professionals can justify their decisions and also by which patients or their families can pursue criminal or civil cases. Therefore, notwithstanding any hospital guidelines, there is still a need for a legal framework providing reliable guidance for patient rights claims and professional accountability.

[20] See, for example, Governor Celestino Gallares Memorial Hospital, "Patients Right", https://gcgmh.doh.gov.ph/patients-and-visitors-corner/patients-right and Karmelli Clinic and Hospital Corporation, "Patients Rights", https://karmellihospital.wordpress.com/patients-rights/.

[21] See, for example, Capitol Medical Center, Inc., "Patient's Guide", www.capitolmedical.com.ph/patients/patients-guide/ and Makati Medical Center, "Patient Reference: Advanced Directives", www.makatimed.net.ph/patient-and-visitor-guide/patient-reference/.

this chapter, existing laws fail to provide a sufficient legal framework. Further, even when legal provisions are in place, there appears to be room for conflict, for example, in relation to next-of-kin laws.

10.4.1 *Types of Advance Directive*

Taking their cue from their foreign counterparts, including those in the United States, many hospitals in the Philippines explicitly mention "advance directives", "advanced medical directives", "advance care", "living wills" and/or "do-not-resuscitate" (DNR) orders in promoting the services they make available to patients.[22] For example, The Medical City,[23] a well-known private hospital in the Philippines, provides a detailed discussion on its website, defining an AD as a "written document (form) that tells what a person wants or doesn't want if he/she in the future can't make his/her wishes known about medical treatment".[24] The hospital further describes an AD as detailing what a patient's wishes are depending on his or her condition in the future, for example, in the event that he or she is in an unconscious state, a coma or a state that is likely to be terminal.

Hospitals recognise ADs of different kinds: (1) a living will, (2) declaration to withdraw or withhold treatment and (3) a DNR order.

10.4.1.1 Living Will and Declaration to Withdraw or Withhold Treatment

A living will details a patient's preferred treatments in the case of a serious or terminal illness.[25] The patient's stated wishes may include such details as "comfort measures only", "Do not transfer to ICU" or "Do not give IV antibiotics".[26] A living will does not allow a patient to appoint someone to make decisions on his or her behalf; such appointment is instead enabled by a "special power of attorney for

[22] See, for example, Luzon Medical Center, "Patient's Right", https://luzonmedicalcenter.com/patients-right/ and Bataan St. Joseph Hospital & Medical Center Corp., "Patient's Responsibilities", www.stjosephhospitalbataan.com/patients-responsibilities.

[23] As one of the most prominent hospitals in the country (with multiple branches inside and outside the Metropolitan Manila area), The Medical City sets trends in hospital practices that tend to be followed by others.

[24] The Medical City, "Advance Directives and Do-Not-Resuscitate Orders", www.themedicalcity.com/news/advance-directives-and-do-not-resuscitate-orders.

[25] Ibid.

[26] The Medical City, "Myths and Facts of Palliative Care", www.themedicalcity.com/news/myths-and-facts-of-palliative-care.

healthcare".[27] A "declaration to withdraw or withhold treatment" is a type of AD mentioned by the Makati Medical Center on its website.[28] Such a declaration is useful in cases where a patient suffers from an incurable condition and life-sustaining treatments would only prolong dying. It seems to be similar to a living will.

The fact that different hospitals offer different types of documents to patients reflects the absence of AD legislation, as well as the expectation that, by giving patients and their families a sense that their decisions are being respected, legal controversies can be minimised. Patients and their families are generally expected to make use of whatever documents are on offer at the institution in question.

10.4.1.2 Do-Not-Resuscitate Order

In addition to a living will and declaration to withdraw or withhold treatment, a DNR order can be implemented in the context of a specific AD. Unlike DNR or do not administer cardiopulmonary resuscitation (DNACPR) orders, which are typically instigated by healthcare professionals on the grounds of futility, a DNR order in this context indicates that the patient does not want CPR if his or her heart or breathing stops.[29] Further, as part of an AD, a DNR order is decided by the patient while competent or by his or her next-of-kin in the event of incompetence.

A cancer-related statement issued by the Tumour Board of Ospital ng Maynila Medical Center Hospital gives doctors four criteria to help them decide when to advise terminally ill cancer patients and/or their guardians to make a DNR order: (1) when there is a high probability of the patient going into cardiopulmonary arrest because of cancer, (2) when the patient is in a vegetative state, (3) when the treatment burdens outweigh the benefits and (4) when the patient and/or guardian wants a DNR order.[30] Such an order is important because in the absence of one, healthcare professionals will continue to administer life-saving treatment.[31] A DNR

27 See note 24.

28 Makati Medical Center, note 21.

29 See note 24.

30 Ospital ng Maynila Medical Center Hospital Tumor Board, "Statements on Certain Cancer Issues", https://omtumorboard.tripod.com/capalliationmgt.htm.

31 See, for example, Calamba Doctors' Hospital, "Patients' Rights and Responsibilities", www.calambadoctorshospital.com/patientsguide/rightsresponsibilities and Makati Medical Center, "Patient Rights & Obligations", www.makatimed.net.ph/patient-and-visitor-guide/patient-references/patient-rights-and-responsibilities.

order instructs healthcare providers not to perform CPR but to continue other treatments.[32] The cessation of other treatments can be specified via a declaration to withdraw or withhold treatment. In the next section, we explore some of the instructions relating to ADs that are typically given by various hospitals to their patients.

10.4.2 Instructions Regarding Advance Directives

This section presents a synthesis of the kinds of instructions on ADs that various hospitals give to their patients.[33] To make an AD, a patient may simply write down his or her preferences, use a doctor-provided form or consult a lawyer.[34] Aside from consulting a lawyer, a patient may also want to talk to his or her doctor, loved ones, caregivers and spiritual advisers.[35] The inclusion of spiritual advisers in the preceding list attests to the importance of religious beliefs in the experience of disease discussed earlier. Doctors usually advise patients to talk to religious authorities to obtain advice and comfort.

Instructions are given that an AD should be made when a patient is still competent to anticipate what decisions ought to be made if he or she loses mental competence.[36] Understandably, the absence of a formal legal framework, even within the NMHA, for determining when decisional capacity has been lost makes it absolutely necessary for the healthcare team to explain how it will be assessed to avoid legal controversy should the family become dissatisfied with certain aspects of the treatment given to the patient.

A DNR order can also be mentioned by a patient to his or her doctor, upon which the doctor writes the order in the patient's medical records.[37] A DNR can also be written on a piece of paper, kept as a card in a wallet or worn as medical jewellery such as a necklace or bracelet.[38]

Patients and their families are also told that any changes made to an AD should ideally be signed and notarised.[39] Notarisation provides legal

[32] Makati Medical Center, note 21; note 26.
[33] However, it should be noted that each hospital publicises its own set of guidelines.
[34] See note 24.
[35] Makati Medical Center, note 21.
[36] Metro Iloilo Hospital and Medical Center, Inc., "Patient's Rights", www.metroiloilohospital.com/patients-rights-and-responsibilities.php.
[37] Makati Medical Center, note 21.
[38] Ibid.
[39] Given that some revocations may occur at the last minute or in otherwise urgent situations, the need to notarise the revocation may be administratively burdensome.

documentation that the AD has been issued upon the patient's authority. Otherwise, the attending physician or family members should be informed of the changes early on.[40]

Patients are told to bring all of their AD documents with them to every hospital admission, with copies provided to all members of the healthcare team.[41] Some hospitals also tell patients to bring their ADs with them if they want them to be applied during a particular admission.[42] There are also hospitals that stipulate that it is patients' responsibility or obligation to bring their ADs or notify their doctor that they have one.[43] More specifically, notifying healthcare personnel of an AD is part of a patient's responsibility to provide complete and accurate information on his or her health status.[44] Details of an AD are usually verified by the healthcare team by checking with the patient's family, a practice that is very much in line with the emphasis on family in the sociocultural context of the Philippines.

Healthcare professionals are instructed to carefully explain to patients how immensely useful an AD can be. Owing to the lack of AD discourse in Filipino culture, such a careful explanation is a necessary step in healthcare delivery. For example, patients are told that preparing an AD can reduce the stress on their family members and doctors in future healthcare decision-making.[45] It is interesting to note that the detailed instructions provided by various hospitals regarding ADs do not appear

Legislating a comprehensive legal framework for ADs is capable of making the process less burdensome by explicitly removing the requirement for notarisation of the pertinent documents.

40 See note 24.

41 Makati Medical Center, note 21.

42 Bataan St. Joseph Hospital & Medical Center Corp., note 22, and Dr Fe Del Mundo Medical Center, "Patient & Visitor Guide", www.fedelmundo.com.ph/patient-visitor-guide/.

43 See, for example, Davao Regional Medical Center, "Do You Know Your Responsibilities as a Patient?", https://drmc.doh.gov.ph/patient-s-corner/patient-s-responsibility, and Chong Hua Hospital, "Patient Rights and Responsibilities", http://chonghua.com.ph/index.php/patients_visitors_guide/patient_rights_responsibilities.

44 San Pablo Colleges Medical Center, "Patients Rights & Responsibilities", www.spcmc.com.ph/patients-rights-and-responsibilities/. Of course, ADs are seen not only as part of a patient's responsibilities, but also as his or her right. Some hospitals explicitly mention the ability to make an AD as a patient's right (see, for example, Bayawan District Hospital, "Patient's Rights", http://bdh-stabayabas.weebly.com/patients-rights.html and Calamba Doctors' Hospital, note 31. An AD is also recognised as part of preserving a patient's dignity (see further Chong Hua Hospital, "Advance Directives", http://chonghua.com.ph/index.php/patients_visitors_guide/advance_directives.

45 Makati Medical Center, note 21; note 24.

to align well with the aforementioned *bahala na* philosophy. One potential reason for this lack of alignment is that hospitals see a practical need for such instructions, perhaps to shield themselves from potential liability, a need that is driving education and awareness of ADs despite the absence of a formal legal regime for ADs and the concept being contrary to *bahala na*.

10.4.3 The COVID-19 Context

The onset of the pandemic provided an opportunity for stakeholders such as healthcare professionals, ethicists, social scientists, policymakers and administrators to underscore the importance of ADs in anticipation of situations requiring quick decision-making by healthcare professionals when patients lack competence and their relatives are not readily accessible. In the knowledge that the triage mechanisms in hospitals need to take patients' autonomous choices into consideration and that relatives were barred from hospitals, internists took the initiative to propose guidelines that were then vetted by other stakeholders committed to promoting ethical decision-making in the face of the existing challenges.

The resulting document, known as the Ethics Guidelines on COVID-19,[46] consists of 30 guidelines, including 4 that address situations that could require the use of ADs. The participants in the consultation recognised that healthcare professionals would soon be swamped with emergency cases for which they needed to be armed with documentary evidence of patients' preferred treatment options.

Guideline 2 recognises "the rights of patients to autonomy, transparency, privacy, and confidentiality of personal information" and provides that ADs should be considered upon admission.[47] Consistent with such recognition, Guideline 6 urges that "advance care planning should be initiated at the earliest appropriate time and preferably even before hospital admission ... and that the patient ... [be] encouraged to accomplish an Advance Directive".[48] The Ethics Guidelines also provide an AD template that is sufficiently specific to offer patients a reasonable indication of possible treatment scenarios and enable specific decisions to be made regarding such options.

[46] University of the Philippines Manila, *Ethics Guidelines on COVID-19: Crisis-Level Hospital Care* (Manila: University of the Philippines Manila, 2020).
[47] Ibid., p. 7.
[48] Ibid., p. 10.

The Ethics Guidelines also include a template for a substitute decision-maker form for use in cases where the patient lacks the competence to accomplish the equivalent form, which implies that an AD is not meant to address disagreements between patients and their families but rather those between patients (and families) and healthcare providers. The guidelines relating to ADs pertain to situations in which timely communication between patients and their families is impossible because relatives are not allowed to join patients in confinement and treatment or medication has to be given very quickly by a healthcare team that may have no opportunity to obtain consent from a patient who lacks mental alertness or competence. Accordingly, decision-makers have to be guided by what they consider to be medically useful or futile while also hoping that ADs will offer them some protection in the event of legal proceedings.[49] In the remote likelihood of legal proceedings (which are rare in the Philippines), healthcare decision-makers can look forward to being protected by acting on the basis of what is professionally determined to be medically useful or medically futile without having to depend on the existence of ADs.[50] This is probably true even with the preponderance of various legal forms in use in medical institutions.

10.5 Conclusion

Although various Filipino hospitals have developed their own guidelines relating to ADs, professional self-regulation is no substitute for a legal framework providing reliable guidance for patient rights claims and professional accountability. In the absence of a clear legal framework that defines the exact parameters for what can be regarded as acceptable documents, ADs are open to inaccurate interpretation and inconsistent application. Legislating a proper framework for ADs would provide consistency in interpretation and, more importantly, greater confidence in the accuracy of the message that incompetent patients are trying to convey to medical professionals and to their families. A legal framework acquires moral significance not simply because it exists and serves as a

[49] Although the Ethics Guidelines cannot replace existing laws, the courts may rely upon them in determining the legal liability of doctors, if any, in absence of explicit laws on the matter at hand.

[50] In addition, the use of the AD template and substitute decision-maker form can provide persuasive evidence that a directive is indicative of a medically accepted procedure or policy and consistent with professional practice, something that the courts may invoke to determine the intent and legal liability of a party.

reliable document in the event of disputes but also because, once it has been sufficiently publicised, people can be presumed to understand that when they write an AD, they know that it will be interpreted in light of the ground rules laid out in the legal framework. The NMHA has signalled to healthcare stakeholders that a legal framework for ADs could serve a useful purpose. In addition to filling a gap in mental healthcare practice, the Act also sends the clear message that legal documents are incomplete without the specific guidance that a legal framework can provide. Moreover, it also provides a legal precedent against which ADs of various kinds in non-mental health contexts can be judged by courts of law in the future. These significant effects of legislation are all the more needed in light of the discussion provided in this chapter regarding the cultural stances to which Filipinos default in healthcare decision-making. The presence of legislation could prompt Filipinos to consider alternative or complementary ways of thinking about such decision-making by themselves or their families.

After all, the importance of the kind of decision-making advocated by ADs is already evident in the way in which hospitals have devised their own ways of justifying and encouraging the use of ADs. In addition to the guidelines of various hospitals, the COVID-19-inspired AD and substitute decision-maker templates constitute initial steps towards formalising and disseminating the use of ADs. However, the Philippines needs to push through with legislation if the full benefits of ADs are to be realised by healthcare professionals and patients alike.

11

Advance Directives and the Turkey Context

YESIM ISIL ULMAN*

11.1 Introduction

Caring for a patient who is at the end of life should ethically be in accordance with human rights and dignity based on the value of life, in the concept's secular sense, meaning that life is a basic good that possesses intrinsic value ranging from the right to life to the avoidance of overly burdensome and futile medical interventions to achieve a death with dignity. It encompasses caring for others with due respect paid to their own choices and preferences on the basis of human rights and dignity.

One way of respecting patient preferences is via an advance directive (AD), the main underlying ethical principle of which is respect for patient autonomy. Such respect is honoured by executing the AD when the person concerned has the capacity to make informed decisions and give consent. Respect for patient autonomy requires that patients have an opportunity to make their own moral choices and achieve their own wishes and preferences. Doing so is a universal and even existential component of being human in compliance with the concept of human dignity, regardless of geographical borders, cultural factors and sociological differences. Such an approach supports the process of advance care planning as a way to improve end-of-life care when decisions are taken openly and straightforwardly in a pluralistic manner with the support of family and relatives, and the role of ADs is to ethically implement and legally document the process.

In the end-of-life context, respect for human dignity, whereby all human beings possess equal and inherent worth, and therefore ought to be accorded the highest level of respect and care,[1] entails paying

* Corresponding author: yesimul@yahoo.com.
Acknowledgments: I am grateful to the editors of this book Assistant Professor Daisy Cheung and Associate Professor Dr Michael Charles Dunn for their scholarly efforts and comments on the piece.

[1] R. Andorno, "Human dignity and human rights as a common ground for a global bioethics" (2009) 34(3) *Journal of Medicine and Philosophy* 223.

particular attention to the decision-making process regarding medical treatment at the end of life as a high-quality procedure, especially for particularly vulnerable patients. Respecting people's views on how they would like to be treated should be considered in terms of the value of life and dying in dignity, both of which extend beyond national borders and cultural features. Palliative care and high-quality end-of-life care are also important components when considering an ethical and legal framework for legislating ADs.

11.1.1 The End-of-Life Context in Turkey

Turkey's life expectancy at birth is comparable to global figures. Whilst the country's birth rate and newborn mortality rate have declined, the elderly proportion of the total population rose by 21.9 per cent over the 2014–19 period.[2] As life expectancy for the elderly has lengthened in Turkey, health problems have changed, and there is greater demand for long-term care and control. According to public health specialist Reyhan Uçku, mortality and morbidity rates have increased in line with global statistics on such non-communicable diseases as cardiovascular diseases, cancer, respiratory diseases and Alzheimer's disease, which has resulted in a rising need for end-of-life care. She has, as a result, called attention to the deficiencies in healthcare delivery for the elderly and end-of-life care in Turkey.[3]

Turkey's low ranking in the Quality of Death Index, 47th amongst 80 countries worldwide according to an Economic Intelligence Unit report, is quite alarming, raising questions about the quality of end-of-life care in the country.[4] Whilst a government-led strategy is in place for the development and promotion of national palliative care, the strategy's milestones are loosely defined, with no targets specified, and the mechanisms for achieving them are also limited. Furthermore, the degree of correlation between Turkey's overall Quality of Death score and per capita healthcare expenditure is also rather low. It is stated in the aforementioned

2 Turkish Statistical Institute (TUIK), "Elderly statistics" (2020) https://data.tuik.gov.tr/Bulten/Index?p=Istatistiklerle-Yaslilar-2020-37227.

3 R. Uçku, "Healthcare provision at the end-of-life: what are the needs and delivery?" [in Turkish] (2016) 31(1) *Toplum ve Hekim* 5.

4 The Economist Intelligence Unit, *The 2015 Quality of Death Index: Ranking Palliative Care across the World* (London: 2015), https://eiuperspectives.economist.com/sites/default/files/2015%20EIU%20Quality%20of%20Death%20Index%20Oct%2029%20FINAL.pdf, pp. 15, 16, 23–25, 32, 37.

report that Turkey falls into the category of government subsidies or programmes being available for individuals requiring access to palliative care services, but the qualification criteria are unclear, and subsidy funds and programmes are limited and/or difficult to access. Moreover, Turkey has a shortage of specialised palliative care professionals, and accreditation for specialist palliative care training is not the norm.[5]

Although end-of-life care is available in Turkey in both the private and public sectors, in accordance with a 2014 regulation, Uçku comments that such care services are far from prevalent, are often poorly organised and are not coordinated or integrated with other components of the healthcare system. There are also shortcomings in capacity. The number of trained, competent healthcare staff is far from sufficient, and health coverage in the field is also insufficient. There is a need for efficient policies that are responsive to needs on the ground.[6] The Ministry of Health has initiated a 2013–23 target plan to increase palliative care capacity by establishing new centres and hospices in Turkey. Medical experts, however, are of the view that palliative care coverage should be expanded. They also recommend that a system whereby certain types of healthcare expenses can be refunded should be realistically implemented and that multidisciplinary healthcare staff, including psychologists, social workers, physiotherapists, spiritual support personnel and volunteers, should be put in place to meet the needs of patients and improve their access to end-of-life care.[7]

In addition to the need for improved end-of-life care, there have also been calls for the development of AD legislation amongst academics and professionals as part of a growing emphasis on patient preferences.[8] Such legislation is a particularly important issue for Turkey, given its ratification of the Council of Europe's Convention on Human Rights and Biomedicine ("Oviedo Convention"), as discussed later. This chapter considers ADs in the Turkish context, beginning with a consideration of the possible legal bases for such directives in Turkey. It then explores the relevant professional guidance from medical associations, as well as empirical data relating to the level of awareness of ADs amongst patients and healthcare professionals. The sociocultural factors that pose potential obstacles to the introduction and implementation of

[5] Ibid, pp. 5–8.

[6] See note 2, pp. 7–8.

[7] A. Bilen, "Palliative care" [in Turkish] (2016) 31(1) *Toplum ve Hekim* 25, 28.

[8] See Section 11.5, The Way Forward for further details.

ADs in Turkey are also discussed, and the chapter concludes with some thoughts about the way forward.

11.2 The Legal Framework

Although Turkey does not have any specific laws dealing with ADs, there are several sources of law that are relevant in considering this issue, as well as end-of-life decision-making more generally.

11.2.1 Oviedo Convention

The first source is the Oviedo Convention. International treaties are one of the sources of written law in Turkey; once such treaties have been adopted by the Grand National Assembly of Turkey, they have the force of law and are hierarchically above national laws.[9] The Oviedo Convention was ratified by Turkey on 4 April 1997, adopted in 2003 and entered into force in 2004 with the name *Insan Haklari ve Biyotıp Sozlesmesi* (Convention on Human Rights and Biomedicine).

The Oviedo Convention provides an ideal framework for the ethical and legal aspects of treating patients with dignity and preserving human rights. With regard to persons lacking capacity, the convention clearly states in Article 9 that "previously expressed wishes relating to a medical intervention by a patient who is not, at the time of the intervention, in a state to express his or her wishes shall be taken into account".[10]

The Guide on the Decision-making Process Regarding Medical Treatment in End-of-life Situations issued in 2014[11] by the Council of

[9] Ö.C. Eren and E.E.V. Lutz, "Turkey and the Council of Europe's Oviedo Convention on its 20th anniversary" (2017) 22(2) *Anatolian Clinic Journal of Medical Sciences* 73.

[10] In addition, the principle of equitable access to health care (Article 3), the requirement of informed consent for any medical treatment (Article 5) and special safeguards to protect persons unable to provide consent (Article 6) present a framework for the inclusion of ADs in the jurisdiction of Turkey based on human rights and human dignity. See I.S. Sogut, "The effect of the Convention on Human Rights and Biomedicine (Oviedo Convention) on domestic law regulations" (2018) 14 *TipHD* 181.

[11] The guide was translated into Turkish in 2014: see further Council of Europe, *Yaşamin Son Döneminde Tibbi Tedavide Karar Verme Sürecine İlişkin Kilavuz [Guide on the Decision-making Process Regarding Medical Treatment in End-of-Life Situations]* (Yesim Isil Ulman, PhD, Trans.) (2014), https://rm.coe.int/CoERMPublicCommonSearchServices/DisplayDCTMContent?documentId=09000016806ad65a. The translated guide is distributed with the support of Acibadem University. The Turkish version of the guide was introduced at a Joint Symposium on the End of Life in collaboration with the Council of Europe and Acibadem University on 25 October 2016. The symposium booklet contained

Europe elaborates on the formal legal arrangements for previously expressed wishes, including as one of the options ADs, or "written documents drawn up by a person having legal capacity (who has attained majority and is able to express a free and informed wish) containing provisions relating to medical treatment in the event that he or she is no longer capable of taking part in the decision-making process".[12] It further states that written ADs are the most direct means of reflecting patients' wishes and, as long as requirements to ensure validity and accessibility are fulfilled, they should take precedence over all other non-medical opinions expressed in the decision-making process.[13] The guide, however, leaves it up to ratifying states to decide whether to give legal binding force to previously expressed wishes.[14]

Although the Oviedo Convention is considered a part of Turkey's internal law, and although its first provision requires signatories to make their domestic law compatible with the convention by making any necessary amendments, Turkey has not yet fulfilled this requirement in full.[15] This is particularly true in relation to Article 9. There remains a lack of legislation on or formal legal regulation of ADs in Turkey, which means that the legal efficacy, content and limits of such documents remain uncertain.[16] Moreover, the Council of Europe's aforementioned guide, which has been translated into Turkish and widely adopted within Turkey, has not been formalised into legal governance requirements concerning how end-of-life care ought to be provided or what role ADs have.

11.2.2 *Additional Legal Frameworks*

Whilst there is no local legislation that deals directly with the subject matter of ADs, there are a number of local laws that sit alongside the

an AD written by Professor Steven Miles to set an example of what an AD is and what the scope and content of an AD can be. I translated this AD into Turkish for the accessibility of academic and public circles in Turkey. See further Council of Europe and Acibadem University, "End of Life Care Symposium" (2016), www.acibadem.edu.tr/doc/EndofLifeCare-kitapcik.pdf.

12 *Guide on the Decision-making Process*, note 11, p. 17.

13 Ibid., p. 18.

14 Ibid., p. 20.

15 I.S. Sogut and E. Tuna, "Legal instruments on patient's living medical wills" (2017) 12 *TipHD* 255.

16 See note 1, p. 223.

Oviedo Convention in Turkish domestic law and that could potentially be interpreted to provide an additional legal basis for ADs.

The first is the 1982 Constitution. Section 2, Article 17 on Personal Inviolability and Material and Moral Existence of the Person states the following.

> Everyone is entitled to right to life, to protect and develop her/his material and moral existence. Personal integrity is inviolable unless there exists any medical necessity and legally binding situation stated by law; no one can be subject to scientific or medical trials without her/his consent. No one can be subject to torture or degrading treatment that is incommensurable with human dignity.

Although not specifically addressing the topic of end-of-life care, the constitutional principles of human rights and dignity contained within this section of the Constitution could provide a foundation for the introduction of ADs.

The second local law is the Civil Code, which some jurists have suggested could potentially be amended to cover ADs in accordance with the Oviedo Convention and Turkish Constitution. For example, Cetinel proposes that Article 23 of the Civil Code, which "protects the personal rights of the individual and states that such rights are indefeasible",[17] could be amended to cover ADs.[18] It has also been suggested, however, that Article 23 might pose difficulties for the refusal of life-saving treatment, which could be seen as a waiver of the rights to life and bodily integrity.[19]

The third local law possibility can be found in the Patient Rights Regulation, which came into effect in 1998. This regulation was issued by the Ministry of Health in light of international covenants, the Turkish Constitution, and other legal documents and legislation with the purpose of allowing patients to exercise rights in healthcare settings in accordance with human dignity and of protecting patients from violations of their

[17] G. Sert and T. Guven, "Examining the ethico-legal aspects of the right to refuse treatment in Turkey" (2013) 39 *Journal of Medical Ethics* 632.

[18] M.U. Cetinel, "Living wills and powers of attorney in view of patient preferences in comparison with Turkish-German Civil Codes, some suggestions" (2019) 3 *3rd International Medical Law Congress, Book of Proceedings* 567, 567 [in Turkish]. Specifically, Cetinel argues that a person's wishes about bodily integrity are not only about physical bodily integrity, but also about his or her own values about their existence as a living being with moral values. Cetinel thus considers Article 23 to be a gateway to ADs and extends her argument through comparisons with the German Constitution.

[19] See note 17.

fundamental rights.[20,21] The Patient Rights Regulation states that a patient's previously expressed wishes should be taken into consideration during any medical intervention and, if the patient's capacity is lost intermittently, that his or her informed consent should be obtained prior to the intervention at a time when he or she is conscious and sane (Article 24). A patient also has the right to reject or withdraw a treatment that is planned or being carried out for him or her except in legally binding situations or when negative consequences may arise from such rejection/withdrawal (Article 25).

Although the aforementioned articles currently provide only for the requirement to obtain informed consent prior to medical interventions, not to prepare ADs with patients,[22] the Patient Rights Regulation is the only document that explicitly refers to the right to refuse treatment.[23] Accordingly, it has been argued that Article 24 provides an appropriate basis for AD legislation in Turkish law.[24] It should be noted, however, that the language of Article 24 contains significant limitations on the exercise of the right to refuse treatment:[25] (i) in cases where treatment has already begun, consent can be withdrawn only if there are no "medical drawbacks" of doing so and (ii) consent cannot be withdrawn in "emergency situations threatening the life or one of the vital organs [of the patient]".[26] It thus appears doubtful that these articles could serve as the basis for ADs without significant amendments. Unfortunately, owing to the low normative status of the Patient Rights Regulation in Turkish law, as a document issued by the Ministry of Health rather than Parliament, provisions contained in higher status laws, including the Constitution and Civil Code, would need to be clarified before the regulation could be amended in any meaningful way.[27] In a similar vein, Irmak elaborates on the refusal of treatment in light of medical

20 Patient Rights Regulation, Article 1.

21 There are studies showing, however, that there is a "marked discrepancy" between patients' rights in principle and how they are applied in practice, with patients stating that these rights are not respected in practice. See further E. Aydin, "Rights of patients in developing countries: the case of Turkey" (2003) 3(1) *Yogun Bakim Dergisi* 37.

22 I. Koşar et al., "Assessment of knowledge and preferences regarding advance directives among patients in university family medicine outpatient clinics" (2020) 6 *Gerontology & Geriatric Medicine* 1.

23 See note 17.

24 See Sogut, note 10, pp. 191–2.

25 See note 17.

26 Ibid.

27 Ibid.

paternalism and proposes reforms in the legal documents defining and regulating patient rights in Turkey to strengthen such rights in relation to patient autonomy.[28]

11.3 Professional Guidance

Given the lack of a specific legislative framework regulating ADs, the professional guidance issued by various professional organisations should also be considered. In addition to the Council of Europe's guidance discussed previously, several Turkish professional organisations have also issued guidance in relation to the end of life.

In 2016, the Turkish Society of Medical and Surgical Intensive Care issued a guidance document entitled "Problems and Possible Solutions Faced by Terminally Ill Intensive Care Patients: Views from the Turkish Society of Medical and Surgical Intensive Care",[29] which affirms the importance of a patient's right to make medically informed, autonomous decisions, as well as the importance of a patient's right to refuse futile treatment. In the document, the society specifically calls attention to the role of ADs in actualising patients' wishes and in respecting patients' self-determination, as expressed in advance with decision-making capacity concerning the withholding or withdrawal of treatment in the circumstances of worsened quality of life at the end of life with a prolonged dying process. Interestingly, the society expresses cultural reservations about euthanasia and physician-assisted suicide, but advises that improved palliative care services and pain control be provided and fostered by psychological and social support via a multidisciplinary approach. Dying with dignity in a peaceful and compassionate way surrounded by loved ones is stated in the document to be the right of everyone at a terminal stage.[30]

The Turkish Society of Intensive Care has taken a similar stance. In its "Opinions and Suggestions of the Turkish Society of Intensive Care on Healthcare during the End-of-Life Period",[31] also issued in 2016, it calls

[28] N. Irmak, "Right to refuse treatment in Turkey: a diagnosis and a slightly less than modest proposal for reform" (2016) 42(7) *Journal of Medical Ethics* 435.

[29] Turkish Society of Medical and Surgical Intensive Care, "Problems and possible solutions faced by terminally ill intensive care patients: views from the Turkish Society of Medical and Surgical Intensive Care" (2016) 31(1) *Toplum ve Hekim* 42 [in Turkish].

[30] Ibid., pp. 44–6.

[31] Turkish Society of Intensive Care, "Opinions and suggestions of the Turkish Society of Intensive Care on healthcare during the end-of-life period" (2016) 31(1) *Toplum ve Hekim* 58 [in Turkish].

for public engagement to be conducted through multilateral dialogue amongst social actors, professional expertise bodies, the Turkish Medical Association, university law faculties and policymakers to enlighten the Turkish people on medical, legal and ethical issues in order to remove the cultural factors that may hinder the acceptance of refusals of futile treatment.[32]

Most recently, and perhaps most importantly, the "Declaration on End-of-Life Decisions" issued by the Turkish Medical Association in 2020 contains two sections that appear relevant to ADs.[33] The first states that, where life support is envisaged, the patient's primary physician should seek the patient's opinion on life support and suggest that the patient express his or her will in advance in situations wherein he or she may lose decision-making ability.[34] Whilst this provision refers to the prior expression of wishes, it is similar to Article 24 of the Patient Rights Regulation and may thus be seen as focusing primarily on the obtaining of informed consent ahead of time in cases in which the patient may lose capacity. It does, however, encapsulate to some extent the normative ethical value of prioritising patient choices in such cases. More importantly, in the second relevant section, which appears under the heading "Living Will", the association provides a clear definition for what appears to be the equivalent of an AD:

> A living will is the patient's verbal, written, and sometimes even witnessing statement about what he wants or does not want to be done, at any stage of the treatment of his chronic disease, after he loses his decision-making ability. These decisions are mostly about terminating treatment that will not provide any benefit to the patient, asking for "Do-Not-Resuscitate" [DNR] when he is unable to regain lost functions, or not continuing life support treatments or artificial nutrition.[35]

This definition demonstrates that the association is supportive of the promotion of an individual's decision-making and self-determination capacity to determine his or her preferences as to whether treatment should be withheld or withdrawn, particularly in the form of an AD. The declaration concludes with an affirmation of the right of every person to

[32] Ibid.

[33] Ethics Committee, Turkish Medical Association, "Turkish Medical Association Ethics Declarations: Statement on End-of-Life Issues, Ankara" (2020), www.ttb.org.tr/kutuphane/etikbildirgeler2020.pdf, pp. 36–40.

[34] Ibid., p. 37.

[35] Ibid., pp. 38–9.

die with dignity. These guidelines have been drafted on the basis of systematic, well-planned, multilateral discussions amongst experts in human sciences, medicine, biosciences, law and social sciences.[36] What is needed at this stage to take steps to implement these principles in practice is the engagement of policymakers.

11.4 The Sociocultural Context of Advance Directives in Practice

Despite the clear endorsement of ADs in professional guidance, available empirical data suggest that there is a relatively low level of awareness of ADs amongst both patients and healthcare professionals. In Koşar et al.'s study of 300 patients in outpatient clinics, 70 per cent of patients were found to be unaware of ADs prior to the survey.[37] Tekpınar and Uludağ's study of 372 healthcare professionals found that more than half (53.8 per cent) had inadequate knowledge of ADs.[38]

Interestingly, however, these studies also found that, upon understanding what ADs are, the majority of participants were in favour of the concept, reflecting the outcomes of similar empirical studies conducted in the United States and China.[39] Of the 300 patients in Koşar et al.'s study, 78 per cent agreed that ADs were useful and necessary.[40] Of the healthcare professionals in Baykara et al.'s study, 77.9 per cent stated that ADs should be clearly legislated, whilst 70.3 per cent supported consideration of the previously expressed wishes of incapacitated patients during a medical intervention, and 52.9 per cent agreed that patients who had signed DNRs should not have their decisions interfered with.[41] These findings suggest that raising the awareness of the population in relation

[36] See, for example, the list of contributors in the Turkish Medical Association Ethics Declarations (see note 33).

[37] See note 22.

[38] By profession, this was 55.9 per cent of the doctors, 71.4 per cent of the assistant doctors and 42.7 per cent of the nurses. See further L. Tekpınar and A. Uludağ, "Perspective of doctors and nurses on the principle of extended autonomy in Konya, Turkey" (2021) 83(4) *OMEGA – Journal of Death and Dying* 884.

[39] L.L. Emanuel et al., "Advance directives for medical care – a case for greater use" (1991) 324(13) *The New England Journal of Medicine* 889; P. Ni et al., "Advance directives and end-of-life care preferences among adults in Wuhan, China: a cross-sectional study" (2021) 21 *BMC Public Health* 2042.

[40] See note 22.

[41] N. Baykara et al., "Factors affecting the attitudes and opinions of ICU physicians regarding end-of-life decisions for their patients and themselves: a survey study from Turkey" (2020) 15(5) *PLoS ONE* e0232743.

to ADs is likely to have a positive impact on the use of ADs in practice if they are legislated or otherwise formally introduced and, prior to that being accomplished, on the likelihood that end-of-life wishes will be clearly expressed by patients.

There are, however, certain sociocultural factors that may affect the implementation of ADs in practice. Most prominently, paternalism appears to be a core feature of the Turkish healthcare context. In their comparative analysis of differing approaches to ADs in Europe, Andorno et al. noted that despite Turkey's ratification of the Oviedo Convention, the use of ADs in the country was practically non-existent in medical practice owing to the strong paternalism that dominates the doctor–patient relationship[42] and that this "culture of paternalism" is in direct contradiction of the Oviedo Convention.[43] Sert and Guven provide further support for this claim, arguing in particular that paternalistic interventions, as well as paternalistic interpretations of provisions that deal with emergency situations, which do not require informed consent, in cases where there is a wish to refuse treatment are often the norm owing to the lack of clear definitions and guidelines on whether patients have a right to refuse treatment.[44]

There are also empirical data that support the claim. In their study of 207 physicians presented with case studies involving the fundamental principles of bioethics, Ersoy and Gündoğmuş found that 83.6 per cent of the participating physicians would try to save the life of a patient who had indicated prior to losing consciousness that he or she did not want to live with the aid of artificial respiration; only 13 per cent said they would respect the wishes, living will or previous consent of the patient.[45] On the basis of these results, the authors concluded that the participants in their study had a low degree of sensitivity to ADs.

This paternalism is manifested not only in approaches towards medical intervention, but also in the choice of whom to communicate with in relation to end-of-life measures. Sert and Guven argue that discussing death with patients at the end of life still appears to be taboo amongst healthcare professionals in Turkey, who often choose to discuss such

[42] R. Andorno et al., "Advance health care directives: towards a coordinated European policy?" (2009) 16 *European Journal of Health Law* 207, 223.

[43] Ibid., p. 227.

[44] See note 17.

[45] N. Ersoy and Ü.N. Gündoğmuş, "A study of the ethical sensitivity of physicians in Turkey" (2003) 10(5) *Nursing Ethics* 472.

issues with the family instead of the patient.[46] Sert and Guven's claim here is that professionals aim to shield patients who are close to death from the difficulties associated with making decisions about their care for their own good, turning to the family as a protective mechanism to relieve patients of any distress resulting from conversations about their care at the end of life. Whilst this behaviour can be seen as in line with the importance of family in Turkey, where familism and collectivism continue to be the leading values, as demonstrated by cross-national value surveys,[47] and where the family is frequently involved in medical decision-making,[48] Guven and Sert argue that simply attributing it to the role of the family in the Turkish social structure "fail[s] to acknowledge the effect of the authority and influence of the paternalist healthcare professional".[49] Thus, professionals' motivation to rely on the family for decision-making in this context is paternalistic rather than grounded in a commitment to patients' meaningful relationships with family members or in the family's status as a decision-making authority independently of a specific patient. Setting the reasons for this behaviour aside, removing the patient from discussions about end-of-life care can result in a patient's desire to refuse life-sustaining treatment being overlooked or disregarded, particularly as anecdotal evidence suggests that families are likely to demand heroic measures in such situations.[50]

11.5 The Way Forward

Whilst paternalism remains a key feature of healthcare professionals in Turkey, it has been argued within Turkey that there should be a move towards a more patient autonomy-centred approach, an argument that reflects the broad consensus in Anglo-American bioethical discourse. Accordingly, the concept of patient rights has become more popular following the issuance of the Patient Rights Regulation by the Ministry of Health.[51]

[46] See note 17.

[47] M.A. Kara, "Applicability of the principle of respect for autonomy: the perspective of Turkey" (2007) 33 *Journal of Medical Ethics* 627.

[48] T. Guven and G. Sert, "Advance directives in Turkey's cultural context: examining the potential benefits for the implementation of patient rights" (2010) 24(3) *Bioethics* 127, 129.

[49] Ibid., p. 130.

[50] See note 17, p. 634.

[51] See Guven and Sert, note 48.

As the evolution of professional guidance over the past few years demonstrates, there is also considerable support for ADs and the valuing of patients' wishes at the end of life from the disciplines of medicine, law and ethics, as well as from medical specialty societies and medical associations. From the viewpoint of family physicians, for example, Kahveci argues that considering patient involvement in the decision-making process and respecting patients' wishes would render healthcare delivery more democratic.[52] Guven and Sert, as discussed previously, have criticised paternalistic practices in the healthcare setting and emphasised the need for coordinated efforts to achieve legislation on ADs and living wills.[53]

In their paper on the ethical approach to end-of-life preferences and decisions, Akpinar and Ersoy argue that fulfilling a patient's previously expressed wishes is an ethical responsibility for healthcare professionals and that it is thus ethically permissible and appropriate for a physician to withdraw or withhold life-sustaining interventions owing to such wishes if they are formulated in a living will.[54] İmamoğlu draws particular attention to the function and effectiveness of living wills and ADs and proposes that they should be expressly regulated by law in order to guide patients, relatives and healthcare professionals in the provision of high-quality end-of-life care to terminally ill patients.[55] Finally, Kalkan and Mirici, two intensive care clinicians, remark in their survey of DNR decisions that the principle of patient autonomy should encompass respect for a patient's previously expressed wishes, namely, in the form of living wills, and that such respect should be promoted to a greater extent to both doctors and patients. They call for consensus to be reached amongst medical, ethical and legal disciplines on the evaluation of living wills in terms of patient autonomy.[56] Importantly, this approach to justifying and developing a more robust AD regime in Turkey, one built

[52] R. Kahveci, "A step towards democratization of health care services: patient involvement in terminal life support decisions" (2007) 15 *Turkiye Klinikleri Journal of Medical Ethics* 90, 93 [in Turkish].

[53] See Guven and Sert, note 48, p. 127.

[54] A. Akpinar and N. Ersoy, "Life-sustaining treatment: when should it be withheld or withdrawn?" (2012) 27(1) *Turkish Journal of Oncology* 37, 38–40 [in Turkish].

[55] S.H. İmamoğlu, "Certain issues concerning patient's will" (2016) 65(1) *Ankara Üniversitesi Hukuk Fakültesi Dergisi* 199, 200–6 [in Turkish].

[56] E.A. Kalkan and A. Mirici, "Opinions of chest physicians about the do-not-resuscitate orders: respect for patient's autonomy or medical futility?" (2018) 9(2) *Yoğun Bakım Derg* 34, 37.

on respect for human dignity and personal autonomy, would also bring Turkey more closely into alignment with other countries.

In practical terms, internationally ratified and legally binding conventions offer an appropriate infrastructure for Turkey in terms of reforming end-of-life decision-making, as well as the inclusion of ADs in legislation on the basis of human rights and dignity. They are an important and necessary starting point for further legislative developments and the formalisation of a legally ratified regime for ADs in end-of-life care. What is also urgently needed is for policymakers to take responsible steps forward to represent the public's views on how the international consensus surrounding end-of-life care and decision-making processes should be tailored to the contemporary norms of Turkish society. However, it is also important to gather the collaborative efforts of medicine, ethics, philosophy, sociology and law in evaluating ADs and designing legislation specific to them. Promoting ethical consultation would be highly valuable to enhancing the end-of-life decision-making process in clinical practice and to addressing some of the paternalistic practices documented previously. Training healthcare professionals in both the concept of ADs and the discussion of end-of-life preferences with patients is also crucial.[57]

In order to develop a legally robust and practically applicable approach to ADs, legislators and professionals in Turkey need to address concerns about how ADs have been put into practice elsewhere. Such concerns include worries about the stability of patient preferences over time, necessitating an ongoing review of any directive made and ensuring an ongoing conversation between the patient and doctor to ascertain any changes that may need to be captured in a revised statement timed in an appropriate manner.[58] As Lo and Steinbrook have argued, it will also be important going forward to not see ADs simply as the fulfilment of a legal process, where the emphasis is on documentation and process. Instead, ADs should be embedded in good clinical practice, where communication between doctor and patient creates a space for a meaningful exchange about the patient's values, perhaps as part of a broader care-

[57] Avcu et al.'s 2018 study found that, in a sample of 443 physicians, a significant majority (84 per cent) had never received any training in relation to discussions with "patients in the last days of life about their last wishes for life". See further R. Avcu et al., "How would doctors want to die if they had a terminal stage illness? A survey study" (2018) 18 *Ankara Medical Journal* 575.

[58] S.E. Hickman et al., "Hope for the future: achieving the original intent of advance directives" (2005) *The Hastings Center Report* S26.

planning process, and within which a discussion about the appropriateness of an AD takes place.[59] Finally, as Brock argues, it is vital that concerns relating to the proper assessment of a patient's competence and his or her full understanding of relevant treatments, consequences and alternatives prior to the AD being made are properly addressed.[60]

There is also a need for in-depth studies exploring social and cultural factors to promote public engagement and public participation led by academe, civil society actors, specialty societies and professional associations. Such studies are likely to aid the development of more patient-centred healthcare provision while simultaneously clarifying the role of family members in the enactment of an AD and in shaping their loved one's end-of-life care more broadly. They might also function to challenge, and subsequently diminish, paternalism and to trigger a public conversation leading to improvements in patient-physician interactions on the basis of trust in balance with patient autonomy and beneficence. This pluralistic way forward, focusing on open dialogue, can ensure that new laws and practices are supported in ways that are feasible, pragmatic and underpinned by a fundamental respect for the values of human dignity and personal autonomy.

[59] B. Lo and R. Steinbrook, "Resuscitating advance directives" (2004) 164 *Archives of Internal Medicine* 1501.

[60] D.W. Brock, "Death and dying: the incompetent patient", in R.M. Veatch (ed.), *Medical Ethics*, 2nd ed. (Sudbury, MA: Jones and Bartlett Learning, 1997), pp. 370–2.

PART III

Non-regulated Jurisdictions

12

Advance Directives in China's Mainland: An Emerging Framework?

BO CHEN

12.1 Introduction

China's mainland is rapidly becoming an ageing society. In 2010 there were 168 million Chinese people aged 60 years of age or above – and the elderly population is projected to increase to 402 million by 2040, representing about 28% of the projected total population of China.[1] Accordingly, it is expected that there will be increased demands for high-quality healthcare in general, and for greater autonomy in end-of-life care. While they have attracted controversy, Advance directives (ADs) are considered as potentially useful legal instruments to promote patient autonomy at the end of life.[2]

This book defines an AD as a statement in which a competent person makes an advance decision in any number of areas (including healthcare, social welfare and any other personal matters), to be implemented in the event that the person becomes incompetent (loses mental capacity) in the future.[3] Even by this arguably narrow definition, it should be stated that China's legal system does not provide a normative framework governing the use of ADs. In recent decades, however, new developments in both law and a professional code of ethics have emerged, and one might reasonably expect these new rules and guidelines will centre patient autonomy, echoing the spirit of ADs.

This chapter explores the emerging normative framework governing the use of ADs in China, which primarily consists of relevant provisions

[1] World Health Organization, *China Country Assessment Report on Ageing and Health* (Geneva: WHO, 2015), apps.who.int/iris/bitstream/handle/10665/194271/9789241509312_eng.pdf?sequence=1, p. 15. "China's mainland" or "Mainland China" is referred to as "China" in the chapter for better clarity.

[2] D. CHEUNG, M. DUNN and R. HUXTABLE, Introduction, in this volume.

[3] Ibid.

from the *Civil Code*[4] and the *Chinese Medical Doctors' Code of Ethics (CoE)*.[5] The chapter argues that where the stakeholders (primarily doctors, and patients' family members who play a part in medical decision-making) choose to respect a patient's will (made before they lost mental capacity), this framework provides such a legal and ethical basis. However, the chapter also observes that such a normative framework is rarely applied in legal proceedings, as revealed by a thorough search of the judicial database for courts' judgments, or in healthcare practice. The chapter will also survey a number of civil society organisations that advocate for the use of ADs in China, before forming a conclusion.

12.2 Making Sense of the Emerging Normative Framework

For the purposes of this chapter, I draw upon a broad definition of ADs to examine the law and professional guidelines in China. The term "advance directive" refers to two types of statements in which the patient may (a) appoint a substitute decision-maker for and by the patient concerned (power of attorney); and/or (b) make specific decisions for future healthcare planning (generally known as a living will). It is the latter meaning of AD that this book adopts, even though recognising its limitations. In this chapter however, given the significance of the adult guardianship system in China, and the general absence of specific laws or regulations on ADs, the norms that apply to both forms of ADs will be considered. This section first explores the relevant provisions of the adult guardianship system as provided in the *Civil Code*, and which I suggest could potentially provide a legal basis for a Chinese version of power of attorney. It then examines the provisions of the *CoE* that direct Chinese doctors to respect the living wills made by mentally competent patients.

12.2.1 Adult Voluntary Guardianship: Chinese Version of Power of Attorney

The enforcement of China's *Civil Code* which adopted provisions on adult guardianship law began on 1 January 2021. The code is not entirely

[4] *Civil Code* of the People's Republic of China (adopted at the Third Session of the Thirteenth National People's Congress on 28 May 2020; entered into force on 1 January 2021).

[5] Chinese Medical Doctor Association, *Chinese Medical Doctors' Code of Ethics* (25 June 2014).

new, however, as it was initially introduced in 2017 by another piece of legislation, the *General Provisions of Civil Law*,[6] as part of a project preparing for the final *Civil Code*.

Adult guardianship authorises a third party (i.e. the guardian) to make legally binding decisions on behalf of another person under their guardianship. The legitimacy of adult guardianship and other forms of substitute decision-making arrangements have been the subject of considerable debates and controversies since the adoption of the United Nations Convention on the Rights of Persons with Disabilities (UNCRPD)[7] and the first General Comment No.1 on article 12 – Equal recognition before the law.[8] China has been a State Party to the UNCRPD since 2008, and the reform of the law regarding adult guardianship is arguably a step towards maximising the autonomy of persons with disabilities, who are often made subjects of adult guardianship.[9] Although the chapter focuses on the current applicable law, it acknowledges the visible gap between domestic law and the relevant requirements made by the UNCRPD.

Before embarking on a closer examination of the adult voluntary guardianship system, it should be noted that the role played by guardians on behalf of those they are responsible for goes beyond mere decision-making. Guardianship in the Chinese context includes the extension of a combination of both rights (or powers) over the person under guardianship, in addition to having a duty of care to ensure the protection of personal rights, property rights and other rightful interests of the person.[10] In practice, guardians also have a duty of responsibility for many aspects of the life of the person under guardianship, such as caring for the person on a daily basis. A guardian may also be liable for the actions of the person under guardianship, for instance, if the person under guardianship causes injury to a third party or their property, and the guardian is deemed not to have fulfilled their oversight duty.[11]

[6] The General Provisions of Civil Law of the People's Republic of China (adopted at the Fifth Session of the Twelfth National People's Congress 15 March 2017; entered into force on 1 October 2017; repealed on 1 January 2021).

[7] United Nations Convention on the Rights of Persons with Disabilities (adopted on 13 December 2006; entered into force on 3 May 2008) 2515 UNTS 3.

[8] CRPD Committee, "General Comment No 1: Article 12: Equal Recognition before the Law" (11 April 2014) UN Doc CRPD/C/GC/1.

[9] B. Chen, "Controversy and consensus: does the UN Convention on the Rights of Persons with Disabilities prohibit mental health detention and involuntary treatment?" (2020) 1 *Foundation for Law and International Affairs Review* 39.

[10] *Civil Code*, art. 34.

[11] Ibid., art. 1189.

In such a context where guardians have a significant responsibility and power over the life of the person under guardianship, the *Civil Code* allows the person under guardianship to be involved in the process of choosing the individual who will be appointed as guardian, while the person retains the mental capacity to make rational decisions.[12] Before moving to the specific arrangements of voluntary guardianship, it is equally important to briefly examine the provisions on mental capacity and adult guardianship in general.

The *Civil Code* adopts the term of "capacity for performing civil juristic acts" that is based on the assessment of whether an adult can "comprehend his own conduct".[13] For adults who are considered as going to lose or having already lost full or partial capacity for performing civil juristic acts, guardians could be appointed in three major methods. The first one is appointing guardians by a legal order of close relatives,[14] where the spouse of the person is the most prioritised candidate of guardian, followed by one's parents and adult children; if all the candidates are inapplicable or unable to take the responsibility, other close relatives or other willing and approved individuals or organisations would also become eligible.[15] Guardians may also be appointed by agreement among eligible candidates of guardianship,[16] and by voluntary or prearranged guardianship.[17] In circumstances where conflict arises over the choice of guardian, the law states that the local village, neighbourhood committee or local government's civil affairs department should intervene, or the issue be resolved in a court of law.[18] As a last resort, in instances where there are no eligible family or others who can take on the responsibility, the local village or neighbourhood committee or local government's civil affairs department would take on the responsibility of guardianship.[19] Since guardianship in the Chinese context consists of both decision-making rights as agent and a duty of care, the legal order prescribed in article 28 of the *Civil Code* serves the purpose of ensuring that the person believed to be in need of such will ultimately be assigned a guardian.

[12] Ibid., art. 21.
[13] Ibid.
[14] *Civil Code*, art. 28.
[15] Ibid.
[16] *Civil Code*, art. 30.
[17] Ibid., art. 33.
[18] Ibid., art. 31.
[19] Ibid., art. 32.

Given that the state does not generally provide guardians with sufficient financial remuneration or other resources to enable them to carry out their guardianship responsibilities efficiently and effectively, to be appointed as a guardian requires a significant psychological and financial commitment.

Voluntary guardianship, or prearranged guardianship, since guardianship can hardly be genuinely voluntary, was introduced in 2017 by the *General Provisions of Civil Law*, and it reflected the principle of maximum respect for the autonomy and wills of persons under guardianship.[20] An official English translation of article 32 of the *Civil Code* reads:

> An adult with full capacity for performing civil juristic acts may, in anticipation of incapacity in the future, consult his close relatives, or other individuals or organisations willing to be his guardian, and appoint in writing a guardian for himself, who shall perform the duties of guardian when the adult loses all or part of the capacity for performing civil juristic acts.[21]

The provision suggests that the appointed guardian will serve the function of a power of attorney, as happens when a competent person appoints a representative to make future healthcare decisions on their behalf, in the event they lose the capacity to do so themselves at some future time. In the context of Chinese civil law, entering a contract of healthcare services with a healthcare service provider, such as a hospital or clinic, deciding on a treatment plan, and, perhaps more controversially, signing on the informed consent documentation are often considered as the so-called civil juristic acts mentioned previously.

It is clear that voluntary guardianship and its terms and conditions must be agreed in writing,[22] but less transparent are the mechanisms to ensure its enforcement. The *Civil Code* does not elaborate on which aspects of decision-making capacity should be assessed and how the capacity for performing civil juristic acts should be assessed and declared. In the context of healthcare services, it seems reasonable to assume that relevant medical professionals are best suited to make such an assessment. However, the Civil Procedure Law contains a section detailing the special procedure for declaring full or partial loss of capacity, a decision which

[20] Ibid., art. 35.
[21] Ibid., art. 32.
[22] Ibid.

must be made by a court.[23] A careful reading leads one to infer that this procedure applies in assessing capacity, since the *Civil Code* is silent on this issue. On the other hand, it has been common practice that public notarisation is sufficient to activate voluntary guardianship, in which case, the aforementioned court proceeding is bypassed or simply ignored.[24] This uncertainty in activating voluntary guardianship might be a factor influencing its utilisation in practice, an issue which will be explored later in the chapter.

Once the guardianship is established, the guardian's action must be based on the Best Interest Principle of the person under guardianship.[25] The *Civil Code* does not elaborate on what actions the guardian is required to fulfil under the Best Interest Principle. One interpretation of this provision given by the Leadership Unit for implementing the *Civil Code* of the Supreme People's Court provides an example of this principle:[26] the guardian may dispose of the property of the person under guardianship only for the express purpose of defending his or her interests, an eventuality that is also provided for in the *Civil Code*. Interestingly, however, such an interpretation also provides that the essence of the Best Interest Principle is to fully respect the wishes of the adult under guardianship, another principle that governs the guardians' actions.

Article 35 of the *Civil Code* obliges guardians to give maximum respect to the true wishes of the person, by supporting the person to undertake matters that are appropriate to their capacity, while refraining from intervention.[27] The principles of "Best Interest" and "maximum respect for true wishes" have the potential to come into conflict with each other; however, the practice as reflected in judicial proceedings and published medical studies seems inadequate to form a basis on which to examine the actual tension, as will be discussed later. These principles might be admittedly more relevant to the daily decision-making for

[23] The Civil Procedure Law of the People's Republic of China (adopted at the Fourth Session of the Seventh National People's Congress on 9 April 1991; amended on 8 October 2007, 31 August 2012, and 27 June 2017), chapter 14, section 4.

[24] Shanghai Notary, "Enforcing my voluntary guardianship when I become confused" (China, 27 August 2018) www.shnotary.org.cn/info/db53f9b27389432fa77177e8242535c7.

[25] *Civil Code*, art. 35.

[26] The Leadership Unit for Implementing the *Civil Code* of the Supreme People's Court, *Understanding and Applying the General Provisions of the Civil Code of People's Republic of China* (Beijing: People's Court Press, 2020), p. 213.

[27] *Civil Code*, art. 35.

persons with intellectual disabilities or mental health problems than ADs in end-of-life care or healthcare generally. At the very least, however, the principle of maximum respect for autonomy, as well as other provisions examined previously, demonstrates a clear direction in law that the autonomy of the persons whose mental capacity might be in question should be given serious consideration and respected as far as possible.

12.2.2 Code of Ethics: Respecting for Living Wills at End-of-Life Care

The Chinese Medical Doctor Association, representing 2.3 million members, issued the *CoE* on 25 June 2014. The association claims that the binding force of the *CoE* lies between non-binding declaration and formally binding regulation,[28] the exact implication of which warrants further clarification.

The *CoE* is comprehensive in content, consisting of 40 articles that are divided into the following sections: basic principles, doctor–patient relationship, the relationship with fellow doctors, doctor–society relationship and doctor–enterprise relationship. Patient autonomy is one of the key themes. Article 1 requires doctors to give adequate respect to their patients,[29] and article 9 asks medical professionals to listen to the patients and to strive to build relationships of mutual trust.[30] In doing so, doctors are required to communicate with their patients in a manner that is understandable to the patient.[31] An example here would be the procedure of obtaining informed consent before a surgical operation; it is expected that a special examination or treatment would not be conducted as a mere box-ticking exercise or an excuse for avoiding possible liability.[32]

It is also evident that the framework is grounded in paternalism. The *CoE* allows doctors to conceal information considered to be potentially harmful should it become known to the patient.[33] Guided by arguably competing approaches, some provisions read less clear. For example, article 23 of the *CoE* requires doctors to respect patients' "reasonable"

[28] Chinese Medical Doctor Association, "Promote noble medical ethics and build a harmonious doctor-patient relationship: the Chinese Medical Doctors' Code of Ethics officially released" (China, 25 June 2014) www.cmda.net/bmdt8/9666.jhtml [in Chinese].

[29] *CoE*, art. 1.

[30] Ibid., art. 9.

[31] Ibid., art. 10.

[32] Ibid., art. 12.

[33] Ibid., art. 22.

requests and choices, including their right to accept or decline any medical recommendation.[34] Yet there remain the problematic questions of how to assess "reasonableness" in this context as there is no standard measure, or what consequences should follow when patients decline medical recommendations, both of which requires further research.

The most relevant provision relating to ADs is article 20, the first sentence of which requires doctors to take seriously patients' life-sustaining decisions.[35] It is followed by the second sentence which states that doctors should also respect any wishes expressed by patients through living wills and substitute decision-making arrangements made while patients lost their mental capacity.[36] The text is unclear on whether the endorsement of living wills is limited within the scope of maintaining or withdrawing life-sustaining arrangements. Nonetheless, even for patients whose capacity for performing civil juristic acts is in question, their doctors should facilitate their maximum participation in all aspects of medical decision-making.[37] There does not appear to be any empirical research on how these articles operate in practice, or how doctors have implemented any such living wills (if at all), so it remains unclear whether article 20 has been put into practice and, if so, how this was done, the circumstances, and with what consequences.

12.2.3 Summary

The normative framework governing mental capacity and professional ethics in China represents a mixed package which endorses both paternalistic benevolence and personal autonomy. Maximum respect for autonomy and involvement in healthcare decision-making goes hand in hand with the Best Interest Principle in the *Civil Code* and the "reasonableness" assessment in the *CoE*.

That said, it is equally evident from this discussion that both the voluntary guardianship in the *Civil Code* and the living wills provision in the *CoE* offer at least a possibility that ADs could become functional in China. From a historical perspective, the current normative framework demonstrates a step towards respecting patients' autonomy in healthcare

[34] Ibid., art. 23.

[35] Ibid., art. 20.

[36] Ibid. The chapter notes that substitute decision-making arrangements are not generally regarded as a process authorised to respect prior wishes alongside living wills.

[37] *CoE*, art. 25.

decision-making. For all stakeholders who have concerns about ADs, they at least have something to start with, albeit there remains considerable uncertainty. On the other hand, however, the fact that adult guardianship has undergone recent reform may imply that legally binding ADs are not likely to be introduced in the foreseeable future. The adult guardianship system may reinforce the pre-existing practice and culture which prioritises substitute decision-making arrangements over giving consideration to patients' wishes expressed through living wills. Given these possibilities, the form in which these will ultimately be adopted depends on how this will be practiced on the ground.

12.3 Explanations for Under-implementation

The previous section argued that the current normative framework at least creates the possibility that ADs could be made and respected, both legally and ethically. This section explores the extent to which this theoretical possibility has been realised. It does so firstly by examining the databases of courts' rulings and medical research, specifically seeking evidence that would suggest real-world use and application of the aforementioned legal and ethical provisions.

Before its introduction in 2017 by the *General Provisions of Civil Law*, the actual application of voluntary guardianship was long-awaited. However, based on the search results from *China Judgments Online*, the official publicly accessible database of courts' rulings, there has yet to be a case where the court has been called upon to decide on the legality of voluntary guardianship.[38] Moreover, the *CoE* was mentioned by a plaintiff in only one case, and the court did not address the question of

[38] In January 2021, the author conducted keyword searches in Chinese that referred to voluntary guardianship (意定监护), article 33 of the *General Provisions of Civil Law* (民法总则第三十三条) and article 32 of the *Civil Code* (民法典第三十二条). There are dozens of cases that mention these keywords but none of them are about medical decision-making. In one case, however, the court recognised the legality of a power-of-attorney form provided by the hospital and signed by the patient in which the patient appointed one of her children to decide on whether to withdraw or refuse life-sustaining treatment. The court ruled that this form served a similar function of voluntary guardianship but on different legal basis. At the very least, the case suggests the power-of-attorney practice exists and its legality could be accepted in court, though on an individual basis. See the case of Beijing Second Intermediate People's Court No. 7645 Civil Case of 2020–Final Judgment (Case reference code is translated by author from 北京市第二中级人民法院(2020)京02民终7645号民事判决书). Further research is required to explore the extent to which this practice is widely adopted nationwide.

whether the *CoE* had been breached. The search results suggest rare, if not non-existent, application of the current normative framework of ADs in Chinese courts. Healthcare services appear not to utilise the normative framework either. Extensive and close searching of *CNKI.NET*, the largest electronic database for academic papers, failed to identify any research studies on the actual application of ADs or the *CoE* provision. Most of the several dozen relevant papers are either theoretical or seek to promote its regulation by introducing foreign law on ADs. The following sections will explore why implementation has been weak, firstly by presenting the factors in the normative framework, followed by a discussion on attitudinal and cultural underpinnings.

12.3.1 Legal Uncertainty and Practical Unnecessity

In the previous discussion of the normative framework, I briefly touched on the matter of legal uncertainty. The *Civil Code* does not specify who should be appointed to assess the extent of incapacitation, or the procedure for activating voluntary guardianship. Moreover, the *CoE* fails to clarify the determination of the concept of reasonableness in patients' wills, or whether the respect for living wills applies only in end-of-life decisions. Even though awareness of ADs has been growing, it would be reasonable to assume these uncertainties do not encourage patients or doctors to invest their time and energy in these matters. This would be particularly the case when they are unsure of the legal or practical consequences that will follow.

Risks exist in the application of ADs in light of other relevant rules. For example, faced with a living will that outlines a refusal of life-sustaining treatment, the doctor will be placed in a dilemma: on one hand, the *CoE* imposes an ethical duty on the doctor to respect the living will, if they are convinced that the patient's refusal of treatment is "reasonable" and all other conditions are met.[39] On the other hand, the doctor has a legal obligation to save lives, and, moreover, the law does not appear to allow exceptions, even where living wills specify the patients' refusal of life-saving treatment. For example, the Law on Practicing Doctors (LPD) explicitly requires doctors in China to adopt emergency treatment measures, and stipulates that doctors cannot refuse to give

[39] *CoE*, art. 20.

emergency treatment.[40] The penalties for non-compliance range from suspension for 6–12 months, to having their medical license revoked, to facing even criminal prosecution if their (in)actions result in delays in the rescue and treatment of patients in emergency and critical condition, and serious consequences due to negligence.[41] Similar provisions are also to be found in lower-ranking regulations, such as the *Administrative Regulations on Medical Institution* in 1994[42] and *The Guiding Opinions on the Establishment of an Emergency Relief System for Diseases* in 2013.[43]

It could be argued that respecting the refusal of life-sustaining treatment through a living will does not violate these general rules. Front-line practitioners, however, appear to feel assured when they are explicitly guided by clear rules that support their legal and ethical obligations to comply with the living will.[44]

In addition to these legal uncertainties in the rules and their legal consequences, substitute decision-making by formal voluntary guardianship may be seen to be unnecessary in practice. It has been widely acknowledged that the procedural requirement established by the *Civil Procedure Law* for declaring the capacity for performing civil juristic acts, the precondition for validating adult guardianship in theory, is facing significant practical difficulties.[45] More importantly, family members are granted considerable rights to information and decision-making in healthcare services.[46] Since in most cases, it is family members

[40] The Law on Practicing Doctors of the People's Republic of China (adopted by the third session of the Standing Committee of the National People's Congress on 26 June 1998; entered into force on 1 May 1998), art. 24.

[41] LPD, art. 37.

[42] The State Council of China, *Administrative Regulations on Medical Institution* (adopted on 26 February 1994; amended on 6 February 2016), art. 31, www.nhc.gov.cn/fzs/s3576/201808/f674e82257a2471a9a68f5c369403042.shtml.

[43] The State Council of China, *The Guiding Opinions on the Establishment of an Emergency Relief System for Diseases* (1 March 2013) section 4(2), www.gov.cn/zwgk/2013-03/01/content_2342656.htm.

[44] Y. Sun, *Research on Advance Health Care Directives* (Beijing: Legal Publishing House in China, 2019) pp. 8–9.

[45] S. Zhang, "Predicament and solution in the implementation of intended guardianship system" (2020) 2 *Oriental Law* 121.

[46] C. Ding, "Family members' informed consent to medical treatment for competent patients in China" (2010) 8(1) *China: An International Journal* 139; V.L. Raposo, "Lost in 'culturation': medical informed consent in China (from a Western perspective)" (2019) 22(1) *Medicine, Health Care and Philosophy* 17.

who serve as the substitute decision-makers, proceedings before the court would not be regarded as necessary.[47]

12.3.2 *Attitudinal and Cultural Factors*

In addition to the previous analysis, there also exists a body of literature that explores attitudinal and cultural factors that drive the slow translation of ADs into practice. For example, the low awareness-rate of ADs among all stakeholders (including the persons themselves, their family members, and doctors and nurses), the tradition of avoiding discussions about death, and the parent–child relationship under Confucianism are widely believed to be the main social and cultural factors relevant to the promotion of ADs.[48] This proposition appears to be supported by empirical studies conducted in China in recent years.

Although there are no available national studies, some medical research papers have explored stakeholders' attitudes towards ADs with relatively small samples or at the local level. For example, a study on the acceptance of ADs consisting of 280 senior patient-participants with chronic disease living in the community suggests that educational level and attitudes to death have the most significant influence on acceptance level.[49] Those patients with higher educational levels indicated a higher acceptance level towards ADs in their responses. Participants who indicated that they had a higher level of acceptance of death as a natural consequence of life also had a higher level of acceptance of the use of ADs (mainly being more open to the idea of and use of ADs).[50]

[47] B.Y. Huang et al., "The do-not-resuscitate order for terminal cancer patients in mainland China: A retrospective study" (2018) 97(18) *Medicine* e0588.

[48] Y. An and M. Zou, "An assessment of advance directives in China: the 'coming of age' for legal regulation?" (2018) 20(1) *Marquette Benefits & Social Welfare Law Review*; Y. Zhou, "Care issues at the end-of-life in China" (2016) 45(2) *Development and Society* 231; M.C. Stuifbergen and J.J.M. Van Delden, "Filial obligations to elderly parents: a duty to care" (2011) 14(1) *Medicine, Health Care and Philosophy* 63; Y. Yang, "A family-oriented Confucian approach to advance directives in end-of-life decision making for incompetent elderly patients", in R. Fan (ed.), *Family-Oriented Informed Consent* (Springer, 2015), pp. 257–70.

[49] Z. Yang and H. Zhang, "Acceptance of advance directives and influencing factors among elderly patients with chronic diseases in the community" (2020) 23(31) *Chinese General Practice* 3949.

[50] The authors suggest that patients who perceive death as an escape may be less willing to discuss ADs with their family because this may lead to conflicts in the process of decision-making, namely because the Chinese concept of filial piety is likely to cause family members to want to keep them alive at all costs. This does not appear to be a convincing

Another study of 249 family members of stroke patients investigated their attitudes towards setting up ADs.[51] Only 40% of participating family members agreed with the idea of setting up ADs; a quarter of participants explicitly disagreed and the remaining 35% preferred not to answer for a variety of reasons. The reasons for family members' disapproval of ADs included the following: "the patients' choice is not necessarily reasonable" (33.3%), "family members cannot accept that their relatives would be left to die" (25.2%), "our family cannot afford a free choice among different types of cares" (14.3%), "the medical decision should be made by me (or other family members)" (12.9%) and "family members concern that doctors would not actively rescue the patients with ADs" (13.6%). Interestingly, the study also asked whether participating family members would themselves have ADs. Of 128 family members who answered "no", 67 respondents believed doctors and family members were capable of making wise decisions on their behalf, while 60 respondents stated that they did not have adequate information to make ADs. In addition to the low awareness, it also reflects an evident attitudinal and cultural preference that favours substitute decision-making arrangements over respect for patients' autonomy by ADs. Such a cultural preference likely also stems from what has been described as the family-based decision-making model prevalent in Confucian Chinese societies, where the family, rather than the individual patient, is seen as the primary unit of medical decision-making.[52]

A study in 2020 explored attitudes of 530 healthcare professionals towards ADs.[53] Its findings revealed that awareness of ADs among healthcare professionals is still low; only 44.5% of the participants knew about ADs. That study adopted a broader definition of ADs, including both types of living wills and powers-of-attorney. Of the participating

explanation, however, given that this kind of conflict with family members is likely to be present regardless of the patient's attitude towards death.

51 X. Wu et al., "Study on family members' attitudes towards setting up advanced directives for stroke patients" (2020) 637 *Medicine and Philosophy* 18.

52 See, for example, X. Chen and R. Fan, "The family and harmonious medical decision-making: cherishing an appropriate Confucian moral balance" (2010) 35 *Journal of Medicine and Philosophy* 573; R. Fan and B. Li, "Truth-telling in medicine: the Confucian view" (2004) 29 *Journal of Medicine and Philosophy* 179; R. Fan, "Self-determination vs. family-determination: two incommensurable principles of autonomy" (1997) 11 *Bioethics* 309.

53 W. Ma and Q. Xue, "Factors associated with attitudes and behavioural intention concerning advance directives among physicians and nurses" (2020) 23(31) *Chinese General Practice* 3935.

professionals, 84% and 70.4% approved of living wills and powers-of-attorney respectively. Regarding living wills, the reasons for approval include respect for patients' right to choose (98.2%), reducing unnecessary suffering (91.7%) and over-treatment (77.3%), avoiding conflict of opinions among family members in resuscitation (74.4%), reducing family members' financial (74.4%), psychological/ethical (73.7%), and caring (72.6%) burden and improving patients' quality of life (73%).

Similar considerations shaped reasons for approving of powers of attorney, but, interestingly, some other reasons were also mentioned, for example, "avoiding the difficulties among different choices faced by doctors" and "saving time for treatment". Among those who disapprove of ADs (16% for living wills and 29.6% for powers of attorney), legal uncertainty represented the shared reason, 68.2% and 66.2% respectively. Regarding living wills, other major reasons for disapproval include losing opportunities for resuscitation, depriving the patient's right to life, conflicts of opinions between patients and family members, violating professional ethics, being uncomfortable discussing the topic with patients, hindering technological progress and lack of time for doctor–patient communication. Among those who disapproved of powers of attorney, there were concerns that "the patients' decision to refuse treatment could be changed by their agents" and "the patient might lose autonomy if the power-of-attorney is signed under pressure". A particularly potent reason was that "family members would become the agent in decision-making automatically", meaning powers of attorney are unnecessary.

While further empirical research is needed, particularly at the national level, existing studies provide a glimpse into the role that ADs may be able to play in China. Although resistance from family members to the idea of ADs is likely to pose a challenge to the uptake of ADs, healthcare practitioners appear surprisingly supportive of living wills in particular, which may be a positive factor in facilitating further awareness and support of ADs in China over time.

12.4 Ongoing Projects Promoting Advance Directives in China

Nonetheless, the attitudinal and cultural factors discussed here are subject to change. As well as a critical review of the literature explaining the status quo, the chapter also considers some pilot projects that promote ADs and were initiated by civil society organisations. These projects are still in their early stages, and their scope is largely limited to urban areas and particular social groups. But they are potential change-makers through their active engagement with social discussions and practice.

12.4.1 Promotion by Beijing Living Will Promotion Association

Beijing Living Will Promotion Association (BLWPA) was established in 2013 as a non-governmental organisation with the ultimate goal being to promote the idea of "die with dignity" and living wills.[54] In addition to distributing information booklets and public advocacy through mass media, one of its key works is supporting more people in thinking about their end-of-life decisions and making their living wills.

BLWPA's official website (www.lwpa.org.cn) provides a tool by which people can complete a form indicating their wills and preferences regarding their end-of-life decisions. Informed by "My Five Wishes" in the United States, BLWPA guides its users to consider their wishes for wanting (a) certain elements involved in medical treatments (such as "I do not want any treatment or examination that would increase pain even when doctors and nurses believe it to be beneficial" and "I do want to keep my body clear all the time"); (b) life-sustaining treatment (including applying Cardiopulmonary Resuscitation, feeding tube, or expensive antibiotics); (c) how other people will treat me (such as "I want to die at home if possible" and "I do not want to be disturbed by volunteers"); (d) what I want my family members and friends to know (such as "I want my family to know I love them" and "I do not want any memorial service"); and (e) who will help me (appointing a substitute decision-maker to ensure these wishes would be respected as much as possible). Users need to register with BLWPA's website to access the form, which requires that the contact information of relevant family members or friends be provided. The default setting is that the wills are activated only when two medical professionals believe the person concerned has become incompetent. BLWPA also recommends its users to notarise their wills, the purpose of which is most likely to enhance the wills' legal status, so that doctors are more likely to follow the directives set out within the wills. That said, BLWPA acknowledges that the wills are not legally binding, as China has not enacted any law that clarifies the doctors' roles and responsibilities in acceding to the directions stipulated within the wills.

[54] Zhou, note 48.

It remains unknown how many people have used BLWPA's service. However, arguably due to BLWPA's advocacy, directly or indirectly, the Chinese Government initiated a pilot project on palliative care in 76 cities or districts nationwide in 2019.[55] Legal recognition of living wills is not mentioned in the policy document of the pilot project. Nonetheless, the development of such services would be expected to have an impact on the social attitudes towards end-of-life care and surrounding legal arrangements.

12.4.2 Active Use of Voluntary Guardianship by the LGBT Community in China

The process of civil law reform in China has provoked deep concerns from among interest groups and stakeholders, among these groups being China's lesbian, gay, bisexual, and transgender (LGBT) community. In the final text of the *Civil Code*, neither same-sex marriage nor civil partnership is legalised. Thus, there exists the need for other legal tools or formal arrangements that would help to ensure a legal bond between homosexual couples in China. Voluntary guardianship, therefore, has become a heated topic within the community and has raised some scholarly concerns.[56]

Yanhui Peng, a community leader from the group LGBT Rights Advocacy China, shared in an online panel in 2020 that they are exploring whether voluntary guardianship could be helpful in gaining control in a variety of issues faced by the LGBT community in China. By setting up voluntary guardianship, community members seek to make their partners legitimate agents or decision-makers on medical treatment, living arrangements as they become older, property and litigation.[57]

Facing the legal uncertainty discussed here, Peng also recommends notarising the voluntary guardianship documents. To promote voluntary guardianship among the community members and to advocate for

[55] National Health Commission of the People's Republic of China, "The Notice of Second Pilot Projects of Palliative Care" (China: 2019) www.nhc.gov.cn/cms-search/xxgk/getManuscriptXxgk.htm?id=efe3ed3d9dce4f519bc7bba7997b59d8 [in Chinese].

[56] S. Zhang and G. Wu, "Exploring the legal application of voluntary guardianship to homosexual community" (2019) 2 *Cross-strait Legal Science* 70.

[57] EqualRights.hku.hk, "Adult guardianship and autonomous decision-making" (Hong Kong: 2020), www.equalityrights.hku.hk/post/成人監護與自主決策-代表與被代表的那些事（上）.

equal rights of the LGBT community, LGBT Rights Advocacy China actively works with notary agencies in different areas. Through their active engagement, Nanjing Public Notary Office has publicly promoted their services in setting up voluntary guardianships for medical decision-making to the LBGT community in their social media accounts.[58]

How these voluntary guardianship arrangements function in practice, especially in the healthcare setting, requires further observation. The efforts from the community, nevertheless, are creating or expanding the possibility that the normative framework of ADs could be activated, thereby changing social attitudes and awareness of ADs.

12.5 Conclusion

This chapter has drawn on related practice and scholarly literature to examine the current semi-normative framework for ADs in China, including related practice and scholarly discussion. Without specific legislation that acknowledges and gives binding force to ADs, China's new *Civil Code* nevertheless sets out legal criteria by which a person may be assessed as lacking in decision-making capacity, and guidance on the appointment of substitute decision-makers for such people. The *CoE* requires Chinese medical practitioners to respect patients' expressed wills made at a time when the patient was of mental capacity and able to make rational decisions, and to ensure patients' maximum participation in the decision-making process, even when the patients are considered to be beyond capacity. The chapter presents a discussion of such a framework of norms that may potentially have a positive impact on practices related to advance healthcare directives.

Existing evidence derived from judicial proceedings and medical research literature suggests it is rare, if not non-existent, that the framework has actually been translated into medical practice. The chapter considers the legal, attitudinal and cultural factors that hinder the implementation of ADs. In addition, it has also surveyed two leading examples

[58] But the article was later deleted without explanation, see D. Wang, "I notarise voluntary guardianship for same-sex couples" (China: 2019), www.sohu.com/a/330829888_120146415 [in Chinese]. The deleted post could be found at Nanjing Public Notary Office, "Notarising voluntary guardianship (for LGBT community)" (China: 2019), mp.weixin.qq.com/s/nT9jmcf5jYe1PBlRSOsxsw?fbclid=IwAR2de0PFyxuWJ4vrihYZQxXqcCTgkXnWrRv8Jq7xMxvPR7sdZyXJRHHVKms.

of civil society-led pilot projects that promote ADs in China, presenting a wider landscape of the relevant practice. With only a vaguely promising prospect that the social attitudes of stakeholders will become more friendly to broader implementation of the power of attorney and living wills in their current form, it is argued that the current legal, policy and economic-social context in China appears unready for the legislation of legally binding ADs.

13

Guideline-Based Approach to End-of-Life Care Decisions in Japan: Practice, Regulation and the Place of Advance Directives

REINA OZEKI-HAYASHI, FUTOSHI IWATA, SATOSHI KODAMA & MIHO TANAKA

13.1 Introduction

End-of-life decision-making has become an increasingly important issue in Japan, where the super-ageing of the population is progressing. To date, no legislation that specifically addresses medical considerations related to end-of-life care (e.g. advance directives [ADs]), forgoing life-sustaining treatment) has been enacted. End-of-life decision-making on care and medical treatment continues to be dealt with primarily according to the Ministry of Health, Labour and Welfare guidelines, which make no mention of ADs, although they are based on the ideas of ADs and advance care planning (ACP).

Despite the lack of formal AD regulation by way of laws or guidelines, and therefore uncertainty about their place in the end-of-life care context and the potential legal implications of AD implementation, empirical data suggest that ADs are in fact discussed and used in Japanese practice. How these data should be interpreted, however, is far from straightforward. There is evidence, for example, that whilst attitudes towards ADs have become more positive over time, there is still a large discrepancy between such attitudes and AD practice. In light of all this, how do ADs fit into the Japanese legal and sociocultural context, and the end-of-life process in particular? This is one of the questions we consider in this chapter, which begins with an examination of issues related to the withdrawal of life-sustaining treatment through court cases and incidents in the past few decades. We then discuss the process guidelines on end-of-life decision-making, national attitude surveys on end-of-life issues and sociocultural factors that have a potential impact on ADs and ACP in Japan.

13.2 A Brief History of Court Cases Dealing with End-of-Life Decisions

The past 30 years have seen some of the most important issues concerning decision-making on end-of-life care raised in Japan. There is no specific statute that recognises the legally binding nature of end-of-life decisions about ADs and do not attempt resuscitation (DNAR) orders and no legal definition of ADs, and only a few court cases have interpreted the basic murder provisions of the substantive criminal law (Penal Code s. 199)[1] and the general negligence provision (Civil Code s. 709)[2] that governs end-of-life discussions. Furthermore, no official entity (e.g. public advocate, ombudsperson, public guardian) is tasked with protecting the rights of the elderly and the validity of the medical decision-making process.[3] The illegality of active euthanasia has been established in a few cases.[4] One of the most important developments in this area was the creation by the Ministry in 2007 of so-called process guidelines (see Section 13.3), which are formulated around end-of-life care and treatment more broadly.[5] Several medical colleges also subsequently created guidelines based on the process guidelines. However, because these guidelines are not legally binding,[6] it may remain difficult in practice for a patient/family to align a medical care team's strategy with the patient's decision and to obtain judicial relief if the team intentionally

[1] Keiho [Penal Code], Act No 45 of 24 April 1907.

[2] Minpo [Civil Code], Act No 89 of 27 April 1896.

[3] In Victoria, Australia, the Public Advocate is an independent statutory officer who promotes and safeguards the rights and interests of people with disabilities and investigates allegations of abuse of vulnerable Victorians. See Office of the Public Advocate, "The Public Advocate", www.publicadvocate.vic.gov.au/the-public-advocate. See also the Guardianship and Administration Act 1986 (Guardianship and Administration Act 2019) and Medical Treatment Planning and Decisions Act 2016.

[4] Hanrei-Times No. 877, 148 [in Japanese]. The Tokai University Hospital case was the first case in which a doctor was convicted of homicide, and thus differs from previous cases in which family members were convicted of homicide.

[5] Ministry of Health, Labour and Welfare, "The Decision-Making Process for Terminal Medical Treatment" (Process Guidelines) (May 2007). The title of the guidelines was changed to "The Decision-Making Process for Final Stage of Life" (Process Guidelines) (March 2015) and was changed again to "The Decision-Making Process for Final Stage of Life Treatment and Care" (Process Guidelines) (March 2018).

[6] Our discussion is based on the idea that regulations and law are not limited to case law or administrative guidance with or without penalties. Rather, they include "soft laws", such as guidance provided by medical colleges and professional medical societies. Soft laws can eventually be taken into consideration by the courts when it comes to judgments on the reasonableness of conduct or standard of care or justification (or excuse) in criminal law.

or negligently ignores the patient's wishes,[7] although relief may be provided by the courts by taking into consideration whether the conduct concerned fell below the standard of care in tort cases or can be excused or justified in murder cases. In this sense, the Ministry's process guidelines and medical colleges' guidelines offer a regulatory tool to aid the courts in interpreting relevant laws. There have been calls for enactment of a Natural Death Act (known as the AD Bill) by the Japan Society for Dying with Dignity and non-partisan Diet members, although such legislation has yet to be realised by the Japanese government, and is unlikely to be so in the near future.[8]

Most developed countries, including the United States and Australia, have a similar medico-legal framework to that of Japan, and treatment without patient consent is considered unlawful under civil and, in rarer situations, criminal law. In other words, patients

[7] We understand that there are situations in which statutory protection would benefit patients in terms of respecting their wishes. Yet, given the developments in and limitations of living will (LW) and AD discussions in the United States and other countries over the past 40 years, the enactment of ADs may not be a panacea for improving end-of-life care. Even with such statutory protection, it is clear that many people do not have ADs. Moreover, because people cannot predict their future, greater weight is often placed on family agreement than on a patient's AD. See, e.g., S.M. Wolf et al., "Forty Years of Work on End-of-Life Care – From Patients' Rights to Systemic Reform" (2015) 372 *New England Journal of Medicine* 678.

[8] Interestingly, not only medical professionals but also ordinary citizens are strongly opposed to the enactment of end-of-life legislation (discussed in Section 13.5). In 2012, a group of non-partisan Diet members proposed a draft Bill for Respecting the Patient's Decision in End-of-Life Care Act (provisional name; hereafter, "draft AD Bill") that would offer immunity to physicians if they withheld or withdrew life-sustaining treatment in accordance with a patient's AD. As of 2020, however, the proposed draft AD Bill had yet to be submitted to the National Diet. See note 23. At present, it has no real prospect of being enacted, and, more importantly, there has been strong criticism of the efficacy of this type of enactment and the side effect of such a statute (namely, that physicians may try to strictly follow the literal meaning of the statute rather than considering its main purpose and spirit). Even in the United States, there is strong criticism of the effectiveness of this kind of legislation (e.g. Natural Death Act and ADs legislation) for improving the quality of end-of-life care. Wolf et al. (note 7) argued that the quality of end-of-life care has not improved in the 40 years since enactment of a patient's right to refuse treatment (LWs) and AD legislation. Considering that the enactment of LW and AD legislation in other developed countries has not proved to be a panacea, it is at least debatable whether Japan needs to follow their path in legislating ADs (see note 7). Some researchers and advocacy groups for severely disabled patients are concerned that legislation on death with dignity would not ensure respect for the rights of severely disabled people, specifically their right to receive life-supporting treatment. See further E. Nakazawa et al., "Why Can't Japanese People Decide? Withdrawal of Ventilatory Support in End-of-Life Scenarios and Their Indecisiveness" (2019) 11 *Asian Bioethics Review* 343, 344.

have the right to refuse treatment at any time, especially before treatment is initiated, which is basically the same as what the informed consent theory requires, although courts in Japan typically do not use the expression "informed consent". However, it is debatable whether the right of patients to refuse treatment automatically guarantees the withdrawal – upon patient request – of life-sustaining treatments to which they themselves consented. The Japanese courts view the withholding and withdrawal of treatment to impose different duties on medical professionals;[9] that is, once they start treatment, it is their duty to continue it to preserve the patient's life. Many doctors believe that a patient with amyotrophic lateral sclerosis (ALS), for example, can legally refuse ventilator support; however, once the patient is placed on ventilator support, doctors are legally bound to continue using the ventilator even if the patient asks them to remove it unless the patient's condition becomes terminal (the courts use the expression "imminence of death"). Whilst there is no case law or legislation that definitively resolves this matter, it could be argued that an answer, at least to some extent, can be found in the Ministry's process guidelines, an argument we make in this chapter.

Several provisions in Japanese criminal law address the protection of human life, such as prohibiting homicide (Penal Code s. 199) and aiding suicide (Penal Code s. 202), although suicide itself is not punishable by law. These two provisions are generally understood as making it clear that terminating one's life cannot be justified simply as an autonomous decision because the Penal Code prohibits assisting death, even if it is the victim's autonomous wish. In light of these provisions, the most important question for our purposes is how much leeway is allowed, or to what extent the withholding or withdrawal of treatment should be considered permissible.

Two criminal cases, the 1998 case of Kawasaki Kyodo Hospital and the 2000 case involving Imizu Municipal Hospital, were the major drivers of the development of the Ministry's process guidelines, which embody the concept of patient autonomy, with the medical care team taking on a facilitating role. Uncertainty over whether medical professionals would face legal consequences as a result of withdrawing medical treatment was

[9] T. Irie [Former Judicial Research Officer of the Supreme Court of Japan], "Saikosai Tokino Hanrei: Keiji (Saikousai Heisei 21 12/7 Kettei) [Supreme Court Recent Case: Criminal]" (2012) 1446 *Jurisuto* 91, 93 [in Japanese].

a central focus of both cases, pushing the Ministry to address end-of-life care more extensively by creating the process guidelines.[10]

The most important judgment concerning the withdrawal of treatment and active euthanasia in Japan is the 2009 Supreme Court ruling in the Kawasaki Kyodo Hospital case. In that case, an attending physician had removed an endotracheal tube from a patient who was in a comatose state owing to bronchial asthma with the consent of the patient's family. The physician had then administered intravenous muscle relaxants to ease the patient's death.[11] The physician was charged with and convicted of murder by the court in 2005. In 2007, the Tokyo High Court reduced the sentence in half, to one year in prison, suspended for three years, a sentence affirmed by the Supreme Court in 2009. This was the first Supreme Court case concerning the issue of end-of-life decisions. The court decided that it was premature to consider whether the physician's conduct (i.e. withdrawing the tube and injecting lethal drugs) was justifiable or excusable as an exception to murder. According to the court, only after objective criteria have been met can the issue be considered (e.g. the "imminence of death" condition was not clearly established in this case). More specifically, because no brain death test had been conducted, and no consultation with the hospital president or peer physicians had been sought, the court maintained that it did not need to discuss the validity of withdrawing treatment as an exception to the murder provision. Even assuming that the removal of the endotracheal tube had been done with the family's consent, the physician's explanation was considered legally insufficient and inaccurate, that is, not a valid basis for consent, because the physician was not herself aware of the patient's medical diagnosis and prognosis.

In its ruling in the case, the Tokyo High Court (one of eight appellate courts) included the following frank statement: "A fundamental solution to the problem of death with dignity in such cases would require the enactment of a Death with Dignity Act, or alternatively, a set of guidelines". ("Namely, the court felt uncomfortable ... creat[ing] leeway to allow active euthanasia and/or [the] withholding and withdrawal of treatment through interpretation", explained Judge Kunio Harada, one of the three judges.[12]) In other words, the issue of death with dignity

[10] This is relevant to our discussion of ADs because, like ADs, the process guidelines on end-of-life patient care are predicated on the central concept of patient autonomy.

[11] *Hanrei-Times* No. 1185, p. 114; >*Hanrei-Times* No. 1237, p. 153; *Hanrei-Times* No. 1316, p. 147 [in Japanese].

[12] K. Harada, "Shumatuki-iryo To Keiho [Terminal Stage and Criminal Law]" (15 April 2009) 1377 *Jurisuto* 86, 109 [in Japanese].

should be the subject of a broader national consensus, the outcome of which should be a law or set of guidelines rather than something to be decided by the courts amidst their prevalent deference to the legislative and executive branches.

In the Imizu Municipal Hospital case, which occurred in 2000, an attending physician had discontinued the use of a ventilator in seven terminally ill patients at the request of the patients or their families. All of the patients died following the discontinuation of ventilator support.[13] In response to media reports, the hospital director publicly apologised for the physician's "unethical" decisions. The police subsequently investigated the patients' deaths and filed a report with the local prosecutor's office in 2008 indicating that there was no need for punitive action. The case was dropped in 2009 on the ground that causation could not be established (i.e. the causes of the deaths were unclear).[14] This case understandably created considerable confusion and uneasiness in the medical field.

In 2007, soon after the Tokyo High Court decision on the Kawasaki case and the reporting of the Imizu case, the Ministry issued process guidelines on the withdrawal of life-sustaining treatment,[15] followed by the publication of more specific end-of-life care guidelines[16] by several professional associations.

13.3 The Process Guidelines

The Ministry's process guidelines, which came into force in 2007, are not linked to any legislation and have no penalties,[17] nor are ADs explicitly mentioned therein. Nevertheless, these guidelines are widely regarded as

[13] "The Suspicious Death: The Hospital in Toyama Prefecture 'Seven Patients Euthanised' 50-Year-Surgeon Switched off Artificial Ventilators from Patients" (25 March 2006) *The Mainichi* [in Japanese]; "The Hospital 'the Physician Withdrew Treatments' after Switching off Artificial Ventilators from Seven Patients; They Died 'Ethically Problematic'" (26 March 2006) *The Asahi Shimbun* [in Japanese].

[14] "Removing Artificial Ventilators in the Imizu Municipal Hospital: Two Physicians Not Prosecuted" (21 December 2009) *The Yomiuri Shimbun* [in Japanese].

[15] See note 5.

[16] The "2014 Guideline on End-of-Life Care in Acute Care and Intensive Care" (compiled collaboratively by the Japanese Association for Acute Medicine, Japanese Society of Intensive Care Medicine and Japanese Circulation Society), the "2007 Guideline on End-of-Life Care" (Japan Medical Association) and the "2012 Guideline for Decision Making Process of Elderly Care: Focusing on the Use of Artificial Hydration and Nutrition" (Japan Geriatrics Society).

[17] Although the conduct of healthcare professionals in breach of these guidelines is not directly punishable, whether or not they acted in accordance with them may matter if

representative of the Ministry's official position on end-of-life care issues, and are thus the currently most influential document in this arena. The process guidelines consist of two core elements: (1) respect for patients' wishes, which is stated as the most important principle in the guidelines[18] and (2) decision-making led by the healthcare team (i.e. not by the attending physician alone). The guidelines stipulate that the healthcare team shall make healthcare decisions through repeated discussions with the patient and his or her family, with particular emphasis on respect for the patient's choice. They also specify that if a patient cannot express his or her wishes, then the healthcare team shall decide on the best course of care in light of the family's wishes. The guidelines further recommend that if it is difficult for the healthcare team to reach consensus with the patient/family, a committee comprising multiple experts should be set up for consultation purposes.[19] In this manner, the process guidelines place significant emphasis on consensus-building amongst those involved in the patient's end-of-life care. Notably, it is clearly stated that the issue of active euthanasia is outside the scope of the guidelines, meaning that no change is imposed by the guidelines regarding the illegality of active euthanasia (i.e. administration of lethal drugs).

The process guidelines purposely specify only procedural matters in relation to end-of-life treatments, rather than the substance of those treatments, which is why they are referred to as "process" guidelines. There are two main reasons why the guidelines do not prescribe which treatments can be withheld or withdrawn: (1) it is difficult to prescribe which treatments are permissible/impermissible, as a variety of situations exist depending on patients' type of illness and prognosis, their wishes and family situation, and their relationships with doctors, nurses and care workers (also, because existing guidelines rarely address these issues, the relevant committee in the Ministry responsible for developing these guidelines felt that it was up to medical and care specialists/societies to develop specific guidelines as appropriate); and, more importantly and (2) to improve the quality of care at the end of life, it is necessary to

they are accused of having civil, criminal or administrative liability. In that sense, the process guidelines are loosely binding on healthcare professionals.

18 Process Guidelines, para. 1.1.

19 Whilst informed decision-making by the patient and family is a key aspect of the guidelines, the fact that consensus must be reached between the healthcare team and the patient suggests that patient wishes are perhaps not the most important consideration therein.

consider a longer process of dying without limiting the question to whether to start or stop a particular treatment.

The guidelines also call for improvements in palliative care. The Japanese government responded to that call by implementing measures to promote palliative care and ACP. The Cancer Control Act[20] was enacted at almost the same time as publication of the guidelines. The PEACE (Palliative care programme Emphasizing symptom management and Assessment for Continuous medical Education) Project, an educational programme for basic palliative care, was also subsequently initiated. In 2014, revisions to the medical insurance reimbursement system made it a requirement to calculate the "cancer patient management guidance fee". The mandatory participation of at least 90 per cent of oncologists at each institution in the PEACE Project workshop led to a rapid increase in the number of programme participants.[21] With regard to ACP, E-FIELD (Education for Implementing End-of-Life Discussion), an educational programme aimed at facilitating ACP, was launched in 2014. Despite these efforts by the government, there is still an insufficient number of medical practitioners who can implement ACP. In 2018, the Ministry revised the process guidelines to bring the idea of ACP into focus and to broaden the scope of the guidelines to include all care settings, such as nursing homes and home care, emphasising the importance of healthcare proxies. It is interesting to note here that even though the 2018 revisions focus on good practice in ACP, there is still no mention made of ADs, although they are based on the ideas of ADs and ACP.

13.4 Issues with the Process Guidelines

The process guidelines fall short in three respects. First, there is no clear definition of what constitutes the "end of life", or terminal stage of illness, in the main body of the guidelines, even though their title contains the phrase "end-of-life treatment". Thus, there is ambiguity over when a patient is considered to be "terminal", and the judgement of whether a patient is facing the end of his or her life is left to the discretion of the

[20] A law to promote comprehensive measures against cancer, the leading cause of death in Japan.

[21] T. Morita and Y. Kizawa, "Palliative Care in Japan: A Review Focusing on Care Delivery System" (2013) 7 *Current Opinion in Supportive and Palliative Care* 207.

healthcare team members assessing the patient's condition.[22] The committee responsible for development of the process guidelines felt it was better to leave the issue to the professional discretion of medical specialists, as end-of-life situations vary depending on illness, age and other factors. For example, in neurological diseases such as ALS, it is difficult to define the end-of-life stage owing to the chronic and incurable nature of the diseases, and whether the concept of "end of life" is applicable in this context is a highly complex question. As this lack of clarity may result in inconsistencies in application, further discussion is needed to address this issue.

Second, there have been discussions regarding the ambiguity of whether healthcare professionals who withhold (or withdraw) life-sustaining treatment according to the guidelines should be held liable under criminal or civil law. The process guidelines are not legally binding because, although issued by the Ministry, they lack supporting statutes. Some scholars, including two of the authors of this chapter (Kodama and Tanaka), believe that legislation is necessary to ensure immunity for healthcare professionals who discontinue life-sustaining treatment.[23] Indeed, the Guidelines for the Treatment of Amyotrophic Lateral Sclerosis acknowledge that removal of ventilator support is a difficult issue, as it is currently unclear what the legal basis for doing so would be. Further discussion is warranted to reach social consensus on this issue.[24,25] Having said that, however, to the best of our knowledge (although no official statistics are available), there has been no instance of a police investigation or prosecution concerning the withholding or withdrawal of life-sustaining treatments since the establishment of the process guidelines in 2007. Even prior to that year, no case of withheld treatment was subjected to police investigation or prosecution. In fact,

22 Ministry of Health, Labour and Welfare, "Press Release Regarding the Revised Guideline on Medical Decision-making Process at the Final Stage of Life: Commentaries on the Guidelines for the Decision-Making Process for End-of-Life Treatment and Care" (2018), www.mhlw.go.jp/file/04-Houdouhappyou-10802000-Iseikyoku-Shidouka/0000197702.pdf [in Japanese].

23 M. Tanaka et al., "Forgoing Life-sustaining Treatment – A Comparative Analysis of Regulations in Japan, Korea, Taiwan, and England" (2020) 21 *BMC Medical Ethics.*

24 Japanese Society of Neurology (eds.), *Clinical Practice Guideline for Amyotrophic Lateral Sclerosis 2013* (Tokyo: Nanko-do, 2013), pp. 138–9 [in Japanese].

25 Social consensus is key here, as the correct formulation of a law that is fundamentally about ethical uncertainty about which people in Japan could reasonably disagree arguably requires a public consultation process as part of the development of overarching governance of the issue.

no case of withdrawn treatment *not* categorised as active euthanasia (i.e. use of lethal injection, discontinuation of ventilator support in non-terminal patients) has ever been subjected to criminal prosecution (in the 1996 Kokuho Keihoku Hospital case, the police investigated the use of muscle relaxants on a terminal cancer patient but decided not to prosecute). Moreover, only a few police investigations have been conducted in cases involving the withdrawal of ventilators (i.e. 2004 Hokkaido Haboro Hospital case, 2006 Wakayama Medical University Kikoku Hospital case). There is some anecdotal evidence suggesting that healthcare professionals are unlikely to be held liable, criminally or civilly, as long as they follow the process guidelines and subsequent guidelines.[26] According to some jurists, including one of the authors of this chapter (Iwata), the process guidelines are broadly interpreted to permit the withdrawal of end-of-life treatment in cases where patients state their clear wishes,[27] and even in cases where patients do not explicitly express their wishes. Although some areas of ambiguity remain, there is growing recognition that no penalty will be imposed for withdrawing life-sustaining treatment in accordance with the guidelines. Further qualitative and quantitative research covering healthcare professionals, as well as national data on treatment withdrawal, is needed to understand the impact of the guidelines on the practice of healthcare professionals, however.

Third, while the process guidelines are an important, if problematic, development in determining the framework for end-of-life patients, the lack of proper legislation on ADs in Japan remains a concern, as patient-

[26] For example, the "2012 Guideline for Decision Making Process of Elderly Care: Focusing on the Use of Artificial Hydration and Nutrition" (Japan Geriatrics Society) has an appended list of lawyers and law professors, including four former and one current Supreme Court Justices and a former High Court Judge who was involved in the 2007 Kawasaki case decision, which supported the guideline, and the following statement: "It is practically unlikely to have any judicial intervention if medical teams withdraw AHN [artificial hydration and nutrition] and treatment based on the draft Guidelines. If there was any judicial intervention, it would be highly inappropriate", www.jpn-geriat-soc.or.jp/proposal/pdf/jgs_ahn_gl_2012.pdf [in Japanese].

[27] In Japan, there is no standard "AD form" that is provided by law or administrative guidelines. There is, however, a notarial system that can be used for such purposes, and there are also various AD documents prepared by healthcare systems, local governments, regional medical associations, the Japan Death with Dignity Association and other public institutions and private companies. Patients and their families can share these documents with healthcare professionals in the hope that they will inform treatment decisions. Although there is no law governing the handling of such written documents, they are usually included in patients' medical record.

centred decision-making can be difficult to enforce without it. In the specific context of emergency care settings (ambulance transport), for example, there may be significant gaps between the attitudes of, and measures taken by, paramedics and municipal ambulance departments and processes for respecting the wishes of the patient as set forth by the guidelines. For example, a family member in distress in the face of an emergency situation may request ambulance transport against the prior wishes of the patient, with resuscitation being attempted as a result. In other words, ADs may not be utilised in the field of emergency transport. What should be done when a person who does not wish to receive cardiopulmonary resuscitation (CPR) is rushed to hospital with cardiopulmonary arrest? This issue concerning DNAR has been debated since the 2010s.[28] If a patient with DNAR wishes experiences a sudden physical change, his or her family may call an ambulance, even though doing so runs contrary to the patient's wishes. In other situations, such as those in elderly care facilities, facility staff may not be fully aware of every resident's wishes regarding CPR. Once an ambulance arrives, paramedics provide emergency treatments (e.g. life-prolonging treatments) even if the patient has written a living will (LW) or the family has conveyed the patient's wish not to receive CPR, with the doctor's confirmation (it is widely and wrongly believed that paramedics are legally required to administer CPR). Studies show that when elderly individuals suffer cardiac arrest, they are unlikely to recover even with aggressive treatment. At best, they become vegetative or comatose. Nonetheless, CPR is still sometimes performed by the paramedics of some ambulance departments, who believe that doing so is a legally binding duty, despite the development of a national policy to respect a person's wish at the end-of-life stage, including the inclusion of the ACP concept in the revised 2018 process guidelines.

Moreover, the importance of legislation, guidelines and other measures by local medical control councils to educate paramedics on the provision of medical treatment and to review their practices has been highlighted by the Ambulance Department's committee on this issue. The current prevailing interpretation is that it is "not illegal" to transport a patient without performing CPR, or to not transport him or her at all in accordance with his or her wishes, if those wishes are confirmed by the

[28] Y. Nakagawa et al., "Do Not Attempt Resuscitation Order in Japan" (2017) 4 *Acute Medicine & Surgery* 286.

attending physician.[29] In the emergency context, procedures vary by locality, and there are no uniform national rules. In the event of an emergency, confirmation of the patient's intentions should be sought from the attending physician (family doctor), and, if the attending physician cannot be reached, the relevant decision may be made by an online medical control physician.

13.5 Public Attitudes towards Advance Directives

In this section, we discuss the attitudes of the general public and health-care professionals towards ADs and ACP. It is interesting to note that in some Japanese publications, AD is not used in its conventional sense to refer to something prepared by the individual in question, but rather to an individual's presumed intentions based on discussions with family members, which makes it difficult to perform cross-study comparisons. Hence, a broader understanding of the concept of ADs may be more appropriate in the Japanese context, especially given the emphasis on the role of the family in patient-centred care, which will be further discussed in Section 13.6.

First, we examine the results of a national attitude survey on end-of-life issues administered by the Ministry in 2018. National attitude surveys are conducted every five years. Although ADs are not legally binding, they were included in the survey because of the efforts of the Japan Society for Dying with Dignity, which has been calling for the discontinuation of futile life-sustaining treatments in Japan since the Quinlan[30]

29 The final report of the Ambulance Agency (Ambulance Service Planning Division of the Fire and Disaster Management Agency) working group on DNAR, of which Iwata was a member, was issued in 2018. The 2018 report includes the details of initiatives by a number of prefectural ambulance departments (e.g. Hiroshima City). According to the Hiroshima City Ambulance Service initiative, paramedics can transport patients with DNAR wishes without any aggressive treatment or leave the scene without any intervention if the patient's doctor confirms that he or she is in fact at the end-of-life stage and wishes to receive no CPR. This is the service's way of respecting patients' wishes, as made clear by the patients' own writing or a family statement. For further details, see N. Higuchi, "Kyukyugenba-to-DNA: Houteki-kenen [The Scene of Emergency and DNA: Legal Concern]' (2021) 33 *Pure-Hosupitaru Kea* [Prehospital Care] 22 [in Japanese].

30 In 1975, Karen Ann Quinlan lost consciousness and stopped breathing after returning home from a party. She had no prospect of recovering consciousness. Her parents filed a lawsuit to stop the life-sustaining treatment, because Karen did not want to live on a ventilator. In March 1976, the New Jersey Supreme Court ruled 7–0 that the right to privacy guarantees the right to withdraw life-sustaining treatment, and in this case, the parents could make the decision for Karen. The Quinlan case shed light on the difficult

case in the United States. Furthermore, the Science Council of Japan and other organisations also took up the issue of ADs in the wake of the Tokai University Hospital case. Both the general public and physicians (66 and 77 per cent, respectively) expressed support for ADs in the survey. However, within these groups, only 8 and 6 per cent, respectively, responded that they had completed their own ADs.[31] The AD completion rate in Japan is quite low compared to that in Western countries (e.g. 36.7 per cent in the United States[32]), a phenomenon discussed in further detail later in the chapter. The rate of agreement with AD legislation was almost the same for physicians and the general public, with 20 per cent supporting AD legislation, 40 per cent responding that such legislation was unnecessary and 10 per cent opposing it. With respect to the use of written ADs, almost 50 per cent of healthcare professionals responded that they do not use any specific document, but discuss patients' wishes regarding end-of-life treatment when patients ask them to do so.[33] It has been suggested that these results reflect traditional Japanese attitudes; that is, the Japanese consider it more "comfortable" to have things decided in a certain way through family conversations rather than through written ADs.[34]

Second, we consider the attitudes of physicians towards ADs, as demonstrated by various studies over the past two decades. In a study conducted in 2003, nearly 70 per cent of general practitioners responded that they would not change their treatment even if informed of the

question of what should and should not constitute life. The right-to-die movement is trying to help the courts better define the boundaries between life and death and fulfil their mission of preventing murder while respecting the desire to preserve human dignity. For further details, see I.M. Kennedy, "The Karen Quinlan Case: Problems and Proposals" (1976) 2(1) *Journal of Medical Ethics* 3.

31 These figures correspond to the results of a 2018 study by Tsuda et al., which found that only 1.9 per cent of patients had written ADs and that 32 per cent entrusted their decision-making to doctors or family members (see further S. Tsuda et al., "Impact of Patients' Expressed Wishes on Their Surrogate Decision-Makers' Preferred Decision-Making Roles in Japan" (2018) 21 *Journal of Palliative Medicine* 354).

32 K.N. Yadav et al., "Approximately One in Three US Adults Completes Any Type of Advance Directive for End-Of-Life Care" (2017) 36 *Health Affairs* 1244, 1247.

33 Ministry of Health, Labour and Welfare, *Report of the Awareness Survey on End-of-Life Medical Treatment* (2018), pp. 89–90, www.mhlw.go.jp/toukei/list/dl/saisyuiryo_a_h29.pdf [in Japanese].

34 M. Mori and T. Morita, *The Evidence of Advance Care Planning* (Tokyo: Igakushoin, 2020), p. 135 [in Japanese].

presence of an LW[35] for the following reasons: (1) official formats for and the regulation of LWs are lacking; (2) the process for ascertaining the wishes of patients with dementia or interpreting what death with dignity means to individual patients according to their LWs is unclear; (3) the timing for the use of LWs is unclear; and (4) an ethical challenge to following LWs arises when patients and/or their families decline a treatment based on a misunderstanding of its effectiveness.[36] A 2010 survey of palliative care physicians found the proportion of physicians who "always" or "very often" ask their patients about existing ADs to stand at 46.9 per cent. The proportions who "always" or "very often" recommend that patients designate a healthcare proxy or complete an AD in the event they lose their decision-making capacity were 40.4 and 30.3 per cent, respectively.[37] The discrepancy in physician attitudes in the two studies is likely explained by the very different study populations: the 2003 study focused on general practitioners, whilst the 2010 study concerned specialised palliative care physicians.

Interestingly, an annual survey of the bereaved families of patients with LWs conducted in 2019 by the Japan Society for Dying with Dignity (which promotes the use of LWs) revealed that 85 per cent of the families had provided the patients' LWs to their healthcare providers and that 94 per cent of LWs were honoured, although the survey provided no details on what changes had been made to treatments or which wishes were followed by doctors.[38] Whilst these data demonstrate a high degree of respect for LWs amongst healthcare providers, members of the Japan Society for Dying with Dignity often use a prescribed form of LW that is well recognised by healthcare providers, which makes it much more likely that their LWs will be respected and implemented.

Third, we discuss research conducted in nursing home settings, in which ADs play an important role. A relatively high proportion of ADs are created in nursing homes, presumably because the residents of geriatric healthcare facilities are elderly people, many with declining cognitive

35 The term "living will" is used instead of AD in this section on empirical data about public attitudes where that term is employed in the study being discussed.

36 Y. Masuda et al., "Physicians' Reports on the Impact of Living Wills at the End of Life in Japan" (2003) 29 *Journal of Medical Ethics* 248.

37 K. Nakazawa et al., "Palliative Care Physicians' Practices and Attitudes regarding Advance Care Planning in Palliative Care Units in Japan: A Nationwide Survey" (2014) 31 *American Journal of Hospice and Palliative Medicine* 699.

38 The Japan Society for Dying with Dignity, "Goizoku Anketo [Bereaved family questionnaire 2019]", https://songenshi-kyokai.or.jp/archives/2131, p. 9 [in Japanese].

function. Prior confirmation is necessary, as such residents are unlikely to be able to express their wishes should a sudden change in their medical condition occur. In one study of nursing home care providers, 28 per cent indicated that they encourage their residents to express their wishes regarding end-of-life care at the time of admission, regardless of whether they are in the final stage of life, and 70 per cent declared that it is their policy to confirm the wishes of residents at the time of admission.[39] In a recent survey, more than half of nursing homes responded that they have adopted a particular AD format (with some variation). These ADs are basically instructional directives and include documents providing explanations and/or informed consent for end-of-life care in nursing homes.[40] However, personal choice-type directive formats were more often introduced during admission to the nursing homes that took part in the survey. They require the signature of a family member (68.3 per cent), the resident himself or herself (48 per cent) and/or a staff member (31.0 per cent). Amongst explanation-and-consent directives, which are more common in end-of-life care situations, 97.2 per cent require the signature of a family member.[41] Therefore, it appears that, unlike ADs in Western countries, ADs in Japanese nursing homes place heavy emphasis on family involvement, and it is debatable whether such ADs can be considered the equivalent of those in Western countries.

In terms of why ADs appear to be more common in the nursing home setting, additional funding for end-of-life care became available in 2006 as an initial step to provide economic support for terminal care in Japanese nursing homes,[42] and such funding could well have been a catalyst for increasing the number of ADs produced in nursing homes. To be eligible for the funding, nursing homes are required to fulfil five high-level care requirements: employ a registered nurse as the team leader, provide end-of-life care guidelines on admission, operate a 24-hour on-call nursing system, provide staff training in end-of-life care and have private rooms available for residents. Every resident is also required to have a diagnosis of the end-of-life (terminal) stage made by a physician, and informed consent in relation to end-of-life

[39] J. Okochi, "End-of-Life Care at Nursing Homes" (2020) 2 *Geriatrics* 532 [in Japanese].

[40] Y. Takezako et al., "Advance Directives in Japanese Nursing Homes" (2013) 45 *Journal of Pain and Symptom Management* 63, 65.

[41] Ibid., p. 67.

[42] E.g., Minna No Kaigo [Nursing for Everyone], "The Government to Consider Additional Funding for End-of-Life Care in Nursing Homes" (2021), www.minnanokaigo.com/news/kaigogaku/no975/ [in Japanese].

care preferences (e.g. CPR, artificial nutrition) must be obtained from residents or family members. It thus appears that discussions regarding advanced end-of-life care are encouraged in nursing homes to a greater extent than in other settings.[43]

13.6 Sociocultural Factors Related to the Completion Rate of Advance Directives

Finally, we discuss several sociocultural factors that may contribute to the completion and implementation rates of ADs in Japanese medical and care settings.

13.6.1 Family-Centred Decision-Making

In Japan, family-centred decision-making is prioritised because people remain influenced by the family-centric beliefs inspired by Confucianism.[44] In a study examining the facilitators of and barriers to the completion of ADs from the patient perspective, the participants regarded such completion as a parental responsibility owed to children.[45] Amongst the views they expressed were that written ADs allow for a death without any futile life-prolongation and free their children from a caregiving burden should they become disabled. These views motivated the participants to complete ADs. However, some participants expressed negative views concerning how ADs function in actual decision-making. They were aware of the decision-making norm in Japanese society whereby family consensus typically overrides patient autonomy. The study's authors suggested that the participants understood family-centredness to constitute values shared across the generations, as they themselves had fulfilled the responsibilities expected by their families throughout their lives.

Similarly, Nakazawa et al. found that, in addition to concerns over uncertainty and propriety with respect to successful AD implementation, the involvement of cultural preferences in family-centred decision-making near the end of life also influences AD practice by physicians.

[43] See note 41.

[44] J. Kwak and W.E. Haley, "Current Research Findings on End-of-Life Decision Making among Racially or Ethnically Diverse Groups" (2005) 45 *Gerontologist* 634.

[45] S. Tsuda et al., "Group-Based Educational Intervention for Advance Care Planning in Primary Care: A Quasi-experimental Study in Japan" (2019) 18 *Journal of Asia Pacific Family Medicine*.

Whilst the physicians in their study generally expressed positive attitudes towards ADs, their practices with respect to ADs, for example, recommending that patients complete ADs, did not reflect those attitudes.[46]

13.6.2 *Character Traits*

According to some studies,[47] there are several character traits in Japanese culture that may contribute to the low AD completion rate in Japan. First, *omakase* (when someone asks family members, close friends or medical doctors to take responsibility, it is called *omakase*[48]) is commonly seen in elderly Japanese patients. These patients feel unburdened by not having to make difficult decisions for themselves even when they are capable of making their own decisions.[49] This *omakase* character trait is based on the Japanese psychological factor of *amae*. *Amae* in medical practice is manifested in the attitude of patients who do not wish to make any decisions regarding their course of treatment, but instead have someone else decide what is best for them. Patients can thus both avoid making a difficult decision and taking responsibility for it. If patients ask someone else to decide what is best for them, they can live as usual without thinking about their death, and hence they also do not need to think about an AD. In this sense, *omakase* is a likely cultural factor contributing to the low AD completion rate in Japan.

Second, the "reticence" of many elderly Japanese people, which causes them to hide their real thoughts, may also affect the end-of-life decision-making process. This character trait often interacts with the importance of the family in Japanese culture, as discussed previously. Reticence is often observed in people who, for example, want to avoid overburdening

[46] See Nakazawa et al., note 8.

[47] Y. Hirayama et al., "Japanese Citizens' Attitude toward End-of-Life Care and Advance Directives: A Qualitative Study for Members of Medical Cooperatives" (2017) 18 *Journal of General and Family Medicine* 378, 381; note 45; and S. Bito et al., "Acculturation and End-of-Life Decision Making: Comparison of Japanese and Japanese-American Focus Groups" (2007) 21 *Bioethics* 251.

[48] R. Voltz et al., "End-of-Life Decision Making and Advance Directives in Palliative Care: A Cross-Cultural Survey of Patients and Health-Care Professionals" (1998) 16 *Journal of Pain and Symptom Management* 153, 159; K. Hirai et al., "Good Death in Japanese Cancer Care: A Qualitative Study" (2006) 31 *Journal of Pain and Symptom Management* 140, 145; and Nakazawa et al., note 8, p. 381.

[49] R. Ishiwata and A. Sakai, "The Physician–Patient Relationship and Medical Ethics in Japan" (1994) 3 *Cambridge Quarterly of Healthcare Ethics* 60.

their family members, be it financially, physically or emotionally.[50] In addition, Japanese people tend to consider it important to have good family relationships at the end of life.[51] For example, even if elderly patients would prefer to die at home, they often hide their true wishes and agree to a hospital stay recommended by family members or medical providers because they do not want to be a burden or disrupt family harmony. Patients with this character trait are hesitant to write ADs, as the presence of an AD can constrain family decision-making and impose a burden.

13.6.3 Pursuit of a Good Death

The pursuit of a good death is also an important goal in Japanese culture. Interestingly, this goal has both a positive and negative effect on the making and implementation of ADs. On the one hand, Tsuda et al. found that participants regarded ADs primarily as a means to pursue their ideal death. On the other, the "Good Death Study" targeting Japanese people found one of the most common answers to the question "If you were dying, what would be the most desirable or good thing for you to do?" was "not being aware of death".[52] As a result, ADs and ACP are considered "bad luck", and many people avoid writing ADs or talking about the end of life.[53]

13.7 Conclusion

Despite being a familiar concept amongst physicians and patients in the end-of-life context in Japan, as evidenced in practice, ADs do not currently have any formal role in the decision-making process at the end of life in Japan. As explained in this chapter, end-of-life decision-making has been under intense discussion since the late 1990s and facilitated

[50] C. Shimada et al., "Reconsidering Long-term Care in the End-of-Life Context in Japan" (2016) 16 (Suppl. 1) *Geriatrics & Gerontology International* 132, 136.

[51] See Tsuda et al., note 31; and Hirai et al., note 48.

[52] See Tsuda et al., note 31 and Hirai et al., note 48. This notion of the ideal dying process is also seen in other countries. See, for example, Wolf et al., note 7; A. Fagerlin and C.E. Schneider, "Enough: The Failure of the Living Will" (2004) 34(2) *Hastings Center Report* 30, etc. See also M. Sanjo et al., "Preferences regarding End-of-Life Cancer Care and Associations with Good-Death Concepts: A Population-based Survey in Japan" (2007) 18(9) *Annals of Oncology* 1539.

[53] See Nakazawa et al., note 8.

based on guidelines rather than legislation. The development of educational programmes for doctors on palliative care or end-of-life communication and the promotion of ACP to the general public have led to a gradual improvement in the process of end-of-life decision-making in general. However, there are still a number of issues that require further discussion, such as the definition of the end of life, the need for legislation on surrogate decision-makers and ADs, and euthanasia. The lack of any legal force for ADs is particularly problematic because decision-making in Japan tends to be family centred, which can lead to situations in which a patient's own wishes are not respected. Such situations are in fact contrary to the most important principle of the process guidelines, despite there being no provision for ADs within the guidelines themselves. To protect the rights of patients, it is important to continue the discussion on the issue of ADs and the legal weight they have. However, given that many Japanese do not hold positive views on legislating ADs and prefer traditional family-centred decision-making, and given the various sociocultural factors at play, it may be more realistic and practical to explore a more culturally appropriate approach to decision-making based on ACP.

14

Advance Directives in Macao: Not Legally Recognised, but…

VERA LÚCIA RAPOSO & MAN TENG IONG

14.1 Introduction

The Macao Special Administrative Region (SAR) is one of two special regions of the People's Republic of China (PRC). According to the PRC principle of "one country, two systems", Macao is vested with its own executive, legislative and judicial powers. Macao law rests on many different legal theories and practices, and is heavily inspired by the Portuguese legal tradition, which differs from that of the PRC. Although the Joint Declaration on the Question of Macao, which was signed into effect on 26 March 1987, provided for the transfer of sovereignty from Portugal to the PRC on 20 December 1999, Macao's law has remained largely unchanged following the handover of power.[1] The profound influence of the previous Portuguese administration means that it appears natural that courts in Macao should adopt solutions from Portuguese doctrine and case law to support their judicial decisions. However, new legal trends from the PRC and nearby countries, and the growing influence of Chinese values imposed by a predominantly Chinese community, are being added to this Portuguese tradition. All of these factors have created in Macao a legal framework that blends the West and the East.[2]

Regarding informed consent theory more generally, most of the solutions in place in Portugal are also applicable in Macao. As in Portugal, Macao's main informed consent solutions reside in its Criminal Code (CC)[3],

[1] Joint Declaration of the Government of the Portuguese Republic and the Government of the People's Republic of China on the Question of Macau, Number 23/1988, 6 June 1988, Article 2(4), https://bo.io.gov.mo/bo/i/88/23/out01.asp#1.

[2] For explanations of the legal and cultural particularities of Macao law, see V.L. Raposo, "Macao Report: Informed Consent in a Multilingual and Multicultural Region: A Bioethical Challenge" (2018) 27(3) *Cambridge Quarterly of Healthcare Ethics* 385.

[3] Decree 58/95/M, 14 November 1995, which approved the Macao Criminal Code, https://bo.io.gov.mo/bo/i/95/46/codpenpt/codpen0001.asp#1.

specifically in Article 150 (which requires prior patient consent for medical acts) and Article 151 (which requires referred consent to be fully informed). However, they depart in similarity in the domain of advance directives (ADs), which is a branch of the right to informed consent. Although ADs have been legally recognised in Portugal since 2012,[4] Macao has not followed this legislative step. Even though members of the Ethics Committee for Life Sciences under Macao's Health Bureau agreed that ADs should be implemented in Macao in 2019,[5] efforts to legislate ADs have now reached a standstill.

To date, no legal document has dealt with ADs in Macao or with the professional regulation of, or guidance for such directives. However, this does not mean that ADs have no application in this small territory. The present chapter analyses the legal relevance of ADs in the Macanese CC, the applicability of ADs in Macao, the ways in which doctors and family members can affect their applicability, the attitudes of the Macao government and Macanese residents towards the current application of ADs and the possible features of a future legislation.

14.2 The Legal Relevance of Advance Directives in the Macanese Criminal Code

One of the most relevant provisions in the Macanese CC is Article 150, which provides for the crime of "arbitrary medical-chirurgical interventions".[6] Number 1 of this norm states that "[t]he people mentioned in Article 144 that in view of the purposes referred to therein, perform effective intervention or treatment without the patient's consent shall be punished with imprisonment up to 3 years or a fine".[7] In contrast with

[4] Recognised by Law 25/2012, 16 July 2012, www.pgdlisboa.pt/leis/lei_mostra_articulado.php?nid=1765&tabela=leis&nversao=.

[5] Macao Health Bureau, "2nd Meeting of Ethics Committee for Life Sciences" (3 December 2019), www.gov.mo/pt/noticias/217173/.

[6] For analyses of Articles 150/1 and 2 of the Criminal Code, see M.T. Iong, "Criminal Liability for Violation of Informed Consent in Macao" (2020) 22 *UMagazine* 62; M.O. Leal-Henriques, *Anotação e Comentário ao Código Penal de Macau (Parte Especial). Vol. III* (Macao: Centro de Formação Jurídica e Judiciária, 2014), pp. 262–6; V.L. Raposo, "Informed Consent in China and Macao" in T. Vansweevelt and N. Glover-Thomas (eds.), *Informed Consent and Health – A Global Analysis* (Cheltenham, UK: Edward Elgar Publishing, 2020), pp. 151–3; V.L. Raposo, "Quando o paciente diz não: sobre o artigo 150. do Código Penal de Macau (Intervenções e Tratamentos Médico-Cirúrgicos Arbitrários)" (2015) 36 *Boletim da Faculdade de Direito da Universidade de Macau* 59.

[7] The expression "people mentioned in Article 144" refers to any "doctor or other legally authorized person", and the expression "in view of the purposes referred to therein" refers

the situations in nearby jurisdictions, such as Hong Kong, the PRC or Taiwan, in Macao, a doctor who does not obtain lawful consent for medical interventions or treatments commits a criminal offence: the crime of arbitrary medical-chirurgical intervention. According to the wording of the norm, the criminal penalty applies even if the patient's health condition improves, and even if their life is saved by the doctor. In practical terms, however, it is unlikely that the doctor would be condemned; certainly, in Macao, there are no instances of legal suits having been brought against doctors, based on this norm, and the instances of such legal suits in Portugal are few in number.

However, obtaining lawful consent is not an absolute requirement for doctors. Lawmakers have accepted that in certain scenarios it is not possible to obtain the patient's prior consent, and thus Article 150/2 includes two exceptions. The first refers to a situation in which consent can be obtained, but would require that the medical intervention be postponed, an eventuality that would involve danger to life (simple danger) or serious danger (qualified danger) to body or health. The second involves a situation in which consent has been given for a certain intervention or treatment, but it is later discovered in the course of treatment or surgery that a different procedure must be performed (due either to new information on the patient's medical situation or to actual changes in the patient's condition) to avoid danger (simple danger) to life, body or health. However, for the doctor to avoid criminal prosecution, an additional condition is set for both exceptions: the existence of circumstances which lead to the certain conclusion that consent would be refused. Such circumstances include conversations with the patient's family members, relatives or friends, and the existence or discovery of ADs or similar documents. A hypothetical danger that is not likely to occur is not an adequate basis for medical intervention or treatment; otherwise, it would be acceptable to invoke presumed consent each time a doctor wanted to override a patient's wishes.[8] Doctors must be able to safely conclude that the patient would not have rejected the proposed medical interventions or treatments if they were in a condition to express their will.

This requirement – the absence of circumstances leading to the certain conclusion that consent would be refused, provided in Article 150/2 of the CC – is called "presumed consent". This solution is established in

to the "intention to prevent, diagnose, defuse or alleviate illness, suffering, injury or bodily fatigue, or mental disorder", as clarified by Article 144 of the Criminal Code.

[8] Raposo, "Informed Consent in China and Macao", note 6, p. 152.

Number 2 of Article 38 of the same code,[9] which provides the legal regime of consent for most situations, whereas Article 150/2 provides a specific regime that is only applicable to the medical domain.[10] The relation between these two norms is one of *lex generalis/lex specialis*. However, there is a difference between the two: Article 38/2 considers the conduct lawful whenever the surrounding circumstances lead to the conclusion that the holder of the legal interests protected (the person whose consent is required to prevent the agent's criminal liability) would have provided his/her consent, whereas Article 150/2 considers the conduct lawful unless the surrounding circumstances lead to the conclusion that if the interest holder were in a position to express their will, consent would have been refused. Thus, Article 150/2 permits broader scope for some interventions to be made without consent than does Article 38/2.[11]

Presumed consent cannot become an instrument used to override the patient's refusal of a medical act in favour of the relatives' wishes or the doctor's assessment. Article 150/2 of the CC clearly centres on the patient's true wishes, as demonstrated by a systematic interpretation of the CC and the inclusion of this criminal provision in the chapter regarding self-determination. Accordingly, the legal value protected in Article 150 of the CC is self-determination in health matters – that is, regarding the healthcare that the patient desires to receive (or not).

There are, of course, some situations where the patient's doctor does not have any knowledge of the patient's wishes. When there is doubt surrounding the patient's presumed decision, doctors must intervene and provide the required medical intervention or treatment, in line with the *in dubio pro vita* principle,[12] that is, in case of doubt, the doctor should act on decisions that will safeguard the patient's life.

14.3 The Applicability of Advance Directives

As discussed previously, ADs are not subject to specific legislation in Macao. Moreover, they are seldom studied or mentioned in local

[9] "There is presumed consent when the agent acts on the reasonable assumption that the holder of the legally protected interest would have effectively consented to the fact had he known the circumstances in which it is practiced".

[10] Moreover, not all medical acts are regulated by Article 150 of the CC; only those that meet the requirements of Article 144 of the CC. Cf. Raposo, "Quando o paciente diz não", note 6, 64–6.

[11] Cf. Raposo, "Quando o paciente diz não", note 6, 70; though this legal mechanism is known as "presumed consent", the concept is closer to the idea of "no presumed refusal".

[12] The same clarification in Raposo, "Quando o paciente diz não", note 6, 68.

doctrine.[13] There is therefore an absence of explicit legal guidance or provision to direct the outcome if a patient presents an AD, more correctly, something similar to an AD. The absence of a legal concept of AD in Macao prevents a definition of what would be considered an AD in this jurisdiction, and which requirements would have to be fulfilled. In this study, we will consider written ADs because we believe these to be the form most likely to be accepted in Macao, a very conservative jurisdiction in this regard.

Because there is no specific legal standard, the legal value of ADs must be assessed considering other applicable norms, namely those addressing informed consent and presumed informed consent. Under Article 150/2 of the CC, doctors are required to consider any indications given by the patient about the medical care that they would or would not wish to receive. ADs typically contain the patient's wishes, which doctors must take into consideration. Here, to take "in consideration" merely means to acknowledge its existence, though there is no binding requirement.

The only situation in which doctors may violate the criminal standard occurs when they completely disregard the AD, for instance, where the doctor is alerted to the existence of an AD, but does not read the document. By contrast, if the doctor reads the AD but acts against the wishes expressed within, this is not necessarily interpreted as an act of non-compliance. The doctor can always argue that they were not sufficiently convinced that the wishes contained within the AD were true reflections of the patient's actual wishes. Thus, even when the doctor has considered the AD, the freedom of assessment granted by law empowers them to disregard its contents and to decide to proceed as they see fit to do. In sum, there is no law that forces doctors to be bound by ADs in Macao[14] and moreover, the extant regulations indicate that current documents lack binding force. Consequently, ADs are valid only if

[13] Nonetheless, some Macanese authors defend the implantation of legislation on ADs in the near future, including its binding nature in the Macanese jurisdiction. See, for instance, M.T. Iong, *Directivas Antecipadas de Vontade: Um Regime Existente em Macau?* (Brazil: Novas Edições Acadêmicas, 2017), pp. 13, 28, 71, 110–11; M.T. Iong, "Please Allow True Self-Decision under Macao Law" (2019) 38(2) *Medicine and Law* 183.

[14] Portugal, as the original source of Macao's doctrine and legal practices, has a different situation because Law 25/2012, 16 July 2012, imposes the binding power of ADs; thus, if doctors do not respect the content of ADs without proper justification, they may be criminally punished.

doctors believe them to be the authentic expression of the patient's current and true will, leaving the decision to the doctor's discretion (and eventually to the court's assessment in case of litigation).[15]

Another major obstacle to compliance with an AD in light of Article 150/2 of the CC is the requirement that the patient's consent shall be actual – that is, consent must be given concurrently with the medical act.[16] This rule excludes consent given years, months or even weeks in advance. By nature, ADs involve advance (often well in advance) consent/refusal, which raises issues regarding the timeliness of the decision. A possible interpretation of this requisite is that all decisions remain up to date – that is, valid – as long as the AD is not changed by the patient. However, this legal interpretation is open to debate. This requirement has been circumvented by some jurisdictions by requiring revalidation of the AD after a certain number of years to ensure that it remains the patient's will.[17] This could be a possible solution for a future law on ADs in Macao.

In conclusion, the Macanese legal framework has not determined the legal status of ADs,[18] but this "omission" does not affect their validity. ADs can be regarded as a legitimate indicator of the patient's acceptance or rejection of medical care, according to Article 150/2 of the CC. However, they have no binding power over doctors. Besides their non-binding nature, the patient's wishes as expressed in ADs can be affected by factors that inform their actual decision, and which may actually contradict such wishes, such as information provided by relatives or friends to the doctor.[19]

[15] This same interpretation in light of existing law in Macao was advocated by Raposo, "Quando o paciente diz não", note 6, pp. 71–2.

[16] V.L. Raposo, *Do Ato Médico ao Problema Jurídico (Breves Notas sobre o Acolhimento da Responsabilidade Médica Civil e Profissional na Jurisprudência Nacional)* (Coimbra: Almedina, 2013), pp. 220–1.

[17] See, for instance, Article 7/1 of Law 25/2012, which regulates ADs in Portugal, and that establishes a validity period of 5 years.

[18] Interestingly, this is despite the fact that Macao generally adopts solutions from Portuguese legal doctrine, and Portugal has already legislated on ADs in 2012. See also J.P. Meneses, "Gentlemen, please think about this...", Macau Business Media (24 February 2020), www.macaubusiness.com/gentlemen-please-think-about-this/.

[19] Regarding the last example, see Iong, "Please Allow True Self-Decision", note 13, p. 186. In this example, this author proposes the binding nature of prior will and the use of sychiatric ADs for the specific case of mentally ill patients in Macao (Iong, "Please Allow True Self-Decision", note 13, pp. 186–90), but the reasoning can be transposed for other situations.

14.4 The Triumvirate Relationship between Family Members, Doctors and the Patient

In Macao, according to Numbers 2 and 3 of Article 37, consent is always a personal act. Except in the case of minors and incompetent adults – both of whom should have legal representatives empowered to act on their behalf and in their best interest – consent can be given only by the patient.[20] In theory, then, ADs should represent the exclusive decision of the patient, made freely, and without the influence of others.

In practice, however, the patient's stated desire as expressed in the AD may be informed by others, especially by the wishes and decisions of family members and doctors. Medical decisions frequently involve a triangular relationship between family members, doctors and the patient. In the majority of cases, the extent to which the patient's expressed desires (specifically as stated within the AD) may be considered an autonomous decision, or to which their desires will be wholly or partially followed depends on the interventions of family members and/or doctors. In jurisdictions such as Macao, where family members can exercise major influence over their relatives' medical decisions, we envisage that they will be able to affect the patient's desires as expressed in their AD.

Familism is a cultural practice which in China facilitates and encourages the family to play a decisive role in the healthcare of family members.[21] Chinese familism has its philosophic roots in Confucianism (although other more practical factors explain familism in modern Chinese society), and still plays a major role in Chinese communities.[22] Based on the social and cultural specificities of the territory, it is fair to assume that family wishes continue to be critical actors in the process of actually instigating ADs, in shaping doctors' perceptions of the content of an AD, and in determining the extent to which the doctor takes the patient's wishes into account.

Presumed consent must be assessed considering – among other criteria – information regarding the patient taken from their relatives.[23]

[20] Raposo, "Informed Consent in China and Macao", note 6, p. 151.

[21] See note 2 and the references quoted in that study.

[22] Ibid., pp. 391–2.

[23] There are no specific guidelines in Macao on how to assess the patient's presumed consent, so we used the existing guidelines in Portugal, see Entidade Reguladora da Saúde, *Consentimento Informado-Relatório Final* (May 2009), www.ers.pt/uploads/writer_file/document/73/Estudo-CI.pdf.

When assessing an AD, doctors normally take several elements – including conversations with family members – into consideration in order to determine whether the content of the AD is consistent with the patient's current and true desire. In this regard, the family's reaction is often a primary factor shaping doctors' perceptions. In certain situations, family members may want to keep the patient alive even though their relative's AD expresses their desire to reject essential medical interventions or treatments. In this case, family members may attempt to influence the doctors' perception of the veracity of the patient's wishes as expressed in the AD. The prevalence of familism is such that within Chinese culture, doctors believe that family members possess knowledge of their relative's true desire and are thus able to confirm whether the desire stated in the AD is true and current.[24] Moreover, when confronted with an AD that rejects a medical treatment – especially if that intervention is life saving – doctors will probably disregard it, fearing potential litigation by family members, and the likely outcome of a conservative (pro-life) judgment of any court assessing the conflict. Thus, in defending a refusal to comply with the AD, the doctor might argue, for instance, that the patient's desire expressed in the AD was indeed taken into consideration, but that it did not correspond to the patient's current or true will. Under Macanese law, relatives are not called upon to make medical decisions for the patient, but in actuality the concept of presumed consent is operationalised in such a way that relatives can influence the way the AD (or any other "sign" to be considered in light of Article 150/2) is understood by the doctor. This is likely to happen in individualist communities (see the case of Portugal, with this very same norm), but the likelihood of this occurring increases in more collectivist communities such as Macao. It can be confidently argued that the triangular relationship in healthcare (patient, doctor, family) enables family members to influence doctors' interpretation of the ADs.

Given the power of the cultural influence of familism within Chinese healthcare provision, and decision-making, patients' wishes can be affected by erroneous (and very discretionary) interpretation of ADs by healthcare providers. That ADs must be given binding force is therefore imperative if patients' autonomy is to be respected and protected. Further legislation to clarify the legal status of ADs and to enforce binding power

[24] C.Y. Tse and J. Tao, "Strategic Ambiguities in the Process of Consent: Role of the Family in Decisions to Forgo Life-sustaining Treatment for Incompetent Elderly Patients" (2004) 29(2) *Journal of Medicine and Philosophy* 207.

in Macao is required, considering that Article 150/2 of CC does not provide sufficient mechanisms to protect the patient's decisions as expressed in the AD.

14.5 Advance Directives and Palliative Care

The Hospice & Palliative Care Centre in Kiang Wu Hospital is Macao's sole healthcare institution providing hospice and palliative care[25] for terminal cancer patients.[26] Local residents (holders of Macao identity card) who receive diagnoses of terminal cancer can receive hospice and palliative care at the centre. Patients who require such care are typically experiencing extreme physical and emotional suffering. The centre provides palliative care which includes painkillers, morphine injections and acupuncture (traditional Chinese medicine), to eliminate or at least relieve pain. On a spiritual level, the centre organises events such as birthday parties and tea gatherings. In addition to patient care, the centre provides psychological counselling for family members.[27] Care is provided free of charge, as it is paid for by the Macao SAR government.

Before admission to the centre, cancer patients must sign a document called "Consent for the Hospice & Palliative Care Centre",[28] which is intended to allow doctors the right to not intervene should the patient's condition require specific urgent medical action, such as cardiopulmonary resuscitation, electrical cardioversion, tracheal intubation or cardio tonic injection. The literal translation of the document is "Consent for…", but in practice, it is not a document for patients to authorise the provision or non-provision of medical procedures, but an acceptance of the hospital's terms and conditions, which include the non-provision

[25] The World Health Organization (WHO) defines palliative care as an approach that improves the quality of life of patients and family members who face life-threatening illness by preventing and relieving suffering by way of early identification and accurate assessment and treatment of pain and other problems, whether physical, psychosocial or spiritual. Cf. WHO, "Palliative Care" (5 August 2020), www.who.int/news-room/fact-sheets/detail/palliative-care.

[26] Kiang Wu Hospital, *Brochure Hospice & Palliative Care Centre – Introduction.* Information also available at www.kwh.org.mo/medical%20center.php.

[27] Detailed information regarding the centre's operations was obtained from a conversation with a nurse who worked in the centre. There are no formal official documents in this regard.

[28] In the past, patients who were admitted in the centre were required to sign a document called "Do-Not-Resuscitate Declaration". Currently, the "Consent for the Hospice & Palliative Care Centre" document integrates the previous document.

of these medical procedures. The decision to sign – or to not sign – the document is usually made by the family, not by the patient, and to withhold a signature is considered a rejection of the centre's services and conditions, and thus the patient cannot be admitted. Notably, the consent form required by the Hospice & Palliative Care Centre is the closest formally recognised mechanism to an AD in Macao, and it appears that the form has binding force only when used at the Kiang Wu hospital. However, its ambit is narrow: (i) it includes only the rejection of medical interventions, not acceptance and (ii) it covers only medical acts standardised in the document, rather than covering the full range of medical acts.

A further drawback to this document is evident: the signatory to the "Consent in the Hospice & Palliative Care Centre" is not the patient, but a relative (in the presence of a witness).[29] This document can thus regarded more as a "family AD", where the AD represents the wishes of the family, rather than those of the individual patient. However, under Article 150/2 of the CC in Macao, third parties cannot give consent to the refusal of medical interventions –particularly life-saving medical interventions – a right reserved solely for the patient, except for some specific cases where a legal representative is assigned by the court. Not only does this document demonstrate profound disregard for the rights and autonomy of patients who are already vulnerable due to their terminal state: there is a glaring contradiction, for the fact that a relative is required to sign this document in order to indicate consent to the refusal of medical interventions for the patient represents an act that is in clear violation of Macao law.

14.6 The Current Position of the Macao Executive on Advance Directives

To date, the Macao Executive[30] has taken a cautious approach towards ADs, accepting (or tolerating) these instruments, but yet not investing

[29] This information was obtained from the "Consent in the Hospice & Palliative Care Centre" document.

[30] Macao is, together with Hong Kong, a special administrative region of the People's Republic of China. It has its own government and Chief of Government (the Chief Executive). As for Article 2 of the Macao Basic Law, "The National People's Congress authorizes the Macao Special Administrative Region to exercise a high degree of autonomy and enjoy executive, legislative and independent judicial power, including that of final adjudication, in accordance with the provisions of this Law". See António Katchi, *As Fontes de Direito em Macau* (Macau: Faculdade de Direito da Universidade de Macau, 2006), pp. 273–408.

them with binding force. It has been reported that given Macao's ageing population, and in light of the adoption of AD legislation in over twenty countries including the United States, Australia, Canada and Singapore, the Executive has recognised the need to legislate ADs. Such binding legal instruments will not only help to enhance the quality of life and to protect the dignity of patients at the end of their lives, but will also reduce unnecessary medical expenses.[31] On 3 December 2019, the Macao Health Bureau, under its sub-entity the Ethics Committee for Life Sciences, introduced "Questions and Future Policy Guidelines for ADs" in Macao and agreed to legitimise ADs.[32]

Despite agreement over the implementation of ADs, the Executive insists that discussions over ADs remain at the preliminary stage. This hesitancy may reflect the bureau's fear of difficulties and controversies surrounding plans for their implementation.[33] These barriers to implementation arise from low public awareness regarding the legislation of ADs, the possibility that the patient could change their mind as the end of life approaches, and the willingness of the patient's family to comply with their relative's desires. The bureau holds that extensive and in-depth public education in the social, academic and legal fields is needed, and that a law introducing ADs can be implemented only after obtaining consensus from all sectors.[34]

In response, it is possible to argue that the Executive's position lacks proper justification. First, the kind of consensus invoked to postpone a regulation on ADs is not possible to achieve, given the multiplicity of legal, ethical and even religious views on the matter. Second, even if such a consensus could be achieved, the Executive has not taken steps to encourage or facilitate discussion or awareness among the population.[35] This was

[31] All about Macau Media, "The Claim that the Legislation Is Not Yet Due to 'Low Public Awareness' – Health Bureau's Reply and Public Response" (29 August 2020), www.cyberctm.com/zh_TW/news/mobile/detail/2620690#.YRko4y3R1QI.

[32] Macao Health Bureau, "2nd Meeting of Ethic Committee for Life Sciences" (3 December 2019), www.gov.mo/pt/noticias/217173/.

[33] All about Macau Media, "Before Existing 'Advance Directives' – Healthy and Undisturbed Centre that Allows End-of-Life Patients to Have a Choice (II)" [in Chinese] (13 July 2020), tinyurl.com/3f5wyu3m.

[34] Ibid.

[35] The only noticeable step is the promotion of ADs by some public and private entities. For example, the Macao Social Welfare Bureau promotes the use of ADs by the elderly when educating them on life-and-death matters (Macao Social Welfare Bureau, *Macao Pension Status and Policy Research Report* (2015), www.ageing.ias.gov.mo/uploads/file/a8387e568125adacb3c4d280d5354985.pdf), and the Geriatrics Society of Macao held an

demonstrated in a recent study exploring the willingness of Macao Chinese people to make ADs.[36] The study found that the lack of information about ADs was the main factor deterring individuals from making ADs. The study also found that 73.6% of the sample (n = 724) were willing to complete an AD if the document had legal recognition. Together with recent media coverage of this issue with voices supporting patients' choices regarding end-of-life decisions,[37] these findings suggest that the questions raised by the formal recognition of ADs are clearly of concern to residents. Two grounds for their concern are apparent: first, the patient's well-being, for in Macao it is common for healthcare delivery to extend until the patient's death, at the cost of much physical and mental pain for the patient and distress to the family; and second, the financial burden of such futile medical treatment, either for the patient or for the hospital. Notwithstanding these important and prevalent concerns, there remains a great deal of resistance – from certain groups of Macao residents and from the Executive – to the implementation of proper regulations on ADs. One possible reason for this hesitancy is the fear that formally legislating ADs could lead to euthanasia, a practice forbidden in Macao,[38] even though the two situations are clearly different.[39]

Academic Annual Meeting in 2019 with teaching on how ADs are put into practice in clinical work for the elderly (Cheng Pou Journal, "Geriatrics Society of Macao Held Its Inauguration Ceremony and Academic Annual Meeting" (26 November 2019), www.chengpou.com.mo/dailynews/183073.html).

36 S.M. Leong et al., "Prevalence and Predictors of Willingness to Make Advance Directives among Macao Chinese" (2021) 18(15) *International Journal of Environmental Research and Public Health* 7942.

37 All about Macau Media, "Claiming No Legislative Time Due to 'The Public's Low Awareness' – Macao Health Bureau's Response and the Public's Response" [in Chinese] (29 August 2020), tinyurl.com/3756nz38. See also All about Macau Media, "Do Patients and Their Family Members Have the Right to Terminate 'Invalid Medical Treatment?' – The True Story of Miss Lam and her Family Members" [in Chinese] (1 May 2020), tinyurl.com/yckfdm3x.

38 It is not completely clear whether all forms of euthanasia are legally forbidden. Regarding the legality of euthanasia in Macao SAR, see Iong, *Directivas Antecipadas de Vontade*, note 13, pp. 54–67. For the same discussion in light of the Portuguese law, whose Criminal Code is the same as the one of Macao in this regard, see V.L. Raposo, "Doctor's Criminal Liability and Medically Assisted Death – The Portuguese Case" (2019) 26(3) *European Journal of Health Law* 240.

39 For a distinction see Macao SAR, Iong, *Directivas Antecipadas de Vontade*, note 13; V.L. Raposo, "No Dia em que a Morte Chegar (Decifrando o Regime Jurídico das Diretivas Antecipadas de Vontade)" (2013) 22(24) *Revista Portuguesa do Dano Corporal* 79; V.L. Raposo, "Directivas Antecipadas de Vontade: Em Busca da Lei Perdida" (2011) 32(125) *Revista do Ministério Público* 169.

It is imperative that the Executives regulate ADs, namely, to clarify some legal voids, such as the requirements to be met in order for them to be legally operational. The decision on whether ADs should be merely indicative or truly binding is the most controversial feature. The binding nature would clearly be in syntony with patient's autonomy, the cornerstone of modern healthcare law, and would also be the most adequate solution from a human rights perspective. Moreover, the binding nature of ADs is also the solution most compatible with Article 150/2 of the CC and with the Portuguese legal heritage that still largely shapes the Macanese jurisdiction. In that respect, a regulation such as that stated in Portugal (Law 25/2012, 16 July 2012) could be a viable option. However, the hazards of legal transplants are well known and it is not clear whether binding ADs would indeed be congruent with the general values of a predominantly Chinese community, still very grounded in and attached to familism. Further studies are required to clarify this and other issues, for example, there are no data on the estimated number and implementation of ADs in Macao's jurisdiction, and there is an urgent need for research studies that explore doctors' perspectives on ADs.

14.7 Conclusion

Macao represents an interesting case study from legal, ethical and sociological perspectives: the existence and application of predominantly Western (Portuguese-inspired) legislation does not always meet the expectations of a community composed primarily of Chinese people[40] nor of an Executive that aims to implement a "not so Western law". However, it is unclear whether the Executive's decision to put a pause on AD legislation actually has the support of the population, especially considering the empirical evidence suggesting that a large percentage of the Macanese population is likely to be willing to complete an AD if legalised, and the growing number of voices in favour of legally binding ADs in the PRC.[41]

[40] A detailed description of this disconformity is provided in Raposo, note 2.

[41] K.Q. Wang et al., "On Legislative Protection of Living Will in China" (2017) 38(6A) *Medicine and Philosophy* 67; Q.S. Qi and J.Q. Xu, "Reflection upon the Legislation of Living Will in China" (2019) 35(8) *Journal of Jilin Engineering Normal University* 71; Y.P. Luo et al., "Promotion of Living Will: Practice and Suggestions" (2020) 41(22) *Medicine and Philosophy* 6; X. Bai and X. Liu, "On the Implementation of Living Wills in China" (2019) 11(1) *Medicine and Jurisprudence* 10; H.M. Zhang et al., "Evidence from Clinical Trials of the Changed Status in Living Will over the Past Twenty Years" (2020) 41(22) *Medicine and Philosophy* 13; S. Sui, "Discussion on the Issues of Living Will" (2014) 22(2) *China Health Law* 10.

While there is currently a mechanism whereby the content of ADs may be taken into consideration, via Article 150/2 of the Macanese CC, there remains some uncertainty as to how effective ADs will be, particularly in light of the fact that doctors are likely to disregard any AD rejecting life-sustaining treatment, as discussed previously.

In Macao, the AD discussion is almost non-existent. Without clear and transparent discussions that include experts and assessments of sound legal arguments, there will be no related legal developments concerning the nature, scope and use of ADs in the near future.

15

Advance Directives in Pakistan: Religious, Cultural and Social Influences

MOHAMMAD ASIM BEG, ERFAN HUSSAIN, NOSHIN KHAN, ASMA HAMID & MUHAMMAD ATIF WAQAR

15.1 Introduction

The Islamic Republic of Pakistan falls into the category of developing nations. Pakistan is abundant in human resources. According to United Nations (UN) data, it is the fifth most populous country in the world, with a total population of 223,103,549 as of January 2021.[1] The median age is 22.8 years, and life expectancy is 67.79 years.[2] With approximately 90 per cent of the population currently under the age of 54, only a very small number of Pakistanis are elderly.[3] The country's very high birth rate creates innumerable challenges, as well as compromised living conditions and a poor quality of life. According to the UN's Human Development Index (HDI) 2020, Pakistan ranks 154th out of a total of 189 countries.[4] Such a low position on the HDI reflects the condition of the population in terms of health, education and well-being. With its rapidly increasing population, inadequate healthcare facilities, low literacy rates and extreme poverty, Pakistan is in a predicament. Although the country is blessed with the demographic dividend of a large youth population, palliative and end-of-life care cannot be ignored, as terminal illness can strike at any age or stage of life. The relatively short life expectancy and poor health conditions in Pakistan demand better healthcare policies and the ability to delegate responsibility appropriately in the event that a person loses the capacity to make decisions.

1 "Pakistan Population (LIVE)", *Worldometer*, 17 January 2022, www.worldometers.info/world-population/pakistan-population/.
2 Ibid.
3 Ibid.
4 M. Haider, "Human Development Index 2019: Pakistan Ranks Lower than All South Asian Countries", *The News*, 12 December 2019, www.thenews.com.pk/print/582826-human-development-index-2019-pakistan-ranks-lower-than-all-south-asian-countries.

Advance directives (ADs) are an important way of specifying the type of treatment a person would like to receive at the end of his or her life. Owing to a range of economic, social, cultural and medical factors, however, no laws or legislation on ADs have thus far been passed in Pakistan. This chapter explores the many influences, perspectives and challenges pertaining to ADs to examine why they have not yet surfaced on the legislative agenda. The remaining sections of chapter are laid out as follows. Section 15.2 describes the governance system, healthcare structure and legislative process in Pakistan. Section 15.3 details the subtleties of the factors creating obstacles on the path to AD legislation, including religious, socioeconomic, cultural and medical factors. Section 15.4 discusses the key issues affecting the feasibility of legislating and implementing ADs in the context of Pakistan, and Section 15.5 concludes.

15.2 Governance, Healthcare Structure and Legislation

Pakistan lags behind other countries in legislating many important issues. Healthcare is a largely neglected sector, and the lack of legislation thereon results in a complex situation. The absence of laws and legislation on such important issues as ADs is due in part to Pakistan's convoluted governance system and its multi-tiered, mixed public and private healthcare system. To gain insight into the lack of AD legislation, it is important to outline the governance structure, map out the healthcare system and briefly describe the legislation related to individual autonomy in healthcare.

15.2.1 Governance Structure

Healthcare was a federal matter in the 1973 constitution, but the 18th constitutional amendment in 2011 transferred healthcare to provincial health departments.[5] Accordingly, the four provinces of Balochistan, Punjab, Sindh and Khyber Pakhtunkhwa assumed legislative and executive responsibility for healthcare in their provinces.[6] The federally

[5] "Cabinet Approves Devolution of Seven Ministries", *Dawn*, 28 June 2011, www.dawn.com/news/640139/cabinet-approves-devolution-of-seven-ministries.

[6] S. Nishtar, *Health and the 18th Amendment. Retaining National Functions in Devolution* (Islamabad: Heart File, n.d.), www.heartfile.org/pdf/HEALTH_18AM_FINAL.pdf.

administered territory of Islamabad was left to the federal mechanism even though the federal Ministry of Health (MoH) was dissolved.[7] After dissolution of the federal MoH, its remaining functions were dispersed across several other federal institutions, including the Planning Commission, Federal Bureau of Statistics and newly established Inter-Provincial Ministry.[8] This decentralisation of the healthcare system created a plethora of issues, including national coordination of global health commitments, drugs licensing and the regulation of medical and nursing professionals.[9] To mitigate the challenges being faced at the federal level, the Ministry of National Health Services Regulation and Coordination (MoNHSRC) was created in 2012.[10] However, the MoNHSRC has struggled to establish legitimacy, as its creation has been contested by both provincial governments and the other federal entities to which its functions were originally assigned.[11] Further, not having a federal MoH means that there is no federal health minister. Pakistan is likely one of the few countries in the world to lack a permanent health minister at the federal level.[12] The devolution of healthcare to the provincial level has created a vacuum, as the lack of a federal health minister has resulted in the absence of coordination and advocacy on health-related issues in the federal cabinet or two upper houses: the National Assembly and Senate. The absence of a federal minister for health has created unsurmountable challenges for the healthcare system. Even though legislative and executive authority now lies with the provinces, the lack of a central authority leaves a significant gap in the development of overarching policy norms, provision of health information and management of interprovincial regulation and coordination, which are roles ascribed to the federal government.[13]

[7] S.A. Khan, "Situation Analysis of Health Care System of Pakistan: Post 18 Amendments" (2019) 7 *Health Care Current Reviews* 1, 2.

[8] S.A. Zaidi et al., "Health Systems Changes after Decentralisation: Progress, Challenges and Dynamics in Pakistan" (2019) 4 *BMJ Global Health*, e001013, 3–4.

[9] Ibid.

[10] Ibid.

[11] Ibid., p. 3.

[12] Khan, note 2, p. 2.

[13] Ibid. Although the MoNHSRC is a federal entity, it is limited in its scope of work and is used to manage specific issues such as issues related to the COVID-19 pandemic. It is unable to take on a more holistic role owing to its contested legitimacy and opposition from the provincial assemblies.

15.2.2 Healthcare Structure

In addition to governance issues, Pakistan has a convoluted healthcare system. The system is multi-tiered and multifaceted, comprising a large network of government health facilities, private individual practitioners, philanthropic organisations and private medical entities.[14]

Public sector healthcare service delivery is organised into three tiers: Basic Health Units and Rural Health Centres form the core of primary healthcare, whereas Tehsil Headquarters and District Headquarters are the spine of the secondary care structure.[15] Both primary and secondary healthcare are supported by tertiary care from teaching hospitals.[16] Although public sector hospitals are the lifeline of the underprivileged and provide critical and tertiary care, a large percentage of the population, approximately 78.08 per cent, depend on private healthcare facilities.[17] Healthcare delivery in the public sector, although free, is not the preferred choice of most, as it is basic and of mediocre quality.[18]

Private sector healthcare facilities are generally favoured over those in the public sector owing to the latter's poor performance.[19] Private facilities also offer a swifter service,[20] although the service provided can be placed on a continuum ranging from extremely low to very high quality.[21] Private healthcare fees are unregulated and depend on the physician, infrastructure and quality of care.[22] A number of private philanthropic organisations also offer reasonable quality treatment to the underprivileged segment of society.[23]

15.2.3 Laws and Legislation

In light of the aforementioned issues with governance and the unsatisfactory healthcare system, it is perhaps unsurprising that there are

14 Zaidi et al., note 8, pp. 1–8.

15 A. Hassan et al., "Healthcare System of Pakistan" (2017) 1 *International Journal of Advanced Research and Publications* 170.

16 Ibid.

17 S. Nishtar et al., "Pakistan's Health System: Performance and Prospects after the 18th Constitutional Amendment" (2013) 381 *The Lancet* 2193, 2193.

18 Ibid.

19 M.T. Abdullah and J. Shaw, "A Review of the Experience of Hospital Autonomy in Pakistan" (2007) 22 *International Journal of Health Planning and Management* 45.

20 Zaidi et al., note 8, pp. 1–8.

21 Nishtar et al., note 17, p. 2193.

22 Ibid., 2201.

23 S. Kassim-Lakha and J. Bennett, "Philanthropic Funding for Health in Pakistan" (2013) 381 *The Lancet* 2236.

currently no laws in Pakistan that deal with ADs.[24] The concept of respecting patient autonomy in a healthcare setting, however, can be seen in two pieces of legislation: the Mental Health Ordinance 2001 and the Transplantation of Human Organs and Tissues Act 2010. Both are noteworthy because they espouse to a certain extent the concept of individual autonomy in the healthcare context. They are briefly described here to provide a sense of what that concept means in Pakistan.

Mental Health Ordinance 2001 – Prior to our discussion of this legislation, it should be noted that the Mental Health Ordinance 2001 is in fact a lapsed ordinance. Ordinances do not become valid laws in Pakistan if they fail to pass Parliament; they remain presidential orders and lapse after three months if left idle.[25] This was the case for the Mental Health Ordinance 2001, although, unlike in other jurisdictions where lapsed ordinances hold no value in the legal landscape, in Pakistan ordinances form a crucial part of the law, so much so that they carry the same weight as any Act passed by Parliament.[26] Accordingly, the Mental Health Ordinance 2001 can still be said to be of influence.

The purported purpose of the ordinance was to consolidate the laws pertaining to the care and treatment of mentally disordered persons and to make better provisions for their care and treatment and the management of their property and affairs and matters connected therewith or incidental thereto.[27] Although the Mental Health Ordinance 2001 was a step towards giving individuals autonomy by affording mentally disordered persons the right to make decisions about their care, specifically the course of their treatment, the mental health legislative framework remains fragmented and ineffective.[28] The ordinance assumes that such persons have the capacity to comprehend their diagnosis and prognosis.[29] It also fails to define capacity or specify how it should be measured,

24 See also other factors discussed in Section 15.3.

25 A.I. Gilani et al, “Psychiatric Health Laws in Pakistan: From Lunacy to Mental Health” (2005) 2 *PLoS Medicine* e317, 1106.

26 Ibid., pp. 1106–7.

27 Ibid.

28 This ordinance is also sparingly implemented in practice (see Gilani et al., note 25). Despite the fact that health has shifted from a federal to a provincial matter since the 18th amendment of the Constitution, only three provinces have enacted mental health acts replacing the Mental Health Ordinance 2001, namely, Singh, Punjab and Khyber Pakhtunkhwa (see further S. Dey et al., “Comparing Legislation for Involuntary Admission and Treatment of Mental Illness in Four South Asian Countries” (2019) 13 *International Journal of Mental Health Systems* 1, 4).

29 Gilani et al., note 25, pp. 1105–9.

leaving it open to debate and discretion,[30] which may in turn raise concerns in relation to mentally disordered persons' right to access healthcare. Nevertheless, the granting of the right to make their own decisions about healthcare constitutes an important step towards recognising the value of individual autonomy in the context of medical treatment decisions.

The Transplantation of Human Organs and Tissues Act 2010 – This Act is a major milestone for two reasons: firstly, it is a step towards recognising individual autonomy, and, secondly, it goes against long-standing Islamic ideology. The Act facilitates individual autonomy by granting the right to donate one's organs after death.[31] Whilst this legal regulation is not directly relevant to ADs, as the decision takes effect only after a person dies, the Transplantation of Human Organs and Tissues Act 2010 affords individuals the autonomy to decide what is to happen to their body after death. Most people in Pakistan believe that performing any kind of medical procedure on a dead body constitutes mutilation of the body.[32] Some Muslim sects even discourage the performance of an autopsy or post-mortem, as the removal of organs is believed to be unIslamic.[33] This legislation thus demonstrates the significance of respecting individual autonomy in relation to one's body even when doing so may conflict with established religious principles.

Thus, although AD legislation does not yet exist in Pakistan, respect for individual autonomy, upon which the concept of ADs is typically predicated, is gaining recognition. This suggests that despite the factors discussed in this chapter that may make AD implementation difficult, there may well be room for the development of ADs in Pakistan. Having considered the laws and healthcare structures in place in Pakistan, we now turn to its religious, socioeconomic, cultural and medical contexts.

15.3 Factors Influencing Legislation on ADs

The religious, socioeconomic and cultural environments in Pakistan exert a strong influence on both its legislative structure and healthcare delivery system. It is imperative that the factors related to these

[30] Ibid.

[31] Transplantation of Human Organs and Tissues Act 2010.

[32] M.A. Al-Bar and H. Chamsi-Pasha, *Contemporary Bioethics: Islamic Perspective* (Cham: Springer Open, 2015), pp. 250–7.

[33] Ibid.

environments be charted in detail to understand the possible reasons for the absence of legislation on ADs. For example, as an Islamic country, religion features prominently in all spheres of life in Pakistan, including legislation, and religious beliefs intertwined with cultural influences, societal attitudes and socioeconomic structures have served to undermine both the importance and relevance of ADs.

15.3.1 Influence of Religion on Legislation

The Islamic Republic of Pakistan is a majority Muslim state that is guided by Islamic laws. In the Constitution of Pakistan 1973, Part IX: Islamic Provisions, Article 227 states that

> All existing laws shall be brought in conformity with the Injunctions of Islam as laid down in the Holy Quran (the holy book of Muslims) and Sunnah (the ways of prophet Mohammad), in this Part referred to as the Injunctions of Islam, and no law shall be enacted which is repugnant to such Injunctions.[34]

According to this provision, all laws enacted, or legislation promulgated, have to be in accordance with Islamic teachings. Although there are many sects in Islam, and each sect interprets the religion according to its own understanding, there is consistency of interpretation amongst most Islamic jurists in the belief that life is sacred. As interpreted by some and believed by many, refusing invasive treatment is tantamount to hastening death, which is contradictory to the teaching of the Quran.[35] Saving lives is a duty, and taking lives unjustifiable.[36] In addition, clerics, who exert a strong influence on society, believe that the withholding or withdrawal of treatment is contrary to religious ideology. In fact, according to the Council of Islamic Ideology in Pakistan, "life is sacrosanct and one should do everything possible to save it".[37] This directive to sustain life at any cost can be understood to be in direct conflict with the concept of ADs, as ADs give individuals the right to refuse life-sustaining treatment. There are, however, interpretations consistent with the concept that do not run contrary to the sanctity of life. For example,

[34] "Part IX: Islamic Provisions" (*The Constitution of Pakistan*), www.pakistani.org/pakistan/constitution/part9.html.

[35] Al-Bar and Chamsi-Pasha, note 32, pp. 250–7.

[36] Ibid.

[37] "Herald Exclusive: When Life Meets Death", *Dawn*, 26 April 2011, www.dawn.com/news/623972/herald-exclusive-when-life-meets-death.

some believe that life is given and taken by God and that the provision or withdrawal of treatment cannot prolong life or hasten death because the time of death is preordained; hence, death will occur irrespective of the treatment choice.[38] The religion may thus allow a person to make decisions on their course of treatment based on personal choice.[39] Given these differences in interpretation, families often rely on the advice of religious scholars before making decisions about end-of-life treatments for terminally ill patients because they lack confidence in their own knowledge of what is permissible in the Quran. In hopeless situations, religious scholars may allow families and patients to take decisions regarding the course of treatment, not with the intention to hasten death but to refuse treatment that is emotionally and financially exhausting and painful, in addition to being of no benefit.

Another aspect worth exploring is the assignment of responsibility for the elderly and women in the Quran. Some Quranic injunctions place such responsibility on the male members of the family. Islam encourages a sense of obligation towards caring for elderly parents and being responsible for women while also emphasising the inherent goodness of looking after the sick. Chapter 17 of the Quran, Al-Isra', states: "Allah has ordered you to worship none except Him, and to be good to your parents. If either or both of them attain old age with you, do not say 'fie on you', nor rebuke them, but speak to them with words of respect". Chapter 4, An-Nisa, discusses the husband's role as "protector and maintainer". Verse 34 of An-Nisa states: "Men are the caretakers of women, as men have been provisioned by Allah over women and tasked with supporting them financially". A *hadith* (saying of the Prophet Mohammed) narrated by Muslim [2699] on caring for the sick reads as follows: "The one who stays with the one who is sick, and takes care of him and looks after him has done good by serving him and caring for him, and Allah, may He be glorified and exalted".[40] These Quranic verses and *hadith* are indicative of the responsibilities of male family members.[41] Whether those responsibilities are limited to specific situations or extend to all matters is unclear.[42] However, prevailing religious values give male members of the family the right to make decisions on

38 Al-Bar and Chamsi-Pasha, note 32, pp. 250–7.
39 Ibid.
40 R.I. Khan, "Palliative Care in Pakistan" (2017) 2 *Indian Journal of Medical Ethics* 37.
41 Ibid.
42 Ibid.

healthcare matters for the elderly (primarily parents) and women. This automatic assignment of rights suggests that ADs have little role to play, as the male members of the family are essentially substitute decision-makers in end-of-life situations.[43] Hence, issues related to patient autonomy, ADs, end-of-life medical treatment and other matters have perhaps not been addressed by the legislature based on the assumption that such decisions lie with male members of the family.

This section thus demonstrates that whilst religion generally has a guiding influence on legislation in Pakistan, different interpretations of Islamic teachings result in varying attitudes towards ADs. It is perhaps for this reason that no AD legislation has thus far been discussed. Legislators may well feel that they are in no position to make decisions on such a controversial subject rooted in religious ambiguity.[44]

15.3.2 Economic, Social, Cultural and Medical Landscape

A medley of religious values, social and cultural norms, and economic stratification has resulted in a distinct economic, social, cultural and medical landscape in Pakistan. Both patriarchy and hierarchy feature heavily in Pakistani society, owing to which the family takes centre stage as opposed to the individual. The patriarchal system is supported by religious beliefs, traditions, and local social and cultural values, which in turn result in extended families that expand horizontally and vertically across generations. These beliefs and values further reinforce familial prioritisation and solidify the role of the family in undertaking decisions on terminal illness for competent and incompetent patients alike. Familial hierarchy, patriarchy and, as mentioned previously, religious teachings all select the oldest or most competent male family member as the pivotal decision-maker.[45] As a result, all healthcare decisions, including end-of-life care and treatment, are generally made by the selected male family member, leaving little space for individual autonomy and eroding the need for ADs. This power imbalance in itself reflects inadequate representation of the interests and perspectives of female family members, who, ironically, are often the primary caregivers

[43] F. Moazam, "Families, Patients, and Physicians in Medical Decisionmaking: A Pakistani Perspective" (2000) 30 *The Hastings Center Report* 28.

[44] J. Akhtar, "Living Wills in Health Care: A Way of Empowering Individuals" (2010) 60 *The Journal of the Pakistan Medical Association* 240.

[45] See note 43.

in such situations. The patriarchal system is likely also rooted in socio-economics, with limited resources often dictating that the survival of the family as a whole takes precedence over individual autonomy.[46]

Furthermore, many patients themselves refuse to discuss death or terminal illness, and thus the responsibility falls on the family members who decide whether patients are to be informed of their diagnosis or prognosis.[47] Families channel their love and compassion by hiding painful realities or cloaking diagnoses in abstraction. Medical professionals accept this state of affairs as well, respecting family decisions and refraining from revealing the diagnosis to the patient.[48] Disease and death are viewed as happening to families rather than individuals, with the family of the individual in question playing a significant role in decision-making and responsibility.[49] For example, children are socialised to believe that caring for parents and grandparents is their duty, with sons often expected to live with their parents and take care of them in their old age.

This emphasis on the family in end-of-life decision-making may make it difficult for individual-oriented ADs to be accepted and used, as demonstrated by a study on advance care planning conducted amongst 57 South Asian individuals (including Pakistanis), which found that many of the participants considered planning ahead to be unnecessary because of close family ties and predefined familial roles and trust in the context of medical decision-making.[50] Most participants believed that one should focus on concrete activities, with advance care planning thought to be irrelevant, vague and unnecessarily worrying.[51]

In addition to the role of the family, that of healthcare professionals is also relevant. A substantial number of people in Pakistan are uneducated and lack the ability to comprehend complex medical conditions, meaning that they depend on the advice of physicians. Physicians and nurses in Pakistan are often drawn towards taking on a decision-making role owing to a combination of factors. In line with the centrality of the family in Pakistan, healthcare providers are often symbolically "inducted" into the family in such a way that they end up directing

[46] Ibid.

[47] Ibid.

[48] See note 40.

[49] See note 43.

[50] P.D. Biondo et al., "Understanding Advance Care Planning within the South Asian Community" (2017) 20 *Health Expectations* 911.

[51] Ibid.

rather than facilitating medical interventions and care.[52] In addition, physicians hold an esteemed position in Pakistani culture owing to their knowledge and expertise. Perhaps as a result of this status, as well as a lack of training in communication skills and ethics education, healthcare professionals assume responsibility for making decisions, often sharing limited information with family members and refraining from fully disclosing a diagnosis or prognosis to patients or doing so only in ambiguous terms, as they do not want to convey bad news to patients. Deeply entrenched in cultural values, medical professionals often ignore ethical values.[53] Undoubtedly, accepting cultural norms is easier and less exhausting than critiquing them or forging an alternative involving patients' informed consent.[54] According to one study, nurses and physicians often adopt the role of care provider, counsellor and, most commonly, decision-maker.[55] Most physicians view themselves as independent decision-makers, particularly with regard to patients in a critical condition, assuming that they are best equipped to understand the needs of an incapacitated patient.

Recognising this practice as unethical, several healthcare organisations across the nation have formulated and implemented do-not-resuscitate, end-of-life care and withdrawal of life support policies and practices at an institutional level.[56] Palliative care services have been established in many of the leading tertiary care hospitals and comprehensive cancer care centres in the nation. Palliative care providers tend to have lengthy discussions with patients and their extended families to explore the goals of such care.[57] These discussions are often transcribed and documented in the patient's medical record. Although such records serve to facilitate patient care, they hold no validity in the courts.[58] It is also unclear whether the goals transcribed in these informal records are met.

It can thus be seen that the economic, social, cultural and medical landscape of Pakistan erects numerous obstacles to the introduction of ADs. In addition to the role of the family in end-of-life decision-making,

[52] See note 43.

[53] R.I. Khan, "End of Life Care in Pakistan; Some Ethical Issues" (2012) 22 *Journal of the College of Physicians and Surgeons Pakistan* 745.

[54] See note 43.

[55] Ibid.

[56] See note 53.

[57] W. Zafar et al., "Preferences regarding Disclosure of Prognosis and End-of-life Care" (2016) 30 *Palliative Medicine* 661.

[58] Ibid.

healthcare professionals in Pakistan have also taken on the role of decision-maker even in situations where doing so may not be ethical. We consider possible solutions to these issues in the following section. Whilst some steps are being taken to involve patients and their families in processes akin to advance care planning, their effectiveness cannot be ensured without a more formalised regime.

15.4 Discussion

The current scenario in Pakistan presents an image that points towards the non-acceptance of ADs. The governance structure, laws and legislation, and the healthcare system, along with the religious, social and cultural landscape, seem to be unprepared for the legislation and implementation of ADs. Although such legislation/implementation in Pakistan appears to constitute a daunting and time-consuming task, we believe there is a dire need to start a conversation about AD legislation given the importance of respect for autonomy. In the following, we lay out five key issues that require further examination and discussion in the Pakistani context.

15.4.1 Perceived Taboo versus Patients' Actual Preferences

The belief that death is preordained and inevitable is prevalent in the Pakistani community, and yet talking about death remains a taboo and to-be-avoided subject. There is an overemphasis on optimism and a widespread belief that speaking negatively will give life to what is feared. Healthcare issues thus generally have a negative connotation and are considered bad news. Perhaps as a result, decision-making on and discussions of end-of-life care take place at a relatively late stage or do not take place at all.[59] As discussed previously, families generally want to ensure that their loved one maintains a positive outlook until the end, and the perceived taboo surrounding death often prompts families to collude with healthcare professionals to "protect" the patient from anxiety, stress and fear of losing hope by keeping a terminal illness diagnosis and prognosis from the patient, thereby avoiding any discussion of what course of treatment the patient would want in the event of incapacity. In certain circumstances where the patient has some knowledge of his or her diagnosis, the extent of the disease, its terminal or

[59] See note 53.

life-limiting nature, as well as the prognosis, may not be disclosed to the patient. Physicians also respect the wishes of the family and refrain from discussing end-of-life care and treatment in such situations.

There are limited data suggesting that this perceived taboo may not in fact be in line with patient preferences and that some patients would prefer to be informed of their prognosis and life expectancy.[60] In one study, 13 per cent of respondents reported feeling uninformed about their medical condition, and more than half expressed the importance of being informed about their medical condition, prognosis and management options. About two thirds wanted their families to be actively involved in decision-making on management options, and half wanted their families to make medical decisions if they themselves ever became incompetent, with 27 per cent preferring their physician to make decisions on their behalf. Whilst two thirds said they were comfortable discussing end-of-life care, 81 per cent said that they had never discussed life expectancy with their physician, and 42 per cent reported no discussions of choices concerning end-of-life care in the past year. Fifty-six per cent of the patients studied wanted to discuss end-of-life care only should the need arise. Many said they wanted to know their prognosis but only a few reported ever having had such a discussion.[61] This study thus seems to demonstrate a mismatch between patient preferences and actual practice in relation to end-of-life discussions, which may be a result of the taboo described previously. If the reluctance to discuss end-of-life matters is indeed merely perceived, then it would appear that engaging in larger conversations with the public about legislating ADs would be well worth the effort.

15.4.2 Unclear Legislative Responsibilities at the Federal and Provincial Level

That being said, beginning a conversation about ADs at the legislative level is likely to prove challenging. Between the constitutional role of the federal government and the devolution of power to the provinces following the 18th amendment, healthcare has sunk into great confusion, particularly with regard to who will legislate and regulate policies. The healthcare legislative process has suffered immensely from the unclear

[60] Ibid.

[61] F. Saeed et al., "Dialysis Decision Making and Preferences for End-of-Life Care: Perspectives of Pakistani Patients Receiving Maintenance Dialysis" (2020) 60 *The Journal of Pain and Symptom Management* 336.

demarcation of federal and provincial roles and responsibilities.[62] Thus, as a consequence of the 18th amendment, it is not always clear whether it is the responsibility of the federal government or provincial governments to promulgate laws and legislation for the welfare of the people, and important issues are often left unlegislated by either. Some of the reasons attributed to such apathy are rooted in provincial governments' lack of capacity.[63] The situation is further complicated by the influence of such factors as illiteracy, a lack of understanding and poor critical-thinking skills permeating all tiers and strata of society, including the legislative assemblies. Elected representatives are not required to have any educational attainments or qualifications.[64] Low literacy and education levels and a lack of exposure to the external world limit thinking capacity and logical reasoning ability, which is reflected in the absence of imperative legislation.[65] Building up the capacity of the provincial legislatures is thus key to promulgating laws on important healthcare issues.

15.4.3 Lack of Resources

Although legislating for ADs will inevitably be an uphill battle, ADs could well play an important role in the delivery of end-of-life care in Pakistan owing to the general lack of resources. Apart from a few cases of malicious intent and family disputes, the premature withdrawal of treatment is generally the result of insufficient financial resources. Much of Pakistan's large population lives on very meagre resources, with many struggling to afford two meals a day. Although public sector hospitals are available, they are few in number and poor in quality, forcing people to turn to private sector hospitals,[66] which offer better facilities but are expensive. Seventy-eight per cent of the underprivileged resort to costly private healthcare, placing families in a precarious position.[67] Many struggle between expending all of their finances on treating and sustaining the life of a loved one and making ends meet. The lack of an option to formally specify in advance that one wishes to have life-sustaining treatment withdrawn at a particular stage of the end-of-life process

[62] Khan, note 7.
[63] Ibid.
[64] T. Ahmad, *National Parliaments: Pakistan* (Washington, DC: The Law Library of Congress, February 2017), https://tile.loc.gov/storage-services/service/ll/llglrd/2016478970/2016478970.pdf.
[65] Ibid.
[66] Nishtar et al., note 17.
[67] See note 40.

unnecessarily prolongs the agony of patients and places families in a dire financial situation, with many burdened with a large amount of debt to pay back.[68] In these circumstances, the ability to make an AD would be beneficial for both patients and their families.

15.4.4 Physicians and the Implementation of ADs

If and when the legislative bridge is crossed and legislation on ADs is promulgated, the task of making that legislation implementable and acceptable will come into play. The implementation of ADs will not be easy, but training healthcare professionals in effective communication skills and medical ethics would pave the way for wider societal acceptance. Such training needs to occur in at least two key areas. The first is in relation to the AD concept itself. Although there is a scarcity of research data, a few studies have explored medical practitioners' understanding of ADs. For example, one study revealed medical professionals to have a limited understanding of ADs, to be unaware of proxy decision-making and to believe that ADs are prepared only for the terminally ill.[69] After being given an explanation of what ADs are, however, they recognised them as an important component of end-of-life quality of care, and almost all of those surveyed said they favoured ADs for themselves. One physician stated that more palliative care services need to be established before ADs can be followed.[70] The medical professionals in the study as a whole emphasised that legal mechanisms, infrastructure, mass education and renowned hospitals taking the lead are all crucial to pave the way for ADs in Pakistan.[71] The barriers that they identified with respect to ADs included ineffective communication, inadequate and inappropriate information and a delay in information being given to patients and families, the paternalistic culture, the possibility of document forgeries, and inequitable resource availability.[72]

The second area in which training is required is how to break news to patients and families and discuss diagnoses and prognoses, as well as end-of-life treatment and palliative care, which are important

68 N. Panjwani, "Advance Directives: A Policy Required in the Asian Countries" (2013) 3 *I-manager's Journal on Nursing* 30.

69 N. Panjwani et al., "Physicians' and Nurses' Perspectives on the Importance of Advance Directives in Tertiary Care Hospitals" (2019) 1 *Journal of Shifa Tameer-e-Millat University* 3.

70 Ibid.

71 Ibid.

72 Ibid.

prerequisites to the development of ADs. Unless patients feel confident in their ability to make decisions, they will be unable to document their preferences with regard to end-of-life treatment and care. Formal ethics education would assist medical practitioners in dealing with ethical dilemmas and difficult end-of-life decisions.[73] Whilst issues such as end-of-life care, palliative care and ADs are recognised and taught in many undergraduate and postgraduate medical and nursing schools nationally, such courses are often optional or elective.[74] The regulatory bodies do not require them to be a mandatory part of the core teaching curriculum.[75]

Training in these two areas would be particularly helpful in relation to the issue of healthcare practitioners, at times problematically, taking on a decision-maker role, as discussed previously. As some healthcare professionals working with terminally ill patients have expressed, appropriate training would be highly beneficial to themselves and the patients they treat.[76] In the absence of formal training, medical care practitioners often do not know how to define their role; they either become overly involved and assume the role of a family member or prime decision-maker or distance themselves to the point that the patient and family feel abandoned.[77] Healthcare professionals' understanding of their role in relation to decision-making is highly important because whilst the superior medical knowledge of physicians vis-à-vis patients and families is beyond question, the risk of physicians misinterpreting patients' wishes and infringing upon autonomous decision-making cannot be ignored.[78] Owing to the unchallenged power and authority that physicians possess against the backdrop of a population that is largely illiterate, financially insecure, unaware of individual rights and without access to judicial redress, a physician's decision to continue life-sustaining treatment without any clear benefit may not be disputed. The absence of a comprehensive framework for ADs may therefore exacerbate the exploitation of unchallenged clinical discretion, which can be cloaked in references to divine predestination.[79]

[73] See note 53.
[74] See note 43.
[75] Ibid.
[76] See note 68.
[77] See note 53.
[78] See note 43.
[79] Ibid.

15.4.5 Religious Interpretation

With an array of interpretations on the meaning of Islamic teachings, as discussed previously, whether ADs will be viewed as permissible remains an open question. A healthy debate involving people from all walks of life is needed, including religious scholars who could review relevant clauses in the Quran and put forward a comprehensive proposal on AD legislation. In light of technological advancement, interpretations of Quranic texts may need to be reviewed to determine what exactly is meant when it comes to using technology for end-of-life treatment and how laws on ADs fit into the religious context. An updated interpretation of the Quran and a major shift in mindset are imperative if ADs are to be placed on the legislative agenda in Pakistan.

15.5 Conclusion

The complex governance structure and healthcare system in Pakistan, together with various religious, cultural, social and medical factors, have contributed to a distinct local context that makes the adoption and implementation of ADs extremely difficult. Given the growing importance of individual autonomy, as demonstrated by the Mental Health Ordinance 2001 and the Transplantation of Human Organs and Tissues Act 2010, and interpretations of Islamic teachings that are consistent with the use of ADs, however, we believe there is room for the development of ADs. There remain a number of hurdles to be overcome, and in this chapter, we have put forward suggestions for how we believe this can be accomplished. Despite the many challenges that lie ahead, we feel that ADs are an important goal to work towards. Not only would ADs educate healthcare practitioners about patient choices concerning end-of-life care and treatment, but they would also empower individuals, safeguard patient autonomy and ensure compliance with individual choices. In light of the patriarchal and hierarchical nature of the Pakistani family structure, ADs would also empower women to make decisions related to their healthcare. Accordingly, we believe it is worth deliberating on the viability and effectiveness of ADs, as well as advocating for them, within the context of Pakistan.

16

Advance Directives in Saudi Arabia: An Islamic Approach and Practical Implications

GHAIATH HUSSEIN & ABDULLAH ADLAN

16.1 Introduction

Saudi Arabia (SA) is an Islamic country in the southwestern part of Asia. It leads the Sunni Islamic world in many aspects, the most important of which is its responsibility for custody of the two holiest mosques in Islam. Making sense of advance directives (ADs) in SA, and the regulatory frameworks governing healthcare more generally, requires a careful understanding of the traditional Islamic religious legal framework of *Shari'ah*.

The main objective of this chapter is to offer clarity on how well-established principles, and Islamic statements of permissible and impermissible behaviour, should be reasoned through to provide an underpinning governance framework for healthcare practices at the end of life. We also review published evidence on the practical application of ADs in SA, and go on to examine the social and cultural factors that may explain the limited uptake of ADs. We then conclude with two arguments about how an appropriate role for ADs might be realised in the future – one concerning the need for legal clarity and the other concerning how to bring about improvements in professional knowledge and understanding.

16.2 Basic Legal Framework and the Role of Religion

The foundation of the Saudi legal system is *Shari'ah* law, or traditional Islamic law, which is supplemented by royal decrees, statutes, regulations and other legislative and policy documents in specific areas of law. As the Basic Law, or the Saudi equivalent of a constitution, states in Article 7: "Government in the Kingdom of Saudi Arabia derives its authority from the Book of God and the Sunnah of the Prophet

(PBUH), which are the ultimate sources of reference for this Law and the other laws of the State".[1]

Because there are no specific laws or other legislative and policy documents derived from *Shari'ah* on ADs or end-of-life care and decision-making more generally, general *Shari'ah* principles apply. *Shari'ah* law is derived from two primary sources, the Quran and the Sunnah, or the practices and sayings of the Prophet Muhammad, as well as a number of secondary sources, including *Ijma*, or the consensus of Muslim scholars on particular issues, and *Qiyas*, or reasoning by analogy. To understand the permissibility of ADs under Islamic law, which is further discussed here, scholarly interpretations of the relevant parts of the Quran and Sunnah must be studied.

Actions in Islamic law are generally categorised within a scale of permissibility rather than the dichotomy of "do" and "do not". That scale includes the following categories:

1. Must do (*Wajib*)
2. Permitted (*Halal/Mubah*)
3. Favoured (*Mustahab*)
4. Detestable (*Makrouh*)
5. Forbidden (*Haram*)

Any given act is judged within one of these categories based on a ruling by a scholar, usually based on one of the Islamic jurisprudential (Fiqhi) schools of thought known as Madhahib. The four main schools in the Sunni Muslim tradition are Hanafi, Shafiite, Maliki and Hanbali, named after the main Imam who developed that madhab. The main Fiqhi school followed in SA is the Hanbali, named after Imam Ahmed ibn Hanbal (who died in AD 857).

The categorisation of an act under any of the five foregoing categories is based primarily on the presence of a text (in the Quran and/or Sunnah) that discourages or forbids that act. In the absence of such a text, the act is considered permissible (mubah) based on the Fiqhi principles of "the original status of things is permissibility" and "nothing is forbidden except with a proof". Such proof can be an *Ayah* (or verse) from the

[1] More on the legal system in SA and its religious basis can be found in A. Babgi, "Legal Issues in End-of-Life Care: Perspectives from Saudi Arabia and United States" (2009) 26 *American Journal of Hospice & Palliative Medicine* 119.

Quran[2] or a *hadith*, a record of the sayings or teachings of the Prophet Muhammad. Lower levels of proof include reasoning by analogy (*Qiyas*), whereby scholars reach a judgement that something is not permissible because it shares the same reasons as those of a known forbidden thing. For example, recreational drugs (e.g. heroin, cocaine, cannabis, etc.) are unanimously forbidden[3] using *Qiyas* despite the absence of any text that forbids them, given that they share the effect of "covering the mind" caused by alcohol.

One of the most common forms of Islamic legal guidance is the "*fatwa*" (plural: "*fatawa*/*fatwas*"), which is a religious/legal non-binding opinion issued by an authentic scholar or group of scholars usually through the so-called Fatwa Complexes. In SA, the highest – and only – authority is the Authority of the Grand Scholars (aka Council of Senior Scholars), led by the Mufti of the kingdom. Members of this authority are allowed to issue personal fatwas on individual affairs if asked to do so.

It is important to emphasise here that *fatawa* are the intellectual outcome of a meticulous process known as *Ijtihad*, which ensures that these rulings are aligned to Islamic scripture and the purposes of *Shari'ah* Law (*Maqasid*), as we have discussed elsewhere.[4] The five higher goals of *Shari'ah* can be summarised as preserving the faith, body/soul, mind/intellect, lineage/progeny and wealth/property. The morality and legality of any act is measured against these goals; the more the goals are achieved by the act, the more legal and moral it becomes and vice versa (see previous discussion of the scale of permissibility). In the event that two or more of the goals contradict one another, for example, if someone were dying of thirst and the only drink he or she could find was alcohol, then the priority would be placed on saving the person's life within the limitations detailed in the sub-principles of the major Fiqhi maxims, as described in the next section. The preservation of any one of the goals is attained both by the provision of its maintaining factors, such as the importance of staying healthy and abstaining from

[2] For example, "And do not kill your children for fear of poverty. We provide for them and you. Indeed, their killing is ever a great sin" (Quran, 17:31), which is used as proof that abortion is forbidden (unless there is a genuine cause).

[3] Y.H.M. Safian, "An Analysis on Islamic Rules on Drugs" (2013) 1 *International Journal of Education and Research* 1.

[4] N. Alsomali and G. Hussein, "CRISPR-Cas9 and He Jiankui's Case: An Islamic Bioethics Review using *Maqasid al-Shari'a* and *Qawaid Fighiyyah*" (2021) 13 *Asian Bioethics Review* 149.

anything that could endanger one's life. Saving a life, according to the Quran, is rewarded as if all human lives were saved: "and whoever saves a life, it will be as if they saved all of humanity" (Quran, 5:32).

16.2.1 *Healthcare Context: Lessons for the End of Life*

Emphasis on the sanctity of life, as demonstrated by the importance the Quran places on the saving of a life, is particularly significant in the healthcare context. As with all other religions, life is sacred in Islam and Muslims are obliged to safeguard it, and the preservation of life is amongst the highest purposes of *Shari'ah*. Moreover, life is believed to be given and owned by Allah, and hence only He can take it. In other words, no Muslim is allowed to take his or her own life, or to help anyone else, Muslim or not, to take his or her life, although, as we shall see, there are instances in which the withdrawal or withholding of futile treatment is permitted or even required.

Illness is generally believed to be a test from Allah, a test of His servants' patience and a means of helping them to erase some of their sins. Whilst all suffering and death is determined by the will of Allah,[5] however, that does not mean that suffering and death should be sought or tolerated unnecessarily, with many *hadith* encouraging Muslims to seek remedies for their illnesses. Examples include the following:

> Narrated by Abu Huraira: The Prophet (□) said, "There is no disease that Allah has created, except that He also has created its treatment" (Sahih al-Bukhari: 5678).
>
> Narrated by Usamah ibn Sharik: The Prophet (□) said, "Make use of medical treatment, for Allah has not made a disease without appointing a remedy for it, except for one disease, namely old age (aging)" (Sunan Abi Dawud: 3855).

Scholars have proposed differing views in relation to the treatment that should be sought. For example, a very prominent scholar, Imam Ahmed ibn Taimiya (who died in AD 1328), stated that seeking treatment can itself fall anywhere on the aforementioned scale of permissibility based on the weighing of its benefits and harms, as follows:[6]

[5] See, for example, Quran, 57:22.

[6] M.M. Malik, "Islamic Perceptions of Medication with Special Reference to Ordinary and Extraordinary Means of Medical Treatment" (2013) 4(2) *Bangladesh Journal of Bioethics* 22.

1. If the treatment is more harmful than the disease or the person believes that he will be cured by the medicine (not by the will of Allah), then it is forbidden (*haram*);
2. If the treatment has equal value to no-treatment, then it is permissible (*mubah*);
3. If the treatment is likely to be beneficial, then it is favoured (*mustahab*); and
4. If the treatment is necessary to stop the harm to oneself or others, then it should be done (*wajib*).

Other scholars have divided the seeking of treatment into three categories: obligatory (where the disease is treatable or is a communicable disease that could be harmful to others), optional (where the treatment is experimental or the overall benefit is unclear) and abstinence (where the treatment would be futile or even harmful).[7] It thus appears that in situations in which a treatment could be futile or harmful, Islamic law principles would generally dictate that the individual not seek treatment, which is consistent with the withholding or withdrawal of futile or burdensome life-sustaining treatment at the end of life. This view is also in line with the concept of death in Islam. Muslims believe that death is like crossing a bridge between this temporary life (of action) and the eternal hereafter life (of judgement and rewards).[8] In other words, Muslim patients should not expect to be immortal or believe that they can delay death, which further supports the idea that the artificial and futile prolonging of life is not consistent with Islamic principles.

In addition to such principles and interpretations, *fatwas* are also a source of guidance in the healthcare context. Most of the leading *fatwas* related to organ donation, blood transfusion, cardiopulmonary resuscitation (CPR)[9] and many others were the result of doctors or patients submitting questions in pursuit of religious fatwas from the Council of

[7] M.A. Albar, "Seeking Remedy, Abstaining from Therapy and Resuscitation: An Islamic Perspective" (2007) 18 *Saudi Journal of Kidney Diseases and Transplantation* 629 (as cited in H. Al-Jahdali et al., "Advance Medical Directives: A Proposed New Approach and Terminology from an Islamic Perspective" (2013) 16 *Medicine, Health Care and Philosophy* 163).

[8] Death is described in the Quran as the "true life" or the "life indeed" (Quran, 26:64).

[9] The Permanent Committee for Scholarly Research and Ifta', "Fatwa no. 8926: Ruling on Cardiopulmonary Resuscitation", in *Fatwa Collections* (Riyadh: General Presidency of Scholarly Research and Ifta', 1988), Group 1, Vol. 25: Miscellaneous Fatwas 2, pp. 71–5, www.alifta.gov.sa/En/IftaContents/PermanentCommitee/Pages/FatawaChapters.aspx?cultStr=en&View=Page&PageID=9745&PageNo=1&BookID=7.

Senior Scholars.[10] Arguably, this is a unique feature of the Saudi context in that clinical/medical decisions are not made solely within the confines of the doctor–patient relationship, as the scholars who are expected to rule by way of *fatwas* are mainly non-medical by profession. It is important to acknowledge the challenges associated with this feature of the Saudi context: because it is essential in Islamic jurisprudence for Islamic scholars to fully comprehend an issue in order to judge its suitability, they require a healthcare expert to explain the issue to them in lay terms and to answer their questions. That expert is usually a medical doctor. Whilst this is entirely understandable, the problem is that those providing the requested explanations are usually physicians, who may have their own preferences in the matter, which could result in experts advocating for what they think is right. The end result could be an indirect form of medical paternalism, aggravated by the religious cover it may have if the decision-making authority seems to have moved from a physician to a religious scholar.

The most relevant *fatwa* in the end-of-life context is likely the famous Fatwa No. 12086 issued on 28/3/1409 (H) (i.e. AD 1989) by the Presidency of the Administration of Islamic Research and Ifta', Riyadh, KSA. This *fatwa* relates to do-not-resuscitate (DNR) orders and states that "if three knowledgeable and trustworthy physicians agreed that the patient condition is hopeless; the life-supporting machines can be withheld or withdrawn. The family members' opinion is not included in decision-making as they are unqualified to make such decisions".[11] This *fatwa* is a good example of the unique role that *fatawa* play in the Saudi legal system: although they are not laws per se, they can be used as legal evidence in the absence of law. This is demonstrated by the fact that, despite there being no mention of DNR orders in any Saudi law, the practice of DNR in Saudi hospitals has been reported for more than

[10] The Permanent Committee for Scholarly Research and Ifta', "Fatwa no. 19165: Ruling on Using Euthanasia to End Suffering", in *Fatwa Collections* (Riyadh: General Presidency of Scholarly Research and Ifta', 1988), Group 1, Vol. 25: Miscellaneous Fatwas 2, pp. 84–91, www.alifta.gov.sa/En/IftaContents/PermanentCommitee/Pages/FatawaChapters.aspx?cultStr=en&View=Page&PageID=9748&PageNo=1&BookID=7.

[11] The Permanent Committee for Scholarly Research and Ifta', "Fatwa no. 12086: Ruling on Cardiopulmonary Resuscitation", in *Fatwa Collections* (Riyadh: 1988), Group 1, Vol. 25: Miscellaneous Fatwas 2, pp. 79–82, www.alifta.gov.sa/En/IftaContents/PermanentCommitee/Pages/FatawaChapters.aspx?View=Page&PageID=9746&CultStr=&PageNo=1&NodeID=1&BookID=7.

20 years[12] and the only reference "legalising" this practice over the years is the aforementioned fatwa. *Fortunately*, there has not been a single case of the family of a patient who died while under a DNR order suing the patient's doctor and/or the hospital at which he or she was admitted. It would be interesting to see how the Saudi courts would handle such a case and whether the *fatwa* alone would be sufficient to clear the doctor/hospital of liability.

16.2.2 Advance Directives

The foregoing discussion of the end-of-life care context in SA demonstrates the general permissibility of withholding or withdrawing futile or harmful life-sustaining treatment, as well as the very specific *fatwa* guidance in relation to DNR orders. Given that there are no laws or *fatwas* directly addressing the issue of ADs, however, how should we understand the permissibility of preparing and implementing ADs under Islamic law?

At least two sources of religious guidance can be drawn upon in understanding ADs under Islamic law. The first, which aids understanding of the individual's own role in end-of-life decision-making, is a well-known *hadith* about the Prophet Muhammad's illness and death:

> This Hadith Narrated by Ibn ʿAbbas and ʿAisha (R.A): Abu Bakr kissed (the forehead of) the Prophet when he was dead. ʿAisha added: We put medicine in one side of his mouth but he started waving us not to insert the medicine into his mouth. We said, "He dislikes the medicine as a patient usually does". But when he came to his senses he said, "Did I not forbid you to put medicine (by force) in the side of my mouth?" We said, "We thought it was just because a patient usually dislikes medicine". He said, "All of those who are in the house will be forced to take medicine in the side of their mouth while I am watching, except for Al-ʾAb-bas, for he had not witnessed your deed". (Translation of Sahih Bukhari. Book of Medicine, *Hadith* number 2012)[13]

This *hadith* demonstrates both a patient's right to refuse treatment and the fact that this right cannot be overridden by the wishes of others, even his or her closest relatives. Al-Jahdali et al. further interpret the *hadith* as conveying three principles: (i) Muslims are permitted not to receive

[12] A. Mobeireek, "The Do-Not-Resuscitate Order: Indications on the Current Practice in Riyadh" (1995) 15 *Annals of Saudi Medicine* 6.

[13] Al-Jahdali et al., note 7.

treatment, especially if they have an incurable disease; (ii) those taking care of patients are not permitted to force a patient to accept a certain treatment, especially when they know that the patient does not want it; and (iii) those persons will be held accountable for their actions if they do force the patient to do so,[14] or, in other words, a patient whose right has been unlawfully overridden has the right to seek retaliation for the (ab) use of his or her state of unconsciousness.

In the context of ADs, these principles can be understood as providing patients with the right to specify beforehand what they do not want to be done to them at the end of life, including choosing whether or not medication or other treatment options will be administered to them. In addition, they demonstrate that ADs should not be overridden and that those who attempt to do so can be held accountable for that attempt, even if made in good faith.

The second source of religious guidance comes from Fiqhi principles, which represent a practical framework for legal and moral decision-making through the categorisation of general rules under which there are sub-principles that are derived primarily from the text of the Quran and Sunnah.[15] Next, we discuss the five main Fiqhi principles agreed upon by most Sunni scholars, as well as some of their main sub-principles, and our interpretation of how they might be applied in the AD context.

I. The Principle of Intention (*Qaidat Al Niyyah*)

This principle states that actions are judged by (or based upon) their intentions. Any act of a human being must come from and is based on his or her will and intention. Under this principle, there is a sub-principle which states that "the means are judged as the ends", or, in other words, the means are judged using the same criteria as those used to judge the intention. Thus, if the intention is wrong, the means will also be considered wrong. In the AD context, this sub-principle can be understood to mean that when a person writes an AD, he or she cannot request illegitimate interventions to achieve a legitimate purpose or legitimate interventions to achieve an illegitimate purpose. For example, even if further treatment would be futile, burdensome or harmful, and the patient would die from the legitimate withdrawal of life-sustaining

[14] Ibid.
[15] See note 4.

treatment, he or she cannot in his or her AD request extensive doses of analgesics that could lead to death.

II. The Principle of Certainty (*Qaidat Al Yaqeen*)

This principle states that certainty cannot be removed by doubt; that is, what is known to be a fact cannot be overridden by what is doubtful. Under this principle, there is a sub-principle which states that what is proven by evidence is valid unless denied by contrary evidence of equal or better strength. In the AD context, this can be understood to mean that where an AD is considered to have been validly made (e.g. the patient was considered competent to make the AD at the time of its drafting) or is considered to apply (e.g. the patient has lost capacity), doctors should implement the AD unless they have contrary evidence of equal or better strength, such as strong evidence that the patient was not competent at the time he or she made the AD.

III. The Principle of Injury (*Qaidat Al Dharar)*

This principle states that harm may be neither inflicted nor reciprocated in Islam. Harm must be eliminated but not by means of another harm. Under this principle, there is a sub-principle stating that harm is to be prevented to the greatest extent possible. In the end-of-life context, where continuing treatment would be futile in terms of recovery and would be burdensome or even harmful in terms of pain and suffering, an AD can be seen as a way to prevent and limit the harm caused to the patient. That view would, of course, be based on the view that the infliction of such prolonged pain and suffering would bring greater harm than bringing about death more quickly by following a patient request in an AD to withhold or withdraw life-sustaining treatment. This is the case because another sub-principle states that an injury cannot be relieved by inflicting or causing a harm of the same degree, which suggests that any option that could inflict some kind of harm, such as the withdrawal or withholding of life-sustaining treatment that would ultimately result in death, would need to be assessed as to whether it might cause equal or greater harm to the patient than what he or she is currently suffering, as well as what the projected outcomes might be.

IV. Principle of Hardship (*Qaidat Al Mashaqaat*)

The basic principle here is that difficulty calls forth ease, and is the basis for allowing an exception to the rules where adherence to the rules would result in great hardship.[16] Whilst this principle deals primarily with what exceptions are permissible in situations of necessity, a sub-principle which states that "what is allowed for a cause (justification) goes with the cause" may be relevant in the AD context: if the AD's validity and applicability are justified by the patient's loss of capacity, they should become void as soon as he or she regains capacity.

V. The Principle of Custom or Precedent (*Qaidat Al Urf*)

This principle states that custom or precedent has legal force. What is considered customary is what is uniform, widespread, predominant and not rare. Customary practices are those that are acceptable to people of a sound nature and enjoy universal or general acceptance by a given country or generation. Custom in a given society can take the form of words, actions, abstinence or a mixture thereof. Under this principle, there is a sub-principle stating that only known customs, not rare ones, are recognised; in other words, transient customs are not recognised. In the wider healthcare context, this sub-principle could be understood as a form of norm-setting by clinical professionals, which in turn renders the customary practice legitimate. Thus, in so far as a practice is customary, it sets a precedent that should be followed. In the more specific AD context, it would mean that if healthcare professionals used ADs customarily, that usage would constitute a bottom-up approach to the legitimisation of the use and implementation of ADs as professionally acceptable, or even required, behaviour.

Another sub-principle states that things are defined by customs, not only by language, and that the way in which people use words can be used as evidence. In the context of ADs, this sub-principle can be understood as follows: where patients use terms in their ADs that are ambiguous or capable of being interpreted in more than one way, the most common, or public, interpretation should be used. For example, if a patient expresses a desire to have all care withdrawn in the face of a life-limiting diagnosis, it would be appropriate for the phrase "all care" to be interpreted in terms of medical treatment interventions rather than basic

[16] J. Auda, *Maqasid Al-Shariah: A Beginner's Guide* (Richmond, UK: International Institute of Islamic Thought, 2008), https://iiit.org/en/book/maqasid-al-shariah-a-beginners-guide/; A.H. Thahir, *Ijtihād Maqāṣidi: The Interconnected Maṣlaḥah-Based of Islamic Laws*, I. Haaz (ed.), (Geneva: Globethics.net, 2019), www.globethics.net/documents/10131/26882166/GE_Theses_30_isbn9782889312207.pdf/5b3a4fd5-b30f-b5d6-8c07-19251ccaacc4?t=1587732852812.

palliative care support that mitigates pain or suffering in the last moments of life. This is the case because despite the fact that "all care" could reasonably incorporate all healthcare interventions, laypersons would be unlikely to interpret the phrase in those terms.

With respect to the specific content of an AD under Islamic principles, Albar and Chamsi-Pasha have identified four elements that can be included: (i) a request to discontinue treatment; (ii) an instruction to switch off life-support equipment; (iii) the inclusion of organ donation; and (iv) power of attorney (*wakalah*).[17] In relation to the discontinuation of treatment, these authors argue that treatment can be discontinued if continuing it would not improve the patient's condition or quality of life and the intention is not to hasten death but rather to refuse "overzealous treatment". This argument is in line with the principles and interpretations discussed previously, which consider the withdrawal or withholding of treatment to be permissible where treatment is futile. Albar and Chamsi-Pasha also argue that palliative care aimed at maintaining personal hygiene and basic nutrition should not be discontinued, which is in line with the idea that only futile or harmful interventions can and should be stopped. Care that is beneficial, at least in terms of quality of life, should remain as a treatment or "remedy" that should be sought when ill.

The instruction to switch off life-support equipment pertains primarily to the case of brain death, for which several *fatwas* provide guidance,[18] and organ donation, which is beyond the scope of this chapter. In terms of power of attorney, or *wakalah*, Albar and Chamsi-Pasha contend that it would be prudent for Muslims to entrust someone (their *wakil*, or authorised representative) with the power of attorney in their living will. Should the person in question subsequently become incompetent, the *wakil* would be responsible for conveying the wishes stated in his or her living will. Accordingly, it can be seen that the term "power of attorney" as used here goes beyond the conventional sense of an individual being granted the power to make decisions on behalf of another, extending it to the role of the *wakil* as a conveyor or even interpreter of the content of an AD. It should be noted that the content of a living will should not include any clauses that contrast with or contradict the rulings of *Shari'ah*; as long as that is the case, there

[17] M.A. Al-Bar and H. Chamsi-Pasha, *Contemporary Bioethics: Islamic Perspective* (Springer, 2015).

[18] See further chapter 14 of Al-Bar and Chamsi-Pasha, note 17.

would arguably be no justification for ignoring the directive.[19] Moreover, the *wakil* is committed to following the instructions in an AD without any alteration or hiding.[20] The *wakil* is considered a witness to the wishes of the person making the AD and is legally and morally bound to express and convey those wishes to others, including healthcare providers.[21]

16.3 Practice and Sociocultural Context of Advance Directives in Saudi Arabia

In the previous section, we have considered how ADs would likely be regulated under Islamic law, although we should again emphasise that there are no specific laws, regulations or *fatwas* on this issue as yet. Moreover, there are no guidelines produced by healthcare professional bodies that mention an explicit role for ADs. We now turn to consideration of the situation relating to ADs on the ground. In particular, this section considers (i) knowledge of and attitudes towards ADs and (ii) the sociocultural factors that affect their acceptance in SA.

In terms of knowledge of ADs, whilst there appear to be no clear data on patient awareness, Baharoon et al. found in 2019 that there was a general lack of understanding on the part of patients about their illness and their options. Of their sample of 300 patients, only 25.3 per cent understood that their disease was incurable, and 54.7 per cent inaccurately thought that their disease was curable. Twenty per cent of the sample reported that their doctors had not discussed their prognosis with them directly. Less than 8 per cent understood the meaning or potential outcome of CPR, intubation or mechanical ventilation or how these interventions were relevant to their condition.[22] This general lack of understanding on patients' part about their illnesses and options is likely to affect their ability and desire to engage in advance care planning.

With respect to healthcare practitioners, a 2019 study on the knowledge and attitudes of physicians and nurses towards ADs for cancer patients found that 64.9 per cent of the participating physicians provided

[19] See note 17, p. 256.

[20] See "Then whoever alters the bequest after he has heard it – the sin is only upon those who have altered it. Indeed, Allah is Hearing and Knowing" (Quran, 2:181).

[21] See note 17, p. 256.

[22] S. Baharoon et al., "Advance Directive Preferences of Patients with Chronic and Terminal Illness towards End of Life Decisions: A Sample from Saudi Arabia" (2019) 25 *Eastern Mediterranean Health Journal* 791.

correct definitions of ADs, whereas the figure for the nurses was significantly higher, at 82.4 per cent.[23] The nurses in the study thus had a much better understanding of ADs, interestingly, with the independent predictors of AD knowledge being female sex and level of education. In terms of attitudes, a 2018 study on the knowledge and attitudes of emergency department and intensive care physicians towards DNR orders found that even though only 13.4 per cent of the sample of 112 mostly Muslim physicians had made ADs themselves, 86 per cent believed that every patient should have an AD. In an earlier study in 2010,[24] Tayeb et al. found that although some medical staff, including physicians, were unaware of what an AD is, most of their participants (who included a range of persons involved in end-of-life care) agreed with the concept of ADs after it had been explained to them. In discussing these findings, the authors argued that ADs were underused in their hospital and that their adoption should be encouraged given that the practice was widely accepted by their sample of 284 Muslim participants.

The data thus far seem to suggest that the concept of ADs is not unknown or unwelcome to physicians. Nevertheless, the few data we have regarding the use of ADs in SA suggest that they are not commonly used in practice. Beyond the likely lower levels of awareness amongst patients, which can be deduced from the aforementioned study conducted by Baharoon et al., do sociocultural and religious factors also play a role?

16.3.1 Role of the Family

Available empirical data suggest that the family plays a significant role in medical decision-making in SA. In a 2012 study on end-of-life practices in a tertiary intensive care unit in Saudi Arabia, it was found that in 88 per cent of their sample of 135 patients who had died after an end-of-life decision, the family or surrogates had been informed and were involved in these decisions.[25] This finding is consistent with the description in Tayeb et al. of the distinct nature of the Saudi family and

23 I.N. AlFayyad et al., "Physicians and Nurses' Knowledge and Attitudes towards Advance Directives for Cancer Patients in Saudi Arabia" (2019) 14 *PLoS ONE* e0213938.

24 M.A. Tayeb et al., "A 'Good Death': Perspectives of Muslim Patients and Health Care Providers" (2010) 30 *Annals of Saudi Medicine* 215.

25 A.S. Aldawood et al., "End-of-Life Practices in a Tertiary Intensive Care Unit in Saudi Arabia" (2012) 40 *Anaesthesia and Intensive Care* 137.

its composite interrelations and strong ties, whereby the patient and family are seen as one unit,[26] as well as the view of Al-Jahdali et al. that illness is considered a "whole-family affair" in Muslim culture.[27] Al-Jahdali et al. further argue that family members may even prefer that a patient not be directly informed of a life-threatening diagnosis or prognosis,[28] and may demand to make end-of-life medical decisions for the patient, decisions that often involve heroic interventions that the patient may not have wanted.[29]

This is perhaps the reason why, despite the cultural significance of the family, studies have shown that a considerable percentage of patients prefer not to consult their family members on end-of-life decision-making. For example, in the previously described study by Baharoon et al., 25 per cent of the sample wanted to be the sole decision-maker, with 55 per cent wanting their family to participate in decision-making.[30] In a 2009 study by Al-Jahdali et al. of advance care planning preferences amongst dialysis patients,[31] one survey question asked participants what they would wish to do if they were transferred to hospital and told by a doctor that their chances of survival were hopeless/dismal. One of the response options queried whether the participant would, in such a scenario, wish to consult their family members before making a decision, and 28 per cent of the sample stated that they would not.

Whilst it is interesting that a significant percentage of patients appear *not* to want to involve their families in end-of-life decision-making, the importance of the family in Muslim cultures such as that of SA and family participation in (or in some cases, takeover of) decision-making in the majority of cases may create difficulties for the use of ADs in SA, at least in a format that emphasises the role of the individual as the sole or primary decision-maker.

[26] See note 24.

[27] Al-Jahdali et al., note 7.

[28] This argument is also consistent with the view of Baharoon et al. that there is a strong belief amongst Saudi citizens that discussing serious illness openly with the patient will cause unnecessary depression or anxiety. As a result, relatives may require physicians to offer hope to the patient or at least request that the patient not be informed of the seriousness of his or her condition, corresponding with their data indicating that many patients are not aware of or informed about their terminal prognosis (see further note 22).

[29] Al-Jahdali et al., note 7, p. 165.

[30] See note 22, p. 794.

[31] H.H. Al-Jahdali et al., "Advance Care Planning Preferences among Dialysis Patients and Factors Influencing their Decisions" (2009) 20 *Saudi Journal of Kidney Diseases and Transplantation* 232.

16.3.2 *Difficulties Concerning Discussions about Death and Dying*

Another relevant factor emerging from the limited empirical research available is the perception that death is not a favoured topic, with discussion of it sometimes avoided, which affects the willingness of doctors and patients to engage in advance care planning more broadly. For example, in the aforementioned study by Tayeb et al., the following was reported: "Some focus group members were concerned about our society's tendency to consider death as taboo, something that human beings cannot interfere with. Participants informed us of cases in which healthcare providers avoided end-of-life discussions because they believed that it is beyond our control as humans".[32]

This view aligns with the perception, mentioned by Baharoon et al., that Arab patients prefer not to discuss ADs owing to a fear of discussion of death and all news related to it,[33] as well as with the problems of palliative care in SA discussed by Alshammaray et al., which include a general unwillingness to discuss issues of death and dying.[34]

There is, however, preliminary evidence from Baharoon et al. suggesting that Arab patients may be more willing to discuss end-of-life decisions, as well as ADs, than previously thought.[35] Although the authors found the majority of their sample to lack knowledge and understanding of their illness and options, as discussed previously, they also found that their patients were generally willing to engage in end-of-life care planning with their doctors and to make decisions about end-of-life care.[36] Despite their participants' limited knowledge of CPR or mechanical ventilation, the majority were capable of making sensible judgements about end-of-life matters, and, when asked directly about their end-of-life preferences, 90 per cent of the sample had formulated opinions on whether resuscitative care would be desirable.[37] Given the limited scope of the study, however, more research is required to substantiate the authors' observation. Nevertheless, avoidance of discussions of death and dying may well contribute to the general lack of discussion surrounding end-of-life care and decision-making, which in turn renders the use of ADs in SA more difficult.

32 See note 24, p. 217.
33 See note 22, p. 794.
34 S. Alshammaray et al., "Development of Palliative and End of Life Care: The Current Situation in Saudi Arabia" (2019) 11 *Cureus* e4319.
35 See note 22, p. 794.
36 Ibid.
37 Ibid., p. 795.

16.4 The Way Forward

In considering the way forward, there are two key points to highlight. The first is that the lack of specific legislation or guidance on ADs is problematic and that, in this area, reliance on "on-call" *fatwas* may not be the best way forward. We argue that what is needed is the empirically guided development of clear policies related to ADs that are supported by a clear legal framework clarifying the roles and responsibilities of the patient, the family and caregivers through enacted laws. To achieve such development, we believe that relevant issues pertaining to ADs (amongst other end-of-life care issues) need to be identified, analysed and explained to the scholarly authorities to allow them to provide caregivers with an outline of how to approach the concept of ADs within the limits of Islamic guidance. Further, previous works within and beyond the *fatwas* need to be gathered, studied and summarised to develop guidelines for this practice. As stated earlier, not all *fatwas* are articulated as laws, although they can be used as supporting defence, if needed, as in the aforementioned example of DNR orders. We do not think that this is an ideal situation. The role of *fatwas*, and more broadly of the *fatwa*-issuing bodies, should be clarified, and these should be incorporated into mainstream guidance, as with the example of the National Guidelines for Informed Consent.[38]

The second point to highlight relates to the training of healthcare professionals on the concept and application of ADs, as well as on end-of-life issues more generally. The studies discussed here suggest that healthcare professionals in SA do not often initiate or engage in discussions of poor prognoses or end-of-life issues with their patients, possibly owing to misconceptions about patients' willingness to discuss such issues. This leads to a lack of understanding on the part of patients about their illnesses and their options, which includes the possibility of indicating a preference beforehand via an AD. Comprehensive and uniform training on ADs and end-of-life issues, including training on how discussions of such issues should be conducted, would be helpful in increasing both patient awareness and the use and implementation of ADs in SA.[39]

[38] Saudi Ministry of Health, *Saudi Guidelines for Medical Informed Consent* (Riyadh, 2019), www.moh.gov.sa/en/Ministry/MediaCenter/Publications/Pages/Saudi-Guidelines-for-Informed-Consent.pdfwww.shc.gov.sa/en/CouncilDecisions/Pages/Decisions260.aspx#.

[39] See also AlFayyad et al., note 23, p. 9, which also recommends more uniform training on ADs for doctors and nurses, as well as access to AD registers.

16.5 Conclusion

Owing to the absence of a specific legislative framework, policy or religious guidance on the topic of ADs (despite the presence of guidance on other end-of-life care-related issues), uncertainty remains over the acceptability and role of ADs in SA. In this chapter, we have considered how Islamic Fiqhi principles might apply. Although there is a general emphasis on the sanctity of life in Islam, Islamic principles concerning the seeking of treatment and the Muslim concept of death provide the basis for an interpretation that could permit ADs in situations where treatment would be futile or even harmful. Fatwa No. 12086, although specifically addressing the issue of DNR orders, supports this interpretation.

However, although there appears to be a general acceptance of ADs in Islamic law, and although empirical data suggest that the concept of ADs is not unknown or unwelcome to healthcare practitioners in SA, clear evidence of AD practice on the ground is lacking. Whilst the absence of specific laws or policies pertaining to ADs is likely a contributing factor, the paucity of ADs in practice may also be the result of such sociocultural factors as the significant role of the family in decision-making or the observed difficulties of engaging in discussions of death and dying. We concluded the chapter with some specific recommendations for how SA might approach ADs moving forward, including the formulation of clearer laws, policy and/or guidance, as well as comprehensive and uniform AD training for healthcare professionals.

17

Advance Directives in Asia: Towards "Generative Accommodation"

DAISY CHEUNG & MICHAEL DUNN

17.1 Introduction

This edited collection has surveyed the law and practice of advance directives (AD) in 16 Asian jurisdictions. In this final chapter, we offer some comparative analysis and tentative concluding comments. We begin with an examination of different aspects of the law and practice of ADs in these jurisdictions, identifying similarities and trends. With this summary of the various connections between these jurisdictions, we then offer some broader reflections on two key features common to Asian jurisdictions, the role of religion and the role of the family. We conclude with a critical examination of this emerging picture of ADs in Asia, arguing that these insights suggest that distinctive patterns of "generative accommodation" are observable as a way of aligning international consensus with localised traditions and expectations in a more nuanced account of the meeting ground between the East and the West.

17.2 Overall Observations

In order to provide an overarching thematic structure to the book, we categorised the 16 jurisdictions into "well-regulated", "semi-regulated" and "non-regulated", according to the extent to which ADs are formally legally regulated in that jurisdiction. The following table picks out the key relevant legislative frameworks and/or guidelines in each jurisdiction.

	Jurisdiction	Key relevant laws/guidelines
Well-regulated	Israel	Dying Patient Law (2005)
	Singapore	Advance Medical Directive Act (1996) Mental Capacity Act (2008)
	South Korea	Act on Hospice and Palliative Care and Decisions on Life-sustaining Treatment for Patients at the End of Life (2016)
	Taiwan	Hospice Palliative Care Act (2000) Patient Right to Autonomy Act (2019)
	Thailand	National Health Act (2007)
	India	Guidelines from *Common Cause* decision (2018) Mental Healthcare Act (2017)[1]
Semi-regulated	Hong Kong	Legislative Proposal (2019 consultation paper: End-of-Life Care: Legislative Proposals on Advance Directives and Dying in Place) Guidance for Hospital Authority Clinicians on Advance Directives in Adults (2020)
	Iran	Iran Charter of Patient Rights (2009) General Guidelines of Professional Ethics (2020)
	Malaysia	Guidelines on Consent for Treatment of Patients by Registered Medical Practitioners (2017) Code of Professional Conduct (2019) Guidelines for Resuscitation Training for Ministry of Health, National Committee on Resuscitation Training (2016)
	Philippines	Various hospital guidelines Ethics Guidelines on COVID-19 (2020) National Mental Health Act (2018)[2]
	Turkey	Patient Rights Regulation (1998) Turkish Medical Association's Declaration on End-of-Life Decisions (2020)
Non-regulated	China	Chinese Medical Doctors' Code of Ethics (2014)
	Japan	The Decision-Making Process for Final Stage of Life Treatment and Care (Process Guidelines) (2018)
	Macao	Article 150/2 of the Criminal Code (1995)
	Pakistan	[n/a]
	Saudi Arabia	[n/a]

[1] This legislation regulates psychiatric advance directives only, and not advance directives at the end of life.

[2] See note 1.

We begin with some general observations about each category, and then proceed to hone in on patterns that can be observed across all the jurisdictions.

17.2.1 Well-regulated Jurisdictions

The well-regulated jurisdictions are those jurisdictions with a clear set of legal rules focused on, or encompassing, ADs. These jurisdictions are described as "well regulated" simply because the legal regulation of ADs in these jurisdictions is relatively formal, and not on the basis of any normative assessment of the quality of this legal regulation.

All of the jurisdictions in this category have detailed legal rules regulating ADs, but each jurisdiction faces its own problems in terms of implementing its framework. The over-specificity of Israel's law, for example, has led to a paradoxical limiting of its application. The scope of the law in Singapore is arguably too restrictive, and replete with too many formalities, whereas Thailand's legal framework lands on the opposite extreme. Despite South Korea's principled attempts to endorse patient preferences, it is comparatively difficult to execute a patient's wishes due to the need for verification of such wishes prior to implementation, and the relative ease with which they can be overridden by family. India's framework, which is the only one in this category that takes the form of judicial guidelines, is overly complex and administratively burdensome.

Except for Taiwan and Thailand,[3] jurisdictions in this category have frameworks that are restrictively limited to patients with terminal illness and the withdrawal/withholding of futile treatment, a feature that, as will be discussed, appears to be common among the Asian jurisdictions in this book. In addition, despite the detailed frameworks in these jurisdictions, there generally appears to be a low level of awareness and take-up of ADs.

17.2.2 Semi-regulated Jurisdictions

The semi-regulated jurisdictions are jurisdictions with other forms of regulation on ADs. Iran falls between the well-regulated and semi-regulated

[3] Both Thailand and Taiwan permit ADs to be implemented for terminally ill patients, but also for patients with incurable disease for which medical treatment will merely prolong an inevitable death (Thailand) and patients with four specific clinical conditions that are unbearable, incurable and have no other appropriate treatment options (Taiwan).

jurisdictions given the legally binding nature of its Charter of Patient Rights and General Guideline of Professional Ethics, but was nonetheless placed in this category because these documents fall under the lowest, or tertiary, level of legal regulation in Iran. Turkey is also anomalous in that the guidance it has on ADs is significantly less than any of the other jurisdictions in this category, but it was nonetheless included due to the specific reference that the Turkish Medical Association's Declaration on End-of-Life Decisions makes to ADs.

The jurisdictions in this category employ different approaches to the regulation of ADs, including the use of (i) professional guidelines in the Philippines, Hong Kong, Malaysia and Turkey and (ii) official regulations in Iran. Two additional points are worthy of note here. The first is that, interestingly, two of these jurisdictions, the Philippines and India, have a formal legislative framework for psychiatric ADs despite not having an equivalent framework for ADs governing treatment for physical illnesses, and end-of-life care in particular.

The second point is that, for some of these jurisdictions, in particular the Philippines and Malaysia, there is what can be called a "bottom-up" approach to regulation via guidelines issued by professional societies. In such jurisdictions, there are generally sociocultural and/or religious reasons why the state has not pushed to regulate ADs, or why AD legislation has failed to pass, but there is nonetheless taken to be a need for such regulation in practice. In the Philippines, for example, religious and sociocultural influences have resulted in failed attempts to pass AD legislation, but mounting pressure on healthcare resources, and the corresponding need for healthcare professionals to have the confidence to withdraw or withhold life-sustaining treatment in certain cases, have created a practical need for ADs – a need which has been further exacerbated by the onset of the COVID-19 pandemic. In response to this, hospitals have stepped in and drawn up their own institutional guidelines to regulate the making and implementation of ADs, in what can be considered a pragmatic and decentralised "bottom-up" regulatory strategy.

Similarly to the well-regulated jurisdictions, both awareness and utilisation of ADs appear to be low in these semi-regulated jurisdictions, where data are available. This is despite guidelines about ADs being in place. The authors often make the claim that sociocultural and religious influences have a sizeable effect on the acceptance and use of ADs, which indeed is a common feature across all jurisdictions, although there is a significant lack of empirical evidence about practice on the ground in the semi-regulated jurisdictions.

17.2.3 Non-regulated Jurisdictions

The non-regulated jurisdictions are jurisdictions with no AD-specific guidance, although broad principles generally exist within other regulatory spaces that pay regard to the importance of patient preferences at the end of life. The format and formality of such principles vary among the jurisdictions, although Japan is anomalous in the level of detailed official governmental guidance it has in the area of end-of-life decision-making.

Like the semi-regulated jurisdictions, there is a dearth of empirical evidence about the practice of ADs (if any) on the ground in these jurisdictions, and in some cases, evidence about attitudes towards ADs as well. In Pakistan and Saudi Arabia, the lack of sufficient empirical data on attitudes may have a particularly significant impact, given preliminary data suggesting that the perception that patients are unwilling to discuss death and end-of-life preferences may not in fact always be true, and that patients in these countries may be more willing to have end-of-life discussions and be informed of their prognosis and life-expectancy than previously thought. This, in turn, suggests that further research may support the goal of increased efforts in promoting end-of-life discussions with patients.

Once again, sociocultural and religious influences are similarly thought to have a significant effect on the acceptance and use of ADs in these jurisdictions, and, for some of them, this has resulted in a need for more training for healthcare professionals concerning ADs and end-of-life discussions with patients and family members. The latter observation is particularly important where there may be the aforementioned possibility of a misperception in patients' willingness to discuss death and end-of-life decision-making.

17.3 Key Comparisons: Patterns and Observations across the Jurisdictions

We now turn to discuss some of the broader patterns observed across all 16 jurisdictions in more detail. We show similarities are present across Asian jurisdictions, frequently in ways that transcend the degree of regulation in place. We also consider two significant points of variation among the jurisdictions, in terms of the level of specificity of AD regulation and the formalities involved. These patterns are of course to be expected; we would be surprised not to see significant variations amongst the jurisdictions of such a vast continent. Indeed, intra-regional variations around the norms, values and practice of ADs are a feature of other international settings as well.[4]

17.3.1 *Conservative Features*

A clear trend across these jurisdictions is the conservative approach that has been adopted in relation to the governance and use of ADs. This approach is characterised by various overlapping features common to many jurisdictions. For example, while different forms of legal and/or professional regulation exist, the acceptability of ADs seems generally limited to patients with terminal illness, with the notable exceptions of Taiwan, Thailand and the proposed legislation for Hong Kong.[5] In some cases, such as Singapore, South Korea and India, this is further limited to instances of determined medical futility, which, as Chan suggests, "adds little deliberative value to the decision to withdraw life sustaining treatment".[6]

A conservative approach is also demonstrated by the requirements for further confirmation that exist in some of these jurisdictions prior to the implementation of the AD, and more generally, what appears to be a lack of concern for the implementation of the patient's wishes in emergency situations. Thailand, South Korea and India, for example, all have procedures for further confirmation prior to implementation. Thailand and South Korea both require further verification of the patient's wishes with the patient prior to implementation where the patient is conscious and retains capacity, and where the patient lacks capacity, South Korea requires the doctor to obtain the agreement of a second doctor, and the confirmation process typically involves a discussion with the family about the authenticity of the AD. In India, the procedures for confirming the AD are exceedingly lengthy and complicated, involving a Judicial Magistrate First Class (JMFC), the formation of a hospital medical board comprising multiple experts from various fields of medicine and the formation of a further medical board with the Chief District Medical Officer and other medical experts. While Malaysia does not have formal

[4] See e.g. R. Horn, "'Why Should I Question a Patient's Wish?' A Comparative Study on Physicians' Perspectives on Their Duties to Respect Advance Directives" (2017) 24 *European Journal of Health Law* 523.

[5] All three jurisdictions include some categories of patients without terminal illness. Hong Kong includes a general category of "other end-stage irreversible life-limiting condition[s]". See note 3 regarding Thailand and Taiwan.

[6] T.E. Chan, Singapore, in this volume, p. 52.

procedures in place, a similar lack of concern for emergency situations is demonstrated by the fact that the Malaysian Medical Council guidelines give physicians a wide scope of discretion to continue treating the patient in their best interests until they can obtain legal advice regarding the validity of the AD. This can be a lengthy procedure due to the lack of clarity surrounding how an AD can be demonstrated to be valid in Malaysia.

A further feature is the relative lack of duties and/or punishment imposed where there is a failure to implement an AD, in particular as compared to the presence of protections against liability where ADs are carried out.[7] Taiwan is the only jurisdiction with strict penalties for the violation of a patient's AD, but only under its Hospice Palliative Care Act 2000. Under the more recent Patient Right to Autonomy Act 2019 (PRAA), there are notably no penalties for physicians, and a very wide scope to opt out of implementing ADs without a duty to refer the patient to someone else who will implement it instead.[8] Singapore also imposes a duty to implement an AD, but without mention of penalties if this is not complied with. India only imposes a duty on a physician to implement a psychiatric AD, with no similar duty in the case of end-of-life ADs. Not only is there no duty to implement, there are jurisdictions in which physicians are given significant discretion in deciding whether to implement at all. In Malaysia, for example, the Malaysian Medical Council guidelines only state that physicians "should" refrain from providing treatment contrary to an AD, and there is a flexibility not to comply with the AD if this decision is taken in consultation with the family. In Macao, physicians are required only to *consider* any patient wishes under Article 150/2 of the Criminal Code, and not necessarily to implement such wishes.

17.3.2 *Lack of Awareness, Understanding and/or Utilisation*

Another clear trend across the jurisdictions of this book is the general lack of awareness and understanding of ADs, even in jurisdictions where there

[7] See e.g. Singapore, Thailand, Taiwan and Hong Kong's proposed legislation.

[8] This is in contrast to Israel and Singapore. In Israel, a physician can conscientiously object to implementing the AD, but is required to refer the patient to another physician who is able to do so. See further M. BENTWICH, Israel, in this volume. Singapore similarly allows a physician to register an objection against implementing an AD, but requires the physician to "take all reasonable steps as soon as practicable" to transfer the patient to someone else who has not registered an objection (see further Advance Medical Directive Act 1996, s. 10(5)).

is a clear, detailed and comprehensive legislative framework for ADs. All jurisdictions for which there were relevant empirical data indicated that there was a lack of awareness and understanding of ADs among the general public, and in several jurisdictions, such as Israel, Thailand, India, China and Turkey, there was evidence to suggest that there was an inadequate level of awareness and/or understanding of ADs among healthcare professionals as well. In some jurisdictions, there were statistics demonstrating that this had translated into low utilisation of ADs.[9]

Two observations are worth making here. The first is that, while a lack of awareness and understanding of ADs is, in itself, a likely barrier to the use and acceptance of ADs, this may be a particular concern in jurisdictions where there are data showing that increased awareness may lead to a higher uptake of ADs. For example, there were studies from some jurisdictions in which a number of participants who did not previously know about ADs responded positively after being informed about them, and in some cases stated they would want to make one.[10] In Macao, there were data showing that the lack of information was a main reason deterring individuals from making ADs.

The second observation is that this lack of awareness and understanding is in some cases related to, or even a result of, the lack of communication about ADs by healthcare professionals to patients. In some jurisdictions like Pakistan, Saudi Arabia and Iran, this appears to be because of a more general reluctance to discuss issues of death and dying, or end-of-life decisions, with patients due to sociocultural factors or traditions in healthcare culture. In contrast, in Hong Kong the problem seems to be more of an institutional one, with a lack of effective and coordinated communication on the part of healthcare professionals regarding ADs, and in Malaysia, the professional guidance in relation to ADs is mostly reactive, without any encouraging of physicians or other healthcare professionals to initiate such discussions with their patients. The notable exception to this is the Philippines, where healthcare professionals are "instructed to carefully explain to patients how immensely useful an AD can be" as a necessary step in the delivery of healthcare.[11]

There is one final point to make here, connected to the point about the lack of understanding of ADs. Namely that, even at the state level, the way that AD regulation has been incorporated into existing legal and

[9] See e.g. Israel, Taiwan, Singapore, South Korea, Japan and Hong Kong.
[10] See e.g. Hong Kong, Malaysia, Saudi Arabia and Turkey.
[11] L.D. DE CASTRO et al., Philippines, in this volume, p. 203.

regulatory frameworks reflects that the procedural requirements to implement and enact ADs frequently do not appear to have been well thought out or understood. In jurisdictions like Singapore and Israel, there remains uncertainty about parallel regimes and how they apply.[12] While the Philippines does not have end-of-life AD legislation, its psychiatric AD legislation has potential conflicts with existing next-of-kin laws, suggesting the practicalities of how the law is to be implemented have not been well considered. In Hong Kong, the introduction of the proposed legislation would further exacerbate the already very piecemeal approach that is employed in this area of the law.[13]

In particular, many jurisdictions do not appear to have attended carefully to the mental capacity requirements for an AD, and how a person's decision-making capacity is to be assessed. In some jurisdictions, there are mental capacity requirements and assessment criteria, but these are problematic. In Singapore, for example, there is inconsistency between two different legislative regimes, and therefore uncertainty regarding the mental capacity threshold to be applied in the Advance Medical Directive Act. The lack of an overarching mental capacity test in Hong Kong, together with the existence of various different tests in the common law, Mental Health Ordinance and Hospital Authority guidelines, similarly results in ambiguity as to what the test for mental capacity should be in relation to the making of ADs. In India, the court in *Common Cause* does not elaborate on how soundness of mind is to be assessed, even though a specific definition and assessment process exists for psychiatric ADs. Various jurisdictions, such as Malaysia, South Korea and Thailand, do not have guidance regarding how capacity in relation to ADs should be assessed. The assessment procedures in South Korea and Thailand raise particular concern. In South Korea, the lack of requirements on how capacity should be assessed has meant that it is not uncommon for this exercise to be left to nurses or even volunteers at the registering institution, who may not have any experience in this area. In Thailand, there is no requirement for the assessment of capacity at the time of making the AD *at all*, and physicians are only required to

[12] Specifically, there remains uncertainty about how the legislative framework works in parallel with the common law (Singapore) or the judiciary (Israel). Furthermore, our reading of the Taiwan chapter is that there may also be some uncertainty about whether and how the two legislative regimes overlap in the case of terminally ill patients.

[13] See e.g. the separate legislative frameworks proposed for ADs and continuing powers of attorney, in addition to the existing enduring powers of attorney legislation.

examine the patient at the time of receipt of the AD to see whether they were capacitous at the time the AD was made, something which is inherently difficult to do without an examination of the patient at that time.

17.3.3 Sociocultural and Religious Influences

The impact of sociocultural and religious factors on the regulation and practice of ADs is observable across all jurisdictions. The two most significant factors, the role of the family and the role of religion, permeated across some jurisdictions in complex ways, and so will be subjected to further analysis in Section 17.4.

Beyond these two factors, a cultural emphasis on deference to physicians was noted across many of the jurisdictions. For example, Tengaumnuay describes a paternalistic culture in Thailand where Thai people commonly allow physicians to make decisions for them, and are therefore less likely to make ADs. Similarly, there is a general deference to physician expertise in Malaysia, arguably also due in part to Islamic religious influence.[14] In Pakistani culture, Beg et al. describe physicians as holding an "esteemed" position. Physicians and nurses often take on a decision-making role due to various factors, including what is often a symbolic "induction" into families as directors rather than facilitators of care. There is a similarly greater role for doctors and medical paternalism in Indian culture as a result of the influence of Ayurvedic systems, although, interestingly, this has not resulted in a greater reluctance to make use of ADs. Instead, Dhru and Ghooi argue that this "preference for the role of the physician" has resulted in physicians being accorded a key role in overseeing and applying the AD regime.

17.3.4 Variations in Specificity of Regulation

In addition to the similarities observed previously, there were also important differences among the jurisdictions worthy of note. One such difference concerns the degree of specificity provided by AD regulations,

[14] See further Malek's argument that a contextualisation of patient autonomy according to Islamic values would include a prioritisation of the physician's views, since physicians are generally seen to be the decision-making authority for the patient in Malaysian society in S. KAUR et al., Malaysia, in this volume, p. 188.

where concerns were expressed regarding both over-specificity and under-specificity.

In relation to concerns about "over-specificity", South Korea and Israel both define the terminal stage chronologically, and further make a distinction between two stages of dying. Israel distinguishes between a "dying patient" (who has no more than six months to live) and a "dying patient in the final stage" (who has no more than two weeks to live), whereas South Korea differentiates a "terminal patient" (who is expected to die within a few months) from a "dying patient" (who is going to die imminently). This distinction is important in both countries because the specific definitions shape permitted actions in different ways. In South Korea, for example, an Advance Statement for Life-sustaining Treatment (ASLST) cannot be implemented until the patient is a "dying patient", and in Israel, while certain types of treatment can be withheld from a "dying patient",[15] ventilator support, nourishment, palliative care and secondary/accompanying treatment can only be withdrawn or withheld from a "dying patient in the final stage".

As the authors recognise, this level of specificity can be problematic. In the Israeli context, for example, Bentwich argues that the specificity of the timeline associated with these two stages of dying causes difficulty because of the ambiguity it paradoxically creates for physicians. This can be, for example, because prognoses often do not neatly fall into the categories of "less than six months" and "more than six months", or because it is unclear whether an acute disease (like pneumonia) that can cause death within two weeks can be successfully treated, and therefore whether the designation of "dying patient in the final stage" is warranted.

On the opposing side of under-specificity (or over-flexibility), Ozeki-Hayashi et al. argue that the lack of a clear definition of when a patient would be considered to be in the "terminal stage" of illness in Japan's process guidelines causes problems because it creates a reliance on the discretional judgement of the healthcare professionals assessing the patient's condition, and because of the inconsistency in application which is likely to result. It is interesting to note that while the definition

15 See in particular the distinction between "continuous" and "cyclical" treatments. The distinction between withholding and withdrawing treatment has also been made in the Japanese courts, and OZEKI-HAYASHI et al. (Japan, in this volume) refer to the belief among doctors in Japan that ventilator support cannot be removed once the patient has been placed on it, due to the doctor's duty to continue treatment once it has been started.

of "imminent death" in Singapore is similarly left to medical discretion,[16] there is a rigorous process of certification involving three medical practitioners, two of whom are specialists, and a separate panel of three other specialists if the initial three do not agree. While this complex process is likely to result in problems of its own,[17] it may safeguard against some of the concerns relating to inconsistency of application.

The possibility of variation in physician interpretation due to the flexibility in AD regulation is also problematised more widely. Kaur et al. argue in the Malaysian context that the wording of the Malaysian Medical Council guidance provides physicians with the flexibility to disregard explicit patient wishes. In Macao, even though there is no specific regulation on ADs, the fact that physicians are only required to take patient wishes into consideration means that physicians are given wide discretion to disregard such wishes and proceed as they see fit. In cases where life-sustaining treatment is to be rejected, Raposo and Iong hypothesise that physicians in Macao are likely to disregard such wishes due to the fear of potential litigation by family members.

17.3.5 Variations in Specificity/Complexity of Formalities

A further important but distinctive variation was observed relating to the specificity and/or complexity of the formalities placed upon the person making an AD. Here, there were jurisdictions on both ends of the spectrum of specificity and/or complexity, and the problems documented demonstrate how difficult it can be to obtain an appropriate and pragmatic balance between the two.

On one end of the spectrum, we have, for example, the jurisdictions of Singapore, India and Israel, which have very specific procedures and/or requirements in relation to making an AD, such as those relating to prescribed forms, safeguards or registration. The Singapore regime contains a number of formalities and safeguards, including a prescribed form, witnessing requirements, registration requirements, and a number of safeguards aimed at protecting the integrity and voluntariness of

[16] It had been suggested that the term "imminent" be defined chronologically, for example within 6–12 months, but it was decided by the Select Committee for the Advance Medical Directive Act that this was better left to medical judgement. See further T.E. CHAN, Singapore, in this volume.

[17] Such as the difficulties in implementation associated with a lengthy procedure and the need for unanimity among several professionals before the AD can be acted upon.

executing the AD. India's judicial guidelines require an AD to be signed by two independent witnesses and to be countersigned by a JMFC, following which the JMFC must preserve the AD in both paper and digital form, send a copy to the Municipal Corporate or local village council for appointment of a custodian of the AD, inform the executor's family of the AD, maintain a copy of the AD in their office and forward another copy of it to the relevant district court. This involvement of the JMFC renders the process particularly difficult, because, as Dhru and Ghooi argue, there are only a very small number of JMFCs in any given city, and these JMFCs will already be dealing with a significant backlog of cases. In Israel, it has been argued that the lengthy and complex prescribed form for ADs may be too difficult for laypersons to understand and use, in particular due to the inclusion of legal and medical jargon. Interestingly and also somewhat confusingly, it appears that this form also contains built-in options that allow individuals to include conditions (amounting to "unbearable suffering") that do not comply with definitions under the law, and it is unclear what effect the specification of these conditions might have.

On the other hand, however, a regime which is flexible in terms of the formalities it requires presents difficulties of its own. A good example of this is in Thailand. Tengaumnuay claims that the regulatory procedures of this regime are so flexible that a number of specific practical problems arise, despite this approach being more supportive of patient autonomy in general terms. As there is no specific format for the AD, no requirement for medical or other witnesses and no registration system for ADs specified in the law, Tengaumnuay argues that physicians are less likely to be aware of the existence of an AD without a registry, and they are likely to be uncertain about the validity of the AD, especially whether the AD was made when the individual had capacity.

17.4 Broader Considerations: The Distinctive Role of Religion and the Family in the Asian Context

Two distinctive and common features impacting on ADs were shared by many, if not most, of the Asian jurisdictions examined in this volume: the role of religion and the role of the family. As these were thought to have a significant but complex impact on the law and practice of ADs in local contexts, we offer some detailed reflections on these two broader trends. With regard to religion, the jurisdictions in this volume were defined by a range of religious traditions, which included those from Christianity,

Islam, Judaism, Buddhism, Hinduism and Jainism. One feature of several of these religions is the principle of the "sanctity of life",[18] which is particularly noteworthy in its influence in this context. However, the impact of this principle, as we shall demonstrate, is not straightforward, and religion more generally has influenced the acceptance and regulation of ADs in these jurisdictions in different ways.

17.4.1 The Role of Religion: Sanctity of Life

The sanctity of life operates as a key principle governing jurisdictions with Christian, Jewish and Islamic influence. While in some cases, like Israel and the Philippines, this principle is given utmost importance, it does not appear to have precluded the development of ADs. In Israel, for example, ADs were formally included as part of the Dying Patient Law 2005, despite this legislation being primarily grounded in ultra-orthodox Jewish values, which include a "commitment to preserving and saving human life, regardless of the individual's desires".[19] The influence of such values does, however, appear to have resulted in a more restrictive scope for ADs. For example, Bentwich contends that the term "dying patient" has been defined very narrowly in the legislation, to the exclusion of patients with chronic illnesses such as dementia or amyotrophic lateral sclerosis (ALS) that do not have a clear prognosis, which appears to conform to the more orthodox view that the sanctity of life is a fundamental principle, and a key foundation of the Dying Patient Law. Similarly, Bentwich explains that the withdrawing and withholding of treatment and care is permitted in the Dying Patient Law in cases where the patients have reached the "final stage", or where their bodies are undergoing acute systems failure, which corresponds to a *Halakhic* religious exception where refraining from treatments is allowed where "three or more systems in the human body have failed, and it is clear from a

[18] We use this phrase broadly to refer to the idea, shared by several of the religious traditions discussed in this volume, that life has intrinsic value and thus that preserving life must be prioritised.

[19] M. BENTWICH, Israel, in this volume, p. 23. It is interesting to note that this ultra-orthodox Jewish influence was not an inevitable consequence of the country's religious traditions. See M. BENTWICH, Israel, in this volume for a discussion of how ultra-orthodox Judaism is not in fact the religious tradition of the majority of citizens in Israel, but how ultra-orthodox Jewish values were adopted in the Dying Patient Law primarily due to political reasons.

medical perspective that death is inevitable sooner or later".[20] Similarly, in the Philippines, de Castro et al. argue that there will likely need to be a finding of medical futility before an AD could apply.[21]

Despite the heavy influence of the sanctity of life in these jurisdictions, however, there appears to be a tension between such overarching religious principles and the needs of practice on the ground, which has resulted, in some cases, in a bottom-up approach to ADs, as discussed earlier in this chapter. This is true of both the Philippines and, to a lesser extent, Israel. In Israel, Bentwich argues that there remains a tension between the Dying Patient Law, a law grounded in strict religious values, and the practice of the law on the ground, which is shaped extensively by medical professionals and the more secular perspectives of patients and their families. We might view this in terms of there being a recognised, pragmatic need for more "practical" solutions to work around the rigidity of the law. The 2014 case of *Ploni [John Doe]* v *The Attorney General*, where a patient with ALS requested to be disconnected from a ventilator, for example, appears to be a case where a practical "workaround" was devised by the Attorney General of Israel to try and resolve this tension.

In other jurisdictions where the sanctity of life is not necessarily of utmost importance but still a fundamental principle, such as the Islamic countries of Iran, Pakistan and Saudi Arabia, this principle (i) is subject to varying interpretations with different outcomes and (ii) is not the only major religious principle that is relevant in this area. In relation to (i), Syed et al.'s analysis demonstrates that the rule requiring the preservation of life can be interpreted using a three paradigm conception of death that views the last stage of life as part of a "dying" (*al-ihtiḍār*) phase, where the obligation to preserve life no longer exists because the individual "is now approaching (destined) death and therefore is not the intended subject of the obligation to preserve life".[22] Beg et al. similarly argue in the Pakistani context that while life is considered sacred in Islam, there are interpretations of this principle that are not inconsistent with ADs, such as the idea that the time of death is determined by God and thus preordained, which means that death will occur as decided by God irrespective of the patient's treatment decision. In relation to (ii), Syed

[20] M. BENTWICH, Israel, in this volume, p. 28.

[21] Although this remains unclear due to the lack of legislation on this issue. See further L.D. DE CASTRO et al., Philippines, in this volume.

[22] Z.A. SYED et al., Iran, in this volume, p. 166. This would, of course, only apply to those in the dying stage, as Syed et al. point out.

et al. and Hussein and Adlan both describe a number of key Islamic principles in addition to the sanctity of life that are relevant in the discussion of ADs and end-of-life decision-making, such as the Rule of No Harm and the Principle of Hardship. Finally, while neither of these three countries have a clear legislative framework on ADs,[23] it should be noted that the analyses of the relevant religious principles in these countries would suggest that if ADs were permissible, they would likely only be permitted where the treatment in question was an artificial and futile prolonging of death.

Thus, while the sanctity of life is recognisably a fundamental religious principle shared among many of these Asian jurisdictions, the principle does not appear to have a uniform effect on how ADs are regulated or implemented in these countries. It should also be noted that, in jurisdictions where religious traditions do not necessarily emphasise the need to preserve life, the influence of these traditions on ADs has also not been straightforward. On the one hand, Tengaumnuay has argued that the Buddhist contemplation and acceptance of death as part of the impermanence of life has led to the acceptance of the view in Thailand that individuals should be able to plan ahead to achieve a "good death". On the other, Dhru and Ghooi argue that while death is seen in Indian religious tradition and philosophy as "a union with the Divine, the greater Self",[24] the desire to avoid pain and suffering is not celebrated, and the use of an AD to reject life-sustaining treatment in order to alleviate pain and suffering would thus likely not be in line with Hindu and Buddhist religious beliefs.

17.4.2 The Role of Religion: Variation in Interpretation

Beyond the principle of the sanctity of life, the authors reveal how the influence of religion on ADs more generally is not necessarily straightforward in their jurisdictions. In our view, one reason for this might lie in variations in the interpretation of relevant religious principles in the process of end-of-life decision-making itself. Bentwich demonstrates, for example, using Justice Elon's judgment in the 1993 *Yael Shefer* case, that *Halakhic* law is capable of supporting different approaches to the withdrawal of life-sustaining treatment, and in particular the withdrawal of

[23] Although unlike Pakistan and Saudi Arabia, Iran's Charter of Patient Rights does make specific mention of ADs.

[24] K.A. DHRU and R. GHOOI, India, in this volume, p. 124.

ventilators. Contrary to the ultra-orthodox view as represented in the Dying Patient Law, which does not permit the withdrawal of ventilators until the final stage, Justice Elon offered in that case an interpretation of *Halakhic* law that would support ventilator withdrawal if the patient was suffering.

Similarly, our sense is that there appears to be some room for interpretation in the application of key Islamic religious principles. As Syed et al. demonstrate by examining a number of rules that may either negate or favour the respect of an AD to limit life-sustaining treatments, such rules can often be subject to varying interpretations, and in some cases even used to support opposing contentions.[25] Beg et al. argue that the study of relevant Islamic teachings has resulted in varying attitudes towards ADs amongst the interpreters of these teachings, which they hypothesise may be a reason why AD legislation has not been discussed. As they argue, "[l]egislators may well feel that they are in no position to make decisions on such a controversial subject rooted in religious ambiguity".[26]

Related to the issue of interpretation is an interesting point concerning the role and significance of religious legal guidance, specifically *fatwa*, in Islamic countries. While the legal force of a *fatwa* may vary between countries,[27] there is little question that *fatwa* are given primary importance in Islamic countries, in particular where there is no legislation on the topic. There appear to be, however, various institutional concerns with the obtaining of "reliable and accurate" *fatwa* on healthcare issues such as end-of-life decision-making. Syed et al. argue, for example, that the unreliability of *fatwa* may be due to several reasons, including the lack of stakeholder consultation or multi-disciplinary input that goes into the making of a *fatwa* and the fact that the derivative reasoning for medical *fatwa* are rarely published and therefore difficult to analyse. Hussein and Adlan raise another concern in the Saudi Arabian context, which is the fact that the Islamic scholars who issue *fatwa* are not generally medical professionals, and as a result, a healthcare expert will be relied upon to explain the relevant issues to them. Because this healthcare expert will usually be a physician, Hussein and Adlan argue

25 See e.g. the Rule of No Harm and how it may be interpreted to either support or reject ADs in Z.A. SYED et al., Iran, in this volume.

26 M.A. BEG et al., Pakistan, in this volume, p. 284.

27 See e.g. the contrast between Saudi Arabia, where it is unclear what the legal role of *fatwa* might be, apart from supporting evidence in some cases (like do-not-resuscitate orders), and Iran, where the Constitution recognises the legally binding nature of *fatwa* in places where there are no statute or by-laws.

that there is a risk that the physician may advocate for their own preferences in the matter, which may lead to an "indirect form of medical paternalism", one with religious cover.[28]

Our examination of the role of the family in these jurisdictions, to which we now turn, gives rise to similar observations. It should first be noted that the literature on the role of the family in medical decision-making in Asia tends to focus on the fact that, as alluded to in the Introduction, individual autonomy is not accorded the same primacy in Asian jurisdictions,[29] and that communitarian, familial models of decision-making are more common,[30] which seem to be contrary to the idea of the individually based AD. The chapters in this volume, however, have demonstrated that the significance of the family, as well as its relationship with ADs, challenges this essentialist, one-dimensional picture in ways that are not often expressed. Although the role of the family is recognised as being highly influential in almost all of the chapters, the *nature of*, and *justification for*, this influence is much more nuanced and complex than is typically recognised. What we can see from the patterns of influence in these jurisdictions is that the family can play different roles in medical decision-making for different reasons, which in turn has varying effects on whether or not ADs are likely to be accepted and adopted.

17.4.3 Family-focused Decision-Making: The Authority to Decide

The most commonly described role, and the one referred to most in the literature, is a family-based model of decision-making in which the family is seen as the authority in, and unit of, decision-making. The family model of decision-making takes two main forms in this context: (i) an approach in which the patient does not possess sole decision-making authority, with the family making shared decisions with the patient as a communal unit[31] and (ii) decision-making directly by

[28] G. HUSSEIN AND A. ADLAN, Saudi Arabia, in this volume, p. 298.

[29] See e.g. R. Fan, "Self-determination vs. Family-determination: Two Incommensurable Principles of Autonomy" (1997) 11 *Bioethics* 309.

[30] D. Martina et al., "Advance Care Planning in Asia: A Systematic Narrative Review of Healthcare Professionals' Knowledge, Attitude, and Experience" (2021) 22(2) *Journal of the American Medical Directors Association* 349.e1.

[31] In addition to East Asian jurisdictions where this is often said to be the case, see e.g. Iran's concept of "family centric patient autonomous" where there is active involvement and inclusion of the family in decision-making; Turkey, where the family is frequently involved in decision-making; and Saudi Arabia, where the family and patient are seen as one unit and illness is a whole-family affair.

the family in ways that can exclude the patient entirely.[32] For example, the application of a family-based model means that, in some jurisdictions, physicians feel comfortable notifying only the family members (and not the patient) of the patient's condition and prognosis.[33] A more explicit example of direct family decision-making is found in Macao, where a family member, and not the patient, is responsible for signing the consent form required by the Hospice & Palliative Care Centre at the Kiang Wu hospital, which is the closest formally recognised mechanism to an AD in Macao. And, while not in relation to the making of the AD itself, Malaysian professional guidance permits a patient's wishes to be overridden by a physician in consultation with family.

17.4.4 Family-focused Decision-Making: The Supportive Role

A very different family-focused approach to decision-making is one where family members are accorded specific supportive roles. In particular, one supportive role is where family members are relied upon to clarify the wishes and intentions of the individual in question. In the Philippines, for example, the details of a patient's AD are verified by checking with their family members, and in South Korea, the family both assist with the verification process of an ASLST and bear witness to the patient's preferences regarding life-sustaining treatment if no ASLST exists. In Macao, the physician has conversations with the family and takes these into account when determining whether the content of the AD reflects the patient's current and authentic desires, and it is the family's reaction that Raposo and Iong argue is most formative in shaping the doctor's views on this. In Thailand, individuals can specify an individual, usually a close family member, who can clarify their intentions as laid out in the AD if there is any ambiguity or confusion. While the family plays an important role in all of these jurisdictions in assisting with the interpretation of the individual's preferences at the end of life, the potential for abuse here must not be

[32] In Pakistan and the Philippines, the male members of the family are the ones who make decisions on behalf of the members of the family (in the case of the Philippines, this would be the eldest male).

[33] See e.g. Singapore, where there is a not uncommon practice of collusion where families and physicians may work together to withhold a diagnosis and/or poor prognosis from a patient; and Taiwan, where the Hospice Palliative Care Act permits the physician to fulfil their obligation by merely informing the family. (The more recent PRAA requires the information to be shared with the patient, though permits physicians to share information with family unless the patient explicitly objects.)

overlooked. Apart from the Thai context, where the individual selects their representative, there is potential, in particular where the individual does not have an amicable relationship with their family, for the individual's wishes to be misrepresented or entirely overridden in these verification or clarificatory exercises.

17.4.5 Family-focused Decision-Making: The Carer Role

A third distinctive approach to family-focused decision-making is one in which family members adopt the role of a carer of the patient, with various implications for decision-making authority. For example, in some jurisdictions, this approach offers a justification for according an overarching decision-making responsibility to family members on the basis of a paternalistic rationale, or because doing so equates with the intrinsic expression of care within the relationship. De Castro et al. argue that, in the Philippines, it can be considered irresponsible for a family taking care of a vulnerable patient to let them make acute treatment decisions, and in jurisdictions like Pakistan and South Korea, families demonstrate their love and care by hiding the truth about poor prognoses from the patient. The family's role as carer can also lead to a corresponding reliance on the family by the individual. In the Japanese context, for example, Ozeki-Hayashi et al. argue that the psychological factor of *amae* and the character trait of *omakase* in Japan can result in the individual preferring to leave the responsibility of making difficult decisions to their loved ones and/or physicians. Finally, related to this carer role is the importance of filial piety in jurisdictions influenced by Confucianism. This can mean that the children of the individual are less willing to initiate difficult end-of-life conversations with their parents,[34] or that they feel the need to do everything to save their parents.[35]

17.4.6 Accommodating ADs in Family-Centric Societies: Some Potential Solutions

Given the significance of the place that the family takes with regard to ADs in these jurisdictions, how have different jurisdictions come up with

[34] D.F. TSAI, Taiwan, in this volume.

[35] D. CHEUNG and R. LEE, Hong Kong, in this volume; LEE, South Korea, in this volume. See also Iran, where this is also the case, though not due to filial piety (see further Z.A. SYED et al., Iran, in this volume).

solutions to accommodate the AD, in particular in light of these different roles that the family plays?

One solution that has been adopted is to incorporate family members officially into the decision-making process. This can be in terms of receipt of information,[36] or in the decision-making process itself, or the wider advance care planning (ACP) process.[37] A second solution gives family members an official supportive or clarificatory role. The Thai regime provides a good example of this, with the option to designate an individual, often a member of the family, to clarify any ambiguities in the AD, as mentioned previously. A third solution has been to go in the opposite direction, drafting legislation that constrains the heavy influence of the family. Article 4 of Taiwan's PRAA, for example, specifically provides that the patient's family are not to prevent the physician from acting on their treatment decisions, a measure which Tsai argues provides the patient with "a rights-based form of resistance against the common phenomenon of family-based decision-making in Chinese culture".[38] In Hong Kong, the government's legislative proposal has stated explicitly that patient autonomy must prevail in case of conflict with family, and in India, a concern about potential abuse by family members has resulted in a judicial regime that relegates family to a secondary level of importance.

17.4.7 *Reflecting on the Distinctive Role of Family*

In light of the preceding discussion, what are the insights that can be gained in relation to the significance of the family in the AD context? Two related points can be made. First, as mentioned at the beginning of this section, the influence of the family, much like religion, is not unidimensional, and there are various ways in which the family can have a significant role to play in every aspect of the AD or its implementation.

[36] D.F. TSAI, Taiwan, in this volume; K.A. DHRU and R. GHOOI, India, in this volume.

[37] See e.g. Taiwan where a family member must be involved in the ACP process. See also Japanese nursing homes, some of which require a family member's signature on the AD form. In the psychiatric AD regime of the Philippines, the inclusion of the role of "supporters", who can access information and attend medical appointments, can be seen as a way to keep family members involved.

[38] D.F. TSAI, Taiwan, in this volume, p. 80. Note, however, that the PRAA also includes provisions that envisage a substantial amount of familial involvement. See e.g. note 33 for a discussion of how the PRAA permits the sharing of information with family as long as there is no explicit objection.

The second point is that, among these different roles, it is important to recognise an often neglected, supportive role that families play. This is in addition to, but separate from, the authoritative, decision-making role that is often taken as the norm in the literature on medical decision-making in the Asian context.

By the term "supportive role" as adopted as a family-focused approach to decision-making in this context, we envisage something much more complex than the general forms of emotional and other social and relational supports typically associated with the family in the healthcare context. Instead, this support, a kind of "support plus" as it were, is broad in scope. It might involve professionals taking steps to actively involve the family in order to bring about the best outcomes for the individual, or it could involve an individual-led approach where the person is encouraged to involve their family members in various kinds of ways. Such approaches typically involve a co-opting of family members into the decision-making process in a mediating role, as facilitators, to allow both the family and the individual to reflect on the kind of support the individual needs, and then also to identify what is best for the individual. Co-opting family members in this way takes different forms across different jurisdictions. For example, like with the Taiwanese regime, the family could be brought into the decision to make the AD as a part of the wider ACP process. As argued in the Hong Kong chapter, the AD itself might also be used as a crux upon which to engender family support for personal preferences. In this way, the making of the AD could be used to initiate family conversations about end-of-life wishes, in particular in jurisdictions where the topic of death and dying is considered difficult to broach, providing an important basis upon which meaningful and well-supported decisions about an individual's end-of-life care can be achieved.

In this way, the construct of the "family", as it features across these Asian jurisdictions in relation to ADs, does not need to be placed in direct contradistinction with the "individual", as is typical in the Asian bioethics literature. The conception of the family as "support plus" renders a focus on the individual (rather than the family) as the decision-maker entirely compatible with a cultural emphasis on the family. In particular, this supportive account of the family's role does not threaten the individual's best interests as the goal of the decision-making process, though the identification and realisation of these interests will of course be heavily dependent on the family's input and participation.

17.5 Making Sense of ADs in Asia: "Generative Accommodation" in Local Context

In the foregoing sections, we described some of the patterns, trends and important variations in the regulation of ADs across the jurisdictions in this volume, followed by an in-depth examination of the distinctive nature of the influence of religion and family. In light of the international backdrop to changing law and practice in relation to ADs that we presented to introduce the book, how should we make sense of the law and practice of ADs in the Asian context?

As the principled foundations and regulatory strategies of ADs have become increasingly codified and implemented internationally in recent years, an emerging pattern of response can be observed across the majority of the jurisdictions included in this volume. Whether explicit or implicit, these responses have functioned to enable ADs to gain a foothold within Asia – in its case law, in its legislative frameworks, in its professional guidelines, or in the ground-level practice of healthcare.

In our view, we might helpfully understand this pattern as one of "generative accommodation". We take these terms in turn, beginning with the idea of "accommodation". The concept here is that, in light of an emerging international consensus in healthcare practice and regulation regarding the value of an AD and its underlying ethical principle of respect for patient autonomy, most of the jurisdictions in this volume have responded in a way that suggests these key concepts and principles are similarly being viewed as important and worthy of incorporation into their own local contexts, whether it be in the form of legislative frameworks, case law, guidelines or practice requirements. A reasonable query at this stage might be why and how we have determined that this is a form of accommodation, rather than something that is more indigenous to the jurisdiction in question. Our view that this adoption can generally be seen as a form of accommodation results from three key reasons.[39] The first is that, while the increase in emphasis on patient autonomy internationally began around the 1950s, the various forms of regulation of ADs and end-of-life care in the jurisdictions of this volume have been put in place or decided upon relatively recently, from the 1990s at the earliest. The second reason is what is, in most cases, an apparent lack of congruence or alignment of the concept of ADs and patient autonomy

[39] While none of these reasons on their own are determinative, together they point away from a conclusion of indigenous development.

with local value commitments or beliefs, such as a heavy emphasis on familial involvement in medical decision-making or religious beliefs that prioritise the preservation of life over other values such as autonomy or individual rights. The final reason is that, apart from a general cultural acceptance in some jurisdictions of death and the importance of a good death, we have not observed strong evidence of any indigenous evolution of the concept of an AD, for example, on the basis of bioethical principles that have also developed importance locally. Indeed, what we do see across the chapters is a broad pattern of internationally agreed-upon ethical principles that are visible across the jurisdictions.

Having said that, however, the qualifier "generative" is equally, if not more, crucial to our understanding of ADs in Asia. We use the term "generative" to refer to the distinctive, locally specific approaches that have arisen, been set in motion, or been proactively produced in ways that are unique to these jurisdictions as they marshal their own commitments and expectations alongside this emerging international consensus. That is, in dealing with the sorts of ways in which the concept of ADs and patient autonomy may be incongruent or even in conflict with local values and/or beliefs, different types of solutions have been created to allow such concepts to exist and develop in these local contexts.

We view the extent to which an approach is generative as falling along a spectrum, with some more generative than others. Moreover, different modes of a generative approach are identifiable in ways that cut across this spectrum in quite complex ways. Taiwan presents a good example of a jurisdiction with a more generative approach, with its PRAA containing provisions that marshal the local cultural emphasis on the role of the family. Interestingly, as mentioned previously, the PRAA both recognises and affirms this role (through the requirement of the presence of a family member in the ACP process) *and* places constraints on it (through the provision that forbids family members from preventing a physician from acting on the patient's treatment decisions). This, we argue, suggests that a significant amount of careful consideration was involved in the attempt to adopt these principles and concepts into the Taiwanese context in ways that retain their essence, but also align with local cultural values.

Also on the side of more generative approaches, Israel presents an interesting example, where we can observe two different modes of generative accommodation within the same country. The Dying Patient Law, espousing the ultra-orthodox Jewish perspective, and the judicial approach to end-of-life decision-making, exemplified by the more liberal religious interpretations of Justice Elon, demonstrate two ways in which generative accommodation has taken place. As Bentwich points out, however, the ultra-orthodox Jewish view is not shared by the majority of Israelis, and this view fails to align with the more secular perspectives of healthcare professionals and patients. This suggests that, while both approaches are generative to some degree, the judicial approach can be said to be more so, in that these court decisions are generating comparatively liberal interpretations of Jewish principles that accommodate the idea of ADs (in the form of prior wishes) and patient autonomy, in ways that allow them to be accepted by the majority of Israelis (especially Israeli Jewish citizens), and in particular the relevant stakeholders in the end-of-life process.

The Philippines provides another example of a more generative approach, but one that manifests itself in the practical spaces of decision-making itself, in the form of grassroots change driven from within networks of healthcare professionals working in specific hospitals. This approach does not focus on aligning the idea of ADs and respect for patient autonomy with local religious and cultural values, such as the Christian commitment to upholding the value of life and cultural attitudes towards disease causation and family. Instead, healthcare professionals and the medical community have brought such concepts directly into the local practice context by way of institutional guidelines, in a way that can meet practical needs and develop good professional practice.

On the end of less generative approaches, Thailand's National Health Act recognises the principle of respect for individual autonomy and preserves the right to make an AD solely for the individual, but the over-flexibility in the rules for making an AD suggest that these concepts have not been introduced into the local context in a way that considers whether ADs can actually be successfully implemented (and respect for patient autonomy thereby upheld). Additionally, apart from the ability to designate an individual, often a family member, to clarify one's wishes as contained in an AD, the Thai regime does little to reconcile their very individually focused AD with the cultural emphasis on family, leading to what is often non-compliance with the patient's AD where family members disagree. India's complex and administratively burdensome judicial regime similarly does not adopt ADs in a way that considers the likelihood of success of implementation, although the courts do appear to have taken the role of the family into consideration, and accordingly relegated family members to a secondary role in the process due to concerns of potential abuse.

Turkey further presents an example of a less generative accommodation process, one that can be said to involve only the painting of a veneer of common purpose and shared agreement, without substantially more. Although Turkey has ratified the Oviedo Convention, Article 9 of which requires a patient's previously expressed wishes relating to medical interventions be taken into account, there remains no legislation or formal legal regulation of ADs in Turkey. This is despite the fact that the Oviedo Convention requires signatories to make their domestic law compatible with it. Suggestions have been made, by Ulman and others, as to how domestic law might be interpreted and/or amended to provide a basis for ADs, but, thus far, the Turkish approach appears to be only a superficial endorsement of the international consensus, without any further attempt to bring this in line with its own local context. It should be noted, however, that some generative accommodation appears to be beginning to occur in ground-level practice: in recent years, professional societies have issued guidelines affirming the importance of patient autonomy, the right to refuse futile treatment and ADs, and have called for public engagement and multilateral dialogue on these issues, so as to remove cultural factors that may hinder acceptance of these ideas.[40] This suggests that, while the state has commenced the process by ratifying the Oviedo Convention, it may be networks of healthcare professionals, like in the Philippines, who are the actual drivers of change – engaging with the values and characteristics of local culture and negotiating the acceptance of autonomy and ADs within this context. In a slightly different way, other modes of generative accommodation can be formulated "on the ground" through grassroots non-governmental organisations (NGO) which are promoting change. This looks to be the case in China. Though the power possessed by NGOs is inevitably limited, and thus the degree of generative accommodation that can be achieved in this way may correspondingly be limited, Chen speculates that the advocacy work of the Beijing Living Will Promotion Association has directly or indirectly led to the Chinese Government's introduction of a pilot palliative care project in 2019.

In this way, different modes of generative accommodation encapsulate attempts to shape the "meeting ground" between international consensus and localised traditions and expectations – a much more nuanced picture than pitching Eastern healthcare practices against Western healthcare practices and identifying essential differences between them. Ways to accommodate, whether occurring explicitly or implicitly, involve picking

[40] See further Y.I. ULMAN, Turkey, in this volume.

up some elements of both components: a commitment to a certain kind of way of decision-making that is increasingly recognised and endorsed internationally but in ways that embrace local manifestations.

Different ways of generatively accommodating ADs in different jurisdictions can, we think, go a long way to help to explain the complex, multiple and different laws, guidelines and practices that are documented across this volume. Just as importantly, the Asian AD journey is likely in fact to be one of a series of unique journeys, regardless of the similarities documented. These journeys are likely to continue to evolve and take shape in ways both that reflect localised commitments, norms and expectations, and that track broader sociopolitical and sociocultural trends and phenomena within and between countries – all subject to ongoing negotiation.

We conclude with some brief reflections in relation to the implications of generative accommodation, and what might be required in the longer term of such an approach. While there may be various forms of generative accommodation, and while some forms may be more generative than others, the key goal underlying all generative accommodations should be to ensure that the adopted principles and concepts relating to ADs are worked through properly, both at the level of legislation and regulation and in ground-level practice, so that they are harmonised and coherent in the local context. It is not enough, for example, to introduce legislation or guidelines promoting patient autonomy and ADs without considering the extent to which they fit in with existing laws and principles, or to design procedures that are too complex or burdensome to realistically carry out. It is also not enough to introduce legislation or guidelines without taking steps to ensure proper operation in practice. As many authors of this volume have argued, AD legislation needs to be implemented consistently, good practice guidelines need to be developed, training needs to be provided to healthcare professionals working in the field, and awareness among both healthcare professionals and the public must be promoted, among others. In short, a failure to follow through in concrete ways with attempts at generative accommodation would be at odds with, and counterproductive to, its goals.

INDEX

For EU product safety concerns, contact us at Calle de José Abascal, 56–1°, 28003 Madrid, Spain or eugpsr@cambridge.org.

www.ingramcontent.com/pod-product-compliance
Lightning Source LLC
LaVergne TN
LVHW011703200926
848484LV00004B/1053

* 9 7 8 1 0 0 9 1 5 2 6 2 4 *